THE EUCHARISTIC LITURGY

A Liturgical Foundation for Mission in the
Malankara Mar Thoma Syrian Church

JAMESON K. PALLIKUNNIL

authorHOUSE®

AuthorHouse™ UK
1663 Liberty Drive
Bloomington, IN 47403 USA
www.authorhouse.co.uk
Phone: 0800.197.4150

Published by AuthorHouse 03/20/2017

ISBN: 978-1-5246-7653-7 (sc)
ISBN: 978-1-5246-7652-0 (e)

Foreword

The Liturgy is the summary of Eastern faith. The Malankara Mar Thoma Syrian Church, as a true heir of Eastern tradition, renewed its liturgical commitment during reformation. Though most of the western understanding of reformation was to do away with liturgy, in contrast, the forerunners of the Mar Thoma Syrian Church took liturgy more dearly and clearly. Liturgy is summary of the Bible, in a poetic form. The pioneers of reformation reviewed the faith and practice of the Malankara Church in the light of a renewed understanding of Scripture. The Church maintains an intrinsic relationship and unity between the liturgy and Scripture in its spiritual life. The liturgy of the word and the liturgy of the Eucharist are inseparably united. The Church gratefully remembers the contributions of the Syrian Church Fathers and values their liturgical heritage. The biblical imageries of Christ, Church, Space, Time, and Mission are weaved together in a rhythmic way in our liturgy. That is the reason we chant the liturgy. Liturgy is not a proposition of confession; it is a poem of faith.

The Mar Thoma Church is a missionary community, and liturgical foundation is at the very source of its Eucharistic life and energy. The Church experiences and encounters Christ in the Eucharist. The 'Christ-experience' of the faithful through the Eucharist strengthens and motivates them to participate in the mission of God. The liturgy enables the people of God to internalize and to enliven this 'Christ experience.' An active participation in the Eucharistic liturgy enables the faithful to take part in the Trinitarian mystery and mission. Mission is not only the conclusion of the Eucharist, but a concrete living out of the mystery of divine love that it symbolizes and celebrates. An active participation in the Eucharist reminds the faithful of their responsibility to witness the salvific act of Christ both individually and collectively. It motivates the Church to impart a Eucharistic presence in the world and thereby accommodates others into a communion with the Triune God. It is a call to incarnate the gospel through an 'active presence' in the day-to-day affairs of the people. The Mar Thoma Church integrates the Liturgy and mission contextually. The Church attempt to incarnate the Gospel through challenging the evils of the caste structure, serving the poor through hospitals and destitute homes, and day care centres for poor children and thus focused on the development of villages though humanitarian programs. In other words, the Church attempts to incarnate wherever needed as a transformative force. As an ancient Christian community, with modern outlook, this Church has rediscovered the essence of its spiritual life by re-reading its historic liturgy and thereby their engagements in the society with its various ministries.

There are numerous ways to study our liturgy. Few attempts have been made by some scholars within India and abroad. But, a focused attempt to study our liturgy through the framework of theology of mission is rarely done. This book, *the Eucharistic Liturgy: A Liturgical Foundation for Mission in the Malankara Mar Thoma Syrian Church* by Rev. Jameson is a novel and noble attempt in this regard. The writer explicitly places how the Eucharistic liturgy of the Mar Thoma Church is observed as the foundation for mission in its course of growth. In order to accomplish this objective, Rev. Dr. Jameson has examined the historical evolution and the developmental process of the Eucharistic liturgy of the Church. In a nutshell, this study is an appraisal of various missiological themes reflected in the Eucharistic liturgy of the Church. This study throws ample light on how the Mar Thoma Church integrated Liturgy and Mission in its course of development. The writer systematically illustrates how the Church made a serious effort to bring missional themes employed in the liturgy into the practical realm by its ancillary organizations, convention gatherings, and socio-charitable works. This volume asserts that an emphasis on Eucharist-centred ecclesiology guides and motivates the Church to enliven a mission-oriented life which is crucial for accomplishing a relevant mission. Rev. Dr. Jameson brings together the liturgical, biblical and missiological aspect of our liturgy in the historical context of the Mar Thoma Church. I congratulate him for publishing the work for the wider audience, for the edification of the church.

I wish, this book may invite more faithful to study the richness of our liturgy and more over people may experience the liturgical spirituality with commitment to mission.

May God bless you all to experience liturgy as a synergy for mission.

Poolatheen, Thiruvalla
20.02.2017

Dr. Joseph Mar Thoma
Metropolitan Malankara Mar
Thoma Syrian Church Kerala,
India

PREFACE

As Christianity continues to become an ever greater global phenomenon and strives to find its home in ever different and diverse contexts, what resources and traditions can Christians draw on to meet this challenge? How can one be a truly Christian and be truly rooted in a particular time and place is a question that faces many Christian communities today. Rev. Dr.Jameson in this study draws on one tradition to answer this crucial question.

The Mar Thoma Church like many of its sister Churches in India is not especially well known outside its immediate homeland and yet it brings together an ancient and venerable liturgical tradition from the Christian East with a reformed theology stemming from the Church of England. With deep roots in the past, it seeks to present its faith in ever changing realities: emigration, a growing diaspora scattered across the world, young believers with little real contact with India, how to welcome new members who are not Indian. Other Christian communities share the same questions in different measures. This study does not ignore such difficult issues but argues that they can be faced and must be confronted not with fear but a hope that is rooted in the very central belief of the Christian faith. Christians celebrate that hope every time when they gather to celebrate the Eucharist, the memorial of Christ passing from death to life and with his passage; we are saved and brought into the very centre of his saving mystery. As Rev. Dr. Jameson argues this Eucharistic celebration is not just to sustain and strengthen the community that comes together on a Sunday, it has an effect for the life of the world. However, it also holds a call for the community that they go beyond what they celebrate on a Sunday and engage with that world and its many joys and sorrows. The mission of a Christian community is a topic that is often discussed and argued about endlessly. Where this mission is rooted, what will sustain it, what can it be measured against? Rev. Dr. Jameson shows that the celebration of the Eucharist itself is one of the greatest impetus for mission in our common faith and yet that it is often ignored or forgotten. It takes someone deeply rooted in ancient liturgical traditions and imbued with reformed sensibilities to analyse how the prayers and gestures of a particular Eucharistic celebration is a call to mission that is to involve every participant. Because this study is rooted in the Mar Thoma Church and the wider West Syrian tradition as found and celebrated in India, it serves as an excellent introduction to these fascinating communities. The Mar Thoma Church has gone through division and reform, and the way the Church has struggled to face these challenges are clearly outlined in this study. Many will welcome Jameson' clear exposition of how liturgical reform and renewal has been central to the life of one particular Church community and no doubt will be invited to look once more at their own ecclesial experience.

Let me commend Rev.Dr.Jameson for his efforts and wish him all the best in his future endeavours. I wish the readers of this book to have a meaningful encounter with the liturgy and mission.

Prof. Dr. Liam Tracey, OSM
St Patrick's College,
Maynooth, Co Kildare
Ireland.

Acknowledgements

It has been a wonderful privilege to pursue my doctoral study at St. Patrick's `College, Pontifical University, Maynooth, Ireland. This book is the revised version of the doctoral dissertation that I submitted as part of the doctoral requirement to the Department of Theology in the St. Patrick's College, Pontifical University, Maynooth. I would like to express my deep appreciation and heartfelt gratitude to all those who have helped out throughout my academic pursuit.

At the very outset let me extend my wholehearted thanks to my thesis guide, Revd. Dr. Liam Tracey for his valuable advice, thoughtful guidance, constructive criticism and unflagging support from the beginning till the end of this research.

I am indeed grateful to the Mar Thoma Metropolitan His Grace Dr. Joseph Mar Thoma who always remain as an inspirational and driving force in my theological journey and ministry. I thankfully remember the encouragement and valued support provided by the Diocesan Bishops, Rt. Rev. Dr. Geevarghese Mar Theodosius and Rt. Rev. Dr. Isaac Mar Philaxinos. I am much indebted to the Hon. Episcopal Synod of the Malankara Mar Thoma Church for the permission to pursue my higher studies in Ireland.

My gratitude also goes to the administrative staff of the Pontifical University of Ireland, St. Patrick's College Maynooth and Faculty of Theology who offered me the opportunity and constant assistance during the course of my research. In particular, I record my gratefulness to the Library Staff at the National University of Ireland, the National Centre for Liturgy, Maynooth, the Cadbury Research Centre, Birmingham, the Basel Mission Centre Switzerland, the Princeton Theological Seminary Pennsylvania, the St. Thomas Apostolic Seminary Vadavathoor, the St. Ephrem Ecumenical Research Centre, Kottayam, the Mar Thoma Theological Seminary

Kottayam, the United Theological College Bengaluru, and the Dharmaram Vidya Kshetram Bengaluru.

I am indebted to numerous persons during this course of research. Let me acknowledge the support of Bishop. Dr. John Fenwick, His Grace Mathews Mar Aprem, Rev. Dr. Michael Mullaney, Dr. Dennis Hainsworth, Fr. Patrick Jones, Fr. Paul Kenny, Sr. Moira Bergin, Revd. Dr. M.J. Joseph, Rev. Dr. George Mathew Kuttiyil, Rev. Abraham Varghese and Rev. Eapen Varghese.

Let me record my sincere thankfulness to Rev. Dr. David Halpin and Mr. C. P. Mathew for proof reading and necessary corrections. Special words of gratitude goes to the members of the Dublin Nazareth Mar Thoma Church, the Belfast Mar Thoma Congregation, the Switzerland Mar Thoma Congregation and all my friends and well-wishers for their support and prayers.

The encouragement, concern and prayers of my beloved parent: Oommen Kunjukunju and Thankamma Kunjukunju, loving siblings and their families are much appreciated. The love, patience and constant support of my wife Honey Rajan, children: Haaran, Darshan and Mahal are beyond words.

Above all,

Let me praise and glorify the name of God Almighty, the one who has called, sustained and guided throughout my faith journey.

Jameson K. Pallikunnil
Maynooth, 25th February 2017

Contents

CHAPTER 7

Missional Aspects in the Eucharistic Liturgy

CHAPTER 8

Paradigms of Mission in the Malankara Mar Thoma Syrian
Church: An Assessment

General Introduction

The Malankara Mar Thoma Syrian Church[1] (MTC) forms part of the ancient Church in India which traditionally traces its origin back to the missionary enterprises of St Thomas, one of the twelve apostles of Jesus Christ which started in 52 CE in the west coast of South India. In the past, this Church had received episcopal oversight from the Church of Persia (East Syrian or Chaldean Church) and used the East Syrian Liturgies.[2] Since 17th century, owing to its association with the Syrian Orthodox Church of Antioch, it has been following a West Syrian Liturgical pattern. The growing influence of Anglican missionaries by the 19th century in India led a group of leaders in the Malankara Church to reform this ancient Church based on some of the key theological doctrines of the Western Protestant reformation, in conjunction with the Church Missionary Society (CMS), London. This led to a revival in the Malankara Church based on a renewed interest in Scripture which began by the revision of the then prevailing liturgy in the Church. Palakkunnathu Abraham Malpan (1796-1845) and Kaithayil Geevarghese Malpan (1788-1855) were at the helm of this revision process. The Church Missionary Society extended a "mission of help"[3] in 1813 CE for the Malankara Church and a Theological Seminary was set up in Kottayam, Kerala with their co-operation in 1815.[4] Through implementing the vision they received in the seminary, with the help of

---

[1] The Malankara Mar Thoma Syrian Church is also known as the Mar Thoma Syrian Church of Malabar or simply the Mar Thoma Church. The name of the Church is hereafter referred to as the MTC.

[2] From the early fourth century the Patriarch of the Church of the East provided India with clergy, liturgy, and ecclesiastical infrastructure, and around 650 CE Patriarch Ishoyahb III solidified the Church of the East's jurisdiction over the St Thomas community. Jacob Vellian, *History of the Syro-Malabar Liturgy* (Kottayam: Powrasthya Vidhya Peeth, 1967), 1-7.

[3] "Mission of help" was mainly focused on the areas of theological education and the revival of the Malankara Church.

[4] It was also known as Kottayam College where English education was first started in Kerala.

the missionaries, they attempted to reform the Malankara Church. The pioneers of reformation process advocated for a sea-change in matters of doctrines and the rubrics of the Eucharistic liturgies. They suggested making changes in the traditions of worship and the life of the Church based on Scripture. The Metropolitan of the Malankara Church, Cheppat Mar Dionysius (1781-1855), the then head of the Malankara Church, viewed the activities of the missionaries and their supporters as a threat to the autonomy of the Malankara Church. He convened a Synod at Mavelikkara in 1836 and the Synod rejected the proposals of the missionaries and asserted the Malankara Church's allegiance to the Patriarch of Antioch. This led to a breach of relationships between the CMS missionaries and the Malankara Church. Abraham Malpan who was teaching in the Seminary took the initiative and a leading role in translating and revising the texts of liturgies of the ancient Church in line with a renewed understanding of the Bible but at the same time tried to maintain the Eastern identity of the Church. Later, he gave up his position as professor in the Seminary and started working for a reformation within the framework of the Church. While the reformers wanted to streamline the Malankara Church by remaining as an integral part of the mother Church, they eventually had to part with the mainstream by forming a separate Church which began to be called as the Mar Thoma Syrian Church of Malabar and had to face many court cases with regard to the ownership of the church properties.[5]

A consequence of the reformation in the Malankara Church is the development of a mission paradigm, which gives equal importance to evangelization, social service, and the struggle for social justice and peace. Until the arrival of the CMS missionaries, there were no external challenges to the Malankara Church to engage in mission. Among Malankara Christians, the MTC is a pioneering Church that took the Word of God (Scripture) and Table (Eucharist) to the remote places where Gospel has not yet been preached and especially to the outcaste sections

---

[5] Abraham Kuruvila, *An Indian Fruit from Palestinian Roots: Towards an Indian Eucharistic Liturgy* (Thiruvalla: Church Sahitya Samithi, 2013), 11.

such as Dalits[6] and Tribal people in the Indian sub-continent by way of its missionary activities. The mission work among the marginalized Dalits in the States like Tamil Nadu, Karnataka, Andhra Pradesh and the Tribal people in Orissa, Madhya Pradesh, Chhattisgarh show that mission is the core and foundation of the Church's identity and witness. Two auxiliary organizations are mainly responsible for mission work within the Church; the Mar Thoma Syrian Christian Evangelistic Association (MTEA) founded in 1888 and the Mar Thoma Voluntary Evangelistic Association (MTVEA) founded in 1924. MTEA is the oldest indigenous Christian missionary movement in India. The annual reports of these organizations reveal that Scripture and the revised liturgy of the Church have been foundational to missionary activities.[7]

A major missiological imperative employed by CMS missionaries in India was solely centred on Scripture. Against this popular understanding, the MTC, through its own reformation process showed that Liturgy can likewise be an imperative for mission. The translation and revision of the Eucharistic liturgy is the basic visible expression of reformation in the Malankara Church. The translation and renewal of the Eucharistic liturgy on the basis of Scripture gave a strong impetus to the Church in its mission. The mission theology of the Church is firmly grounded on the concept of mission as ecclesial proclamation of the economy of salvation here and now. The Church strongly held an approach of mission as "brotherly communion and service." The Mar Thoma Church accepted the supreme Liturgy- Eucharist- as the culmination of mission. An analysis of the mission strategy of the Church demonstrates that a sense of mission flows from the Eucharistic liturgy. This research is an examination of the concept of mission reflected in the Eucharistic liturgy of the Church. A missiological perceptive of the revised liturgy of St. James necessitates a

---

[6] Dalits are the most vulnerable group of people in Indian society who are marginalized and alienated from the main stream of Indian society because of their colour, occupation and social situations.
[7] *The 23rd Annual Report of the Malabar Mar Thoma Syrian Christian Evangelistic Association*, August 1911 (Kottayam: V.G. Press, 1911), 1.

thorough investigation of its roots in the West Syrian liturgical tradition and the impact of reformation on the liturgy. This study will focus on the influence of evangelical principles of the faith of the Church, its liturgical prayers, its practices and its mission. It will seek to understand how the liturgy becomes an integral part of its identity and mission.

The scope of this research is two-fold. Part One addresses the specific missiological significance of Eucharistic liturgy within the West Syrian liturgical tradition, and the approach is through an analysis of Eucharistic liturgy of the MTC. In this process, there comes to light a clear Trinitarian model of mission which emerges from an analysis of the Saint James Liturgy. In this endeavour there arise a number of questions to be answered: *(a)* How did the very identity of the MTC as "missionary" come to light? *(b)* What were the socio-political situations that prevailed within the Malankara Church during the British colonial period, especially, after 1800 CE? How did this whole state of affairs contribute to Church reformation? *(c)* More specifically, what had been the role and influence of the CMS in Travancore State in general and the Malankara Church in particular? What are the major shift that took place in faith, liturgical prayers and practices within the MTC following the reformation process of 1836?

Part Two examines how the Eucharistic liturgy influences the mission of the Church. Through its mission-work and revised liturgy, the Mar Thoma Church took a pioneer role in the formation and nurturing of new Christian communities in India and different parts of the world.[8] Mission is, in fact, the life blood of the Church. Accordingly, this second part reflects on the role of liturgy and its influence on the missionary undertakings of the MTC. It elucidates how the revised liturgy functions as a basis for mission. With a living experience and profound theological understanding, this ancient but reformed Church has something unique to offer to the whole Christendom.

---

[8] The MTC has missionary works and outreach programs in more than twenty states including two union territories of India and other parts of the world such as Nepal (1945), Tibet (1972), and Malaysia (1980).

Methodology

The history of the MTC and its Eucharistic liturgy can only be understood against the social, religious and political background of Kerala in general and of the Malankara Christians in particular during the 19th and 20th centuries. The method of investigation is a historical survey[9] of the reformation in the Malankara Church which includes the formation of its identity, liturgy and its mission activity. The mission of the Church will be analyzed by examining the missionary activities, mission strategy and engagements of the Church in general and its ancillary mission organizations in particular. The method of study is historical, liturgical and theological. In the course of development, a descriptive and analytic study on West Syrian liturgical texts, Liturgical commentators and other literature related to the subject matter and content are examined. Visits to the archives of the Church Missionary Society in the University of Birmingham for primary sources, interview with the scholars in the field of Liturgy, mission and history of the Church, analysis of the reports of the Church and its ancillary organizations are done. A number of interviews with distinguished scholars of West Syrian liturgy namely John Fenwick and Phillip Tovey, will be part of the research along with interviews with scholars in the Malankara tradition, e.g. Mathews Mar Aprem, M.J. Joseph, George Mathew Kuttiyil, the Metropolitan and bishops of the Church. The

---

[9] The historical method of the Church History Association of India that is the commonly accepted historical method in reconstructing the history of Christianity in India. The Church history Association of Indian (CHAI) highlighted the role of Indian Churches and Indian Christians in the development of Christianity, by the process of historical-critical analysis of the data available for the reconstruction of Indian Christian history. It deals with different aspects of Christianity-social, cultural and ecumenical-in relation to other religious and cultural movements. The CHAI has published six volumes on comprehensive history of Christianity in India using this method. See John Webster, "History of Christianity in India: Aims and Methods," *Indian Church History Review* 13, no.2 (December 1979): 87-122. Kaj Baago, "Indigenization and Church History," *Bulletin of the Church History Association of India* (February 1976): 24-28. A. Mathias Mundadan, "The Changing Tasks of Christian History: A View at the Onset of the Third Millennium," in *Enlarging the Story: Perspective on Writing World Christian History,* ed. Wilbert R. Shenk (New York: Orbis, 2002), 44. George Thomas, *Christian Indians and Indian Nationalism 1885-1950* (Frankfurt: Peter D. Lang, 1979), Mathias Mundadan, "Changing Approached to Historiography," *Indian Church History Review* (June 2001): 51-55.

annual reports of the missionary agencies of the MTC will also be analyzed and studied.

Limitations of the Study

In this study, investigation has been limited to the anaphora of St James; the other anaphoras do not come within this scope. Admittedly, because of conflict between traditionalists and liberals uniformity is lacking in terms of observance of fast, feast, rituals, signs and symbols. Also, be it clearly repeated and understood that the term "reform tradition" used in this study is employed in that general sense of all churches adhering to the reform ideals of Martin Luther, not in the tighter sense of a particular reformed church tradition. The usage of the term "Syrian" is not intended in an ethnic sense; it is used in relation to its liturgical identity and heritage. The signs, symbols and rubrics in the liturgy will be analyzed and interpreted from a mission perspective. And finally, to date only limited studies have been undertaken towards a greater understanding of the relationship between Eucharistic and Church missionary aspects in the Malankara tradition, and especially in the MTC.

Chapter Categorisation

The purpose of this research is to uncover how the Eucharistic liturgy of the MTC is a foundation for mission. In order to accomplish this task, I have examined the historical evolution and theological development of the reformed Eucharistic liturgy of the Church. In a nutshell, this study is an appraisal of various missiological themes reflected in the Eucharistic liturgy and its implications in the Church. The **first two chapters** mainly deals with the historical development of the nature and identity of the MTC in which the importance of Malankara Reformation is analysed in detail. The Malankara Christians in Kerala attribute the root of their spiritual heritage to St. Thomas and they claim their ecclesiastical existence right from the very First Century. The arrival of missionaries from the West especially the ecclesial powers such as the Persians, the Portuguese, the Dutch, the French and the British made a great impact on the social and religious life of the people of Kerala from time to time. The immigration of a group of people from Persia under the leadership of the merchant Thomas of Cana in 345 CE paved the way for a connection between the Malankara Church and the Persian Church. Until the arrival of Portuguese in 1498 CE, the St. Thomas Christians were in connection with the Persian Church and they followed the prayers and practices of the East Syrian liturgical traditions. The colonisation and the rule of the British by the 17th century had made a great impact in the life of the Kerala society especially in the St. Thomas Christian community. The Church Missionary Society (CMS) from London arrived in India with the aim of revamping the St. Thomas Christians and it was yet another epoch making chapter in the history of the Malankara Church. The influence of the CMS missionaries caused a revival in the Malankara Church and thereby the formation of a reformed Church in the Malankara tradition. Being a reformed Church but at the same time, having some elements of the cultural ethos of the Oriental Orthodox Church, the MTC uses the West Syrian liturgy but follows an Anglican theology. The second chapter further explains the identity and ecclesiastical nature of the Church.

Since, the Church upholds the West Syrian liturgy and worship patterns of the Antiochian Orthodox Church, it is imperative to understand the features of the West Syrian liturgical tradition. The **third chapter** deals with the distinctive characteristics of the West Syrian liturgical traditions and the various theological changes in the present Eucharistic liturgy of the MTC. The translation of the Eucharistic liturgical texts from Syriac to Malayalam was the initial apparent attempt of the reformation process. Later, the availability of the Bible in the vernacular,[10] and the systematic

---

[10] The first attempt to translate the Bible into Malayalam was started by Rev. Claudius Buchanan, who persuaded Malankara Church leaders to translate the holy text into Malayalam and gave guidance to local scholars. At that time Syriac was the liturgical language of Christians in Kerala. In 1811, Kayamkulam Philipose Ramban translated four Gospels from Syriac to Malayalam which is considered as the First version of the Bible that popularly known as "Ramban Bible." After Ramban Bible, it was Benjamin Bailey who continued the effort of translating Bible to Malayalam. He completed New Testament and published it in 1829. Bailey completed the translation of Old Testament and printed it in 1841. Hence, it was Benjamin Bailey who had translated the entire Bible to Malayalam

study of Scripture, helped the reformers to revise the Eucharistic liturgy in line with Anglican theology. Since the reformation, the MTC uses the Liturgy of St. James in its revised form. This chapter examines the historical development of the Liturgy of St. James in detail. The **fourth chapter** mainly deals with the development of the Eucharistic liturgy of the Church. This chapter delves deep into the theology of the Eucharist, the major changes that have undergone in prayers and practices of the liturgy following the reformation, and the historical development of the Eucharistic liturgy in the Church especially from 1835 to 1954. When the Church grew out from Kerala to the other parts of India and abroad by way of evangelisation and emigration, more translations of liturgical text have been made for the use of the members. A historical record of various translations of the liturgy is also analysed in this chapter.

The MTC is a "missionary Church" and hence its Eucharistic liturgy underlines the importance of mission. Since the liturgy of the Eucharist is the foundation for mission, the **fifth chapter** highlights the concept of mission in Scripture, various ecclesial traditions and in the liturgy in details. Since the MTC has both the Protestant and Oriental Orthodox traditions, this chapter looks at mission on the basis of these traditions. Participation in the Eucharistic liturgy enables the faithful to partake in the Trinitarian mystery. The Eucharistic liturgy is a sharing of Trinitarian love and the communion with the Father, the Son and the Holy Spirit. The Eastern understanding of the Trinity is all about God's radical relationship with the humanity and the movement towards the restoration of the whole creation. The *Perichoretic*[11] dimension of the Trinity stands as the paradigm for Christian mission. The mission of Christ and thereby Church is for the entire creation. It can be understood as the work of a community (the Church), with a community (the holy Trinity), for a community (God's whole creation). The Eucharistic liturgy affirms that

---

language. Hermann Gundert updated Bailey's version and produced the first Malayalam-English dictionary (1872).

[11] *Perichoresis*, (Gk) describes the mutual indwelling and the mutual inter-penetration of the Father and the Son and the Holy Spirit.

the community gathered for worship must be dispersed for mission. It orients the believing community towards new responsibilities such as the preservation of creation, witness to Jesus Christ and service to society. The **sixth and seventh chapters** mainly examines various missiological elements reflected in the liturgy. In order to find out the missiological aspects of the Liturgy, the structure, content and theology of prayers, signs, symbols, postures and gestures in the Liturgy are analysed. The Church is commissioned with the privilege and responsibility of participating in the mission of Jesus Christ by the power of the Holy Spirit.[12] Wherever the Church is proclaiming the Gospel, the Eucharistic liturgy happens to be the directive and motive force for its life and mission. The missiological elements in the Eucharistic liturgy play a catalytic role for the mission in the Church. Hence, the **eighth and ninth chapters** mostly deal with a historical and liturgical overview of the mission in the MTC. The revised liturgy of the Church is a liturgical foundation for mission in the MTC. The translation of the liturgy into different languages for the use of the members is a classic example. These chapters present a historical survey of mission in the Church in which the role of Maramon Convention, Ancillary Organizations and Ashrams in the Church are investigated. In order to discover how the Church integrated the liturgy and mission within the background of its historic reformation, various mission models employed in the Church are analysed, from which one arrives at the conclusion that the missiological elements enshrined in the Eucharistic liturgy is the foundation of a renewed understanding of mission in the MTC.

One of the challenges that the MTC faces in the 21st century is to develop itself fully into a global Church by transcending local frontiers set by ethnicity and nationality. The Church is called to be a cross-cultural, inter-racial and inter-generational community responding to the needs of the hour. Responding creatively to the signs of the time marks the relevance of a Church. The Liturgy of the Church is designed in such a fashion as

---

[12] Vincent J. Nugent, "Theological Foundation for Mission Animation: A Study of the Church's Essence," *World Mission* 24, no.1 (Spring 1943): 7-18.

to bring God's life to the people. The liturgy of Saint James is enriched with missional elements and that it is primarily centred on the four-fold pattern of the central Eucharistic act of Christian worship: gathering, word, table and sending. Currently, the mission of the Church is multifaceted, including matters of justice, peace and the integrity of creation, as well as evangelism. An active participation in the liturgy motivates the believers to co-operate with God's economy of salvation. As an ancient Christian community, the MTC with its vibrant life of mission and sacraments for the extension of the Kingdom of God, has a pride of place in the Christendom. As a Church with modern outlook over against an ancient backdrop, this Church has a growing relevance in rediscovering the quintessence of its spiritual life by re-reading its historic liturgy.

Chapter 1

The Malankara Mar Thoma Syrian Church and the Importance of Reformation (1836 CE)

1 - Introduction

The Mar Thoma Church (MTC) is a historic apostolic faith community, strongly rooted in the spiritual heritage of St. Thomas Christians[13] in continuity with the apostolic faith handed on to them from generation to generation. Throughout the centuries, the Malankara Church was connected to the various ecclesial traditions such as the East Syrian (4th C), the Roman Catholic (16th C), the West Syrian (17th C) and the Anglican (19th C). An interaction with these faith communities influenced and shaped the theology, faith and practices of the Malankara Church over the course of the centuries. The arrival of Portuguese in 1498 CE and the spreading of Catholicism among the Malankara Church (the Latinisation) that followed had caused a major division among the St. Thomas Christians. Subsequently, the relationship with the Syrian Orthodox Church in Antioch in the 17th century commenced along with an adoption of the West Syrian liturgy and customs in the Malankara Church.

The 19th century reformation in the Malankara Church was a landmark in the history of the St. Thomas Christians. During the 19th century, because of the influence of the British rule, English education and the activities of the CMS missionaries there was a remarkable change in the

---

[13] The Christians of Malabar is often known as the St. Thomas Christians, the Mar Thoma Christians or the Malankara or Malabar Christians. The name Malabar is derived from the Malayalam term "*Mala*" (mountain) and "*Varam*" (valley), ("bar" being the corrupted form of "*Varam*"). The other names of Malabar are Malankara and Malanadu. Malayalam is the vernacular of the people of Malabar. The term 'Malabar' is derived from the geographical peculiarities of the region. A. Sreedhara Menon, *A Survey of Kerala History* (Kottayam: Sahitya Pravartthaka Cooperative Society, 1967), 21-22.

social, cultural, political and ecclesial landscape of Kerala. The influence of the CMS missionaries caused a revival in the Malankara Church. The translation of the Eucharistic liturgical texts from Syriac to the native vernacular -Malayalam- was the initial apparent attempt of the reformation process. Later, the availability of the Bible in Malayalam and systematic study of Scripture, helped the reformers to revise the Eucharistic liturgy in line with Anglican theology.

The Mar Thoma Church exists as a "hybrid church" by blending the Eastern liturgical elements of the Oriental Orthodox Church and the evangelical ideas of the Protestant Reformation of the 16th century. This Church is a "bridging Church" connecting Protestantism and Oriental Orthodoxy. The theological and liturgical position of the Church marked it as a "special family of Church" among the global Churches, which means this new ecclesial group is rooted in the spiritual heritage of the St. Thomas Christians, its liturgical footings in the Oriental Eastern tradition and theological underpinnings in the European Protestant reformation. The basic understanding of the Church is based on divine authority, the Bible, the Nicene-Constantinople creed, the apostolic tradition and sacraments.[14] The Church accepts the Holy Bible, consisting of the sixty-six books of the Old and New Testaments, as the basis for all matters pertaining to doctrine and faith. This is the premise on which the identity of the Church developed during the reformation. Hence, this Chapter explore the importance of reformation in the Malankara Church and discover how the very nature of the MTC as "missionary" comes to light? In order understand the relationship between the Eucharist and mission it is necessary to explore

---

[14] The word Sacrament is derived from the Latin word *sacramentum* (*mysterion* in Greek) which means an oath or surety. In the Church, each sacrament is administered as a means of God's grace. It is the visible expression of an invisible grace. The MTC recognizes seven sacraments for administration in the life of her members. Of these seven, Holy Baptism and Holy Qurbana are called Dominical Sacraments. These are called so because they are directly commanded by the Lord. Among the sacraments, only Confession and Holy Qurbana are repeated. Michael J. Taylor, ed. *The Sacraments: Readings in Contemporary Sacramental Theology* (New York: Alba House, 1981), 2-3.

the connection of the Malankara Church with other ecclesial traditions and the nature and identity of the MTC in the global ecclesial scenario.

2 - The St. Thomas Christians and Other Ecclesial Traditions

The St. Thomas Christians of Malabar form the most ancient Christian community of India and within the Far East. This community has a large concentration of its members in the state of Kerala,[15] South India. It maintained its relation with the Churches of Persia and Syria prior to the arrival of European missionaries. Though currently they have branched off into various denominations,[16] they were one in faith, spiritual heritage, tradition and organization until the arrival of the Portuguese in the 15th century.

Considering the relationship with the Persian Church, since the migration of the Christians from Persia[17] the Malabar Church was ecclesiastically in

---

[15] Kerala is the South-Western coastal regions of the Indian Sub-continent, lying north to south, measuring about 350 miles in length. It is bounded on the East by the Ghats and on the West by the Arabian Sea; it covers an area of 15,002 square miles. Kerala means the "Land of Coconuts." From ancient time onwards, there was a trade between Greece, Rome and China. P. K. Gopalakrishnan, *The Cultural History of Kerala,* 4th ed. (Thiruvananthapuram: Kerala State Institute of Language, 1991), 2-5.

[16] At present, the St. Thomas Christians are mainly divided into eight denominations namely, the Syro-Malabar rite of the Roman Catholic Church, the Malankara rite of the Roman Catholic Church, the Malankara Orthodox Syrian Church, the Malankara Syrian Orthodox Church (Jacobite), the Malankara Mar Thoma Syrian Church, the Malabar Independent Syrian Church, St. Thomas Evangelical Church and Chaldean Syrian Church of the East (Assyrian Church of the East). *Joseph Daniel, Ecumenism in Praxis: A Historical Critique of the Malankara Mar Thoma Syrian Church* (Frankfurt: Peter Lang, 2014), 23-24. James Aerthayil, *The Spiritual Heritage of The St. Thomas Christians* (Bangalore: Dharmaram, 2001), 8.

[17] During the time of King Shapur II (310-379 CE) of Persia, a group, along with a bishop named as Uraha Mar Yausef, four priests, many deacons and four hundred persons of seventy two royal families migrated to India under the leadership of a merchant Thomas of Cana, known as Knaye Thomman. The native Hindu rulers received them kindly. The migrants were engaged in trade and settled down in Cranganoor (Kodungallur). Another group from Persia landed in Malabar, 823 CE under the leadership of a Persian merchant Marwan Sabriso, with two bishops named Mar Sapro and Mar Prodh. They landed in Quilon, an old trade centre. The native Hindu ruler Cheraman Perumal welcomed and extended them special privileges and rights in the society through a decree. These gifts and privileges were inscribed on two sets of copper plates. Three of these are still in the Old Seminary in Kottayam and two are with the Metropolitan of the Mar Thoma Church, Thiruvalla. These two migrated communities together were known as "Knanaya."

contact with the Churches of Persia and Seleucia-Ctesiphon[18] before the 15th century.[19] The connections with the Persian Church made great impact on the life of St. Thomas Christians. The Malankara Church accepted episcopal supervision by the Persian bishops and adopted East Syrian liturgy in its worship.[20] According to Vellian, "the commercial and colonial relation between Persian and Indian and the ecclesiastical relations between the Indian Church and the Persian Church, point to the probability of the use of East Syrian Liturgy in Malabar."[21] Episcopal supervision entails the mutual recognition of each other as Churches, and the Malankara Church's acceptance of oversight of Persian bishops.

In considering the connection with the Roman Catholic Church, until the arrival of the Portuguese in the 15th century CE, the Malankara Church was one body, one family and one Church. The Portuguese, who came as

---

(Knanaya people). They taught Syriac and it is believed that at this time Syriac became the liturgical language of the early Malankara Christian community and during this time the Church began to use the liturgy of St. James for their Holy Communion service. Jacob Kollaparambil, *The Babylonian Origin of the Southists Among the St. Thomas Christians* (Roma: Pont. Institutum Studiorun Orientalium, 1992), XXIII, 66-67. K. Kuruvilla, *A Brief History of the Syrian Christians of Malabar*, CMS/ C I 2/0148/3 MSS (Birmingham: Cadbury Research Library), 2. James Hough, *The History of Christianity in India: From the Commencement of the Christian Era* (London: R.B. Seeley and W. Burnside, 1839), 107-108. Firth, *An Introduction to Indian Church History,* 30-31. K. Kuruvilla, *A Brief History of the Syrian Church in Malabar,* CMS/C I 2/0148/3, 1. Daniel, *Ecumenism in Praxis,* 60-61. Alfonso Mingana, *The Early Spread of Christianity in India* (Manchester: Bulletin of John Rylands Library, 1926), 45. Daniel, *Ecumenism in Praxis,* 60-61. Alfonso Mingana, *The Early Spread of Christianity in India* (Manchester: Bulletin of John Rylands Library, 1926), 45.

[18] Seleucia was a major Mesopotamian city of the Seleucid, Parthian, Roman, and Sassanid empires. It stood on the west bank of the Tigris River opposite Ctesiphon, which was one of the great cities of late ancient Mesopotamia. Seleucia-Ctesiphon was the capital of the Parthian and Sasanian Empires (247 BCE - 224 CE and 224- 651 CE respectively). Today, the remains of the city lie in Baghdad Governorate, Iraq, approximately thirty five kilometer south of the city of Baghdad.

[19] Susan Viswanadhan, *The Christians of Kerala: History, Belief and A Ritual Among the Yakoba.* (Oxford: Oxford University, 1993), 14.

[20] The earliest document which asserts the existence of the East-Syrian Liturgy in Malabar is Ms. Vatican Syriac 22 written at Cranganore, Malabar, in 1301. This is an *epistolarium* copied for the use of the Malabar Church from a text used in the Cathedral of Beth Koke in Seleucia Ctesiphone. Jacob Vellian, ed., *The Malabar Church: Symposium in Honour of Rev. Placid J. Podipara* (Roma: Pont. Institutum Orientalium Studiorum, 1970), 9.

[21] Vellian, *The Malabar Church,* 9-10.

traders and as missionaries of the Roman Church soon, however, became colonial and ecclesiastical overlords. They came there with two purposes, which were economic and religious. Along with colonial interest, they tried to spread Catholicism in the Malabar region and used their power to bring the Malankara Church under the supremacy of Rome. The Synod of Diamper[22] (1599 CE) and the incident of "Coonan Cross Oath"[23] (1653 CE)

---

[22] Alexis de Menezes, (1559-1617) an Archbishop of Goa, appointed by Pope Clement VIII in 1595, together with his Jesuit advisers, decided to bring the Kerala Christians under the religious jurisdiction and ecclesial obedience in conformity to the Roman Pontiff and "Latin" customs. This meant separating the Christians of Malabar not only from the Catholicate of Seleucia-Ctesiphon, but also from the Chaldean Patriarchate of Babylon, and subjecting them directly to the Latin Archbishopric of Goa. With this intention, by the support of the King of Cochin, he convened a Synod at Udayamperoor, south of Ernakulum, from 20-26 June 1599. This is known as the Synod of Diamper. At this meeting the Archbishop demanded complete obedience and allegiance of St. Thomas Christians to the Bishop of Rome. More than that, Alexis de Menezes officially anathematised the customs and rituals of the Malankara Christians as heretical and condemned Malankara Church's liturgy and manuscripts to be either corrected or burnt. The representatives sent from various parishes in and around Cochin were forced to accept the decrees read out by the Archbishop. Thus, those parishes of the Malankara Church were made part of the Catholic Church under the Bishop of Rome. To strengthen the Pope's authority over the Malankara Church, the Synod also accepted the Council of Trent (1545-1563), which addressed doctrinal, sacramental and ecclesiastical corruption, and the Roman Catholic Court of Inquisition. Kuruvilla, *A Brief History of the Syrian Christians of Malabar*, CMS/ C I 2/0148/3 MSS, 5-8. Mundadan, *Traditions of St. Thomas Christians,* 29. Stephen Neill, *A History of Christianity in India: The Beginning to AD 1707*, vol.1 (Cambridge: Cambridge University, 1984), 27-35, 212-213. Michael Geddes, "Act III, Decree IV of the Synod of Diamper: A Short History of the Church of Malabar Together with the Synod of Diamper," in *Indian Church History Classics - The Nazranis, ed.* George Menacherry (Thrissur: SARAS, 1998), 62-64, 84. Claudius Buchanan. *Christian Researches in Asia: with Notes of the Translation of the Scripture* (London: Ward and Co. Paterson Row, 1849), 108-109. Hough, *The History of Christianity in India,* 462. Vellian, *The Malabar Church*, 9-11. Howard, *The Christians of St. Thomas and their Liturgies*, 39-40.

[23] The Synod of Diamper triggered a wave of unrest among the Malankara Christians against the Roman Catholic Church and the oppressive rule of the Portuguese padroado (patronage) provoked a violent reaction on the part of the indigenous Christian community. In this situation under the leadership of Thomas the Malankara Mooppen, Christians around Cochin gathered at Mattancherry church on 3rd January, 1653 and made an oath that is known as the "Coonan Cross Oath" or "Slanting Cross Oath" (Coonan Kurishu Satyam). The following oath was read aloud and the people touching a stone-cross repeated it loudly. "By the Father, Son and Holy Ghost that henceforth we would not adhere to the Franks, nor accept the faith of the Pope of Rome." Those who were not able to touch the cross tied ropes on the cross, held the rope in their hands and made the oath. Because of the weight it is said that the cross bent a little and so it is known as "Slanting Cross Oath." This historical incident resulted in the formation of two branches

marked as definite historical events that made a new ecclesial identity to the St. Thomas Christians.

The Malankara Church and its relationship with the Antiochian Orthodox Church along with the adoption of West Syrian liturgy and practices is an epoch in the history of the Malankara Church. Those who took the "Coonan Cross Oath," later in the month of May in 1653 held a Council at Alangad in Kerala and chose Archdeacon Thomas as their Spiritual Head by the laying-on-of hands by twelve priests. For the first time, in 1653 Malankara Mooppen was given the title "the Mar Thoma."[24] In order to keep the continuity of the apostolic succession and to preserve the originality and the indigenous nature of Malankara tradition, they sought the help of the Syrian Patriarch of Antioch. Then later, when Mar Gregorios Abd al-Jalil, the Bishop of Jerusalem sent by the Antiochian Syrian Orthodox Patriarch in 1663, the Archdeacon was consecrated as the Bishop of the New Community. Thus, the Mar Thoma I became the first indigenous Metropolitan of Kerala.[25]

This event marked the beginning of a new epoch in the history of the Malankara Christians which resulted in the Mar Thoma party's (*Puthencoor*) joining the Antiochian Patriarchate and in the gradual

---

in the Malabar Church. Those who renounced Papacy became known as the Puthencoor (new community) and those who favoured Papacy became known as the Pazhayacoor (old community). Viswanadhan, *The Christians of Kerala*, 15. Ken Parry, David J.Melling, Dimitri Brady, Sidney H. Griffith and John F. Healey, eds., *The Blackwell Dictionary of Eastern Christianity* (Oxford: Blackwell, 1999), 251-253. Daniel, *Ecumenism in Praxis*, 32-35. V. Titus Varghese and P. P. Philip, *Glimpses of the History of the Christian Churches in India* (Thiruvalla: Christian Literature Society, 1983), 22. Joseph, ed. *Malankara Mar Thoma Syrian Church*, 18, 31-33. Mathew Varghese Thumpamon, ed., *Diary of Puthanpurackal Mathai Kathanar*, (Malayalam) (Thiruvalla: Christava Sahitya Samithi, 2014), 28, 43.

[24] I. Daniel, "The Syrian Church of Malabar," in *Indian Church History Classics, ed.* Menacherry, 406.

[25] Kuruvilla, *A Brief History of the Syrian Christians of Malabar*, CMS/ C I 2/0148/3 MSS, 9-10. The apostolic succession from the Antiochian Patriarchate that continues till date. The present head of the MTC is the twenty-first Mar Thoma. The throne used for the consecration of Mar Thoma I in 1663 is still in the possession of the Church and that is kept in Poolatheen, the official residence of the Malankara Mar Thoma Metropolitan at Thiruvalla, Kerala. It has been used in the installation of every Mar Thoma Metropolitan, to this day, so that the continuity of the throne of the Mar Thoma is ensured.

introduction of the West Syrian liturgy, customs and script on the Malabar Coast.[26] According to Philip, it was a reaction of the Mar Thoma Christians against the liturgical circumvention by the Roman Church.[27] During the period from 1665 to 1877, thirteen bishops led the Church one after another. Among them, the first nine bishops hailed from the Pakalomattom family, a family from which St. Thomas was believed to have ordained priests.[28]

3 - The Malankara Christians: An Outline

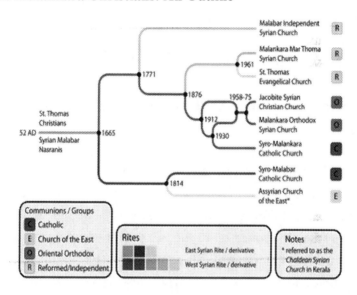

---

[26] More precisely, in 1751, three Antiochian prelates named Baselius Sakrallah, Gregorios and Ivanios and a Cor-episcopos Geevarghese landed at Cochin. They stayed in Mar Thoman church Mulanthuruthy for some time and trained several priests. It was these prelates and the Mulanthuruthy School that introduced the West Syriac script as well as the liturgical rites in the Malankara Church. Baby Varghese, "The CMS Missionaries and the Malankara Church (1815-1840)" *The Harp* XX (2006), 399-401.

[27] When the Synod of Diamper forbade the use of their Syriac liturgy and instead introduced the Latin Liturgy, the Church members did not welcome the new liturgy and practices. A. T. Philip, "Liturgical Imperatives of the Mar Thoma Church," in *A Study on the Malankara Mar Thoma Church Liturgy*, eds., M.V. Abraham, Abraham Philip (Manganam: Thomas Mar Athanasius Memorial Orientation Centre, 1993), 22-42.

[28] Joseph, *Malankara Mar Thoma Syrian Church*, 148-149.

4 - The Reformation in the Malankara Church (1836 CE)

Similar to the European reformations of the 16th century, the reformation in the Malankara Church in the 19th century also drew a new ecclesial landscape in the St. Thomas Christians of Kerala. This reform movement made a drastic influence and change in the moral, structural, doctrinal, and social life of Malankara Christians. The inception of the Malankara Mar Thoma Syrian Church is an outcome of this reformation movement. This Church is the only reformed Church in the ancient St. Thomas traditions of Kerala with Oriental liturgy and reformed doctrines. The reformation owed its origins to a series of attempts to reform the morals and worship of the Church, according to more biblical patterns.

4.1 - Socio-Religious and Political Background of Kerala in the 19th Century

During the colonial period, especially after 1857, the present state of Kerala was divided into three administrative units such as Travancore, Cochin and Malabar. Travancore and Cochin were princely states while Malabar was part of the Madras Presidency under British rule.[29] The present day Kerala State was officially formed on the 1st of November 1956, to unify these three princely states in which the Malayalam language is spoken.[30] Though administrative and economic situations in these regions were different, the social conditions of the lower castes were similar in these areas. The caste system created a hierarchical order and divided society into a number of groups based upon birth and occupation.[31] The status of the individual in

---

[29] During the 19th century, the British consolidated their power in India. The British Government appointed a Resident to take care of the administration of the princely state of Kerala. On November 17, 1795, the English East India Company entered into a treaty with the Travancore. The King of Travancore accepted the British supremacy. According to one of its term, a British Resident was to live in Travancore. Colonel Macaulay was the first resident in Travancore (1800-1809). Colonel John Munro (1810-1819), who succeeded Macaulay, carried out a number of reforms, which changed the history of Travancore considerably. P. Cherian, *The Malabar Syrians and the Church Missionary Society 1816-1840* (Kottayam: CMS, 1935), 33-34.

[30] Menon, *A Survey of Kerala History,* 366.

[31] C. J. Fuller. *The Nayars Today* (Cambridge, Cambridge University, 1976), 10. The "Brahmin" enjoyed the upper class position who were taking care of the activities related

society was determined by the norms of caste.[32] Hinduism became the state religion in all of Kerala with the support of the Hindu Kings.[33] The so-called high caste Brahmanical domination of its society was based on a legend in the Brahmanical tradition about its creation. It is believed that, the Brahmins introduced the caste system into the community structure of the indigenous people. This process is known as "Aryanisation" or "Sanskritization."[34] It is considered that the caste rules and social barriers were the deliberate creation of the Brahmins.[35] According to the caste rules, they became the landowners and gradually a feudal system of society emerged. The Hindus, Christians, and Muslims and various castes and sub-caste together constitute the people of Travancore. According to the Nagam Aiya, there were about 1,050 subdivisions of castes in Travancore during this century.[36] The traditional high caste Hindu-dominated society was not based on the principles of social freedom and equality; rather strict caste rules imposed untouchability and unapproachability upon its people. By this rule, a person from high caste would be polluted if touched by low caste person. An account of the manners and customs of the people of Travancore written in 1860 stated that ritual pollution infected a person in three ways: "by approaching, touching, or eating with an inferior."[37] The above-mentioned account states the rule regulating the distance that people of different castes had to maintain between each other. According to Robin Jeffrey, Nayars and Nambudiris were the chief landowners in

to religion and study. "Kshythria" mainly warriors and rulers, "Vaishyas" who were engaged in trade and commerce. "Sudras" who indulged in other menial works. There was another group casteless; who were considered as impure and placed in the lower strata of the society.

[32] R.N. Yesudas. "Christian Missionaries and Social Awakening in Kerala," *Journal of Kerala Studies* 7 (March- December, 1980): 199.

[33] Gopalakrishnan. *A Cultural History of Kerala*, 280.

[34] A cultural domination of pre-Aryan people by a Brahmanical culture by which non-Aryan people gradually adopted Vedic practices and Brahmanic authority.

[35] K K. Kusuman, *Slavery in Travancore* (Trivandrum: Kerala Historical Society, 1973), 25.

[36] Nagam V. Aiya, *The Travancore State Manuel*, vol.2. (Trivandrum: The Travancore Government, 1906), 245.

[37] A.H. Day, *Dawn in Travancore: A Brief Account of the Manners and Customs of the People and the Efforts that are being made for their Improvement* (Kottayam: CMS, 1860), 9.

Travancore. The Nayars kept slaves, and in the pre-British period (1857) they were responsible for maintaining law and order. In the administration of Travancore, they held more than sixty percent of the posts, and by the mid-nineteenth century, they were about one fifth of the population.[38] The caste Hindus branded the low castes as untouchables and outcastes. The high caste always kept a distance with the low caste to avoid ritual pollution.[39] Samuel Mateer, a missionary of the London Missionary Society who worked in Travancore observes that "the very touch of the degraded pariah or Pulayan, (outcaste) even their shadow falling on the food of the Brahmin conveys pollution."[40]

Robin Jeffrey points out that while Christians had no leading role in the political system, they enjoyed a respectful place in the Hindu-dominated society in their contacts with the English missionaries and with the new rulers of India during that time.[41] Eugene Stock reported that the Syrian Christians were among the best educated and most prosperous of the people.[42] When Buchanan visited Travancore in 1806, he saw a substantial number of Syrian Christians living there, and there were fifty-five Syrian churches[43] and about 200,000 Christians in the whole of South India.[44]

---

[38] Robin Jeffrey, *The Decline of Nayar Dominance* (New York: Holmes and Meier, 1976), xvii.

[39] For example, pulakuli (defilement removal bath) was a ritual bath practiced among the people related to death ceremony. This Malayalam term is a combination of two words "pula," means defilement or pollution and "kuli" means the bath in water. It is a ritual bath taken by the relatives of the deceased in order to free them from the defilement caused by the death of a family member. John Moolan, "Death Rite Customs of St. Thomas Christians in Malabar," *Studia Liturgica* 38, no.2 (2008): 203. 197-205.

[40] Samuel Mateer. *The Land of Charity: A Descriptive Account of Travancore and its People* (New Delhi: Asian Educational Services, 1991), 28.

[41] Jeffrey, *The Decline of Nayar Dominance*, 19.

[42] Eugene Stock, *The History of the Church Missionary Society: its Environment, its Men and its Work,* vol.1 (London: MS, 1899), 250.

[43] Claudius Buchanan, *The Works of the Rev. Claudius Buchanan: Comprising His Christian Researches in Asia* (New York: Whiting and Watson, 1812), 69, 77. http://search.library.utoronto.ca/details?1445955 (accessed March 20, 2014).

[44] Buchanan, *Christian Research in Asia, Proceedings of the Church Missionary Society for 1818-1819* (London: CMS College, 1819), 81.

The socio-educational changes[45] that occurred in the princely state of Travancore shaped the life and mission of the Malankara Church. Travancore, especially its north and central sections, became the cradle of reformation among the Syrian Christians. Many scholars have studied the society of Kerala and observed that during the 19th century an awakening emerged within Kerala for a radical social and religious change in its caste structure.[46] This awakening prepared the people to question the validity of the caste structure and to fight against its oppressive manifestations. Education led to the emergence of a new middle class under the influence of both traditional and Western ideas, which directly influenced social change. Significant changes in the administrative and economic structure and land relations contributed to the emergence of social reforms in Kerala. Employment opportunities in the public works department and plantation industries were given to the backward communities.[47] The Church Missionary Society (CMS)[48] missionaries through their mission strategies began to break the caste mentality of the Syrian Christians and lessen their prejudices against the outcaste. They motivated the Malankara Christians to spread the Gospel to all people irrespective of caste status. There was a strong impetus for a social and religious change within the community and society. There is a consensus among the scholars that the British, the

---

[45] By consolidating their administrative power, the British government terminated the high caste domination and its tyranny over the community. People began to enjoy freedom from the oppression of high castes. Oppressed communities gained their rights. Colonel Munro reloaded the administrative services and a fair judicial system was established for assuring justice and equality. They introduced English education system and established schools. The government gave considerable support to the mission societies for their educational work. Gopalakrishnan, *A Cultural History of Kerala*, 506. Agur, *Church History of Travancore*, 694-695.

[46] Jeffrey, *The Decline of Nayar Dominance,* 14-19. C. P. Mathew and M. M Thomas, *The Indian Churches of St. Thomas* (Delhi: ISPCK, 1967), 14-17. Koli Kawashima, *Missionaries and a Hindu State: Travancore 1858-1936* (Delhi: Oxford University, 1998), 83.

[47] P. Chandra Mohan, "Growth of Social Reform Movements in Kerala," in *Perspectives on Kerala History, Kerala State Gazetteer,* vol. II, ed. P. J. Cheriyan (Trivandrum: Government, 1999), 458.

[48] The Church Missionary Society is hereafter referred to as CMS.

Travancore government, and the Western missionaries acted as catalysts for the emergence of a new awakening in the Kerala Society.[49]

4.2 - Backdrops of the Reformation Movement in the Malankara Church

An analysis of the reform process in the Malankara Church reveals that the reformation was a response to the living situation, of theology, practice and actions in the Malankara Church. The reformation movement in the Church was a reaction to the lived reality of the people and the circumstances of the Church in the 19th century. This period is marked as the "dark age" of the Malankara Christians.[50] During this period, the customs and practices of the Malankara Church were a mixture of Persian, Roman Catholic, Antiochian and indigenous cultures. They found that some practices like the unethical conduct of the clergy, the practice of celebrating sacraments as a source of income and so on, of the Malankara Church were inconsistent with the Christian faith. Moreover, the celebration of the liturgy was written in Syriac was found to be an unknown language to the laity. This inevitably brought about a general recognition of the need for liturgical translation and reforms in the light of Sacred Scripture. The lack of sound theological training and teaching, the overemphasis of rituals, the Church-centred life of the leaders etc., were the realities of the time. The majority of the people

---

[49] Alex Thomas, *A History of the First Cross Cultural Mission of the Mar Thoma Church 1910-2000* (Delhi: ISPCK, 2007), 2.

[50] In general, there lacked spiritual guidance and liturgical discipline in the Church. According to Abraham, an Indian church historian, "at the beginning of the 19th century the Syrian Church was in a state of decline. Life within the state and the Church was grievously disturbed by various factors such as political, social and theological issues. Lack of leadership qualities, absence of theological insights, poor knowledge of the Bible, loose moral life, enforced celibacy of the priest, unscriptural doctrines etc., weakened the Church day by day. Besides, all sorts of superstitious beliefs that were rampant among people that caused a fatal break in their spiritual life. Ignorance, immorality and false beliefs were the reality of the Church at this time." During this period, the Malankara people were satisfied with observance of certain "rites" and ceremonies. It is believed that by praying to the saints and by celebrating special festival connected with them, benefits could be derived and evil could be avoided. This was very much like the festivals observed by the non-Christian community around them. T. Abraham, "Mar Thoma Syrian Church of Malabar," in *The Mar Thoma Church: Tradition and Modernity,* ed. P.J. Alexander (Thiruvalla: Mar Thoma Syrian Church, 2000), 148-149.

were not in a position to distinguish or grasp the real meaning of the liturgy and Church life according to the context. In reality, the Church was at the depth of corruption.[51] In one sense, the reformation was not a movement against the Church, but against the decadence of its practices. Hence one can say that the reformation movement was not primarily based on any concrete theological thinking on the liturgy, but was primarily a protest that emerged in the context of certain practices and spiritual problems in the Malankara Church. According to Philipose Mar Chrysostom, "Luther's reformation emerged from a theological thinking, whereas ours was a protest in the context of certain practical situations in the Church."[52]

Until the middle of the 19th century, the Malankara Church was under the shadow of various practices and traditions such as praying for the dead, veneration to Mary and saints, secret confession. The erroneous traditions, doctrinal misapprehension, striving for power, ignorance of the priest about the biblical truths, over emphasis of tradition, exaggerated rituals and ignorance of the believers were anathema of the Church. The Church was embroiled in a crisis with regard to doctrinal and practical levels, and there existed a lot of contradictions both spiritually and morally. In this juncture, the Metropolitan and the Malankara Church felt the need for assistance from the CMS missionaries which proved fundamental for a renewal in the Church. Buchanan's book lists three major reasons for the reforms in the Malankara Church. First, the CMS missionaries inspired a new desire in Mar Thoma Christians to infuse missionary fervour in the life and witness of the Church. This prompted the Malankara Church to institutionalise certain changes with a view to fostering a mission-oriented programme of action. Secondly, the need to revise and translate the Syriac liturgy became inevitable as the use of Syriac, a language totally unknown to the laity, was in use in the Church. The laity welcomed the liturgical translation into Malayalam and it was also accepted by the then Metropolitan Mar

[51] Joseph, *Malankara Mar Thoma Syrian Church,* 19.
[52] Jesudas M. Athyal and John J. Thattamannil, eds., *Metropolitan Chrysostom on Mission in the Market Place* (Thiruvalla: Christava Sahitya Samithi, 2002), 37.

Dionysius I (1760-1808). Third, the need to protect the autonomy and independence of the Malankara Church from the Antiochian Patriarch.[53]

The reformation movement in the Syrian Church was spearheaded by two Syrian Christian priests, Palakkunnathu Abraham Malpan[54] of Maramon and Kaithayil Geevarghese Malpan of Puthupally, Kottayam. Abraham Malpan was a professor in the theological seminary at Kottayam.[55] By coming into contact with the missionaries of the CMS of England, and by studying the Bible carefully, they realized that there were many errors in the liturgy and practices of the Church.[56] They encountered them and tried to remove some of the practices from the Church especially from the liturgy. The reformists instilled an evangelical fervour in the Malankara Church and this effort was managed in cooperation with the CMS, by way of a "Mission of Help" agreement formalized between the then Metropolitan Dionysius I and the CMS missionaries in 1816.

4.3 - The Church Missionary Society (CMS) and the Malankara Church

The reverberation of the Western reformation produced a great influence in the mission and ministry of the Church of England and its laity. The evangelical zeal and enthusiasm to fight against moral corruption influenced a group of the Church of England's members in 1875. They were popularly known as British Evangelicals. Charles Grant (1746-1823), William

---

[53] Letter to Benjamin Bailey to the Secretary of CMS, dated 10th November 1818, cited in the "*Extracts of Communication from the Rev. Benjamin Bailey and the Rev. Thomas Norton,* Respecting the Syrian Christian," in *Christian Research in Asia,* Buchanan, 321. Buchanan, *Christian Researches in Asia,* 64-65. Daniel, *Ecumenism in Praxis,* 75-76.

[54] Abraham Malpan (1796-1845) hailed from Palakunnathu family in Maramon and became a priest at the age of sixteen. In 1836, when the Synod of Mavelikkara took place he was a teacher of Syriac at the Old Seminary, Kottayam. He was one of the priests appointed by the missionaries to revise the Syrian liturgy and is also known as the "Luther of the Malankara Syrian Church." Actually the ripples of reformation process started in the Church by the sanction of the then Metropolitan and by the approval of the general body, met on December 3, 1818. K. N. Daniel, *Malankara Sabhayum Naveekaranavum* (Malayalam), vol. 1 (Thiruvalla: K. N. Daniel, 1949), 68.

[55] M.J. Joseph, ed., *Malankara Mar Thoma Syrian Church: Sabha Directory 2015,* 4th ed (Thiruvalla: The Ma Thoma Syrian Church, 1915), 19.

[56] Cf. Chapter 2, 4.2 and 4.3

Wilberforce (1753-1833) were the chief promoters of this movement.[57] They prepared the Anglican Church for mission. Their passion for missions led to the formation of the CMS. This missionary organisation was officially established by a group of sixteen evangelical clergymen and nine laymen on 12th of April 1799 in London for the propagation of the Word of God around the world.[58] The CMS, being an evangelical society, began as a small voluntary group, professing loyalty to the established Church of England. Gradually this society gained a secure and valued place within the life of the Church of England. The existence of the CMS helped to revivify the older Anglican mission societies and was crucial in the global spread of an Anglican communion. From the beginning of the 19th century, with the strenuous work of missionaries, support of the Anglican Church and the active initiatives of the local people, the CMS could plant churches in various parts of the world. The local people were often the driving force in the work of evangelization, the Bible translation, creating education and health facilities and building up and providing pastoral care for the community.[59] By 1899, the CMS had become one of the largest Protestant mission agencies in terms of resources, personnel, and influence.[60]

The first CMS corresponding committee of India was established in Calcutta in 1807.[61] The arrival of the Anglican missionaries at the beginning of the 19th century, and their proposal of the "Mission of Help" apparently to reinvigorate the ancient Malankara Church had far-reaching consequences in the Malankara Church and Kerala society. Under the British colonial rule, Kerala witnessed an all-round Renaissance in education and social order. The main intention of the CMS missionaries was to reform the Malankara Church, which was under the jurisdiction of the Syrian Church of Antioch,

[57] Andrew Walls, *The Missionary Movements in Christians History* (New York: Orbis, 1996), 240-245.
[58] Stock, *The History of the Church Missionary Society,* 69-71. The CMS archives now deposited at Birmingham University, are one of the richest and best ordered of all missions resources.
[59] Kevin Ward and Brian Stanley, eds., *The Church Mission Society and World Christianity: 1799-1999* (Cambridge: William B. Eerdmans Publishing Company, 2000), 7.
[60] Ward, *The Church Mission Society and World Christianity,* 1-2.
[61] Ward, *The Church Mission Society and World Christianity,* 228.

in the line of the Anglican Church.[62] Actually the seeds of reforms were planted when the then Metropolitan Mar Dionysius I (1760-1808) welcomed the CMS missionaries in the Malankara Churches and cooperated with them for the translation of Scripture and liturgy in the vernacular. In 1806, Governor General Lord Wellesley sent Claudius Buchanan (1766-1815), a chaplain of the East India Company, to investigate the life and conditions of the Malankara Christians. He visited Travancore and Cochin in 1806-1807. This was to be the first important British ecclesiastical contact with the Syrian Christians in Kerala.[63] Claudius Buchanan was very much interested in the ancient Church of Malabar and published a book in England entitled *Christian Researches in Asia*. By reading this book, the CMS missionaries got interested in the Malabar Church.

Buchanan's book lists three major reasons for the reforms in the Malankara Church. First, the CMS missionaries inspired a new desire in Mar Thoma Christians to infuse missionary fervour in the life and witness of the Church. This prompted the Malankara Church to institutionalise certain changes with a view to fostering a mission-oriented programme of action. Secondly, the need to revise and translate the Syriac liturgy became inevitable as the use of Syriac, a language totally unknown to the laity, was in use in the Church. The laity welcomed the liturgical translation into Malayalam[64] and it was also accepted by the then Metropolitan Mar Dionysius I (1760-1808). Third, the need to protect the autonomy and independence of the Malankara Church from the Antiochian Patriarch.[65] British Resident Colonel Munro[66] (1810-1819), a staunch evangelical, also did everything possible to assist the Malankara Church. He invited the CMS missionaries to start mission work among the Malankara Christians

---

[62] Cherian, *The Malabar Syrians and the Church Mission Society*, 365.
[63] Visvanathan, *The Christians of Kerala*, 18.
[64] Letter to Benjamin Bailey to the Secretary of CMS, dated 10th November 1818, cited in the "*Extracts of Communication from the Rev. Benjamin Bailey and the Rev. Thomas Norton*, Respecting the Syrian Christian," in *Christian Research in Asia*, Buchanan, 321.
[65] Buchanan, *Christian Researches in Asia*, 64-65. Daniel, *Ecumenism in Praxis*, 75-76.
[66] Colonel Munro was the then British Resident in Travancore and Cochin from 1810-1819.

in 1814, in line with Buchanan's understanding with Dionysius I.[67] Munro hoped that "a respectable body of native clergy could be procured for the propagation of Christianity among the people of other religions."[68]

The founding of the Kottayam College, presently known as "Old Seminary at Kottayam" by Pulikottil Joseph Mar Dionysius II in 1813, with the help of the British Resident, Colonel Munro and the Travancore Royal family was a major landmark in the cultural and educational history of Kerala. Another notable contribution from the side of the British Government was the institution of a trust fund of 3000 pagodas with a bank at eight percent of interest rate to benefit the community in October 1808. The Metropolitan of the Syrian Church was the beneficiary of the fund on behalf of the community.[69] The government initiated an endowment fund 10,300.00 Indian Rupees for the training of the clergy in the Malankara Church. Missionaries established a printing press at Kottayam to publish the Bible and a complete version of Malayalam Bible was released in 1841. Along with this, they founded many primary and higher education schools in and around Kottayam.[70] Colonel Munro requested the help of the CMS to improve the conditions of the Kerala Christians. The first CMS missionary, Rev. Thomas Norton came to Alleppey[71] in 1816. Three more missionaries: Rev. Benjamin Bailey, Rev. Joseph Fenn and Rev. Henry Baker came after Rev. Norton. Colonel Munro further appointed Benjamin Bailey at

---

[67] Colonel Munro had a plan to found a college for the education of the Malankara Church clergy and laity in Kerala. He induced the ruler of Travancore for a free gift of land and money for the construction of the college. The King of Travancore granted 20,000.00 Indian Rupee and a land at Kallada in Quilon district for the specific purpose of promoting education among Christians, Menon, *A Survey of Kerala History*, 279. Thomas, *Mar Thoma Sabha Directory*, 41-44.

[68] Buchanan, *Christian Research in Asia*, 169. Cherian, *The Malabar Syrians and the Church Missionary Society*, 26.

[69] The endowment instituted for the training of the clergy is known as "Vattippanam." The first principal of the seminary was Joseph Fenn, one of the first missionaries from the 'Mission of Help' sent by the Church Missionary Society of the Church of England. Geevarghese Mathew, "Mar Thoma Theological Seminary: A Retrospective Reading," *Mar Thoma Seminary Journal of Theology*, vol.1, no. 1 (June 2012): 10, Vishwanadhan, *The Christians of Kerala*, 19.

[70] Kuruvila, *A Brief History of the Syrian Christians of Malabar*, CMS/ C I 2/0148/3 MSS, 10-11.

[71] Then Alleppey was a famous seaport, known as the Venice of the East.

Kottayam[72] to be in charge of the work of Bible translation. He founded a printing press in Kottayam and made two dictionaries for the Malayalam language and also translated the Bible and the Book of Common Prayer into Malayalam. The CMS missionaries extended full support to contemporise the Malankara Church by imparting missionary consciousness. They also felt the need for reforms within the Malankara Church to equip it for missionary work in India. These missionaries prepared the ground for reforms and they were well received by the Metropolitan[73] and the Church. The missionaries propagated the doctrine of the Anglican Church through regular instructions and sermons in the Malabar Churches themselves,[74] for which they were generously permitted by the Metropolitan Punnathra Mar Dionysius (1785 - 1825) and through conventions, publications of the Book of Common Prayer, of the Anglican Liturgy etc., in the vernacular. The CMS missionaries condemned the practices of and customs of the Malankara Church such as the celibacy of the clergy, adoration of images, auricular confession, veneration of saints, prayer for the dead, and prayer towards St. Mary.[75] The CMS missionaries encouraged the clergies of the Malankara to get married.[76] The Metropolitan under the influence of the missionaries declared that the custom of celibacy was not binding on the clergy.

---

[72] Benjamin Bailey, *Cottayam Report: 1st October 1825. MS, CMS/C 12/0 110/4* (Birmingham: Cadbury Research Library). "The Mission of Help" from the Anglican Church of England came to Travancore in 1816-1817. The first batch of the missionaries of the mission known as the "Kottayam Trio" (Joseph Fenn, Benjamin Bailey and Henry Baker) made valuable contributions to the church and the society through their active involvement in the different fields of evangelism, theology, education, Bible translation and printing. T. P. Abraham, *"The Mar Thoma Syrian Church of Malabar,"* 149-150. Joseph, *Malankara Mar Thoma Syrian Church,* 19, 37-39.

[73] Metropolitan Mar Dionysius II (1816-1817) and Mar Dionysius III (1817-1825) had close relation with the CMS missionaries. However their successor Dionysius IV (1825-1852) did not follow the same policy of friendship with the new CMS missionaries especially with Joseph Peet, who came to Kerala after Benjamin Bailey, Joseph Fenn and Henry Baker. See. T. C. Chacko, *The Concise History of the Mar Thoma Church,* 5th ed. (Thiruvalla: Episcopal Jubilee, Institute, 2001), 73-74.

[74] *Travancore High Court Judgement* 459/1064.No. 137), 57. E. P Mathew, ed., *The Indian Church of St. Thomas* (Thiruvalla: Mar Thoma Church, 1929), 265.

[75] Daniel, *Ecumenism in Praxis,* 80.

[76] Cherian P, *The Malabar Syrians and the Church Mission Society,* 283.

The CMS missionaries followed an attitude of missionary paternalism by implementing liturgical and custom changes without the prior consent of the then Metropolitan. The paternalistic attitude of the CMS missionaries and Colonel Munro turned the context of reform into one of confrontation. The missionaries found that many practices were not in line with the evangelical fervour that they sought to impart and decided to banish them, tracing those practices to the Roman Catholic Church. However, they failed to see the fact that such practices are also cherished by the Orthodox Church of Antioch and thereby the Malankara Church too.

The missionaries also hoped that the Church could easily be transformed by means of a sound education, circulation of the Bible in vernacular, use of translated copy of the Book of Common Prayer and the spread of the evangelical doctrines. With this intention, they translated the Book of Common Prayer into Malayalam and used it for Sunday public worship services at the Kottayam Old Seminary Chapel. Inevitably, this strained the relationship of the Metropolitan Dionysius IV with the CMS missionaries. The missionaries' acts overstepped the boundaries of religious neutrality and their agreement with the Metropolitan Dionysius I. They did not give attention to studying the importance given by the Church to its age-old traditions, liturgical practices, religious ethos, signs, symbols, rituals, and liturgical elements when the new liturgy and practices were introduced without the consent of the Metropolitan.[77] The missionaries failed to see the place of traditions in the Malankara Church before attempting to strain customs and practices irrespectively into the mould of the rule of Scripture.

4.4 - The Malankara Reformation and the Formation of the Mar Thoma Church

The first missionaries had a very cordial relationship with the Metropolitans Pulikot Mar Dionysius (1816-1817) and Punnathara Mar Dionysius

---

[77] The missionaries seemed to be under an anti-Catholic and strong protestant fervour which blinded them to the rich heritage and practices in the Malankara Church's liturgy and customs. Cyril Bruce Firth, An Introduction to Indian Church History (Delhi: ISPCK, 1961), 176-177. Daniel, Ecumenism in Praxis, 80-82.

(1817-1825) at that time. But after the arrival of two young missionaries Rev. Joseph Peet and Rev. W. J. Woodcock tension developed between the Metropolitan and the missionaries. The English missionaries accepted the independent status of the Malankara Church, but they were keen to reform the Malankara Church,[78] especially in its liturgy, rituals, faith, and practices. The CMS missionaries had great interest in reforming the liturgy and theology of the Church. They were not interested in ecclesiastical politics and power.[79] Mar Dionysius IV[80] (1825-1852), unlike his predecessors, was unfriendly to the missionaries. He was against missionary paternalism and decided to confront the missionaries and even Abraham Malpan, for his efforts to revise the liturgy. He was not in favour of reforms within the Malankara Church. The Metropolitan Mar Dionysius IV (1825-1852) feared that it would tilt the Church towards the Western reforms. Conversely, the new missionaries were hasty in implementing reforms without seeking the support of the Metropolitan.[81] As a reaction to the Metropolitan, the Anglican Bishop Daniel Wilson of Calcutta (1832-1858) approached Mar Dionysius IV in 1835 and suggested six points, for reform for the Metropolitan's consideration, in order to make peace between CMS missionaries and the Metropolitan.

The Anglican Bishop of Calcutta Daniel Wilson put forward certain reform measures for the consideration of the Metropolitan, the most important of them being the following.

---

[78] Bailey, *Cottayam Report: 1st October 1825. MS, CMS/C I 2/0 110/4.*

[79] Philip Tovey, *Essays in West- Syrian Liturgy* (Kottayam: Oriental Institute of Religious Studies, 1997), 23.

[80] During the first two decade of the 20th century, the Malankara Church witnessed the demise of four Metropolitans, Mar Dionysius I passed away in 1808. He was succeeded by Mar Thoma VII (1808). But he died on 4th of July 1809 and he was succeeded by Mar Thoma VIII (1809-1816) and Mar Thoma IX (1816-1817) and when he died in 1817, Mar Dionysius III (1817-1825), became the Metropolitan. He was friendly with the missionaries and the world of Abraham Malpan, whom he authorize to take leadership in the revision of liturgy and other literary work. Daniel, *Malankara Sabha Naveekaranavum,* (Malayalam) 68-69.

[81] Joseph Peet and W. J. Woodlock boldly criticized the Malankara Church's ritual and practices without realizing the authority of the Metropolitan in the Church. Juhanon Mar Thoma Metropolitan, *Christianity in India and a Brief History of the Mar Thoma Syrian Church* (Madras: Thompson and Company, 1952), 20.

(a) To appoint the natives as priests after the completion of seminary education.

(b) To keep the accounts of receipts and payments of the Church and conduct annual verifications.

(c) To provide a salary to the clergy instead of depending on uncertain payments at the time of services in the Church.

(d) Schools should be established in connection with every parish.

(e) Insist that the clergy give some exposition of the Bible in parishes on every Sunday divine service.

(f) Conduct prayer and worship in vernacular Malayalam instead of Syriac.[82]

The Metropolitan Cheppat Mar Dionysius was not willing to implement the above recommendations proposed by the Missionaries.[83] The Metropolitan and the Church leaders suspected that the intervention of missionaries in Church administration would lead to another ecclesial hegemony. On January 18, 1836, the Metropolitan convened a meeting of all Church representatives at Mavelikkara to discuss the recommendations, on the pretext of considering the proposals of the Anglican Bishop, but with the real intention to suspend the CMS "Mission of Help" and stop the reforms in the Church. At this meeting, the Syrian Church unanimously rejected the proposals by Bishop Daniel Wilson and decided as follows:

"We the Jacobite Syrians, being subject to the supremacy of the Patriarch of Antioch, and observing as we do the liturgies and ordinances instituted by the prelates sent under his command,

[82] Joseph, *Malankara Mar Thoma Syrian Church,* 37-38. Mathew and Thomas, *The Indian Churches of St. Thomas,* 66- 68. Thumpamon, *Diary of Puthanpurackal Mathai Kathanar* (Malayalam), 56.

[83] The Metropolitan had any moral or legal obligation to give assurance to the Anglican Bishop about the norms of ordination or any other matters of the Church, including the accounts, as he was not under any obligation to the British Resident or CMS missionaries. These attitudes of the missionaries were considered by the people as their deliberate plan to poke in to the affairs of the Malankara Church. Thomas, *Mar Thoma Sabha Directory,* 89-91.

cannot deviate from such liturgies and ordinances and maintain discipline contrary thereto…"[84]

By this declaration, the Malankara Church officially accepted Orthodox West Syrian Liturgy and discipline. Besides, it decided that, "The Syrian traditions and liturgy are not to be changed or modified."[85] The Metropolitan was under no obligation at that point to continue the relationship with the Anglican Bishop or CMS missionaries. Nevertheless, the Mavelikkara Synod, decided to surrender its autonomy before the Antiochian Orthodox Church.[86] The Metropolitan sent a circular letter to all the parishes prohibiting any association with the missionaries. In this juncture both parties decided to separate. This is known as the Mavelikkara Padiyola.[87] The Church properties were partitioned on the 4th of April 1840 by arbitration. Hence the cooperation between the Malankara Church and CMS missionaries came to an end.[88]

The CMS Missionary Council held on 22nd March 1836 had entrusted four priests including Palakkunnathu Abraham Malpan to introduce the reformation in the liturgy, after the Mavelikkara Synod. The teachings of the missionaries very much influenced Abraham Malpan and he began to reform the Church in line with the reformed principles of the Anglican Church.[89] He edited the Eucharistic liturgy on the basis of Scripture and celebrated it in Malayalam at the Maramon Parish. This was contrary to the practice of celebrating the communion in Syriac.[90] This led to a crisis. A new faction, later called "reform party," evolved in the context of the

[84] The resolution unanimously accepted at the Mavelikkara Synod held on 18th January 1836 at the Mavelikkara Puthiyakavu St. Mary's church is known as "Mavelikkara Padiyola." Thomas, *Mar Thoma Sabha Directory*, 89-91. Cherian, *The Malabar Syrians and the Church Missionary Society*, 390-391. http://www.stgeorgecheppaud.org/mscr/chathuruthil/mavelikara__padiyola.htm (accessed June 11, 2013)
[85] Thomas, *Mar Thoma Sabha Directory*, 89-91.
[86] Daniel, *Ecumenism in Praxis*, 81-82.
[87] Thumpamon, *Diary of Puthanpurackal Mathai Kathanar* (Malayalam), 57- 58.
[88] Viswanadhan, *The Christians of Kerala*, 21-22.
[89] Kuruvilla, *A Brief History of the Syrian Christians of Malabar*, CMS/ C 1 2/0148/3 MSS, 9-10.
[90] Thomas, *Mar Thoma Sabha Directory*, 12.

Church reformation. In reality, the decisions in the Mavelikkara Synod led to the third schism in the Malankara Church. One group decided to continue the reforms within the Church and to keep its autonomy and independence from the Antiochian Patriarch. The second group decided to establish an alliance with the Jacobite patriarch of Antioch, while the third group decided to have a communion with the CMS missionaries.[91]

The reform party also puts forward some demands to the Metropolitan. The key demands are followed:

(a) Worship in vernacular language
(b) Total participation of the lay- people in worship
(c) Appointment of educated clergymen in parishes

In 1836, Abraham Malpan and eleven other priests submitted a memorandum to the British Resident Colonel Fraser, requesting him to make the necessary changes in the Malankara Church. They mainly highlighted twenty four points which they thought contrary to the Bible, which have no sanction in the canons of the Church.[92] The memorandum contained complaints against such practices as prayer for the dead,

---

[91] Leslie W. Brown, *The Indian Christians of St. Thomas: An Account of the Ancient Syrian Church of Malabar* (Cambridge: Cambridge University, 1956), 139-140. After the decision of the Synod of Mavelikkara, the CMS missionaries continued their mission work among the Malankara Christians separately. Concerning the question of the administration of properties, which jointly operated by the Metropolitan and CMS missionaries, the then Resident appointed arbitrators consisting of the representatives from the Government, the Metropolitan and the CMS missionaries. They announced their award, dividing the property into two lots-one to the CMS missionaries for the sole benefit of the Mar Thoma Community and the other to the Metropolitan in 1840.The CMS mission had started a separate Anglican Church and later it was elevated as the Anglican Dioceses of the Travancore and Cochin in 1878. When the Church of South India was formed in 1948, the Anglican dioceses of Travancore and Cochin merged into the CSI. Currently it is the Central Kerala Dioceses of the CSI. Juhanon Mar Thoma, *Christianity in India as a Brief History,* 22.

[92] "Letter to Colonel Frazer by the reformers of the Malankara Church in 1836," CMS/ C I, 2/0 253/ 59/19. MSS in CMS Archives, Cadbury Research Centre, Birmingham. Thomas, *Mar Thoma Sabha Directory,* 82-89. Zacharia John, *"The Liturgy of the Mar Thoma Church of Malabar in the Light of its History"* (Master's Thesis, University of Durham, 1994), 115-118.

keeping of relics of the saints in churches, the failure to use Scripture for instruction.[93] The memorandum submitted to the Resident is considered as the "Trumpet Call of the Reformation."[94] But the British Resident[95] could not make any changes and the Metropolitan Cheppat Mar Dionysius was not in favour of any reform in the Malankara Church. He adhered strictly to the old beliefs and the supremacy of the Antiochian Church and Patriarch over the Malankara Church. On hearing about the activities of Abraham Malpan, Metropolitan Mar Dionysius suspended him from religious duties and refused to ordain deacons trained under him. It was a real blow to the movement started by Malpan. However, Malpan continued his reformation work.

Abraham Malpan wanted to reform the Malankara Church without joining the Anglican Church. They tried to uphold their own heritage and traditions. But there was no Bishop to give leadership for the reformation movement. Later on, they felt the need to have an episcopal sanction for the clergy and congregation, which opted for revised liturgy and vernacular expressions of prayers and petitions. Abraham Malpan sent his nephew Deacon Mathew to the Syrian Orthodox Patriarch of Antioch, Elias at Tur Abdin in Syria in 1841. The Patriarch was impressed by Deacon Mathew and ordained him as a priest and later consecrated as Metropolitan, with the name Mathews Mar Athanasius in 1842. After a short period as acting bishop of Mosul, he came back to Kerala in 1843.[96] In 1852, Mathew Mar Athanasius was confirmed as the Metropolitan of the Malankara by the Royal edict of the Travancore Kingdom.[97] Even though, first he celebrated

---

[93] Vellian, *The Malabar Church*, 34-35.
[94] Juhanon Mar Thoma, *Christianity in India and a Brief History,* 23. John, *The Liturgy of the Mar Thoma Church of Malabar*, 58-59.
[95] The Residencies of British India were political offices, each managed by a Resident. The Resident was a permanent reminder of the subsidiary relationship between the indigenous ruler and the British Government.
[96] Parry, et al., *The Blackwell Dictionary of Eastern Christianity,* 249. Juhanon Mar Thoma, *The History of the Mar Thoma Church*, 45. A. T. Philip, *The Mar Thoma Church and Kerala Society* (Thiruvananthapuram: Juhanon Mar Thoma Study Centre, 1991), 36-37.
[97] Juhanon Mar Thoma, *The History of the Mar Thoma Church*, 45.

the Holy Communion with the old liturgy, later he gave an active leadership in reforming the Church. The believers, those who had been influenced by the evangelical teachings, remained in the Syrian Church and argued their point of view. Ultimately, the Patriarch of Antioch himself had to act in the Church scene.[98] The Patriarch himself came to Kerala and convened a Synod at Mulanthuruthy in 1875. This Synod authorised the Patriarch of Antioch to exercise the spiritual and temporal authority over the Malankara Church. This led a schism within the Church and those who upheld the autonomy and independence of the Malankara Church (the reform party) felt that it was a departure from the traditions of the St. Thoma Christians.[99]

After the demise of the Metropolitan Mathews Mar Athanasius in 1877, Thomas Mar Athanasius became his successor.[100] During this period, Joseph Mar Dionysius who was very conservative and who opposed the reformation move, filed a suit against him in 1879 to recover the Church properties. It was of special significance that, there was no reference to doctrinal differences or liturgical practices of the reformed party; rather, the complaint was about the acceptance of the supremacy of the

---

[98] In order to prevent the Reformers taking control of the Malankara Church, Pulikottil Joseph Môr Dionysius invited H.H Ignatius Mar Peter IV the new Patriarch of Antioch, to India On 17 May 1875 the Patriarch arrived at Bombay, accompanied by Môr Gregorios Abdullah, Metropolitan of Jerusalem. Patriarch Peter IV summoned the Mulanthuruthy Synod to meet at Mar Thoman Church, Mulanthuruthy from 29 June until 1 July 1876. Representatives from 103 parishes (130 priests and 144 lay men) participated in the Synod. The Synod adopted 18 canons for the administration of the Church. On August 17, 1876 the Mulanthuruthy padiyola was registered. Through the canons approved by the Synod of Mulanthuruthy, the relation between the Malankara Church and the Syrian Patriarchate grew closer than ever before. Parishes and bishops executed bonds declaring their loyalty to the Orthodox faith and to the Patriarch. The Patriarch also divided the Malankara Church into seven dioceses, consecrating a further six Metropolitans to preside over them. The Metropolitans and the dioceses are: Kadavil Paulose Mar Athanasios (Kottayam), Konat Geevarghese Mar Julios (Thumpamon), Ambat Geevarghese Mar Coorilos (Ankamaly), Chathuruthy Geevarghese Mar Gregorios (Niranam), Murimattim Paulose Mar Ivanios (Kandanad), Karot Simon Mar Dionysios (Cochin). Pulikottil Joseph Môr Dionysius V was allocated the diocese of Quilon, but retained the rank of chief Malankara Metropolitan and President of the newly constituted *Suriani Christiani* Association, with the Patriarch as its patron. Patriarch Peter IV sailed back from Bombay on 16 May 1877.
[99] Daniel, *Ecumenism in Practice*, 73.
[100] Juhanon Mar Thoma. *The History of the Mar Thoma Church,* 46.

Jacobite Patriarch over the Malankara Church.[101] The prominent figures of the reformed wing in the case were Thazhatthu Punnathra Chandapilla Kathanar and Kottayam Palathunkkal Mathai Kathanar.[102]

After ten years of litigation, the Royal Court of Appeals (comprising three judges) gave the final verdict (the two Hindu judges, in favour of Joseph Mar Dionysius, confirming the authority of the Patriarch and the one Christian judge, Mr. Ormsby, in favour of Thomas Mar Athanasius) declaring that the Church had throughout been independent.[103] It was this judgement in 1889 that finally caused the split in the Malankara Syrian Church between the Conservatives and Reformed. Henceforth the reformed section became known as the Mar Thoma Syrian Church of Malabar[104] and the other faction as the Malankara Syrian Orthodox Church[105] also known as the Jacobite. With regard to the final separation, T. V. Philip writes:

> "Though the court judgement of 1888/89 led to the final break between the two parties, the question of heresy was not an issue. What happened in 1888/89 was a schism between two groups. It is now commonly regarded that schism is not outside the Church but within. So the question 'which is the original mother Church."[106]

---

[101] Milne. *The Syrian Church in India*, 329.

[102] Thumpamon, *Diary of Puthanpurackal Mathai Kathanar* (Malayalam), 86.

[103] K.K. Kuruvilla, *A History of the Mar Thoma Church and its Doctrines* (Madras: Diocesan, 1951), 23. Juhanon, *History of the Mar Thoma Church*, 46.

[104] The designation Malankara Mar Thoma Syrian Church is also used. (*Mar Thoma Syrian Church of Malabar: Constitution*, Thiruvalla: Mar Thoma, 1984), 1. Juhanon Mar Thoma, *History of the Mar Thoma Church*, 48.

[105] As a result of the decree of the Royal Court, the Mar Thoma party lost its right over the Seminary and much of the property of the Church. For a few years, then, the training of the clergy of the MTC was done at the CNI (Cambridge Nicholson Institute) run by the CMS missionaries. Further, the Reformed group got only two churches, i.e. Maramon and Kozhencherry and five other churches were to be used by both groups on alternate Sundays. The only parish held without contest was of Kottarakkara, where the whole congregation favoured the reforms. Alexander Mar Thoma, *The Mar Thoma Church*, 21. Varghese Mathew, "Mar Thoma Theological Seminary: A Retrospective Reading," *Mar Thoma Seminary Journal of Theology* 1, no. 1 (June 2012):10.

[106] T. V. Philip, *The Mar Thoma Church in the St. Thomas Christian* (Thrissur: National, 1973), 90.

A joint meeting of the priests and lay people of the reformed group met at Maramon in the month of January 1890 under the leadership of Thomas Mar Athanasius. In this meeting, they reiterated the traditions and spiritual heritage of the St. Thomas Christian that is confirmed in the Arthattu and Kandanadu Councils (padiyola), and rejected the supremacy of the Patriarch of Antioch over the Malankara Church. In keeping the continuity of the spiritual traditions of the St. Thomas Christians in Malankara, they accepted the title "the Mar Thoma Church "as the official name of the Church. Further, they decided to buy property in the name of the head of the Church Mar Athanasius, for constructing church buildings and to conduct regular prayer meetings and liturgical celebrations as a reformed Church within the Malankara Church.[107]

The basic difference between Mar Dionysius and the reformists was seen in their view of the goal to modernize the Church. While Mar Dionysius IV aimed at the adoption of the West Syrian liturgy and canon into the Malankara Church. The aim of the reformers were the removal of unscriptural practices, liturgical translation to Malayalam and church modernization, based on western theological insights.[108] The senior Metropolitan of the Church, Philipose Mar Chrysostom comments on Abraham Malpan's reforms as: "a Protest initiated by Western theological insights against the practices in his own church; he did not discard eastern theology to adopt a Protestant theology."[109] The reformists revised the liturgy for the first time in the Malankara Church. This is indeed also the first time the liturgy was revised in any of the oriental Churches in India.[110] In this sense one can call the MTC a reformed[111] Oriental Church.

---

[107] Thumpamon, *Diary of Puthanpurackal Mathai Kathanar* (Malayalam), 103.

[108] Daniel, *Ecumenism in Praxis*, 83-84.

[109] Athyal and John, *Metropolitan Chrysostom on Mission in the Market Place*, 42.

[110] Daniel, *Ecumenism in Praxis,* 84.

[111] The term "reformed" denotes a type of Protestantism developed in Switzerland by Zwingli and John Calvin in the 16th century. Later it had its roots in Europe and elsewhere. They are active in the World Alliance of Reformed Churches, which includes the Presbyterian and Congregational with their headquarters in Geneva. They also share the basic teachings of Protestant Reformations as propounded in Martin Luther's writings in 1520. The word reform tradition used in this study, is in general sense of all churches

4.4.1 - The Reforms Made by Palakkunnathu Abraham Malpan

Abraham Malpan was a devoted churchman who was very loyal to the traditions of the St. Thomas Christians. He was a visionary leader who was very ardently devoted to his tradition and antiquity. He wanted to revive the Malankara Church in accordance with the apostolic and evangelical traditions of the early Church. The CMS missionaries' opinion on Abraham Malpan was, "a godly man who was a burning and a shining light in the Syrian Church."[112] He draws a clear line of thought and initiated a spiritual revival based on the Bible in the Malankara Church with the influence of the CMS missionaries. Malpan was very eager to amend and adapt a scriptural centred spirituality rather than a ritualistic piety in the Malankara Church. His biographer Rev. M. C. George Kassissa calls him a "Wycliffe of the East."[113] The Metropolitan Juhanon Mar Thoma calls Malpan as "Luther of the Syrian Church."[114]

Abraham Malpan's reformation ideas emerged from three sources: from his study of the Bible, from his association with the missionaries and from the decadence of the practices of the Malankara Church. He approached the liturgy with Bible and carefully studied the existing liturgy and detected many unscriptural prayers and practices like praying for the dead and of the dead, veneration to saints, mediation of Virgin Mary and saints, the practice of bowing down before the statues etc., which has no biblical support.[115] Malpan had many limitations in his reformation venture. The main limitation was that he did not have the resources for a systematic analysis of the situation and a proper response to it, and neither did he have able assistance. Even though he was a professor, his associates did not have the privilege of a refined academic background. He eliminated all the unscriptural prayers and practices from the liturgy. His

---

that hold the reformation ideals of Martin Luther, not in the sense of the reformed church tradition' in its strict sense.

[112] Kuruvila, *A Brief History of the Syrian Christians of Malabar*, CMS/ C I 2/0 148/3 MSS, 13.

[113] John Wycliffe (1328-1384) was one of the leaders of the Western Reformation.

[114] Martin Luther (1483-1546) was another leader of the Western Reformation.

[115] Viswanadhan, *The Christians of Kerala*, 21.

reform purpose was based on his vision for restoring the Church to what he considered to be its position before the Synod of Diamper. He strove hard for the abolition of auricular confession (confessing sin to a priest), prayers for the departed souls, invocation of saints and over the ritualistic veneration (giving deep reverence or respect) of the sacraments. Further, he emphasized the reading and study of the Bible, family worship and evangelistic work. He also insisted on a high moral standard of conduct for laity and clergy alike. The main intention of Abraham Malpan was to effect reform in the ancient Malankara Church based on scriptural truth. He held firmly in the conviction that salvation is by faith in Jesus Christ alone as revealed in Scripture. The preaching of the missionaries and the printing and distribution of the Bible in the local language (Malayalam) went a long way in opening the eyes of the people to understand the biblical and spiritual truths of the Christian teachings. This also paved the way for a reformation in the Malankara Church. Abraham Malpan was a social reformer too. He wanted to emancipate his people from the superstitions of his time. The removal of the Muthappan[116] statue from the Maramon church was a good example of this. All this created ferment in the Church and its effects are still discernible in the Syrian Church as a whole.

---

[116] Maramon Muthappan: In 1685 CE Mor Baselios Yeldo Bava a Syrian prelate came to Kerala and died at Kothmangalom immediately just a few days after his arrival due to travel in his old age and ill health. (This bishop is considered as a Saint by both Orthodox and Jacobite Churches in Kerala - is called Kothamangalom Bava). The Syrian Christians of Kerala used to come to his graveyard each year for prayer and special favours. It was a place of pilgrimage. As people from Mavelikkara, Chengannur, Maramon of southern Kerala had difficulty in travel up to Kothamangalom in those days, southern people decided to make a local festival in his name and chose Maramon church for that. The people brought soil from Kothamangalom to Maramon. They made a three feet wooden doll in the shape of a human, made in memory of Mor Baselios Yeldo Bava and called the statue Muthappan (means old grandpa). The members of the Maramon Parish used to celebrate the festival of Muthappan every year. Offerings and prayers were conducted in front of this statue. The people believed that the cause of all their prosperity and blessings was because of this semi-god, Muthappan. The priests including Malpan Abraham used to venerate this idol. Large crowds used to attend this yearly festival, which was a good source of income for the Maramon parish. When Malpan Abraham realized the truth from the Bible by the influence of the CMS missionaries, he urged the people to leave such practices. On 4th of October 1837, the day before "Muthappan Festival," Abraham Malpan threw "the god Muthappan" into the well situated in the Church compound and put an end to this festival forever in Maramon, starting the reformation process.

The following are the reforms made by the strenuous activities of Abraham Malpan in the Malankara Church

(a) Worship services including Holy Communion were conducted in Malayalam.
(b) Prayers to the saints and prayers for the dead were removed from the liturgy.
(c) Changes made in various prayers in the prayer books incorporating the divine light received through the study of the Bible.
(d) Sunday school classes for the children were started in many parishes. The practice of ordaining young boys without any training as priests was stopped.
(e) Theological education became necessary for the priesthood.
(f) Importance was given to the Word of God. People started to read the Bible in their own language. Prayer groups were established to study the Word of God. The Bible became the sole source of faith and practices. Any beliefs or practices that were detrimental to Scripture were discontinued.[117]

5 - Importance of the Reformation in the Church

The MTC believes that the reformation was going back to the original doctrine and practices of the independent St. Thomas Church (Malankara Church). It was an affirmation of the autonomy and independence of the Malankara Church. The reformers were focused on eliminating the errors of their liturgy and its practices, which did not have a biblical rooting. The reform party was convinced that they continued in the apostolic faith brought to India by the Apostle, St. Thomas. Abraham Malpan or Mathews Mar Athanasius founded no new Church. They claim continuity with the independent Church formed in 1664, after the Coonan Cross and also with the Church founded by the Apostle St. Thomas.[118] According to Metropolitan

---

[117] Joseph, *Malankara Mar Thoma Syrian Church,* 40-41.
[118] Juhanon Mar Thoma, *The History of the Mar Thoma Church,* 31.

Juhanon Mar Thoma, the reformation in the Malankara Church is a return
to the faith of the Independent Malabar Church established by the Apostle
St. Thomas. It is a process of correcting the doctrines and practices of the
Church, rooted in the Malankara Church by the influence of the Roman
Catholic and Antiochian Orthodox Church throughout the centuries.[119] As
a reformed Church within the Oriental Eastern tradition, the MTC upholds
Scripture and tradition together in its life and mission. The reformation in
the Malankara Church is not just a historical act, but it has been a process.
Thus, MTC is a reformed as well as a reforming Church. The following
are some of the pertinent aspects of reformation in the Malankara Church.

4.5.1 - Sociological and Political Aspect of the Reformation
During the end of the 19th century, the traditional society of Kerala
encountered a tremendous change or awakening due to various reasons.
Mainly four agencies facilitated the emergence of this awakening,
namely, the British government, the Travancore government, the Western
missionaries, and the English educational system. These agencies caused
the emergence of a new society by restoring the dignity of the lower caste
people, especially the Dalits, through spreading the principles of equality,
liberty, and freedom.[120] The reformation within the Malankara Church was
not a spontaneous overflow of emotion of the marginalized sections, but
was part of the socio-political transformation in the Kerala society.

The activities of the CMS missionaries and the 19th century social reform
movements in Kerala,[121] inspired and challenged the St. Thomas Christians

---

[119] Juhanon Mar Thoma. *The History of the Mar Thoma Church*, 55.
[120] The reformation movement challenged the age-old caste-ridden social structure of the
region. It constituted a public sphere, which catered to rational democratic discourses
and launched social reform movements. During this time, the Christian faith stood out as
an ideological tool in the determination of the freedom struggle of the region. Thus, the
reformation in the Malankara Church was a struggle for identity and for the protection of
the age-old faith of their ancestors. Alex Thomas, *A History of the First Cross Cultural
Mission of the Mar Thoma Church 1910 – 2000* (Delhi; ISPCK, 2007), 1.
[121] In the social sphere, there were movements of caste reform or caste abolition, equal
rights for women, a campaign against child marriage and a ban on widow remarriage,
a crusade against social and legal inequalities. In the religious sphere, there sprang up
movements which combated religious superstitions and attacked idolatry, polytheism and

to re-examine and reconstitute their identity and social status. It provided distinctive transformations in the ecclesial identity of the Malankara Church. C. P Mathew and M. M Thomas pointed out that the CMS missionaries began to break the caste mentality of the Syrian Christians and lessen their prejudices against the Dalits and underprivileged. They also point out that those CMS missionaries motivated Christians to spread the Gospel to all people irrespective their caste status.[122] The Western missionaries acted as catalysts for the emergence of the awakening.[123] The reformation enabled the Church and its members to step into the changing social context of the 19th century Kerala society with transformed individuality and with new discourses of societal change. Consequently, it equipped the Syrian Christian community to reach out to the Dalit communities of Kerala with a renewed vision and mission.[124] The vernacular liturgy movement or the reformation movement of 1836 was the beacon for a number of social reform movements in Malabar. Liberal values, freedom of worship and due dignity to human beings were the notable practices followed herein. Thus, a wave of democratization was generated from the struggles of the people to define their faith and social identity.[125] The reform faction wanted to redefine their identity in the course of the struggle. Thus the newly evolved Church declared its identity as the Mar Thoma Syrian Church of Malabar (*Malankara Mar Thoma Suriyani Sabha*) and had its liturgy in Malayalam. The name of the Church affirmed its regional linguistic identity and the

hereditary priesthood. These movements, in varying degrees, emphasized and fought for the principles of individual liberty and social equality and stood for nationalism.

[122] Mathew and Thomas, *The Indian Churches of St. Thomas*, 28-29.

[123] Thomas, *A History of the First Cross-Cultural Mission of the Mar Thoma Church,* 2.

[124] K. E Geevarghese and Thomas T. Mathew, eds., *Beyond the Diaspora: Mar Thoma Church: Identity and Mission in the Context of Multiplicity* (Thiruvalla: Mar Thoma Church Dioceses of North America and Europe, 2014), 58.

[125] The main issue that evolved in the course of the reform movement was purely the question of social identity. Their liturgy in Syriac language defined their identity as the Syrian Christians or Malankara *Nazarani* (Christians) in the same way the Brahmins- the upper class Hindus viewed their language Sanskrit as superior. The caste name *Nazarani* closely linked to the liturgy of the Syriac. The adoption of Malayalam liturgy meant a conscious abandoning of the caste identity, because Malayalam was considered to be a socially "low language," unaccepted in the literary public sphere, and even it was, moreover, the language of the untouchables and outcaste people.

tradition of St. Thomas that it followed. The Church attached the word "Syrian" not in caste identity, but to express its liturgical identity. Above all, critically one can say the MTC reclaimed the caste identity by the addition of the term "Syrian."

4.5.2 - Theological or Doctrinal Aspect of the Reformation

The reformation in the Malankara Church had decisively helped the Church to reconstitute its identity more symbolically and seriously as a result of revisiting the biblical teachings. The reformation in the Malankara Church had several elements of the protestant reformation that took place in the 16th century in Europe under the leadership of Martin Luther. The Protestant Reformation initiated a renewed interest in the understanding and hermeneutical aspect of Scripture. The slogan "Scripture alone" had a great impact on the doctrinal position of the reforming process. This changed approach and new initiative in the study of the Word of God and its consequent practices were more epistemological, raising more 'why' and 'what' questions in the micro and macro social structures and practices. Moreover, the members of the MTC being formed and re-formed within this changed space have had a deeper conviction of their calling and vocation which also helped the growth of the Church along with their own growth in the diaspora.[126] Because of reformation, a new trend emerged in the theological thinking of the reformed wing about their doctrines, spiritual practices and mission. A recovery of the Lutheran maxim of the "priesthood of all believers" and the reclamation of the Christian vocation as the task of the whole Church, signalled a realignment of the nature of ministry and mission. The ministry was no longer solely equated with the activities of the clergy, but rather became something exercised by the whole people of God, in the Church and the world. Instead of clerical paradigm (something oriented towards ordained ministry), theological literacy among the whole people of God is emphasized.[127]

---

[126] Geevarghese and Mathew, *Beyond the Diaspora*, 58, 62.
[127] Tovey, *Essays in West- Syrian Liturgy*, 23-25.

4.5.3 - Liturgical Aspect of the Reformation

The reforms in liturgical prayers and practices were the focus and most evident aspect of the reformation process in the Malankara Church. The reformers made concrete changes in the liturgy to make it more simple for active participation. In practice, the reformers preferred to avoid the dramatization of the Holy Qurbana. Their intention was to make the worship more easy and meaningful. They avoided the excessive use of ritualistic elements from the original liturgy. The removal of the procession, the kissing of the altar, the removal of *Marvahuza* (a fan with bells on its sides which is used at the most solemn moments of the Holy Qurbana such as before reading the Gospel, Epiclesis, and the fraction to draw the attention of the people), the continued act of veiling and unveiling of curtain in the *madbaho* etc., are some examples of this. The motive behind this was to make the communion service simple and uncomplicated.

The contact with the CMS missionaries and their reformed theology had a tremendous influence on the leaders of the Malankara reformation. In the initial stages of reformation, the Anglican preachers like Walker and later on by Presbyterian and Baptist evangelical preachers like Wordsworth, Billy Graham and others influenced the Church in its spiritual journey. Reading and re-reading of the Word of God, rituals, practices, liturgical and sacramental celebrations hold a decisive role in the formation of a new liturgical identity to the Mar Thoma community. The translation of the Bible and the liturgy in the vernacular was an important aspect in this matter. The liturgy used in the Malankara Church was the combination of both Scripture and teaching of the early Church Fathers. Because of the influence of the missionaries and the thorough study of the Bible in later years, the reformers were forced to find a theological position for its prayers and practices. The study of the Word of God led many in the Malankara Church to see the need for reformation in the Church. They understood that the Christian Church as the body of Christ must witness to Jesus Christ and present the light of the Gospel to others. The Maramon Convention was a platform for the spiritual nourishment of the Mar Thoma community since 1895.

4.5.4 - Linguistic Aspect of the Reformation[128]

It is before the inception of the Malayalam language, since the fourth century CE, Syriac became the liturgical language of the Malankara Christians. In the formation time of Malayalam as a script, the Syriac script was used to denote the Malayalam letters and vowels. This script was known as Garshuni script, which traditionally evolved among the Malankara Christians and existed among them till the 19th century.[129] The introduction of vernacular liturgy triggered a series of changes in the society in Malabar. It distorted the notion of "holy language." The structure of Malabar society was anchored because of caste and the notion of holy language. The Hindu community considered Sanskrit as a holy language whereas the Christians regarded Syriac to be so. The use of a vernacular liturgy was a challenge to these holy languages and the accompanying social structure. In the Indian context, social groups were defined as castes and each caste had their own God and language.[130] The use of the vernacular at the sanctum Sanctorum of the Church not only challenged Syriac, but Sanskrit and other holy languages. This was the starting point of anti-caste struggles in Malabar. The placing of untouchable, script-less language in the holy place of the church shocked the social consciousness, and preconceived notions of language. For the first time ever known in the history of Malabar, a faction of people decided to define themselves as a faith community outside the age-old caste structure. The reformation in the Malankara Church reiterated the fact that no language is superior to

---

[128] One of the hallmarks of the European reformation of the 15th century was its insistence on the vernacular. For instance, Martin Luther is often viewed as the leader of vernacular reform in the 16th century, who published his major treaties in German. Swiss reformer Ulrich Zwingli insisted that his own works be published in Swiss-German while second generation reformer John Calvin was published in his native French. Vernacular promotion played a major role within the English reformation as well. The chief architect of the *Book of Common Prayer,* Thomas Cranmer (1556), also supported the vernacular liturgy. The result of such a paradigmatic shift to the vernacular had significant effects far beyond the borders of Reformation Germany, Switzerland or France. Keith P. Pecklers, *Dynamic Equivalence: The Living Language of Christian Worship* (Collegeville, MN: Liturgical, 2003), 127-128.

[129] Thumpamon, *Diary of Puthanpurackal Mathai Kathanar* (Malayalam), 36.

[130] *Pulayabhasha* and *Parayabhasha* are the best examples in this regard, which belongs to the lower class in the Kerala society.

another and that God is not pleased because of prayers in any particular language. It further emphasised that worship should be in the language of the worshiping community for better understanding and effective participation.

4.6 - The Reformation in the Mar Thoma Church: A Critical View

The reformation of the Malabar Church in 1836 is a highly contentious issue in the Church history of the region. The prevailing argument is that the Western colonial intervention was the primary reason for reformation in the Malankara Church. James Hough observed that, reformation is an indirect result of the English - Syrian alliance in the Malabar region. In a critical view, it is not the primary reasons for the reformation. There are other factors such as English education, socio-religious movements of the time, etc., which also caused the formation of reformation process. On the other hand, the movement can be considered as a radical response of the natives to the colonial encounters and their attempt for reclaiming the tradition bequeathed to them from St. Thomas, the Apostle. Simply, it was a return to the purity of life and practice of the early Malankara Church. The reformation was an attempt to cleanse the Malankara Church from the unscriptural practices included in the very life of the Church as a result of its association with overseas ecclesial groups. It is an assertion of the originality of the St. Thomas tradition. The most prominent element of reformation was:

(a) Return to the Gospel message of salvation by faith in Jesus Christ.
(b) Cleansing of wrong ways of living.
(c) Taking up responsibility to be witnesses of Jesus Christ to others.
(d) Focusing on the study of the Word of God.

Abraham Malpan initiated a theological investigation in the Church and his followers upheld that and tried to explore it in depth. In that sense, the theological exploration of the Church into its various prayers and practices was continued after the formation of the Church. It is an ongoing process and the exploration on various prayers still continues. The reformed liturgy is the continuation of the apostolic faith of the Church that is handed down from generation to generation. But the mode of communication and content need to be contextualized for the modern period. When the liturgy becomes contextual, it will influence the people and the total life of the Church will be transformed.

An analysis of the Eucharistic liturgy of the MTC discloses the unique features of the liturgy such as richness of theological content centred around the Trinitarian doctrine, active participation of the congregation, the prayers and petitions that have scriptural support and the presence of the eschatological dimension of salvation.[131] Another aspect of the present liturgy is that it is a God-centred liturgy in the framework of the Church. God loves the Church, and the Church is God's prime arena of work. But we should not forget the importance of the world. Instead, our primary concern should be God-World-Church. God loved the world and because of God's love for the world, God created the Church. The world should write the agenda for the Church. Therefore, the liturgy should not deal only with the acts of God in the past, but must relate to the life situations of today. Edification of people about the role of liturgical prayers and practices is important at this juncture. This helps the participants to worship God while keeping the great heritage and tradition of the Church and satisfying their spiritual needs in connection with their day-to-day life. The Eucharistic community should be a reconciled, renewed and mission-oriented.

---

[131] This does not mean that the reformed liturgy is devoid of any limitations. If one critically observes the reformed liturgy of the MTC, it is evident that it does not consider its context very much. There are several areas where they need further adaptations, changes or renewal of liturgy. A relevant liturgy should reflect the day-to-day affairs of the community, their problems, hopes, and aspirations. A contextual liturgy must address the issues like injustice, poverty, exploitation, discrimination based on caste, colour, gender and so on. The participation in the liturgy should challenge such evil systems in society and enable them to fight against it. Through the liturgy, the real sanctification and transformation of the people have to take place. For better ecumenical relations, the Church should formulate and celebrate an ecumenical liturgy and new modes of communication should be incorporated into the worship for explaining the signs and symbols.

Finally, one can say that the reformation process caused the formation of a simple and uncomplicated liturgy in the MTC. It avoids the intricacy and perplexity of performing rituals, symbols and signs. Moreover, it facilitates an active participation of the laity in worship. Abraham Malpan initiated a theological investigation in the Church and his followers upheld the same and strove for further insights. Hence in that sense the theological exploration of the Church into its various prayers and practices was continued even after the formation of the Church. The reformation is an ongoing process under the guidance of the Holy Spirit, which is never complete.

5 - Conclusion

The Malankara Christians in the Indian subcontinent hold a special place in the ecclesial map of world Christianity because of their unique identity and apostolic nature. The traditions of the Church uphold its footings in the missionary activity of St. Thomas, and later colonialism and its connection with various ecclesial traditions shaped the theology, practices, and liturgy of the Malankara Christians. As already seen, the ecclesiastical history of the Malankara Church is a unique one since the colonialism and the Catholicism had a wide impact in the Malankara Church. The historical events like Synod of Diamper, Coonan Cross Oath etc., sow seeds of reformation in the Church and thereby exposed its desire for autonomy and independence. Here, the process of reformation marked as a decisive incident in the identity of the Malankara Church. The reformation movement in the Church was a call to going back to the original faith and practice of the early Malankara Church since the 52 CE.

The pioneer of reformation, Abraham Malpan was not a westernized Syrian reformer. As cited above, he was an ardent follower of the Eastern liturgical traditions and practices, who considered that translating the liturgy into vernacular on the basis of Scripture is essential for a renewal in the Church. He argued that the liturgy has to be interpreted on the basis of the Bible. For him, reformation movement was an act of going back to the origin and purity of the Malankara Christian tradition and the spiritual heritage of St. Thomas on the background of Scripture. From our analysis, one can come to a conclusion that the purification process initiated by the pioneers of reformation in the Malankara Church was not an outcome of any Western ecclesial activity; rather, it was a spontaneous overflow of the need of the time. The influence of the CMS missionaries accelerated and influenced the reformation process in the Church. They infused a new vision of mission into the Malankara Church by translating the Bible, publication of the Book of Common Prayer and revising the Syriac liturgy into vernacular.

Chapter 2

The Nature and Identity of the Malankara Mar Thoma Syrian Church

The term identity always goes along with culture, race and linguistic line. From a religious perspective, identity is something more than the traditional definition.[132] At present, the identity of the MTC goes beyond cultural, racial and linguistic line and it has an emerging identity in its diaspora regions.[133] The cross-cultural encounters of the Church continue to broaden its ecclesial identity, with its wide-open windows to the world. There is a trend to adapt, adjust, and accept many things in its life, mission, and witness in its arena of global-multi- cultural and linguistic- diaspora existence.

1 - The Mar Thoma Church: Hybrid in Nature

The MTC bears witness to the fact of the Eastern origin of Christianity along with the other "Lesser Eastern Churches."[134] The liturgy, pattern

---

[132] The term identity is presently used in two connected senses, which may be termed "social" and "personal." According to James D. Fearon, an "identity refers simply to a social category, a set of persons marked by a label and distinguished by rules deciding membership and (alleged) characteristic features or attributes. In the second sense of personal identity, an identity is some distinguishing characteristic (or characteristics) that a person takes a special pride in or views as socially consequential but more-or-less unchangeable." James D. Fearon, "What is Identity (As we now use the word)?" Stanford: Department of Political Science Stanford University, 1999), 2. https://web.stanford.edu/group/fearon-research/cgi-bin/wordpress/wp-content/uploads/2013/10/What-is-Identity-as-we-now-use-the-word-.pdf (accessed September 18, 2016).

[133] The MTC has moved away from its traditional cultural social settings to a multi-racial, multi-ethnic, multi-linguistic and multi-generational context. It is no longer a monolithic community. The diaspora and the mission centres' context force the Church to embrace multiplicity. Now this is a unique nature of the Church in general.

[134] The Syrian Orthodox Church, the Coptic Orthodox Church, the Eritrean Orthodox Church, the Ethiopian Orthodox Church, and the Armenian Orthodox Church are the

of worship, its ceremonies, rituals, traditions and theology admit this fact.[135] This has been described in different ways: Metropolitan Juhanon Mar Thoma called it "a Protestant Church in an oriental grab." One of the Church historians Kaj Baago noted that "the Mar Thoma Church is a strange combination of Catholicism and Protestantism, of conservatism and radicalism, of traditionalism in worship and revivalism in preaching."[136] Owing to the exceptional identity of this Church, Metropolitan Alexander Mar Thoma remarks that:

> "The Mar Thoma Church combines evangelical and reformed doctrines with ancient forms of worship and practices. As a reformed Church with progressive outlook, it agrees with the reformed doctrines of Western Churches. Therefore, in the days of ecumenism, there is much in common between the Mar Thoma Church and other reformed Churches. At the same time as it continues the Apostolic Episcopal tradition and ancient Oriental practices, it has much in common with the Orthodox Churches. Thus it is regarded by many in the ecumenical world as a bridging Church."[137]

This Church gives more importance to the participation of the laity, which contributes a lot to the growth of the Church. It is believed that all people are called to share in the royal priesthood of Jesus Christ.[138] The very foundation of the Church is rooted in the idea that the "*Church is creatura Christi and creatura Spiritus*" - in India. The leaders of reformation never attempted to alter this basic understanding of the Church that was based on divine authority, the Bible, the Nicene-Constantinople creed, the apostolic tradition and sacraments. The creeds are understood as summaries of the essentials of Christian doctrine. In conformity with the faith of the

---

lesser Eastern Churches. The common element among these Churches is their rejection of the Christological definition of the Council of Chalcedon (451 CE) which asserted that Christ is one person in two natures, undivided and unconfused

[135] Joseph, *Malankara Mar Thoma Syrian Church,* 16.

[136] Geevarghese and Mathew, *Beyond the Diaspora,* 82.

[137] Alexander Mar Thoma, *The Mar Thoma Church: Heritage and Mission,* 14-18.

[138] Alexander Mar Thoma, *The Mar Thoma Church: Heritage and* Mission, 93.

Christian Church in all ages, the MTC believes in Jesus Christ, who came into the world to redeem humankind from its sins, and in the Triune God. The Church accepts the Holy Bible, consisting of the sixty six books of the Old and New Testaments, as the basis for all matters pertaining to doctrine and faith. This is the premise on which the identity of the Church developed during the reformation.[139]

With regard to the ecclesiology of the Church, it shares the undivided Church's stand that the Church is a communion of believers, revealed to the world through the Trinitarian mystery. The Church firmly held the Orthodox faith regarding the mysteries of Trinity, the incarnation, and the Holy Qurbana.[140] The Church's life is characterized by its participation in fellowship, teaching, witness, worship, and service. Witnessing the redemptive work of Christ is the primary task of the Church. Thus, the missionary mandate of the Church is its primary characteristic nature. It also affirms that the Church is the sign and sacrament of the Kingdom of God. Based on these undivided Church's ecclesiology, the foundation of the faith, mission and practice of the Church are laid. The following are some of the principal values that are regarded as being very important in its identity.

1.1 - Apostolic in Origin and Episcopal in Character

The MTC values the importance of apostolic succession and a celibate episcopacy that is constitutional in nature. Thereby the Church continues in the age-old beliefs and customs of the ancient Syrian Church. The Church stands in the apostolic succession, of which three-fold apostolic ministry of bishops, priest, and deacons is a central expression.[141] The apostolic dimension of the Church also refers to the apostolic legacy that the Church inherited from the Apostle Thomas to the long chain of luminaries

---

[139] *Constitution of the Malankara Mar Thoma Church of Malabar*, English version (Thiruvalla: Mar Thoma Press, 2002), 1-2. Geevarghese and Mathew, *Beyond the Diaspora*, 139-140.

[140] Joseph Thekkedathu, *History of Christianity in India.* vol. II (Thiruvalla: Christian Literature Society, 1983), 30.

[141] *Constitution of the Malankara Mar Thoma Church of Malabar*, 1-2.

including the present Metropolitan and bishops, who adorn the apostolic tradition of St. Thomas in the Church. This Church in principle accepts the authority of the Church over matters of faith and practice and therefore it practices historic episcopacy.[142] It affirms that episcopacy is an essential expression of the wholeness and the historic continuity of its ecclesial life.[143] This Church stands in continuity with the apostolic tradition and succession. This means that whatever the bishop is doing in teaching the Word of God, sacraments, doctrines and faith, must have continuity, going back to the Church Fathers, the first seventy-two disciples, the apostles, to the apostle Thomas and to Jesus Christ.[144] Concerning the apostolic succession, the Church insists that it is not something that the bishop enjoys as private personal possession in isolation from the Church, but it is the grace of God for the Church as a whole.[145] Thus, apostolic succession is in continuity with the Trinitarian mystery of salvation, which brought the Church together with God.[146] This also includes the laying-on-of-hands.[147] For instance, the apostolic authority is handed over to bishops through the handing over of *"Staticon,"* that is, an authorization certificate from

---

[142] *Canon of the Malankara Mar Thoma Syrian Church*, English translation, 10-18. *Constitution of the Malankara Mar Thoma Syrian Church*, 29-32. The MTC affirms and follows the historic hierarchical nature of the Oriental Orthodox Churches, the Anglican Church, the Old Catholic Church, and the Lutheran Churches. The Anglican and Lutheran Churches affirm their apostolicity of the whole Church as gift of God and therefore, the apostolic succession does not confine to the three-fold apostolic ministry of the Church alone, but it extended to the variety of means, activities, and institutions of the Church. Thus for them the apostolicity connects to the whole life of the Church the people of God, who are being baptized into the Body of Christ. But the three fold ministry is a central characteristic of the Church. *The Consultation Report of the Lambeth Conference and the Lutheran World Federation- 1970-1972.* (London: SPCK, 1973), 69 - 81.

[143] *Report of the Metropolitan's Committee*, July 15, 1953.

[144] Unpublished liturgy of the Mar Thoma Episcopal Consecration, *Amalogia*, (Thiruvalla: Poolatheen: handwritten Copy): see Mt.16:18-19, Jn.20:21-23.

[145] The MTC follows the teaching of the early Church Father Irenaeus, who says that, "we should obey those presbyters in the church who have their succession from the apostles and who together with succession in the episcopate, have received the assured charisma of the truth." See Irenaeus, *Against the Heresies* IV, XI, (xxviii) 2, 236. Peter Moore, ed., *Bishops But What Kind?* (London: SPCK, 1982), 12.

[146] *Mar Thoma Sleehayude Edavakayakunna Malankara Suriyani Sabhayude Canon*, 13 -18.

[147] Joseph Mar Thoma Metropolitan, Interview by writer, April 15, 2014.

the Metropolitan at the time of the bishop's consecration; it is most the significant sign of the unbroken chain of apostolic authority, going back to the apostles and Jesus Christ.

The Church affirms the connection between the Holy Qurbana and the bishop, which is a dominant idea of all Orthodox Churches.[148] This understanding has a special significance in the context of various teachings about the celebration and administration of sacraments in the contemporary context. The presiding bishop of the Holy Qurbana acts as a sign and sacrament of the Church's unity.[149] This idea of the Eucharistic unity of the bishops is indebted to the teachings of Ignatius of Antioch (98-170 CE). For him, the bishop is "the one who presides at the Eucharist, acting as a living image of Christ, and so constituting the focus and visible centre of unity within the Church."[150] Ignatius therefore instructs, "let the Eucharist be considered valid, which is celebrated by the bishop or the one whom he appoints. Wherever the bishop is, there let the people be."[151] To keep this tradition in the Church, the Bishop consecrates the wooden block called tablito which reminds us of whose altar on which the priest celebrates the Eucharist, which is considered as requirement for the priest to celebrate the Eucharist in the parishes or in any place of worship. The reform tradition of the Church added a new meaning to the Tablita. It reminds us of the fact that the Holy Qurbana "is a sacrifice without blood"[152] offered on tablito. It is in line with the Syrian ecclesial tradition, the episcopacy of the MTC is celibate in nature. The Church believes that it is quite biblical for a bishop to lead a married life, but traditionally the Church practices episcopal celibacy. The bishopric candidates enter into a life of an ascetic

---

[148] Moore, *Bishops But What Kind*, 2-3.

[149] The Malankara Mar Thoma Syrian Church, *The Constitution*, 3-24 *Edavakayakunna Malankara Suriyani Sabbayude Canon*, 13 -18.

[150] The Malankara Mar Thoma Syrian Church, *The Constitution*, 3-24 *Edavakayakunna Malankara Suriyani Sabbayude Canon*, 2.

[151] Letter of St. Ignatius to the Smyreans, Ch: 8-9; see Archimandrite Kallistos Ware, *Communion and Inter-communion*, (Minnesota: Light and Life Publishing House, 1980), 11- 15. J. Romanides, "The ecclesiology of the St. Ignatius of Antioch," *Greek Orthodox Theological Review* VII (1961): 63-65.

[152] Joseph, *Gleanings*, 39.

(*Sanayasam*), through accepting the consecration as Ramban. According to Mar Theodosius, this aseptic nature is not a withdrawal from the world or from the realities of life.[153]

1.2 - Evangelical and Biblical Emphasis

As mentioned earlier, till the time of reformation, the Malankara Church remained aloof as a privileged group within the caste ridden society of Kerala. An interaction with the CMS missionaries, and the translation of the Bible and the Liturgy facilitated the pioneers of reformation to identify the missionary vocation of the Church as one of the core concerns of the Church. The Church believes that the Bible as a whole contains the message of salvation. Along with it, the Nicene Creed formulated in accordance with Scripture considered as above alteration in any form by anyone. [154] An interpretation of Scripture in the settings of liturgy was a major emphasis of reformation in the Church. Mathews Mar Athanasius is the first Malankara Metropolitan who introduced the practice of reading Scripture and its exposition during the worship service in the Malankara Church.[155]

A great emphasis on teaching the Bible through conventions, study classes and cottage prayer groups in parish units, diocesan and Church at large made a great revival in the community and that triggered a great spiritual growth in the Church. The inception of Maramon Convention for the proclamation of the Word of God is a classic example for this. Hence, one can say that Scripture is the basis of the liturgical revision in the Malankara Church, and thereby the formation of the MTC. The Church, realizing that the renewal is needed continually within the community by the re-reading of Scripture. Reading and re-reading of the Bible, rethinking ritual practise of worship, liturgy and sacraments all play a decisive role in

---

[153] Geevarghese Mar Theodosius, "Eastern Spirituality and Identity of the Mar Thoma Church," in *The Mar Thoma Church: Tradition and Modernity*, 95.
[154] *Constitution of the Mar Thoma Church*, http://www.pcaac.org/wp-content/uploads/2012/11/WCFScriptureProofs.pdf (accessed September 07, 2015).
[155] Juhanon Mar Thoma, *The History of the Mar Thoma Church*, 46.

the construction of the identity of the community and thereby the members who are regularly confronted with the pressures of the changing world.

1.3 - Oriental in Liturgy and Reformed in Practices

The MTC is an Oriental non-Chalcedonian wing of the Universal Church because it stands in continuity with the Oriental Eastern Church, and is reaching out through the medieval period of the Oriental Church to the Fathers and martyrs of the early Church and to the Apostle Thomas. It embodies Eastern Canon, Scripture, the Nicene Creed, three fold ministry, sacraments, and worship pattern (liturgy). The liturgy of the Church opens up doors into a rich world of worship, where beauty, form and wonder offer liberation, joy and freedom of the person. The worship in the MTC is communitarian as well as personal, spiritual along with physical, mediatorial and vicarious. The worship offered by the community of believers along with the cosmic community enjoys the fellowship of both the visible and the invisible dimension.[156] The MTC derives its identity and cohesiveness from the very liturgy it uses. The whole theology of the Church is embedded in its liturgy. The Church also acknowledges its debt to the reformers; it acknowledges that the 19th century missionary movements and the reformation ideals of the CMS missionaries have significantly influenced and shaped the nature of the Church. It is very evident by its emphasis on the paramount place of Scripture, the royal priesthood of the baptized, and the missionary identity of the Church. Therefore, the Oriental and reformed impulses interact with each other within the Church and moderate each other.[157] The Church keeps a balance between its oriental liturgical tradition and the evangelical emphasis on reformation theology.

The MTC exists as a hybrid Church by merging eastern liturgical traditions and the evangelical aspirations of the Protestant Reformation of the 16th century.[158] Even though the Church is rooted in the Oriental Orthodox tradition, its doctrines are slightly different from the Orthodox

---

[156] Alexander, *The Mar Thoma Church: Tradition and Modernity*, 97.
[157] Geevarghese and Mathew, *Beyond the Diaspora*, 142-143.
[158] Joseph, *Gleanings*, 24.

traditions.[159] The Church combines evangelical and reformed doctrines along with ancient forms of worship and practice. For example, in the Church, both the traditionalists and the evangelicals will find mutual space: the ritualists will find satisfaction in chants, prayers and collects, while the evangelicals will find it in the preaching of the Word of God, the extemporal prayers and the singing of hymns and lyrics. As a reformed Oriental Church, it agrees with the reformed doctrines of the Western Churches. Therefore, there is much in common in faith and doctrine between the MTC and the reformed Churches of the West. As the Church now sees it, just as the Anglican Church is a Western Reformed Church, the MTC is an Eastern Reformed Church. At the same time as it continues in the apostolic episcopal tradition and ancient oriental practices, it has much in common with the Oriental Orthodox Churches. Thus, it is regarded as a "bridging Church." This nature of the Church points to its uniqueness when compared to other Churches both in the Malankara traditions and worldwide. However, this position and status of the Church never hinder her from entering into a friendly relationship with the Protestant Churches and other Christian denominations.[160]

1.4 - Indigenous in Nature and Democratic in Function

The MTC is essentially indigenous, self-governing, self-supporting, and self-propagating.[161] It is an autonomous Church in the sense of its being in an independent Church governed by its own Metropolitan, Episcopal Synod, the Sabha Council (Executive Body) and General Assembly (*Sabha Pradhinidhi Mandalam*) and appointing its own Metropolitan. In matters of a proposition dealing with theological questions, the Episcopal Synod of the Church together with the whole body of the Church - priest and laity- have their responsibility to keep the Church in the biblical truth, God's mission and to guard it from errors. For instance, in the event of dealing

---

[159] A detailed description on the doctrines of the Church is mentioned in the following chapters.

[160] Abraham, "The Mar Thoma Syrian Church of Malabar," 151-152.

[161] Alexander Mar Thoma, *The Mar Thoma Church: Heritage and Mission,* 91.

with any new theological proposal, the constitution of the Church demands "the three fourth majority of the laity and clergy of the General Assembly, sitting separately and simple majority in the house of bishops before it can become an act in the Church."[162] Therefore, the Episcopal nature of the Church is both historic and constitutional. This is also in conformity with teachings of Ignatius of Antioch (35-108 CE) and Cyprian of Carthage (200-258 CE), "...as the Lord was united to the Father, and did nothing without Him, neither by himself nor through the apostles, so should you do nothing without the bishop and the presbyter."[163] And "Do not decide without the counsel of the Presbyterium and the consent of the people."[164] For instance, without the simple majority approval of the bishops in the Episcopal Synod, the house of the laity or clergy or both together cannot impose their decisions in matters of faith in the Church. Similarly, the Episcopal Synod by itself cannot impose its decision in matters of faith in the Church. This collective authority of the metropolitan, bishops, clergy and laity holds good for the Church to guard it from errors collectively; collegiality of the bishops also is valued.[165]

The administration of the Church is very democratic. The administrative structure of the Church is a well-defined hierarchical structure, but it also accommodates democratic agencies to formulate and implement the mission life of the Church at the level of the local parishes. The bishop has the role of supervising the deliberations of the people and giving proper guidance. At the same time, the bishop initiates new schemes and dimensions of mission and helps the people to execute them. The required

---

[162] The Malankara Mar Thoma Syrian Church of Malabar, *The Constitution*, 6.

[163] Ignatius of Antioch, epistle to the Magnesians, vii, 1; see Ignatius of Antioch, Epistle to the Philadelphia 7, www.earlychristianwrittings.com/.../ignatius-philadelphians-lightfoot (accessed June 15, 2014).

[164] Cyprian of Carthage, Letter to Ephesians 14:4. Cyprian of Carthage joined with Irenaeus about the charisma verities imparted to the bishops by virtue of their apostolic office, to proclaim the faith. But at the same time Cyprian recalls the basic principle that the bishop is in the Church. In this sense the authority to proclaim the truth belongs to the bishop grounded in his presiding role in the Eucharist. Moore, *Bishops But What Kind*, 18-19; Cyprian letter Iv, Ixxiii. 26.

[165] Abraham, *The Mar Thoma Syrian Church of Malabar*, 152-153. Geevarghese and Mathew, *Beyond the Diaspora*, 146-147.

finance is raised by the people from among them and they support the mission and ministry of the Church.[166]

1.5 - Mission Oriented Church - Missionary in Action

The MTC is a mission-oriented Church. The focus of the Church is to witness the reign of God in the world. The Church always searched for numerous ways to make the mission relevant to the community along with direct evangelism. The efforts in the area of evangelization have followed various patterns of mission because of the diversity of the Church. Globally the Church has to keep on seeking and finding new avenues of service in reaching out with the Gospel.[167] The Church attempted to incarnate the gospel through challenging the evils of the caste structure, serving the poor through hospitals, destitute homes and day care centers for poor children and thus focused on the development of villages through several programmes. The Church attempted to provide education for all people irrespective of their caste or religious status. The humanitarian work initiated by the Church is considered as a part of its wider mission. The Metropolitan Alexander Mar Thoma remarks that, "Jesus Christ came to preach the good news to the poor, to proclaim liberty to the captives, to give sight to the blind and to set free the oppressed. The gospel has to be presented as the power of God that saves individuals and change social structures. It is the duty of the Church to work on both levels."[168]

The reformation in the Malankara Church caused the development of a mission paradigm among the St. Thomas Christians. The Church affirms that she is commissioned to work for the Kingdom of God established through the person and work of Jesus Christ. Evangelism, social service, struggles for social justice and peace, the emancipation of the exploited and depressed class and caste are an inevitable responsibility of the Church.

---

[166] Alexander, *The Mar Thoma Church: Tradition and Modernity*, 95.

[167] A detailed overview of the models of mission employed by the Church is described in the eight chapter. George Poikail, *ST. Thomas Christians and their Eucharistic Liturgy* (Thiruvalla: Christava Sahitya Samithi, 2010), 120.

[168] Alexander Mar Thoma, *The Mar Thoma Church: Heritage and Mission*, 46.

The evangelistic outlook of the Church helps spread the Gospel among the non-Syrian areas too.[169] The Church believes that the Christian mission is both proclamation and engaging in activities that liberate people. Thus, the goal of the mission of this Church is the total redemption of individuals and society. The MTC affirms that the people of God are sent to the entire world and that they are called to participate in the plan of salvation, which is the reconciling work of God "to unite all things in Christ."[170]

A delegation of responsibility and inclusion of all people is fundamental ministerial norms. The Church is understood as a community of fellowship where each one cares for the other. House churches, family prayer, house visits, home care, etc., have found a very important place in the ministerial activity. Prayer groups, Bible study groups, witnessing sessions, worship gatherings and service activities are within the life and witness of the Church and through which the faith community grows and finds meaning in life. Through the organizations of the Church, children, teen, youths, adults, women, aged, all at every level are covered. Ministry is all embracing and corporate; at the same time very personal and intimate. The logo of the Church, "Lighted to Lighten" is indeed a commentary of the pastoral vision of the Church.[171]

1.6 - Ecumenical in Outlook

The MTC has cherished its apostolic tradition and at the same time remained open to fresh insights and ideas from other faiths and Christian denominations. Ecumenical spirit is very much engrained in the identity of the Church. The Church participates very much in the ecumenical arena locally, regionally, nationally and internationally. The ecumenical disposition of the Church can be traced back in history to the time when it

---

[169] Alexander Mar Thoma, *The Mar Thoma Church: Heritage and Mission*, 92.
[170] Joseph, *Gleanings*, 24.
[171] The Metropolitan Juhanon Mar Thoma provided the MTC with an emblem having the motto "Lighted to Lighten." This shows the privilege as Lighted and further responsibility to lighten the global village Zacharias Mar Theophilus, "The Pastoral Ministry of the Mar Thoma Church," in *In Search of Christian Identity in Global Community*, ed. M.J. Joseph (Thiruvalla: The Dioceses of North America and Europe, 2008), 36-37.

channelled its ecumenical outlook in practice by bringing together converts from three ethnic India groups- the Brahmins, the Dravidian[172] and the People of the land[173] - under the ambit of the Church. This ecumenical ethos led to the Church establishing its own unique self-identity. The Church always gives priority to the spirit of tolerance and unity in diversity with other faith communities and Church denominations. The ecumenical outlook of the Church underpins its inherent quality of openness and autonomy. The Church has shown this ecumenical outlook throughout its entire historical development and progress and particularly when it encountered challenges in its engagement with the Persian Church, the Roman Catholic Church, the Antiochian Church, the Malabar Independent Syrian Church, the Anglican Church, the Church of South India, the Church of North India and the worldwide ecumenical movement. According to Daniel, the history of the MTC evolved over the years through its ecumenical engagement with other Churches.[174] This Church emphasizes its commitment to ecumenism through its active participation in the various ecumenical bodies and programmes. The Church is actively engaged with the institutional expressions of modern ecumenism, such as the International Missionary Council (IMC) and later, the World Council of Churches (WCC). This Church is a member of the Joint Council of the Church of North India (CNI), Church of South India (CSI) and the Mar Thoma Church. These churches are in communion with each other and in communion with the worldwide Anglican Church. The Church is also in communion with the Independent Church of Thozhiyoor although the doctrinal positions are not mutually accepted in full.

The year 1936 witnessed a remarkable achievement in the field of Church union movement when the MTC and the Anglican Church of

---

[172] The Dravidians belong to the Mediterranean race. They are believed to be the main racial group in the population of South India and also considered as the descendants of the Indus valley civilization. This race also consists of the scheduled castes: Pulayas, Parayas, Kuravas. Menon, *A Survey of Kerala History,* 44.

[173] The people of the land are the hill tribes of Kerala. They belong to the Dalit community and Adivasis.

[174] Daniel, *Ecumenism in Praxis,* 24-25.

India had established formal occasional inter-communion. Now the Church enjoys full inter-communion relationship with the worldwide Anglican Communion, CSI, CNI and Episcopal churches in the USA and Canada. The Church also maintains friendly relations with other Churches like the Independent Church of Thozhiyoor, The Roman Catholic Church, The Jacobite Church, the Orthodox Churches, the Chaldean Church and interdenominational organizations like the Bible Society, Christian Conference of Asia (CCA), National Council of Churches in India, (NCCI), National Council of Churches in America, (NCCA), Churches Together in Briton and Ireland (CTBI), and Churches Together in Briton (CTB). The Church was an observer in the II Vatican Council of the Roman Catholic Church. [175] The women of the MTC are also active in the inter denomination women's programmes such as the Association of Theologically Trained Women of India, All India Council of Christian Women.

The MTC has been contributing many ecumenical leaders like, Metropolitan Juhanon Mar Thoma (President of WCC), M. M Thomas (President of the Central Committee WCC), Joseph Mar Thoma Metropolitan (President of CCA), Mathews George Chunakkara (General Secretary of CCA), Zacharias Mar Theophilus and Isaac Mar Philaxinos (member of Central Committee WCC) are a few of them. The ecumenical vision of the Church is rooted in Scripture. The divine plan to administer the universe envisages the unity of all things in Christ (Eph.1:10). "To hold things together" is the ultimate goal of the mission of the Church. The spirituality of the Church is embodied in the concept of the Kingdom of God which provides guidelines for an authentic ecumenical identity in the world.[176]

2 - Conclusion

The MTC exists as a hybrid Church by merging eastern liturgical traditions and the evangelical aspirations of the Protestant Reformation. The Church

---

[175] Abraham, "The Mar Thoma Syrian Church of Malabar," 154.
[176] Alexander, *The Mar Thoma Church Tradition and Modernity,* 107.

combines evangelical and reformed doctrines along with ancient forms of worship and practice. The MTC is a mission-oriented Church, which gives importance to corporate worship, fellowship in Christ, witness through service and charity, evangelization, and a moral life standard of its believers. There is a tension between tradition and reformation, between the Orthodoxy and the Protestantism in the Church. This dual identity-Orthodox in liturgical and Protestant in theology- is a mark of the Church. However, it is precisely this ability to comprehend both the Orthodox tradition and the Protestant message which has manifested the importance of the MTC and its significance throughout the entire world. The intrinsic tension in its cultural ethos and spirituality should enable the Church to rise above traditional boundaries.

Chapter 3

The West Syrian Liturgical Tradition and the Eucharistic Liturgy of the Malankara Mar Thoma Syrian Church

The arrival of Portuguese and the introduction of Latinization in the Malankara Church made a tremendous impact in the ecclesiastical life of the Malankara Christians. As mentioned in the previous chapter, the two historical events namely "Synod of Diamper" held in 1599 CE and the incident "*Coonan Kurishu Satyam*" (Slanting Cross Oath) held in 1653 resulted in a split in the St. Thomas Christians. A major faction recognized the Archdeacon Thomas Parambil of the Pakalomattom family as the head of the Church, who, after a valid act of consecration by the Antiochian bishop Mar Gregorios in 1663 was known as Mar Thoma I (1653-1670). This marked the beginning of the Malankara Church's relation with the Syrian Orthodox (Jacobite or *Monophysites*) Patriarchate of Antioch[177] and the gradual introduction of the West Syrian liturgy, customs and script on the Church of Malabar. Generally, two major effects of the Church's relations with the Antiochian Church can be identified. They are (1) the adoption of the West Syrian liturgical traditions and practices and also (2) the Church's approval of the Antiochian Patriarch's spiritual supremacy.[178]

To find out the origin and influence of the West Syrian liturgical tradition in the MTC and to understand an intrinsic relationship between

---

[177] *Mononphysitism* is a theological position to counter the Nestorianism and it held that "there is only one nature in the incarnated Christ" after the union. It was since sixth century; the *Monophysites* separated themselves and called themselves as Jacobites. Placid J. Podipara, *The Thomas Christians* (Bombay: St. Paul's Publications, 1970), 66-69.

[178] The arrival of Mar Gregorios connected the Malabar Church to the Patriarchate of Antioch. Vellian, *The Malabar Church,* 148. Daniel, *Ecumenism in Praxis,* 38.

the Eucharist and mission, this chapter draws attention to the historical nature, theological developments, and distinctive features of the West Syrian liturgy. Since, the translation and revision of the St. James liturgy is a visible expression of the reformation in the Malankara Church and the formation of the MTC, the Liturgy of St. James is analysed in detail.

1 - The West Syrian Liturgical Tradition

The Syriac liturgical tradition forms a distinct Oriental Christian tradition that exists alongside the Greek and the Latin liturgical traditions. Ecclesiologically, it is an indigenous Semitic expression of Christianity. In an ecclesiastical context, the term "Syrian" refers to those Churches for which Syriac was the primary vernacular in which their distinctive liturgical and theological traditions were formed. By extension, the term applies to those communities founded by the ancient churches where Syriac is widely spoken. The Syriac language is a branch of the Aramaic language which was derived from Semitic family of languages.[179] The Syriac literature especially, writings before 400 CE was expressed in Semitic thought forms that have not yet undergone much influence of Greek culture and thought pattern.

2.1 - The Early Syrian Syrian Tradition: An Outlook

Geographically, Syria is halfway between East and West and both the Greek and Semitic cultures had great influence on the life of Syrian Christianity. Politically, Syria was under the servitude of the Assyrians, (from mid-eighth century BCE), the Babylonians (586 BCE) and the Persians (539 BCE). It was a division of the Persian Empire when Alexander the Great (356-323 BCE) conquered and took it into the Hellenistic sphere. Following the death of Alexander the Great, his generals Seleucus and Ptolemy divided Syria between them and founded powerful dynasties. In the month of May 300 BCE, after having defeated Antigonus at Ipsus in 301, Seleucus I Nicator (358-281 BCE) founded Antioch. Antioch, the Seleucid capital,

---

[179] Fenwick, *The Forgotten Bishops,* 24.

was one of the greatest metropolises in the Mediterranean world. Seleucus named the city after his father Antiochus and erected a temple dedicated to Zeus Bottios, who together with Apollo was of special importance for the Seleucid dynasty.[180] This city remained under the control of Seleucid for about a century. Later on the dissolution of the Seleucid Empire and a brief annexation by Armenian king Tigran (95-55 BCE), a large piece of the Middle-East was conquered by Pompey (65-62 BCE) and thus Syria became a Roman province. Septimius Severus (193-211CE) later divided the region into two provinces: Syria Coele and Syria Phoenice. The extent of these provinces was more or less the equivalent of modern Syria, Iran, Lebanon, and division of Iraq.[181]

Antioch was an important city at the time of the emergence of the Christian community. It was noted as the regional capital and equally the administrative core for the Roman authorities at that time. During that period there was a strong Jewish diaspora community living in Antioch. From a Christian point of view, Antioch was the main center outside of Jerusalem, where the first followers of Jesus developed a distinctive voice and organization. The presence of a Christian community in Antioch from the very early period after the death and resurrection of Jesus is beyond dispute.[182] Acts.11:11-30 describes that some of those scattered from Jerusalem following the stoning of Stephen went to Antioch. It is claimed that in Antioch the term "Christian" was first used (Acts.11:26). Apart from Antioch,[183] the cities of Edessa, Nisibis, and Mosul happened to be the cultural centers of the Syriac-speaking people, across the world.

Syriac language was the mother tongue of most of the people before the time of Christ until the 13th century CE, and then Arabic became

---

[180] Magnus Zetterholm, *The Formation of Christianity in Antioch* (London: Routledge, 2003), 19, http://www.timemaps.com/history/syria-500bc (accessed November 10, 2014).
[181] Matti Moosa, *The Crusades Conflict Between Christendom and Islam* (Piscataway, New Jersey: Gorgias, 2008), 341-380, http://rbedrosian.com/Ref/Moosa/mmant1.htm (accessed November 15, 2014).
[182] Martin Stringer, *Rethinking the Origins of the Eucharist* (London: SCM, 2011), 105-108.
[183] http://www.timemaps.com/history/syria-500 BC (accessed on November 10, 2014).

the dominant language. After the Council of Chalcedon (451CE) and especially after the first decade of the sixth century, Syriac speaking Christians throughout those territories organized into three Christian Churches, owning allegiance to three separate hierarchies. These Christian communities claimed the legitimacy of the Patriarchate of Antioch.[184] The life of the Christian communities in Syria showed that there was neither one single Eastern Orthodox[185] Church, nor one doctrinal tradition which could be called Orthodoxy.[186] These faith communities were known as the Church of the East or the Apostolic Catholic Assyrian Church of the East, but often referred to as the East Syrian, the Syrian Orthodox Church or the West Syrian and the Antiochian Syrian Maronite Church usually known as the Maronites.[187] A debate on Christology was the matter of the separation of these Churches. The Church of the East, historically centered on Edessa and then Nisibis and Seleucia-Ctesiphon did not accept the decrees of the Council of Ephesus (431 CE) and Chalcedon (451 CE).[188] The Syrian Orthodox Church was derived from those who accepted the Council of Ephesus, but who regarded the Council of Chalcedon as a departure from the Christology of the Cyril of Alexandria (378-444 CE) as codified at

---

[184] Gordon Lathrop, *What are the Essentials of Christian Worship?* (Minneapolis, MN: Fortress, 1994), 138-139.

[185] The title Orthodox refers to several Churches, which have been in conflict over doctrinal, administrative, and hierarchical matters. The term Orthodox is a combination of two Greek words: *Orthos,* meaning upright or proper, and *doxa* which means both opinion and glory. In Western Christianity, the term Orthodox is used for right opinion. This term is also used to identify groups and individuals known for their concern to maintain strict doctrinal positions. Eastern Christianity uses Orthodox to describe a style of life and worship that is faithful to the Christian message. James R. Payton, *Light from the Christian East: An Introduction to the Orthodox Tradition* (Illinois: Inter Varsity, 2007), 57-58.

[186] John Binns, *An Introduction to the Christian Orthodox Churches* (Cambridge: Cambridge University, 2002), 2.

[187] Further, there are two other smaller Christian communities near by Antioch such as the Syrian Catholic Church, based at Beirut and the Greek Catholic or the Melkites. At present, the ancient city of Antioch is called Antakya and falls within the boundaries of modern Turkey, a city with numerous mosques but no living churches. Binns, *An Introduction to the Christian Orthodox Churches,* 1-2. Bryan D. Spinks, *Do This in Remembrance of Me: The Eucharist From the Early Church to the Present Day* (London: SCM, 2013), 141.

[188] Wilhelm Baum and Dietmar Winkler, *The Church of the East: A Concise History* (London: Routledge, 2010), 20-27, http://www.peshitta.org/pdf/CoEHistory.pdf (accessed November 14, 2014).

Ephesus.[189] Under the leadership of John of Tella (483-538 CE), Severus of Antioch (465-538 CE) and later, Jacob of Baradaeus (500-578 CE), a separate clerical hierarchy was established and the Church flourished in the Syriac speaking frontier of Antioch.[190] The Church was thus a non-Chalcedonian Church. The Maronite Church was a Chalcedonian Church, which gathered around the monastic community of St. Moron and gradually moved south to find protection in the mountains of Lebanon. It was rediscovered by the Latin Crusades, and it was politically useful for recognizing the Roman supremacy.[191] These three Churches had a shared common core. The Syriac version of Scripture commonly known as the Peshitta has been a valuable witness to the textual traditions for both the Masoretic Text of the Hebrew Bible and the *Textus Receptus* of the Greek New Testament.[192]

The characteristics of the Syriac literature are biblical, ritualistic, polemical, theological, historical and traditional. The Syrians were much concerned about generating translations and commentaries on Scripture. Moreover, the books of religious services and prayers which they have composed over many generations testify to their superior taste, high-mindedness and pre-eminence in the theological disputes, which long endured among the Christian sects.[193] The most significant writers in the

---

[189] Christological formula of Cyril of Alexandria, "one nature (*mia physis*) of God the Word, Incarnate," which mentions both the divinity and humanity in Christ but insists on their union. Christine Chaillot, "The Ancient Oriental Churches," in *The Oxford History of Christian Worship,* eds. Geoffrey Wainwright, Karen B. Westerfield Tucker (Oxford: Oxford University, 2006), 131.

[190] Volker L. Menze, *Justinian and the Making of the Syrian Orthodox Church* (Oxford: Oxford University, 2008), 13-20. Binns, *An Introduction to the Christian Orthodox Churches,* 31-32. The Syrian Orthodox Church is sometimes called the Jacobite Church that is after one of the greatest missionaries, Jacob bar-Addai or James Baradaeus. During the middle years of the sixth century he travelled around the Eastern part of Syria and set up an ecclesial structure, consecrating clergy who formed the hierarchy of the Church. The north of ancient Nisibis, the area Tur Abdin was the heartland of this Church.

[191] Matti Moosa, *The Maronites in History* (Piscataway: Gorgias, 2006), 18-24. Paul Naaman. *The Maronite: The Origins of an Antiochene Church* (Collegeville, MN: Liturgical, 2011), xv-xviii.

[192] Fenwick, *Forgotten Bishops,* 27.

[193] Sebastian Brock made a commendable research in the field of Syriac literature. He outlines a detailed record on the Syriac literature into four distinctive periods. Sebastian

58

Syriac tradition, whose works have an influence on the Church at large,
are Aphrahat (270-345 CE), Ephrem the Syrian (306-373 CE), Narsai (503
CE), Jacob of Serug (521 CE), Philoxenus of Mabbug (523 CE), Babai
the Great (628 CE), Jacob of Edessa (708 CE), and Isaac of Nineveh (700
CE).[194] Many of them cultivated a distinctive style of rhythmic prose that
Syriac preachers praised, as well as the metrical hymns and homilies for
which such writers as Ephraim the Syrian (the harp of the Holy Spirit),
and Jacob of Serug (the flute of the Holy Spirit) were later remembered.[195]

2.2 - Historical Groupings

The Orthodox[196] Churches originated from a common background which
had shaped the nature of the life of the Churches.[197] Generally, the Orthodox
Churches were grouped into two families, i.e. The Eastern and the Oriental.
It was in the 20th century ecumenical context that the term Eastern and
Oriental were used to classify these two families. The "Eastern Orthodox"
refers to the family of Churches in the Byzantine liturgical tradition in
communion with the See of Constantinople (Ecumenical Patriarchate) like

Brock, "An Introduction to Syriac Studies," in *Horizons in Semitic Studies*, ed. John
Herbert Easton (Birmingham: University of Birmingham, 1980), 8-10. Mor Ignatius
Aphram Barsoum, *The General Characteristics of the Syriac Literature*, trans. Matti
Moosa, http://syriacstudies.com/AFSS/Syriac_Articles_in_English/Entries/2008/2/22_
THE_GENERAL_CHARACTERISTICS_OF_SYRIAC_LITERATURE_-_Mor_Ignatius_
Aphram_Barsoum.html (accessed November 28, 2015).
[194] Patriarch Ignatius Aprem I Barsoum, in his book, *History of Syriac Literature and
Sciences* outlines a comprehensive historical and liturgical development as well as
illustrating materials of Syriac literature, liturgy and sciences of the Syrian Orthodox
traditions. Ignatius Aprem I Barsoum, *History of Syriac Literature and Sciences* (Pueblo:
Passeggiata, 2000).
[195] Baum and Winkler, *The Church of the East,* 158-164. Fergusson, *Encyclopaedia of
Early Christianity*, 878.
[196] "The Orthodox Churches share the common roots, historical experiences, and cultural
expressions. All these Churches are found in the eastern parts of the Christian world and
therefore are sometimes called the Eastern Churches. The Orthodox Churches affirm a
common Orthodox faith, life, practice and a conciliar nature of unity. While the Orthodox
Church is separated by geographic and administrative jurisdictions rooted in the long
history of Orthodox people across the globe, these Churches are united by shared doctrines
and religious practices across jurisdictional, linguistic, and geographical locations."
Frances Kostarelos, "Short Term Missions in the Orthodox Church in North America,"
Missiology: An International Review 41, no.2 (April 2013): 179-186.
[197] Binns, *An Introduction to the Christian Orthodox Churches*, 1-2.

the Churches of Greece, Russia, Romania, Bulgaria and so on. The Eastern Orthodox Churches have accepted the first seven Ecumenical Councils which define the fundamental doctrines and canon. They share the same liturgical texts and practices. For the Orthodox Churches, the Chalcedonian Ecumenical Council (451CE) was the point of separation between the Oriental Orthodox and the Eastern Orthodox Churches. The other family, namely the Oriental Orthodox, consists of the Armenian, the Coptic, the Ethiopian, the Indian (Malankara) and the Syrian Churches. Very recently, as the aftermath of the political division between Ethiopia and Eritrea, a separate Church called the Eritrean Orthodox Church, formerly part of the Ethiopian Orthodox Church has been formed.[198]

The doctrine of Christ (Christology) was the main area of conflict between these groups. This fact illustrates, how the divine and the human nature were united in Jesus Christ.[199] However, strong political, cultural, and social factors also played significant roles in the conflict between these groups.

---

[198] Oriental Orthodox Churches accept the first three Ecumenical Councils. John Anthony McGuckin, *The Orthodox Church: An Introduction to its History, Doctrine, and Spiritual Culture* (Sussex: Wiley-Blackwell, 2011), 17-20. Chaillot, "The Ancient Oriental Churches," 31-33. Paul F. Bradshaw and Maxwell E. Johnson, *The Eucharistic Liturgies: Their Evolution and Interpretation* (Collegeville, MN: Liturgical, 2012), 137-140.

[199] "The Syrians, who accepted Nestorius's (386-450 CE) teaching and did not follow the canon of Ephesus, were called Nestorians. Nestorius argued that Jesus embodies two persons: God, the logos, and Jesus, the human. Because God cannot be subjected to natural influences, Mary only gave birth to the human Jesus, and therefore she cannot be called "Mother of God" (*Theotokos*). This means that Christ has two persons and two separate natures. The Council of Ephesus (431 CE) rejected this position and condemned Nestur. They were persecuted by the Byzantine Empire. Thus, they fled to the Persian Empire in South-Mesopotamia. In this way the Syrian Church was divided into two. The Syrians living west of the Euphrates were called "Syrians of the West" and they came directly under the Patriarch of Antioch. Those living east of the river Euphrates - also in Iraq - were called the "Syrians of the East," most of them were following the teachings of Nestur. Because of this geographical division, the Syrian language is split into two dialects, namely the West-Syrian and the East-Syrian. The "Syrians of the West" living in the Persian Empire had to suffer heavily under oppression by the Persians. This happened not just because of their faith but because it's spiritual leadership was residing in the hostile Byzantine Empire. They were therefore accused of disloyalty." Patriarch Zakka I, "A Short Overview of the Common History of the Syrian Church with Islam through the Centuries," *Patriarchal Journal* 33, no.146 (June 1995) http://www.syrianorthodoxchurch. org/library (accessed October 15, 2015). Chaillot, "The Ancient Oriental Churches," 31-32.

The differences resulted in the breach of communion between these two Eastern families. Despite the separation, they maintained a remarkable unity in theological approach, liturgical-spiritual ethos, and the general discipline of the Church.[200] The Christological differences between these two families were resolved by a series of unofficial and official dialogues since 1967. Both families acknowledged each other as they were holding the same apostolic faith in spite of the differences in the Christological understandings of the distant past. They were separated since the Council of Chalcedon which was 1500 years ago. These two groups shared common roots, historical experiences and cultural expressions.[201] They used the same liturgy and Scripture in the same Syriac language without distinction or discrimination. The Syriac Fathers of this common period was known as "the true heirs of the Semitic world into which Christianity was born."[202] As a result of the unofficial dialogue between these groups, a consensus emerged regarding its doctrines and traditions. Both sides affirm together the common tradition of One Church in all important matters such as liturgy and spirituality, doctrines and canonical practices, understanding of the Holy Trinity, the Incarnation, the Holy Spirit, the nature of the Church, the communion of saints, ministry, mission, and sacraments.[203]

The West Syrians and the East Syrians have remained faithful to the early Syriac tradition. Generally, Syriac was divided into two dialects namely West Syriac and East Syriac, which are mainly distinguished by their tradition of pronunciation (and also the different scripts). For example 'o' in West Syriac is pronounced 'ā' in East Syriac. (e.g., the name of God which in West Syriac is *Allōho*, is pronounced *Allāhā* in East Syriac; in West Syriac *malko*, (king), while in East Syriac *malka*). A further variation

[200] The liturgical life in these groups have numerous similarities in the symbolically important matters of space, vestments, gestures, liturgical objects, the conduct of the Liturgy and the Daily Offices, and the life of both the laypeople and monastic communities. For instance, the general structure of the Liturgy of the Eucharist remains the same, confession is regularly practiced before communion. Chaillot, "The Ancient Oriental Churches," 134-135.
[201] Binns, *An Introduction to the Christian Orthodox Churches,* viii.
[202] Fenwick, *Forgotten Bishops,* 26.
[203] Fenwick, *Forgotten Bishops,* 26-27.

is found in connection with the type of script used; the east Syrians (also known as the Chaldeans) use the form known as *Estrangelo* (probably from Greek *strongulos*, "rounded"), whereas the Western Syrians employ the *Serto* script (literally "a scratch, character").[204]

The liturgy of the Eastern Churches are divided into two. They are Antiochian liturgy and Alexandrian liturgy. The liturgies of Greek (Byzantine), Syrian and Armenian Churches belong to the Antiochian tradition. The Coptic and Abyssinian (Ethiopian) liturgies belong to the Alexandrian tradition.[205] As mentioned earlier, the division of the East Syrians from the West Syrians was the result of the Christological controversies of the fifth century, particularly by the Council of Ephesus in 431 CE. More precisely, after the Chalcedon council, the majority of monks and clergy of Alexandria and Antioch opposed to the Dyophysite Christology[206] and were called Monophysite[207] or non-Chalcedonian. The non-Chalcedonians of Antioch were known as Jacobites.[208] In the second half of the century, the Monophysite' prevailed in Edessa, and the East Syrians who followed the teachings of Theodore of Mopsuestia (350-428 CE) withdrew into Persia. The city of Nisibis became the main East Syrian theological centre. The expansion of Islam and linguistic differences contributed largely to the isolation of the East Syrian Church from the rest of Christendom for a long period.[209]

---

[204] Brock, *An Introduction to Syriac Studies*, 23.

[205] George Mathew Kuttiyil, *Liturgy for Our Times* (Thiruvalla: Christava Sahitya Samithi, 2006), 29.

[206] The word *Dyophysite* comes from the Greek which literally means two natures. This theological term used in understanding how the divine and human are related in the person of Jesus Christ.

[207] *Monophysites* are those who hold the view that there is only one inseparable nature (partly divine, partly and subordinately human) in the person of Christ. According to this view, Christ had only a single divine nature instead of two natures, one divine and one human, as set forth in the Orthodox or Chalcedonian position of the hypostatic union of Christ. This name comes from a combination of the Greek words *monos*, meaning one or alone, and *physis*, meaning nature.

[208] Baby Varghese, *West Syrian Liturgical Theology* (Aldershot; Ashgate, 2004), 1.

[209] A. Gelston, *The Eucharistic Prayer of Addai and Mari* (Oxford: Clarendon, 1992), 21-22.

2.3 - The West Syrian Liturgical Tradition: Origin and Development

The West Syrian tradition originated and developed in and around the city of Antioch and the centre of the East Syrian tradition was Edessa.[210] Many of the Oriental Orthodox Churches and some of the Catholic Churches of the East followed the West Syrian liturgical tradition.[211] The oldest form of the Antiochian rite was derived from the Greek. It was considered that this version must have been made very early, evidently before the Monophysite schism, before the influence of Constantinople and Byzantine infiltrations had begun. The origin of this rite is the Greek language and later translated into the Syriac language. This point is pertinent because the Syriac liturgy already contained all the changes brought to Antioch from Jerusalem. It is not the older pure Antiochian rite, but the later rite of Jerusalem-Antioch. The Jacobites as well as the Orthodox were upholding the Jerusalem-Antiochian liturgy. This is the main proof that this had supplanted the older Antiochian use before the schism of the fifth century.[212]

It is possible that the primitive form of the West-Syrian liturgy has been derived from two major sources. The *Apostolic Constitutions'* provided a liturgy of the Word that consisted of reading from the Old Testament, singing of the Psalm, reading of the Epistle and the Gospel, Homily, Dismissal of the Catechumens and the Prayers of the Faithful. The *Catechesis of Cyril*, the liturgy of the Eucharist included the anaphora, the Lord's Prayer and the invitation to participate in the communion. The Liturgy of St. James was a conflation of the rites of Antioch and Jerusalem.[213] Both the Eastern and Oriental Orthodox traditions have the same liturgical and spiritual

---

[210] Robert Taft, *The Liturgy of the Hours in East and West* (Collegeville, MN: Liturgical, 1986), 239- 240.

[211] Versions of the West Syrian rite are currently used by Oriental Orthodox bodies including: the Malankara Mar Thoma Syrian Church, the Syriac Orthodox Church, the Malankara Orthodox Syrian Church, the Malankara Jacobite Syriac Orthodox Church, and the Malabar Independent Syrian Church. Some Eastern Catholic bodies including: the Syriac Catholic Church, the Maronite Church and the Syro-Malankara Catholic Church. Bradshaw and Johnson, *The Eucharistic Liturgies,* 139.

[212] Peter D. Day, *The Liturgical Dictionary of Eastern Christianity* (Kent: Burns and Oates, 1993), 132.

[213] Frank C. Senn, *Christian Liturgy: Catholic and Evangelic* (Minneapolis: Fortress, 1997), 119-120.

receptivity and approaches. There were several common elements in the East and the West Syrian liturgies. The West Syrian rite is a synthesis of native Syriac elements, especially hymns and other choral elements with materials translated from the Greek liturgical text of Antiochian and Hagiopolite provenance. This synthesis was the work of Syriac, non-Chalcedonian monastic communities in the Syriac speaking localities of Syria, Palestine, and parts of Mesopotamia beyond the Greek cities of the Mediterranean coast. These Syriac speaking Christians were organized into an independent Church under Jacob Baradai (500-578 CE).[214] The Syriac documents came about the end of the fifth century gave valuable information about the local forms of the rite of Antioch-Jerusalem. The Jacobite sect kept a version of this rite, which is obviously a local variant. The first writer on this rite was Jacob of Edessa (633-708 CE), who wrote a letter to a priest Thomas comparing the Syrian liturgy with that of Egypt. This letter was very valuable and really a critical discussion of the rite. A number of later writers from this group followed Jacob of Edessa (633-708 CE).[215] Overall, this group produced the first scientific students of liturgy. George of the Arabs (724 CE), John of Dara (825 CE), Benjamin of Edessa (843 CE), Lazarus bar Sabhetha of Bagdad (Ninth Century), Moses bar Kepha of Mosul (903 CE), Dionysius bar Salibi of Amida (1171 CE) wrote valuable commentaries on the Jacobite rite.[216] The first Syriac commentary on the sacraments was written by Narsai (503 CE), who used the homilies of Theodore of Mopsuestia as its model.[217] In the eighth and ninth centuries, a controversy concerning the prayer at the fraction produced more acceptable liturgical literature.[218] The chronicle of their

---

[214] Horatio Southgate, *Narrative of a Visit to the Syrian (Jacobite) Church of Mesopotamia* (New Jersey: Gorgias, 2003), vi.

[215] John R K. Fenwick, *The Anaphoras of St. Basil and St. James: An Investigation into their Common Origin* (Roma: Pontificium Institutum Orientale, 1992), 8.

[216] Spinks, *Do This in Remembrance of Me,* 155. Chaillot, "The Ancient Oriental Churches," 155-156.

[217] Baby Varghese, "Some Aspects of West Syrian Liturgical Theology," *Studia Liturgica* 31, no.2 (2001):174-175.

[218] Sebastian P. Brock, "Spirituality in the Syriac Tradition," in *Moran Etho* 2 (Kottayam: SEERI, 2005), 18-36.

Patriarch Michael the Great (1199 CE) discussed the question and supplied valuable contemporary documents. The main liturgical books of the West Syrian rite are the *Ktobo dQurbono* (the missal), *Ktobo dtesmesto* (the diaconal), the *Evangelion* (the Gospel book), and the *Egroto daslihe* (the epistles) together with the *Phenqito* and *Shimo*.[219]

2.4 - Distinctive Features of the West Syrian Liturgy

Among the Christian Churches, the West Syrians have the richest and the largest collection of anaphoras.[220] Though they invariably followed the structure of St. James, in the wording of individual prayers, the anaphoras differ from one another. Sometimes the structure has been disregarded. The anaphoras at present, according to a liturgical scholar, H J. Feulner is eighty three.[221] These anaphoras attributed to the apostles, Early Church Fathers, West Syrian doctors, Patriarchs or famous prelates. All these anaphoras followed the structure of the liturgy of St. James and retained the main themes of the prayers, though the wordings vary considerably changed.[222] The anaphora attributed to Thomas of Harkel (616 CE) had a curious formula that combined the words of institution and anamnesis. In the course of the evolution, litanies were replaced with hymns to assure the participation of the community. It is a common tradition among the Syrians that nobody below the order of a bishop was allowed to compose

---

[219] Parry, et al., *The Blackwell Dictionary of Eastern Christianity,* 474-475.

[220] The *anaphora* is the central part of the Eucharistic liturgy. The Greek word *anaphora* means elevation or the offering presented to God. Offering is a presentation made to a deity as an act of religious worship or sacrifice. In the Eucharistic liturgy, *anaphora* begins with the prayer of peace and ends with the final commendation and a blessing. Geevarghese Panicker, "West Syrian Anaphorae," The Harp 6, no.1 (April 1993): 29. Henry George Liddell, *A Greek-English Lexicon,* 9th ed. (Oxford: Oxford University, 1996). Fenwick, *The Anaphoras of St. Basil and St. James,* 11.

[221] Hans Jurgen Feulner, "Zu den Editionen Orientalischer Anaphoren," in *Crossroad of Cultural Studies in Liturgy and Patristics in Honour of Gabriele Winkler,* eds. Hans Jurgen Feulner, E Velkovska and Robert F. Taft (Rome: Pontificio Istituto Orientale, 2000), 261-274. Spinks, *Do This in Remembrance of Me,* 158. Sebastian P. Brock, *Syriac Studies: A Classified Bibliography (1960-1990)* (Kaslik, Lebanon: Parole de I 'Orient, 1996), 184-208.

[222] Bryan D. Spinks, "Eastern Christian Liturgical Traditions: Oriental Orthodox." in *The Blackwell Companion to Eastern Christianity,* ed. Parry, K., et al (Oxford: Blackwell, 2007), 339-367.

an anaphora.[223] The translation of the anaphora of St. James is the most significant development in the history of the West Syrian liturgy. Not all of these anaphoras are available in one single book, and most are no longer in use. However, this large number of anaphoras witnessed local variations and differences co-existed and continued the tradition of compiling new Eucharistic prayers.[224] Along with *Sedro* various types of theologically rich hymns such as *Qolo* (antiphon), *Bouto* (petitions), *Madroso* (exposition) and *Sugito* (canticle) were invaluable sources for the study of West Syrian liturgical theology.[225]

The monastic movement played a vital role in shaping the liturgical and spiritual traditions of the West Syrians. One cannot perceive liturgical uniformity in this tradition because there was a space for different liturgical books reflecting diverse liturgical practices especially in monasteries. This diversity was regarded as a sign of "spiritual vigour" and "wealth of devotions" which might have rooted in the monastic background.[226] Baby Varghese explains that "the socio-political conditions of the Syrians as a minority made it rather difficult to bring the dioceses and the monasteries under a centralized authority, as in the Byzantine or Latin traditions. People lived in close relationship with the ascetics who always maintained simple faith and traditions of folk wisdom. This has left traces in the liturgical texts and in the commentaries. Liturgical diversity was rooted in the monastic background."[227] Abundance of mystical elements were evident in the West Syrian liturgy. The use of symbols, processions and gestures communicated these mystical expressions. There was a space for active participation of the people in the liturgy because of its responsorial structure. Here religious devotion was very demonstrative. The West Syrian Church Fathers considered the liturgy an intimate matter to one's experience. For them, to be a Christian meant to be a liturgical being. They

---

[223] Panicker, "West Syrian Anaphorae," 33.
[224] Spinks, *Do This in Remembrance of Me,* 158.
[225] Varghese, "Some Aspects of West Syrian Liturgical Theology," 175-176.
[226] Varghese, *West Syrian Liturgical Theology,* 3.
[227] Varghese, *West Syrian Liturgical Theology,* 3-4.

regarded worship as a realization of one's vocation. The liturgy reflects the faith and theology of the Church and participation in the liturgy affirms that faith. In this tradition, the faith of the Church is not articulated in "articles of faith" but embedded in liturgy.[228] The Antiochian liturgy is intensely human with its spontaneity and dramatic way of presentation. The processions, hymns, gestures, people's acclamations and responses make the celebration lively and it ensures the involvement of the entire community in the liturgy, the common work of the Church.[229] This sense of community experience is reflected in every expression of the Antiochian faith.

3 - The Liturgy of St. James and Its Importance

The liturgy of St. James is one of the oldest anaphoras in the Christian circle. It is generally believed that the origin of the rite was in Jerusalem during the fourth century. This liturgy became the liturgy "par excellence" of the Syriac-speaking Monophysites and was to become models for a large number of other rites. By the 17th century, the East Syrian rite was replaced by the West Syrian rite among considerable sections of the St. Thomas Christians in South India.[230] This West Syrian liturgy of the present form is a Mesopotamian version of the Antiochian tradition. This liturgy is called the mother of the most of the Eucharistic liturgies especially of the Oriental and Eastern Churches.[231] According to Baby Varghese, there is no other Eastern anaphora ever seems to have such a wider circulation in the history of the Church. He further points out that, this liturgy has been employed in the Churches of Palestine, Arabia, Syria, Armenia, Georgia, Slavonic countries, Greece, Ethiopia and Egypt.[232] This anaphora may be used on any occasion (unlike other anaphoras) but it is particularly employed on the occasions of all the festivals of the Church, at the ordination of deacons,

---

[228] Kuttiyil, *Liturgy for Our Times*, 58.
[229] Varghese, *West Syrian Liturgical Theology*, 7.
[230] Fenwick, *The Anaphoras of St. Basil and St. James*, 31.
[231] Baby Varghese, "St. James' Liturgy: A Brief History of the Text," *The Harp* 2, no.3 (December 1989): 129.
[232] Varghese, "St. James' Liturgy: A Brief History of the Text," 141.

priests, the consecration of a new church building, the consecration of a bishop and enthronement of a Patriarch/Catholicos. Usually a priest uses the anaphora of St. James' when he celebrates his first holy Eucharist after having been ordained and also whenever he celebrates the holy Eucharist in a church for the first time because of its primacy among the anaphoras in the Syrian Orthodox Church.

3.1 - Authorship and Date of Composition

The authorship of this liturgy is traditionally attributed to St. James, the brother of Jesus Christ, the first bishop of Jerusalem. This belief was deeply rooted among the Syriac writers. Most of the Syriac manuscripts bear the following or similar title: "the Anaphora of St. James, the brother of our Lord and the Apostle, who learned from our Lord in the Upper Room of the mysteries."[233] The shorter version published from Pampakuda (Kerala, India) gives the title: "the Anaphora of St. James, brother of Our Lord, Apostle, martyr, and the first Archbishop of Jerusalem for the year of our Lord."[234] The most ancient Church Father, who attributed a liturgy to St. James is St. Jerome (340-420 CE) and Proclus the Patriarch of Constantinople (434-446 CE). The Sixth and Seventh Ecumenical Councils testified that St. James was the author of the liturgy.[235] Another earliest authentic mention of the liturgy by name occurred in Canon 32 of the Quinisextine Council (in Trullo, 692 CE). This canon speaks of a liturgy composed by St. James "the brother of Jesus Christ and the bishop of Jerusalem."[236] During the same period, Jacob of Edessa (633-708 CE), in his letter to a presbyter named Thomas, gave an outline of the liturgy of St. James.[237] Regarding the reason for the wider acceptance of this liturgy

---

[233] Varghese, "St. James' Liturgy: A Brief History of the Text," 143.
[234] This title is given to the Anaphora which was abridged by Bar Hebraeus (1286 CE).
[235] Panicker, "West Syrian Anaphorae," 35.
[236] Fenwick, *The Anaphoras of St. Basil and St. James*, 31-32.
[237] Frank E. Brightman, *Liturgies Eastern and Western*, vol.1 (Oxford: Clarendon, 1896), 490-494.

Baby Varghese offers two reasons, i.e. the Jerusalemite origin and the attribution to St. James.[238]

Even though the liturgical scholars of the present century agree on the relative antiquity of this liturgy, they have divergent opinions concerning the possibility of its authorship by St. James. There is no early historical evidence of St. James's authorship of the Anaphora in his name. From a critical observation one can understand that the liturgy in its entirety cannot be attributed to St. James. Since he was a pillar of the Jerusalem Church (Gal.2:9) and is the presiding bishop at the Eucharist assembly, his role would certainly have been both formative and definitive in giving shape to the first distinctively Christian mode of worship, the liturgy. But there is a general consensus that the fundamental parts of the St. James Eucharistic prayer have not changed since the fourth century.[239] The present text of the Eucharistic liturgy is a mixture of various cultural, linguistic and theological aspects. Fenwick remarks that "this liturgy is not a single, primitive composition; it is too long, too carefully structured, too theologically and biblically precise."[240] Hence, he assumes that this liturgy is of a late dating, possibility of a fourth or fifth-century date. The Liturgy of St. James has undergone a process of development in the community which used it. However one cannot negate the influence of St. James in the initial stage of the development of this liturgy. One should be careful not to lose sight of the reality that, at its core, the Liturgy of St. James represents an apostolic rite of great antiquity.

Even though the Jerusalemite origin of St. James liturgy had not been questioned, there was no unanimity concerning the date of its composition. Some scholars propose a date at the middle of the third century and some others to the middle of the fourth century.[241] Those who propose fourth century claim that the anaphora had already got its final form when Cyril

---

[238] Varghese, "St. James' Liturgy: A Brief History of the Text," 141.

[239] Ishaq Saka, *Commentary on the Liturgy of the Syrian Orthodox Church of Antioch,* trans. Matti Moosa (Piscataway, New Jersey: Gorgias, 2009), 14.

[240] Fenwick, *The Anaphoras of St. Basil and St. James,* 32-33.

[241] A. Raes, *Introduction in Liturgian Orientalem* (Rome, Pontificio Istituto Orientale, 1947), 20.

(313-383 CE) preached his Fifth Mystagogical Catechesis. The popular belief was that the liturgy was not older than the fourth or fifth century, but its principal elements went back to very early days, if not apostolic times, and it was certainly one of the most venerable rites of the Church. According to Heiming, the Syriac text was finalized between 520 CE and 630 CE. Since the liturgy of St. James was acceptable to both Chalcedonians and Non-Chalcedonians, the period before the Council of Chalcedon (451CE) seems to be the probable date for the fixation of the Greek text.[242]

3.2 - Different Versions of the Liturgy: A Historical Outline

A historical survey of the liturgy of St. James is a complex one. As cited above, this liturgy in its nucleus was brought from Jerusalem to Antioch, and it was from there, the first missionaries took the rite and the liturgical customs to other places. The anaphora survived in many languages, Syriac and Greek being the main. In some places along with Syriac, Greek terms were also used since Church scholars in Syria were bilingual. It also contained expansions, substitutions and the apparent retention of more primitive forms when compared to the extant Greek text.[243] There were different versions of the liturgy of St. James that had commonly been in use in the Christian corpus. They were Greek, Syriac, Georgian, Old Slavonic, Armenian, Ethiopian and Coptic versions.[244] The Greek and Syriac were the most important versions and other forms were dependent either on one or the other. The ancient manuscripts of the Syriac version show that it was translated from a Greek original.[245] The Syriac text retained several examples of literal translation of Greek words and expressions. In the fourth century, the liturgical language of Jerusalem was Greek, as it was evident from the Catechesis of Cyril of Jerusalem. It was considered that

---

[242] Varghese, "St. James' Liturgy: A Brief History of the Text," 145.

[243] Anne McGowan, *Eucharistic Epiclesis, Ancient and Modern* (London: SPCK, 2014), 61.

[244] Fenwick, *The Anaphoras of St. Basil and St. James*, 57-58.

[245] The oldest Greek manuscript belongs to the eighth century and is different at several points from the Syriac text. The Syriac version is made from the Greek manuscripts, which are one or more centuries older than the existing oldest Greek manuscripts. Varghese, "St. James' Liturgy: A Brief History of the Text," 145.

a Syriac version of St. James liturgy existed at least from the beginning of the fifth century.[246] Brian D. Spinks remarked that, the Syriac version of the St. James liturgy was in most places a word-for-word translation from the Greek version, apparently undertook at a time of consolidation of the non-Chalcedonians in the first half of the sixth century, either in the time of John of Tella or under Jacob of Burdana.[247] Since the fourth century, various Church Fathers quoted from the liturgy of St. James. F.E. Brightman gave a list of such quotations and references.[248] This anaphora existed in both Greek and Syriac forms since church scholars in Syria were bilingual, using both Greek and Syriac. However, through time and because of the theological disputes which dominated the fourth and fifth centuries, this text suffered many changes; for example when discussing theological development from the Apostolic Constitutions to the Liturgy of St. James Bouyer notes: "If we look at the Eucharist of St. James as a whole, we are especially struck by the clarity of its Trinitarian theology, which is expressed with much more exacting precision in its structure than could be seen in the liturgy of the 8th book of the Apostolic Constitutions. All the duplications and all the repetitions in thought have been definitively and categorically removed."[249] We know that Jacob of Edessa (d.708) revised it and his revision, except for minor and superfluous changes, is used by the Syrian Church today.[250] In the early 18th century Lebrun produced a French translation of the anaphora of St. James and passages from the commentary of Jacob Edessa.[251] A little before this Renaudot's publication of more than forty West Syriac anaphoras introduced the richness of the Syriac liturgy with a Latin translation.[252] Likewise an English translation of the West Syriac Anaphoras was published by Howard[253] in 1864 and

---

[246] Varghese, "St. James' Liturgy: A Brief History of the Text," 146.
[247] Spinks, *Do this in Remembrance of Me*, 160.
[248] Brightman, *Liturgies Eastern and Western*, liii - liv.
[249] Bouyer, (Eucharist: Theology and Spirituality of the Eucharistic Prayer, 1968), 279.
[250] Fenwick, *The Anaphoras of St. Basil and St. James,* 48.
[251] Pierre Lebrun, *Explication de la messe* (Paris: Lyon Public Library, 1726).
[252] Eusebe Renaudot, *Liturgiarum Orientalium Collectio* (Paris: Coignard, 1716).
[253] George Broadley Howard, *The Christians of St Thomas and their Liturgies: Comprising the Anaphora of St. James, St. Peter, The Twelve Apostles, Mar Dionysius, Mar Xystus and*

Brightmann in 1896.[254] In 1926 Fuchs published one of the oldest Syrian Orthodox anaphoras attributed to John I (648 CE), Patriarch of Antioch.[255] A landmark in the study of the West Syriac Anaphora is Labourt's *Dionysius Bar Salibi* (1172 CE), *Expositio Liturgicae*[256] on the Eucharist and *Two Commentaries on the Jacobite Liturgy*[257] edited by Connolly and Codrington. In the 13ᵗʰ century, Gregory Bar Hebracus abridged the liturgy of St. James and made a shorter version and this text was printed at Pampakuda, Kerala. This is the oldest manuscript of St. James liturgy and it was found in the Malankara Church.[258] Among the Syrian Orthodox Churches, this anaphora is the main liturgy. Although there are many anaphoras, the liturgy of St. James was the model for the rest.

Mar Evannis, together with the Ordo Communis (Oxford: John Henry and James Pakker. 1864). http://cerziozan.ru/the-christians-of-st-thomas.pdf (accessed November 14, 2014).
[254] Brightman, *Liturgies Eastern and Western,* https://archive.org/details/liturgieseastern01unknuoft (accessed November 17, 2014).
[255] H. Fuchs, Die *Anaphora des monophysitischen Patriarchen Johannan I* (Münster: Westfalen. 1926).
[256] H. Labourt, *Dionysius Bar Salibi*, Expositio Liturgicae, CSCO 13-14 (Paris: Harrassowitz. 1903).
[257] Richard Hugh Connolly and Humphrey William Codrington. eds., *Two Commentaries on the Jacobite Liturgy by George Bishop of the Arab Tribes and Moses Bar Kepha: Together with the Syriac Anaphora of St. James and a Document Entitled the Book of Life* (Oxford: Williams and Norgate, 1913)
[258] Varghese, "St. James Liturgy: A Brief History of the Text," 148.

Chapter 4

Development of the Eucharistic liturgy in the Malankara Mar Thoma Syrian Church

1 - Introduction

In the Oriental Orthodox Churches, the Holy Qurbana is considered not merely as one of the seven sacraments, but as the centre of all others. It is also called the "Queen of all Sacraments in the Church," because of its centrality in the life of the Church. In the celebration of the Eucharist, the Church commemorates the divine dispensation of God in Christ with the attitudes of confession, praise, adoration, thanksgiving, and supplication. Everything in the Church leads to the Eucharist and all the things flow from it.[259]

The MTC mainly uses a revised form of the liturgy of St. James in its Eucharistic service. This revised version is a modification of the Syrian Orthodox liturgy in line with Protestant theology.[260] The revision of liturgy is based on scriptural principles. A distinguishing mark of this liturgy is its intimate connection with the Holy Bible. The prayers are resplendent with echoes and idioms of the Bible. The content of this liturgy is simple and easy to follow. It is enriched with elements of solemnity, majesty and mystery. The use of the vernacular for most part of the liturgy helps to maintain a continuous dialogue between the celebrant and the community. The whole liturgy constantly brings before our mind the supreme importance of the mystery of the blessed Trinity in the Eucharistic worship. This liturgy is full of mystical symbolism. The vestments, the sacred ornaments and the

---

[259] Thomas Hopko, *The Orthodox Faith, Worship*, vol. II (New York: Department of Religious Education, 1972), 34.
[260] Phillip Tovey, *The Liturgy of St. James as Presently Use* (Cambridge: Grove Books, 1998), 3.

revered rituals are very meaningful.[261] The development of the Eucharistic liturgy, the major changes in the liturgical prayers and practices, and its theological significance had been a matter of study since the Church was open for accepting the theological position of the Anglican Church in its course of progress during the final decade of 19th century. Also, this chapter deals with the topic of liturgical translations in the Church and its historical and theological progress.

2 - Liturgical Revisions in the Mar Thoma Church: A Historical Summary

The history of liturgical reform in the Malankara Church can be traced from the time of the Metropolitan Mar Dionysus I (1760-1808) who welcomed the CMS missionaries and their "Mission of Help" with a view to revamping the Malankara Church.[262] Hence a seminary was set up in Kottayam in 1815 and CMS missionaries joined there as staff in 1816. Later the Metropolitan, Punnathara Mar Dionysius III appointed a committee to reform the liturgy. A meeting was held on December 3, 1818 at Mavelikkara to consider possible reformations of the Church and also to study the changes that can be implemented.[263] To suggest improvements to be made in the Church, a

---

[261] The influence of the CMS missionaries motivated the reformers to study Scripture thoroughly. The Bible is the norm for the faith and practice of the MTC. Traditions that are considered contrary to biblical teachings were abandoned or amended. The Church has seriously taken the biblical authority over the liturgy and at the same time, they tried to uphold the traditions of the Malankara Church too. Kuruvilla, *An Indian Fruit from the Palestinian Roots,* 12-13.

[262] Daniel, *Ecumenism in Practice*, 74-75. It was during this period the customs and practices of the Malankara Church were a mixture of the Persian, the Roman Catholic, the Antiochian, and the indigenous. Moreover the celebration of the liturgy was in Syriac. There was no liturgical uniformity or ecclesial discipline in the region. The priests were not having any theological training. Even young boys aged 7 or 8 were ordained as deacons at the request of their parents. Prayers to the Saints and Mass for the departed soul's relatives were conducted in the Church. There was no permanent income or salary for the priests. Hence fees were levied for rites and sacraments like baptism and marriage. Scripture was not accessible to the people since there was no Malayalam translation. Religious life was centred on certain ceremonies, festivals and rituals. It made a context of reforms in the Church and need of liturgical translation an inevitable.

[263] Cherian, *The Malabar Syrians and the Church Mission Society,* 229. Brown, *The Indian Christians of St. Thomas,* 135-136. Mathai John, "The Reformation of Abraham Malpan an Assessment," *Indian Church History Review* xxiv, no. 1 (1990): 39.

six-member committee was appointed. Palakunnathu Abraham Malpan, Kaithayil Geevarghese Malpan and Konattu Varghese Malpan were among them.[264] But later, there was a sharp decline of Church reforming efforts during the period between 1825 and 1830 and it reached its peak in 1833.[265]

2.1 - Liturgical Reforms and Revision in the Malankara Church: 1835-1840

The revised version of the Eucharistic liturgy of the MTC has been evolved through a long process of debates, arguments, consultations and theological discussions. There are mainly three incidents that are considered very important in the initial stage of Reformation process. They are: the celebration of the Eucharistic liturgy in the native language (Malayalam) at the Maramon parish by Palakkunnathu Abraham Malpan on 15th August 1836, removal of the statue of Muthappan from the Maramon parish on 4th October 1837, and thereby the cessation of Muthappan Festival and the submission of a Memorandum to Colonel. Fraser, the then British Resident by Malpan and his supporters on 6th September 1836, to rectify the 24 incorrect practices which had prevailed in the Malankara Church. These are the visible expressions of the beginning of liturgical revision and reform in the Malankara Church.[266]

Liturgical reform in the Malankara Church during the period of 1835-1840 could be perceived in two ways. An initial apparent attempt of translation and revision was made by the CMS Missionaries and later by Abraham Malpan. After the Mavelikkara Synod in 1836, the missionaries

---

[264] However, the moves in between eventually led to the suspension of the revision of the Liturgy Committee. K. T. Joy, *The Mar Thoma Church: A Study of its Growth and Contribution* (Kottayam: K.T. Joy 1986), 28. David Daniel, *The Orthodox Church of India* (New Delhi: R. David, 1972), 147.

[265] Zacharia John points out that it is because of the demises of the three venerable Metropolitans and the retirement of the Missionary trio (Baker, Fenn, and Bailey) due to ill health. Mar Dionysius III met with a sudden death in 1825 and in the following year Fenn left for England. Bailey and Baker left on Furlough in 1830 and 1833 respectively. This was the close of the cordial chapter of relationship between the Syrian Bishops and the early English Missionaries. John, *The Liturgy of the Mar Thoma Church of Malabar*, 53.

[266] The MTC celebrated the 175th anniversary of this event at Kozhencherry, near Maramon on 15th August 2010.

translated the Syrian liturgy into Malayalam and revised it in line with the reformed ideas. They have removed the prayers which were contrary to the reformed ideas of Western reformation.[267] In this endeavour, they tried to preserve the liturgical identity and did not attempt to amalgamate them with the liturgy of the Church of England.[268] The amended Syrian liturgy was being written in March 1836. The English translation was mentioned in the minutes of the corresponding committee in November 1836. In his report on the "Mission of Help," Mr. Joseph Tucker, the Secretary of the Madras Corresponding Committee pointed out the errors of the Syrian Church under seven main points.[269] There are records in the missionary letters to suggest that they introduced Morning Prayer from the Book of Common Prayer in Malayalam at the College. Zacharia John comments that "there were daily evening family worships at Bailey's house and public service on most Sundays in the Seminary Chapel in Malayalam according to the Book of Common Prayer. The morning and evening services were read in some of the Syrian Churches also occasionally after the usual Syrian service."[270] This reformed Syrian liturgy had been used in the Seminary Chapel till 1838 and in the parishes of Mallappally, Pallam, Kollad and Kottayam till 1840. This seems to have been attended by Syrian Christians from time to time.[271] Since Abraham Malpan had been working with the missionaries

---

[267] John, *The Liturgy of the Mar Thoma Church of Malabar,* 56-57.

[268] J. Tucker to Bailey, Baker and Peet, March 14 1836, CMS Archive C I 2 / M 12, 466.

[269] They are (1) Transubstantiation (2) The sacrifice of the Mass (3) Prayers for the departed souls (4) Purgatory (5) Worship of the Virgin Mary, supplicating her intercessions, and observing a fast in her honour (6) Worship of saints. (7) Prayers in an unknown tongue. The evidence that he provides for these points is based upon Pete's translation of the Syrian Liturgy, which had been published in *The Madras Church Missionary Record* in 1835 and 1836. J Tucker's Report on the Cottayam Mission, Part 1, Received Feb 1 1836, CMS Archive C I 2 / M 12, 545-557.

[270] John, *The Liturgy of the Mar Thoma Church of Malabar,* 47. Hough, *The History of Christianity in India,* 385-387.

[271] Palakkunnathu Abraham Malpan, Kaithayil Geevarghese Kattanar and Eruthikkal Marcus Kattanar were the Syrian Priests who officiated the liturgy at the Seminary chapel, Kollat and Pallam respectively. John, *The Liturgy of the Mar Thoma Church of Malabar,* 58. Zacharia John, "Vishudha Qurbana Kramam: Maarthoma Sabhayil," (Malayalam) in *Self Formation Through Worship and Sacraments, Mar Thoma Clergy Conference 2009,* Charely Johns ed., (Thiruvalla: Mar Thoma, 2009), 68-74.

at the Seminary from 1816,[272] Tovey argues that Malpan would probably have been one of the persons consulted for the translation of the liturgy by Joseph Peet and would have heard the preaching of the missionaries in the Chapel. The Malpan and Peet probably worked closely together to revise the liturgy.[273] In fact, Tovey gives the impression that Peet was initiating the revision and that Malpan was helping Peet. Records show that in February of 1836, Abraham Malpan was involved in the discussion of liturgical revisions and said that his views entirely coincided with that of the missionaries.[274] On March 14, 1836, a letter from J. Tucker, Secretary of CMS Madras Committee, in response to the Mavelikkara Synod of 1836, indicated that the missionaries were requested to "prepare a suitable liturgy in Malayalam for the use of the Syrians."[275] It is clear that Abraham Malpan and Joseph Peet were partners in the reformation in the Syrian Church and the revisions of the liturgy. This CMS amended or revised liturgy was in use at the Seminary from 1836-1838, which was during Abraham Malpan's tenure.[276] Although this amended Syrian Liturgy was only used for a short time, it expressed the views of the missionaries and demonstrated their hopes for liturgical revision in the Syrian Church.

The second phase of liturgical revision during this period was initiated by Abraham Malpan. Malpan moved from Kottayam Seminary to his home parish in Maramon and continued his reform activity there by celebrating the Holy Communion Service in Malayalam. Malpan recited the prayers -*Promeion* and *Sedro*- while holding and watching the Liturgy in Syriac.

---

[272] John, "The Reformation of Abraham Malpan an Assessment," 40.

[273] Phillip Tovey, "Abraham Malpan and the Amended Syrian Liturgy of CMS," *Indian Church History Review* 29/1 (June 1995): 51.

[274] Tovey, "Abraham Malpan and the Amended Syrian Liturgy of CMS," 51.

[275] Tovey, "Abraham Malpan and the Amended Syrian Liturgy of CMS," 39.

[276] Joseph Peet, who became Principal of the Seminary in 1833, continued in charge till 1838, when he moved to Mavelikkara. Peet had moved the students from the Old Seminary on October 2, 1838 to a shed near the proposed site of the new College. Abraham Malpan taught at the new College for two years, until he resigned in 1840, 'to dedicate himself for the reforms.' Between 1838 and 1852, the Seminary seems to have remained closed. The major event that took place during this period was the Cochin Arbitration Award, which granted the possession of the Seminary to the Syrians. Cherian, *The Malabar Syrians and the Church Mission Society,* 289-90. Baby Varghese, "The CMS Missionaries and the Malankara Church (1815-1840)" *The Harp* XX (2006): 399-446.

He was not using any printed copy and there is no written document of his translation.[277] There is no sufficient historical evidence to prove whether Malpan used the Amended Liturgy of missionaries or his own independent translated liturgy or whether it was just a spontaneous translation of *Sedra* and *Promeion* from Syriac. Tovey, comments that, "unfortunately there is no text of what he did, extant documents authentically from his hand not being liturgical."[278] But Thazhathu Chandapilla Kathanar, a prominent leader of the Conservative party, in his personal letter to the Thaksa Committee of 1927 mentioned that there is a Thaksa of Abraham Malpan.[279] In this letter he appealed to the Committee that, the Thaksa of Malpan had to be considered seriously in the revision of liturgy. But still there lack a concrete historical evidence of the Reformed Qurbana Thaksa of Abraham Malpan. The involvement of CMS in the formation of this liturgy is a debateable question. The important liturgical question is: Was there a revised liturgy of Malpan different from the CMS 1836 rite? It seems highly unlikely that the liturgy used in the Seminary Chapel and that in Maramon were the same. Indeed there was a year of overlap (1837) where the amended liturgy was being used in the Seminary Chapel and Abraham Malpan was using a revised rite in Maramon. In all probability the two liturgies were different. There is no clear evidence of exactly what liturgy was used at each service when it is called a Reformed Qurbana. Later in 1843 Peet reports to Tucker that Deacon Mathew helped Abraham Malpan to draw up the modified rite for Maramon.[280] The most obvious time for this is 1835/36 when they were together in the Seminary. Tovey remarked that the process

---

[277] Brink, *The C.M.S. Mission of help to the Syrian Church in Malabar,* 253.

[278] Tovey, "The Reformed Qurbana of 1873," 253.

[279] A personal letter to the Thaksa Committee on 7th *Makaram* 1102 ME (1927 January) by Thazhathu Chandapilla Kathanar. It is recently found from his house which is kept at the Mar Thoma Museum, Thiruvalla. This letter helps us to understand the tension between the Conservative and Reformed groups within the Mar Thoma Church and their arguments on revisions of the Thaksa. In the biography of Mathews Mar Athanasius, it is mentioned that Abraham Malpan had translated a revised Thaksa and his friend Kaithayil Geevarghese Malpan also used the same Thaksa. J. Varghese Shirasthaar, *Mathews Mar Athanasius: Biography*, 2nd ed, (Malayalam), (Thiruvalla: Mar Thoma Press, 2011, First Impression, 1920), 84.

[280] Letter Rev'd Peet to Rev'd J. Tucker June 12 1843. CMS archive ACC 91 02/05.

of spontaneous translation and omission would seem to be a second form of liturgical revision in the reformation process, and is perhaps as equally early as the Amended Syrian Liturgy as is the Maramon reform. Tovey compares this CMS amended liturgy to the Syrian liturgy and notes the following: The CMS amended liturgy shows that the method of reform was excision. Portions which were theologically unacceptable were removed. Such include relating to saints and to the dead. There were some marginal influences from the Anglican Book of Common Prayer, but virtually no insertion. The ceremonial is radically reduced as there are no crossings, elevations or bells. However, vestments and the incense remained.[281].

Zacharia John argues that, Malpan was interested in reforming the existed customs and practices rather than liturgical revision. Removing the statue of Muthappan and the cessation of *chaatham* (a ritual celebration in connection with death ceremony) are examples for this.[282] He approached the liturgy with Bible and carefully studied the existing liturgy and detected many unscriptural prayers and practices like praying for the dead and of the dead, veneration to saints, mediation of Virgin Mary and saints, the practice of bowing down before the statues etc., which has no biblical support.[283] The major liturgical changes made by Abraham Malpan in 1837 were aimed at restoring the autonomous nature of the Church, with a liturgy that had a distinctly oriental identity.[284] According to Mathai John, the Reformation of Abraham Malpan was an effort to "expurgate, purify and clarify" and not a movement to "renovate or innovate"[285] Zacharia John points out that the major reforms introduced by Malpan may be the following:

"The regular Sunday services were held in Malayalam. Auricular confession, prayers for the departed, invocation of the Blessed Virgin and the Saints and the celebration of the Eucharist when

---

[281] Tovey, "Abraham Malpan and the Amended Syrian Liturgy of CMS," 47.
[282] John, "Vishudha Qurbana Kramam: Maarthoma Sabhayil," (Malayalam), 68-74.
[283] Viswanadhan, *The Christians of Kerala,* 21.
[284] Daniel, *Ecumenism in Praxis,* 85.
[285] John, "The Reformation of Abraham Malpan an Assessment," 63.

there was no one to communicate along with the officiating Priest were all stopped. In administering the Lord's Supper he made it a rule to give the bread and the wine separately to the laity as in the Protestant Churches; but he did not follow their example in introducing the Filioque clause into the Creed. He took care to see that, subject to these innovations, the form and exterior of the Kurbana service and the arrangement of the Public worship were changed as little as possible. Perhaps the greatest change that he introduced was to arrange for the regular reading of the passage from the Old and New Testaments during the service in addition to the Gospel and Epistle for the day and to preach regularly to those who assembled for Divine worship. He adopted plans for the strict observance of the Lord's Day by every member of his congregation. In order to popularise the Reformation, he took special care to have the Bible regularly read and family worship held in the houses of his parishioners."[286]

A transition occurred in the history of the Malankara Reformation during the period between 1836 and 1839. During this period at a few places like Mallappally, Pallam and Kollad the Morning Service was conducted according to the Anglican Liturgy and the Eucharist Service according to the revised Syrian liturgy. In April 1837 Mar Dionysius IV intimated by a circular to all the churches under him that neither the Missionaries nor those who associate with them should be allowed to preach in the Syrian churches and warned that the congregation would be excommunicated otherwise.[287] This circumstance urged the Missionaries to convert the Mission of Help into an open Mission, whose principal object was the proclamation of the Gospel to the non-Christian population.[288] Generally the Malpan and his supporters wanted to reform the Malankara Church from within without joining the Anglican Church. Since 1836, the reform leaders neither subscribed to the decisions of the Synod of Mavelikkara nor joined with the Anglican Church. They stood for the Church's autonomy

---

[286] John, *The Liturgy of the Mar Thoma Church of Malabar*, 61, Cherian, *The Malabar Syrians and the Church Mission Society*, 290-291
[287] Brown, *The Indian Christians of St. Thomas*, 140.
[288] John, *The Liturgy of the Mar Thoma Church of Malabar*, 57.

and renewal.[289] The words of Brown help us to see the viewpoints of reformers for not joining the Church of England. He points out that "it was clear to Abraham Malpan that there was no prospect of widespread acceptance in the Church of the reformed ideas that he had accepted from the missionaries and yet he had no desire to separate himself from the Church of his fathers."[290] Tovey further argues that later there were two divisions in this period. The first was in 1836 between Orthodox and reformers which consisted of missionaries and supporters of reforms under the leadership of Abraham Malpan and, later, the division followed between CMS and Mar Thoma reformers with the decision by the CMS to set up an Anglican Church in Kerala.

2.2 - The Malankara Church Reforms and Liturgical Revision After 1840

When Abraham Malpan left the Seminary in 1840 only a few priests, deacons and laity supported him in his reformed ideas. However he had full support of the entire Maramon parish and the assistance of the Missionaries. There was no uniformity in the celebration of the Holy Qurbana among the reformers since Abraham Malpan, Geevarghese Malpan and others reformers were using the Thaksa with spontaneous translation based on reformed ideas. Therefore a corrected Malayalam

---

[289] Cherian, *Malabar Syrians and the Church Missionary Society*, 390-391. Mathew and Thomas, *The Indian Churches of St. Thomas*, 68-69. People like K.N. Daniel and Phillip Tovey are of opinion that the revision of the Liturgy by Malpan was much more radical than it is upheld; where as those like Punnathra Chandapilla Kathanar and Mathai John are of the opinion that the revision was much conservative than projected.

[290] Abraham Malpan had good relationship with the missionaries. When the CMS missionaries invited Malpan to join them, offering a huge salary, he refused the offer and remained in the Church, determined to reform it from within. In 1840 the Archbishop of Canterbury authorised the Bishop of Madras to supervise the newly formed Anglican congregations. In the same year the disputes between the Missionaries and the Metropolitan on properties were settled by arbitration. The reformed Syrian liturgy has been used in the Seminary Chapel up to 1838 and in the congregations at Pallam and Kollat till 1840. Since 1840 the Syrian services were discontinued and regular Anglican-services were introduced. John, *The Liturgy of the Mar Thoma Church of Malabar*, 57-58. Brown, *Indian Christians of St. Thomas*, 141. Majority of Indian Church historians share the aforementioned view. K. K. Kuruvila, *Mar Thoma Church and its Doctrines*, 14, Chacko, *The Concise History of the Mar Thoma Church*, (Malayalam), 80-81.

Thaksa of uniform nature might not have been produced during this time, which created problems in the future.[291] When Mathews Mar Athanasius, the new Metropolitan returned from Mardin, the Malpan hoped that he would become the leader of the reformers. Contrary to his assumption the new Metropolitan celebrated his first Qurbana with the Old Thaksa.[292] According to John, "the new Metropolitan's intention was to establish his position by ousting the presiding Metropolitan and afterwards to carry out the reforms widely in the Church. This resulted in arousing dispute and unrest."[293] It is interesting to note that Abraham Malpan was not in support of Athanasius' attempt to gain Royal support and approval for him to be the Metropolitan of the Malankara Church.[294] After the demise of Abraham Malpan in 1845, differences of opinion began to arise concerning the points of reform in the liturgy. Later in 1852, the Governments of Travancore and Cochin, after proper investigation, declared Mathews Mar Athanasius as lawful Metropolitan of the Malankara Church. Although since 1852 he became the sole Metropolitan his position was not secure enough. He was in between the conservatives and the reformists. The conservatives were against his reformatory ideas. A major task of Mar Athanasius was to keep both the traditionalists and reformers under the umbrella of the same Church and to this end Metropolitan diplomatically tackled both groups by using the reformed ideas and traditional liturgy side by side.[295] He could not introduce liturgical reforms widely as he wished, owing to various hindrances inside and outside the Church. After the demise of Dionysius IV in 1857, Pulikot Joseph, a native Priest, became the leader of the Conservative group.

---

[291] Sunni E. Mathew, "History of the Development of the Mar Thoma Syrian Liturgy," in *Roots and Wings of Our Liturgy, Mar Thoma Clergy Conference 2008*, A. T. Zachariah, ed., (Kottayam: WiGi, 2008), 36-37.

[292] Shirasthaar, *Mathews Mar Athanasius: Biography*, 51-52.

[293] John, *The Liturgy of the Mar Thoma Church of Malabar*, 64.

[294] It is noted that Abraham Malpan advised Mar Athanasius in the following words: "not to be Metropolitan of Malankara Church rather be the Metropolitan of the Maramon." Shirasthaar, *Mathews Mar Athanasius: Biography*, 52-53.

[295] Shirasthaar, *Mathews Mar Athanasius: Biography*, 66-67, 110-111.

2.2.1 - The Church Reforming Efforts of Mathews Mar Athanasius

The Metropolitan Mathews Mar Athanasius (1852-1877) is the first native of Malabar, who ever received consecration as Syrian Metropolitan of Malabar directly at the hands of the Jacobite Patriarch of Antioch.[296] L.W. Brown's opinion is that in the knowledge of the Scripture and theology, Mar Athanasius was perhaps the most able Metran (bishop) the Christians of St. Thomas ever had.[297] G. Milne Rae pointed out that,

> "for a quarter of a century he had occupied the episcopal throne of Malankara and more than any of his predecessors, had attempted to reform the Church. During his regime, he encouraged the people to read Scripture regularly which is translated by the missionaries and offer prayers in the native language. He was not in favour of veneration to saints and the practice of adoration of relics which was introduced into the Syrian worship by the Roman Catholics. Bible readings, and other active efforts to spread the truth were fostered and encouraged and all the ordinary apparatus of evangelical works were also used for promoting the good of the Syrian Church. He also stopped the custom of burying the bishops within the chancel of the Church."[298]

As the head of the Malankara Christian community, he enjoyed a privileged status in the society and had strong influence even in the Royal administration of Travancore. He stood for social justice, freedom, and equality. He was a man of determination, piety, courage and vision. He encouraged the priests to celebrate the Holy Qurbana[299] in the mother

---

[296] Fenwick, *The Forgotten Bishops*, 433. "Letter of Pratt to Tucker, dated Bombay 16th March 1843," MTS/A/228, CMS/ACC, 91 02/05, MSS in CMS Archives, Cadbury Research Centre, Birmingham.

[297] Brown, *The Indian Christians of St. Thomas*, 145.

[298] George Milne Rae, *The Syrian Church in India* (London: William Blackwood, 1892), 324-325.

[299] In the Oriental Orthodox tradition, the Sacrament of Eucharist is generally known as the Holy Qurbana - the "Sacrament of the Sacraments." The term *Qurbana* is derived from the Syriac word *qurbo* which means offering or sacrifice. It is also known as the *qurbo* means access, signifying that it is through it that humans "draw near to God." The Syrian Christians call it as *roze*, which means mysterious. It is called so, because Christ delivered it secretly to the disciples in the upper room and because by this he exposed to them the mysteries regarding his passion. Geevarghese Panicker, *The Holy Qurbana in the*

tongue and also the distribution of holy elements separately. He exhorted the faithful to keep Sunday as a day of worship and motivated them to gather as a worshipping community to study Scripture and also introduced the system of biblical exposition (sermon) during the Holy Qurbana. He insisted on keeping the parish registers and statement of accounts in all parishes. Mar Athanasius, was against the practice of conducting *perunal* (a religious celebration which was not based on biblical teachings) in the churches, a practice that was in line with Hindu traditions and customs. He seriously withstood people who propagated black-magic and superstitions. He abolished the Hindu religious practices of purification acts such as - *Thrandukulli, Pulikudi, Pulakuli*[300] among the members of the Church. In consonance with the Protestant theology, he was against the practices of offering prayers to saints, prayers for the dead, and keeping statues and pictures of Mother Mary and saints in the Church.[301] Another notable contribution of Mar Athanasius was the codification and publishing of a Canon for the Church in 1857. Its clauses 9 and 10 reveal the attitude of the reformers towards the rites of the departed.

> (9) "That, since all the departed saints, who lived in accordance with the Holy Scripture and instructed the Church by rightly imparting the Words of Truth, are ideal models, their names should

Syro-Malankara Church (Kottayam: St. Ephraim Ecumenical Research Institute, 1991), 18. "The Byzantine Rite uses the terminology of "Divine Liturgy." Among the Syrians, Armenians and Copts the title of the liturgy underscores its sacrificial or offering character with the use of Qurbana (Syriac), Badarak (Armenian), or Prosfora (Coptic)." Bradshaw and Johnson, *The Eucharistic Liturgies*, 141-143.

[300] *Thiruandukuli* or *Thirandukalyanam* is the function conducted when girls attain puberty. Pula and Pulakuli, (pollution) is a compulsory Hindu religious custom observed during birth as well as at death. A few days coming after death of a close relative are considered as Pula. During olden days all Hindus observed Pula for 10 days. The bath taken to remove pula is known as *Pulakuli* rite. *Pulikudy* or *Pumsavanam* is a pre-delivery ritual observed in the seventh month of pregnancy, which is considered an important function during pre-delivery period. http://www.nairs.in/acha_t.htm (accessed November 14, 2015).

[301] Shirasthaar, *Mathews Mar Athanasius: Biography*, 110-118. Joseph, *Malankara Mar Thoma Syrian Church: Sabha Directory 2015*, 43.

be commemorated in prayers and beseech for Divine Grace to follow their footsteps."

(10) "That, since worshipping the angels or saints and praying to the departed saints are not in accordance with the teaching of the Scriptures, the Holy Church must abstain from such worships and prayers."[302]

It is also to his credit that during his episcopate, Rev. Ipe Thoma Kattanar, the Vicar General initiated the printing of the revised liturgy of the Eucharist in1872.[303]

Brink points out that later in 1864, a Committee was set up under the guidance of the CMS missionaries to write down the reformed liturgy. But the committee was unable to provide the liturgy because of the difference of opinion. He further argues that various groups of theological interpreters in the reformed group exercised their own judgement in adapting the liturgy of Syriac St. James for their own use. A bewildering number of practices made their appearance. This affected both the text and practice believed to have been advocated by Abraham Malpan and his supporters.[304] The supporters of Church reforms wanted to make the liturgy and worship meaningful to its participants, to this end they continued the liturgical translation and rejected unscriptural practices in the Church. They advocated the removal of prayers to the saints and prayers for the departed souls as those practices "deteriorated to such an extent that people believed that irrespective of how a person led his life, the priest could, through appropriate rituals, ensure eternal life for him."[305] The three major topics of revisions in the liturgy

[302] *Mar Thoma Sleehayude Edavakayakunna Malankara Suriyani Sabhayude Canon,* (Kottayam, 1857), 14. John, *The Liturgy of the Mar Thoma Church of Malabar,* 66.
[303] *Malankara Mar Thoma Suriyani Sabhayude Qurbana Thaksa* (Malayalam) (Thiruvalla: Mar Thoma, 2009), 71.
[304] Ten Brink, *"The CMS Mission of Help to the Syrian Church in Malabar, 1816-1840: A Study in protestant Eastern Orthodox Encounter"* (PhD Thesis, Hartford Seminary, 1960), 321-322.
[305] Athyal and John, *Metropolitan Chrysostom on Mission in the Market Place,* 37.

were the rejection of celebrating Mass for the souls of the faithful departed, the rejection of the emphasis on representative priesthood and the adoption of the royal priesthood of all baptized.[306]

2.3 - The Holy Qurbana Thaksa of 1872/73

The Qurbana Thaksa of 1872/73 is one of the first public documents of the reform. It shed light on the liturgical reforms of the Malankara Church in the period between the death of Abraham Malpan (1845) and the beginning of synodical reform (1900). It is generally believed that the translation of this Thaksa was done by Kovoor Ipe Thoma Kathanar in the year, 1872.[307] This was published in Malayalam and printed by CMS Press, Kottayam. The publication of this revised liturgy was sanctioned and approved by the Metropolitan Mathews Mar Athanasius. It was used in Maramon and in eight other churches.[308] An English translation of this revised liturgy later appeared in the Madras Church Missionary Record for April and May 1873[309] and it was also included as an appendix in Thomas Whitehouse' *Lingering of Light in a Dark Land.*[310] This liturgy is believed to be developed considerably from the position of Malpan and

---

[306] Thomas, *Mar Thoma Church Directory*, 45-47.

[307] There is no consensus on the provenance of this Thaksa. Thazhath Chandapilla Kathanar, a prominent figure of the traditional school of thought in the reformed group deferred the attribution of this Thaksa to Kovoor Ipe Thoma Kathanar. He says "I understand that the Thaksa of 1872 is not written by Ipe Thoma Kathanar, rather it is the initiative of Henry Baker who made certain revisions and sent to all parishes by the interest of the then British Resident." Thazhath Punnathra Chandapilla Kathanar, *Vilapangalude Cherupusthakam*, (Malayalam) (New Delhi: Dharma Jyothi Vidya Peeth, 2008, 1st Impression. 1946), 42. Contrary to this argument, Mathai John argues that this liturgy was translated by Kovoor in 1872 from a reformed manuscript of Abraham Malpan. Mathai John, "The Reformation of Abraham Malpan," 50.

[308] Thomas Whitehouse, *Lingering of Light in a Dark Land* (London: William Brown, 1873), 313. https://ia801407.us.archive.org/33/items/lingeringslight00whitgoog/lingeringslight 00whitgoog.pdf (accessed March 08, 2014). These churches are Maramon, Kozhencherry, Kottarakkara, Thevalakkara, Kollam Perunadu, Mallappally, Thalavady Padinjarekkara, Chenganoor. Juhanon Mar Thoma, *Bharathathile Christhu Sabhyum, Marthoma Sabhayude Samshiptha Charithravum*, (Malayalam) (Thiruvalla: Christava Sahitya Samithi, 1973), 46-47.

[309] Whitehouse, *Lingering of Light in a Dark Land*, 313-314. Tovey, "The Reformed Qurbana of 1873," 252.

[310] T. Whitehouse, *Lingering of Light in a Dark Land*, William Brown (London, 1873).

that is much closer to the reforms of Abraham Malpan. Therefore, Mathews Mar Athanasius revised the liturgy again to make it slightly closer to the original form of the rite.[311]

Zacharia John points out the position of reform by the statement of the Reform Society in 1878 as "the removal of ignorant practices bordering on hypocrisy, prayers to the Saints, prayers on behalf of the dead and heretical festivities, and the establishments of rules conformable to the holy religion and to the ancient practices of our community and which will contribute to rendering the basis of the true faith:"[312] This Thaksa is considered to be a much more moderate reformed liturgy which is an indicative of the state of reform in 1872/73. Thus Tovey remarks that there are summaries of the Reformation prior to the work of the synods and thus two types of text that are relevant in looking at Reformation progress, the texts which are a summary of principles, and actual liturgical texts.

Tovey observes the following major changes made in the reformed liturgy.

(a) St. Mary and the saints: The prayers addressed to St. Mary and the saints seeking their intercession were removed from the reformed liturgy especially from the preparatory service. Every hymn in veneration of the Virgin Mary was removed from the communion rite, but it is preserved in the liturgy where she is being remembered for her definite role in the economy of salvation. In lieu of the term Mother of God (*theotokos*), the mother of Jesus (*christotokos*) was included. The prayers addressing the saints were removed completely from the liturgy.

(b) The Departed souls: The prayers for the departed souls were removed from the liturgy completely. Prayers for the faithful

---

[311] Tovey, "Abraham Malpan and the Amended Syrian Liturgy of CMS," 54.

[312] The statement issued by the Reform Society in 1878 soon after the death of Metropolitan Mathews Mar Athanasius, inviting the Priests., of the Malankara Parish to join the Reform Society, dated 28th Medom 1053 (1878). John, *The Liturgy of the Mar Thoma Church of Malabar,* 121.

departed were altered to use as a prayer for the faithful living. Instead of praying for them the Church thankfully remembers their lives and asks God for the grace to continue to follow their spiritual path.

(c) Incense: Although the use of incense in liturgy was preserved as an offering that reconciles God and humanity, the frequent use of the same in liturgy was considerably reduced.

(d) Theology of the Eucharist: Major theological emphasis was given to the Eucharist in the liturgy as a sacrifice (oblation), mystery and epiclesis.

(e) The office of the priesthood: The role of the priest was accepted as a representative of the people before God. An emphasis on the priesthood of all believers (the general priesthood) was given more importance in the liturgy.

(f) Ecclesiology: the continuity of the Christian traditions were remembered in its intercession.[313]

A general evaluation of this liturgy shows that there was a progressive continuity of reforms in this liturgy. As mentioned above, this liturgy is believed to be closer to the reformed ideas of Abraham Malpan. In this liturgy the main method of reform was excision. Those passages that were theologically unacceptable were removed. Two areas in particular were deleted, those relating to the saints and to the dead. Hence, the motive for revision was primarily theological. The latter part of the service was drastically curtailed suggesting a shift in Eucharistic doctrine away from the consecration to the forgiveness of sins through the sacramental reception of the elements. This may be particularly seen in the epiclesis and the reception. However, features of Orthodox theology are also retained over against the Prayer Book approach, in the offering language, statements about incense, and the constant use of the term altar. Together with this ceremonial is radically reduced. There are no crossings, elevations or

---

[313] Tovey, "The Reformed Qurbana," 253-268.

bells. But it would appear that customary vestments were worn, incense was retained, and the new ceremonial feature of kneeling at the epiclesis was introduced.

As demonstrated in the previous chapter, with the judgement of Royal Court in 1889 that finally caused the split in the Malankara Syrian Church between the Conservatives and Reformed. Henceforth the reformed section became known as the Mar Thoma Syrian Church of Malabar[314] and the other party as the Malankara Syrian Orthodox Church. In this situation the MTC was forced to make its stand clear in the doctrines and faith. According to the Metropolitan Joseph Mar Thoma, one of the most difficult tasks of that time was to frame a statement of the doctrines of the Church. Therefore, Thomas Mar Athanasius and his colleagues[315] formulated a new doctrinal and faith outline for the Church. The indifference in matters of doctrine and the absence of well-equipped and efficient theological scholars along with a lack of knowledge about the ancient liturgies (which was destroyed by the Roman ecclesiastics after the Synod of Diamper in 1599) had given neither the incentive nor the qualifications for them to develop a theology of their own. Out of the debris of the old, they had to construct the new. It was an attempt to rediscover the old heritage, faith and practices of the Malankara Church. Throughout the centuries the Malankara Church was in connection with different ecclesial centres such as the Assyrian Church of the East, the Roman Catholic Church, and the Syrian Orthodox Church of Antioch. All these Churches had been following diverse theological,

---

[314] The designation Malankara Mar Thoma Syrian Church is also used. (*Mar Thoma Syrian Church of Malabar: Constitution*, Thiruvalla: Mar Thoma, 1984), 1. Juhanon Mar Thoma, *History of the Mar Thoma Church*, 48.

[315] They were mainly thirteen priests who actively participated in the discussion of the Shucheekarana Prasthanam (Purification movement) in the reformed wing. They are G. Philipose Kathanar, a professor at Kottayam Seminary and the vicar of Kozhencerry and Ayiroor church, Theethoos Kathanar of Maramon church, Yakkoob Kathanaar of Nranam Church, Yakkoob Kathanar of Kalluppara chruch, Mathen Kathanar of Anapparampal church, Mathai Kathanaar of Kozhenchery church, Thoma Kathanar of Kozhencerry church, Skariah Kathanar of Elanthoor church, Vaidhyan Kathanaar, the vicar of the Chenganoor church, Abraham Kathanaar of Kumbanadu church, Geevarghese Kathanaar of Kaviyoor church, Alexandriyos Kathanar of Punthala church, Abraham Kathanar of Venmony church.) Joseph, *Malankara Mar Thoma Syrian Church,* 44.

ritualistic and cultural positions. The witness in the course of Thomas Mar Athanasius' examination in court gave a general outline of the faith of the Church in his capacity as head and spokesperson of the reformed group both in doctrine and in administration.[316] The reformers tried to keep the tradition and heritage of the Malankara Church and dropped the doctrines that lacked biblical foundation.[317]

2.4 - The First Thaksa Formation Committee[318] - 1900

After the formation of the Church, the priests, who favoured the reform movement celebrated the Holy Qurbana in Malayalam by using the Syriac liturgy. There was no verbal uniformity in the celebration of the liturgy among the priests since the translation was extempore. In order to avoid terminological variations and to make a uniform liturgical text, Metropolitan Titus I[319] convened a meeting of Thaksa Formation Committee at Maramon in 1900.[320] This committee is known as *"Prarthana Pusthaka Shucheekarana Samithi* - (Prayer Book Reforming Committee) that consisted of eight members with Rev. J.J.B. Palmers of the CMS as Chairman.[321] The committee discussed the following points which are theologically important. To quote K. K. Kuruvilla,

---

[316] A summary of the statement of Metropolitan Thomas Mar Athanasius, in the course of his examination in the Seminary Case, on the doctrinal position of the Reformists are mentioned in the Appendix D of Zachariah John's Thesis. John, *The Liturgy of the Mar Thoma Church of Malabar,* 122.

[317] Metropolitan Joseph Mar Thoma, interview by author, London, April 15, 2014.

[318] The term Thaksa formation is not used in the strict sense of formulating a new liturgy, but it is to denote the renewal, simplification and the formulation process of the existed Syriac version of the St. James liturgy. This term is particularly referred in the personal diary of Thumpamon Mathai Kathanar who was a member of this committee.

[319] Titus I (1843-1909) is the first Mar Thoma Metropolitan after the formation of the MTC.

[320] Thumpamon, *Diary of Puthanpurackal Mathai Kathanar* (Malayalam), 121.

[321] M.C. Chacko, *Thaksa Committee Report* (Malayalam) (Thiruvalla: R.V. 1925), 2, which is kept in the archives of the MTC, Thiruvalla. Brink, *The CMS Mission of Help to the Syrian Church in Malabar,* 321.

(a) The way in which the presence of Christ is realized by the recipient in the sacrament- Is it the physical presence of Christ in the body and the blood or is it the spiritual presence of Christ only?

(b) The significance of the use of "mystery" and the "bloodless sacrifice" in the liturgy.

(c) The meaning of the expression "worthily receives." Does it imply receptionism? [322]

All the doctrinal arguments and discussions were based on the Eucharistic perspective of the Church. Further, they discussed on keeping the cross, candle, incense, vestments as per the worship tradition and practice of the Syrian Church. This Committee drafted a liturgy in 1901, but it did not receive wide approval because it failed to meet fully the points of view of the members of the Committee.[323] The prominent figures who stood for keeping the traditional worship pattern in the committee were Ayroor C. P. Philipose Kasheesha, Kottayam Thazhathu Chandapilla Kathanar, Thumpamon Puthenpurackal Mathai Kathanar, and Kottarakara Aviyottu Yohannan Kathanaar. But Kottayam Ipe Thoma Kathanar and his followers argued to follow the translated form of the Book of Common Prayer and the worship tradition of the Anglican Church. There were tensions between these traditional and liberal wings within the reformed group. The Metropolitan Titus I's diplomatic interference and conviction unified both groups without any concrete revision in the liturgy.[324] Though the members differed a great deal on the explanation of these expressions, there was a consensus on the fundamental principles of the liturgy. The Committee issued a tentative Thaksa for temporary use in the Church in 1901.[325]

---

[322] Kuruvila, *A History of the Mar Thoma Church and its Doctrines*, 31. John, *The Liturgy of the Mar Thoma Church of Malabar*, 68.

[323] Brink, *The CMS Mission of Help to the Syrian Church in Malabar*, 322.

[324] Thumpamon, *Diary of Puthanpurackal Mathai Kathanar* (Malayalam), 121-122.

[325] Chacko, *Thaksa Committee Report* (Malayalam), 2.

2.5 - The Second Prayer Book Revision Committee - 1913

After the demise of the Metropolitan Titus I, Titus II became his successor on the 5th of November, 1909 at Kozhencherry Mar Thoma parish. He convened the first meeting of the clergy who stood for reformation.[326] It was reported that thirty five priests participated in this meeting. This meeting made a few important decisions related to the discipline of the Church, i.e. the introduction of salary system for the clergy, cancellation of handsel (a token fee given as gratitude) to the clergy for conducting worship and sacraments and incorporation of all revenue of each parish to its trustee account.[327]

During the episcopate of the Metropolitan Titus II Mar Thoma (1909-1944), in 1913, the General Assembly of the Church appointed a new Prayer Book Revision Committee to revise the Liturgy. They presented a liturgy to the Assembly which met in 1922, but it did not receive general approval. Hence, the General Body constituted another liturgical revision committee consisted of thirty-six members and a sub-committee of twelve members to study for making the necessary changes in the Thaksa. The members of this subcommittee were Ollasserril Youseph Malpan, C.P. Philipose Kasheesha, George John Kasheesha, K.T. Thomas Kasheesha, K.E. Oommean Kasheesha, Mr. P.J. Varghese, Mr. C.K. Mathen, Mr. K. K. Kuruvila, C.P. Mathew, P.V. Varghese, T C. Varkey, and K.N. Daniel. They produced a report in 1923. On the basis of which a new Committee of twelve people was again appointed for liturgical revision.

2.6 - The Third Liturgy Revision Committee - 1924

This Committee wanted to introduce a Thaksa in line with the teaching of the pioneers of reform moment. But there were no sufficient records related to the reformation activities of Abraham Malpan. Abraham Malpan who left behind him no treaties on his reforms. The posterity was left with only the

---

[326] After the Royal Court Judgement, 28 priests supported the reformed wing in the Malankara Church.

[327] Thumpamon, *Diary of Puthanpurackal Mathai Kathanar* (Malayalam), 126.

expurgations he made. Therefore, the committee tapped other sources of information in this respect. The main topics of research were the following:

(a) The inferences from the negative statements of the Synod of Diamper.

(b) The memorandum from the clergy to Col. Fraser, the British Resident in 1836.

(c) The statement issued by the Reformed Society in 1878.

(d) The advice and suggestions from the CMS missionaries and the Bible.

(e) The deposition of Thomas Mar Athanasius in the Seminary Case.[328]

After careful examination of the above and of serious deliberations, this Committee submitted a revised liturgy along with a report on the points of reform in faith and practices believed to have been advocated by Abraham Malpan and his supporters.[329] According to this report, the Malpan effected ten alterations in Eucharistic liturgy and three changes in practices. They are the following:

(1) All invocations to saints and to the Blessed Virgin Mary were discarded.

(2) All prayers for the repose of the dead (requiem) was omitted.

(3) The prayers beginning with "I hold you, who holds the ends of the earth. I take up you who rules over the deeps. O God, place you in my mouth." were left out.

(4) The prayer "we offer thee this bloodless sacrifice for thy holy Church all over the world" was rewritten to read "O Lord….we offer this prayer for the Church."

(5) The declaration – "offer this living sacrifice…" was altered to read "offer this living sacrifice of grace, peace and praise."

---

[328] Kuruvila, *A History of the Mar Thoma Church and its Doctrines,* 29-30.
[329] Brink, *The CMS Mission of Help to the Syrian Church,* 322.

(6) The declaration "this Eucharist is sacrifice and praise was omitted."

(7) The declaration "Holy Spirit is the sanctifier of the censor" was omitted.

(8) The note that the "censor should be blessed" was left out.

(9) The prayer "May this bread be transformed into the life giving and saving bread." was amended to read "may he (the Holy Spirit) by brooding over it, make this bread the body of the Lord Jesus Christ for those that receive it for the remission of sins and for eternal life."

(10) The statement "this is the flaming rock laid in the sepulchre of Our Lord" was altered into "Thou art the tried and precious stone which the builders reject."[330]

The reforms of the practices are:

(1) It was ordained that Holy Communion should be administered in both kinds.

(2) The practice of obtaining absolution from the priests after having confessing sins to them was abolished.

(3) The practice of celebrating the Holy Communion, even in the absence of communicants was discontinued.[331]

The Committee adopted unanimously the following resolution on Holy Communion as well.

"In the Holy Communion, Christ gives Himself to his believers and we partake in it. But we repudiate the doctrine that any material change occurs in the bread and wine and that Christ is localised in them. Besides, the Holy Communion is a reminder of Christ the incarnate, who offered Himself

---

[330] Chacko, *Thaksa Committee Report*, (Malayalam),1-2., Joseph, *Malankara Mar Thoma Syrian Church*, 40-41, Alexander Mar Thoma, *The Mar Thoma Church: Heritage and Mission*, 16. John, *The Liturgy of the Mar Thoma Church of Malabar in the Light of its History,*" 68-71.

[331] K.T Thomas and Koshy T.N, ed., *Faith on Trial* (Mar Theomotheos Memorial Publishing House, 1965), 156. Joseph, *Malankara Mar Thoma Syrian Church: Sabha Directory 2015*, 41. Brink, *The CMS Mission of Help to the Syrian Church*, 323-324.

up as an eternal sacrifice, for the redemption of the whole world by His death; a sacrificial feast for participating (eating and drinking) in Christ, who offered himself up as a sacrifice; a pledge of the certainty of the redemption through Christ; a means for the incorporation of the believers in Christ and between themselves; a thanks offering declaring our gratitude to God for the redemption wrought through Christ and for all other benefits we enjoy from God; a prayer for all blessings on the basis of Christ's eternal sacrifice; an offering, wherein the church incorporating itself in the offering of Christ, offers itself up as a living, holy and acceptable sacrifice to God. This holy rite was instituted by Our Lord during the most important occasion in His life and the Church has been celebrating it right from Apostolic times, and it occupies the central place in the worship of the Christian Church and no section of Christians, which disregard this rite which is biblical and in conformity with the consciousness of the Church universal, will escape suffering serious deterioration in spiritual life and progress. The blessings of Holy Communion are dependent on conditions spiritual, and those who participate in it without the proper mental attitude do not derive any benefit therefrom, but, it will be curse to them."[332]

By considering the above mentioned matters, this committee published another tentative Thaksa with their report and submitted it in the General Assembly of the Church in 1927. The prominent members in this committee included K.K. Kuruvila, K.N. Daniel and C.P. Mathew.[333] The General Assembly which met in 1927 marks as an important event in the life of the MTC. In this assembly, in the light of the liturgical developments to date in the Church, decided what reforms they would accept and the authority of Abraham Malpan was claimed for. The changes in the Syrian liturgy of St. James were declared by this Assembly as owning the imprint of Abraham

---

[332] Thomas and Koshy, *Faith on Trial,* 17-18.
[333] C.P. Mathew, *Thaksa Nirupanam* (Malayalam) (New Delhi: Dharma Jyothi Viddya Peeth, 2008), 12.

Malpan and his supporters.[334] The changes to be noted in the liturgy relate to the following points:

(1) Incense - the old liturgy gives great importance to this and it gives the impression that it was something, which effects reconciliation with God. "Accept our incense out of thy mercy, O Lord" was changed into "accept our worship, O Lord" and "be reconciled to us through the incense offered by Thy priests" into "attend unto the prayer of Thy priest."

(2) The term "sacrifice" in the liturgy- wherever this word expresses the idea that the sacrifice of Christ is being repeated, it was either dropped or explained. It was replaced by the expression "the bloodless sacrifice of grace, peace and praise."

(3) The meaning of "sacrament" was redefined.

(a) The Words of Institution in the old liturgy were so changed that, only the words of Christ as given in the gospels were retained (Lk.22:19, Mt.26:28). The old liturgy contained the expression. "This is my body which is broken for the remission of sins and eternal life."

(b) The word "mystery" is dropped from all places where it is occurred. It was feared that this word might encourage the worshippers in the belief that some magical change would take place in the bread and wine during the communion service.

(c) Regarding the Epiclesis in the prayer of Institution, different forms were suggested. One form was as in the original Jacobite Thaksa: "May the Holy Ghost descend on this bread and transform it into the body of Christ for those who worthily receive it." The last committee replaced it by the following: "May the Holy Spirit sanctify this bread to be the body of our

---

[334] Brink, *The CMS Mission of Help to the Syrian Church*, 323.

Lord Jesus Christ." A corresponding change is made in the form of the consecration of the wine also.

(d) Regarding the person of Christ, the prayers suspected of Monophysitism were dropped. The following three passages from the prayer of fraction and commixture seen in the liturgy text had been removed: "His soul was parted from his while his divinity in no way parted, either from His soul or from His body." "On behalf of the sins of the entire world, the Son died on the Cross, His soul came and united with His body". "And one is Emmanuel who cannot be divided after the union, there is no division into two natures."

(e) The Priest - In all prayers which the priest offers in his own name for the people, the first person singular is deleted and either the first person plural or the second person plural, signifying the congregation, is substituted. After the prayer for the Holy Ghost, just before the prayer of the institution, the prayer of the priest, "Answer me O Lord, answer me O Lord Answer me O Lord and have mercy upon me" has been changed into "Answer to us O Lord".

(f) After the fraction, the prayer of the priest that "this my service (oblation) be acceptable unto Thee" is changed into "this our service be acceptable to Thee." This change was made in order to emphasize the Priesthood of the Laity. (1 Pet.2: 5, Rev.1:6, 5:10, 20:6) and to affirm that the Church does not recognize its ministers as mediators.[335]

The report and the liturgy were presented for the approval of the General Assembly of the Church in M.E 1102 (1926 December). The Assembly confirmed the summary of Abraham Malpan's reforms, drafted

---

[335] Kuruvila, *A History of the Mar Thoma Church and its Doctrines,* 32-33, John, *The Liturgy of the Mar Thoma Church of Malabar,* 71-73.

by the committee, and also the resolutions on the Holy Qurbana.[336] But it did not arrive at no decisions concerning the revised liturgy. Although, the Assembly did not adopt this liturgy officially, it had the unanimous agreement of the Liturgy Revision Committee. However this liturgy gradually came to be used widely in the Church and eventually became known as the "Liturgy of the Committee."[337] The liturgies currently used in the MTC have been composed after 1102, inconformity with the articles of reforms accepted by the Church at that time.[338]

Even though, the Committee Thaksa became widely used there were tendencies of certain other versions of the liturgy drawn up by differing schools of Eucharistic interpretation began to be in circulation. Hence, there were no liturgical uniformity in general. In order to tackle this issue and to make consensus among traditionalist and liberalists, on the recommendation of the Episcopal Synod, Metropolitan Titus II published the previously mentioned liturgy in 1942 with slight modifications and is known as the "Liturgy of Titus II."[339] It was an attempt to accommodate different groups within the Church. This liturgy was accepted by a large sections in the church without much complaint.

2.7 - The Fourth Thaksa Revision Committee - 1945

In 1945, the Episcopal Synod of the Church appointed another committee to revise the Thaksa, which consisted of fourteen members and this committee unanimously submitted its report in 1951. This committee submitted an agreed revised version of St. James Liturgy which made certain changes in the hope of making it acceptable to the Church as a whole. The present Mar Thoma Eucharistic liturgy dates from 1954. It was the work of the Liturgy Revision Committee appointed in 1945. With the approval of the Episcopal Synod, the Metropolitan Juhanon Mar

---

[336] *The Minutes Book of the Samudayalochana Sabha of M.E 1102, Dhanu 13-15*, Thiruvalla, 274.
[337] Brink, *The CMS Mission of Help to the Syrian Church*,.324. Abraham, *Malankara Mar Thoma Syrian Church*, 420-421.
[338] John, "The Reformation of Abraham Malpan and Assessment." 47
[339] Mathew, *Thaksa Nirupanam* (Malayalam), 12-13.

Thoma published a revised Eucharistic liturgy in 1954. This is known as the "Liturgy of the Synod."[340] There was no fundamental difference in the two liturgies mentioned above. A comparison of the epiclesis in the two liturgies is given below:

The Liturgy of Titus II:

"May the Holy Spirit sanctify this bread to be the Body of our Lord Jesus the Messiah." or "May the Holy Spirit sanctify the wine in this Chalice to be the Blood of our Lord Jesus the Messiah."

The Liturgy of the Synod:

(a) "May the Holy Spirit sanctify this bread to be the Body of our Lord Jesus the Messiah." Or "May the Holy Spirit bless this bread and sanctify it to be, for us, the communion of (participation in) the Body of Christ, thy dear Son and our Lord God Jesus the Messiah."

(b) "May the Holy Spirit sanctify the wine in this chalice to be the blood of our Lord Jesus the Messiah" or "May the Holy Spirit bless this chalice and sanctify it to be, for us, the communion of (participation in) the Blood of Thy dear Son and our Lord God Jesus the Messiah." [341]

Both of these liturgies have been officially accepted and are in common use in the Church now. As we have seen, the revision of liturgy in the MTC is not an instant venture. But it was the result of a long process of critical study on the Antiochian liturgy, serious enquiry into the ideas of Abraham Malpan, debated with liturgical scholars, re-reading of Scripture and close observation of the principles of the protestant reformation in the 16th century.

---

[340] David J. Kennedy, *Eucharistic Sacramentality in an Ecumenical Context: The Anglican Epiclesis* (Aldershot: Ashgate, 2008), 208. Joseph, *Malankara Mar Thoma Syrian Church,* 49-50.
[341] Joseph, *Malankara Mar Thoma Syrian Church,* 50. John, *The Liturgy of the Mar Thoma Church of Malabar,* 73-76.

As noted above, one of the objectives of the reformation in the Malankara Church was to have a liturgy in the native language - Malayalam. However, except for the Qurbana Thaksa of Kovoor Ipe Thoma Kathanar[342] and the order of worship for Sunday morning (Divine service), no other translations were made from Syriac to Malayalam. The Metropolitan Titus II initiated the translation of other liturgies.[343] Among these, Maliekkal Zachariah Malpan translated the liturgy for the Sacrament of Baptism into Malayalam. Currently the Qurbana Thaksa of the MTC contains the following anaphoras: the anaphora of St. James, the anaphoras of Mar Dionysius Metropolitan, the anaphora of Xystus the Patriarch, the anaphora known by the name of the Apostle St. Peter, the anaphora of John the Patriarch, the anaphora of Thomas the Episcopa of Harkkaliya and anaphora of Mar Ivanios Metropolitan.[344] The doctrinal position of the Church in relation to the Eucharist, is embedded in the Thaksa, and it is officially accepted and use for its celebrations; in the offices for the

---

[342] Kovoor Ipe Thoma Kathanar (1842-1927) was the Vicar General of the MTC in 1891. He bought the *Panchayathu Purayidam,* the SCS compound in Thiruvalla that is the Headquarters of the MTC for Rs.600 in 1892. Realizing his leadership qualities, the Maharaja of Travancore nominated him as a member of his Legislative Assembly. When the Metropolitan Thomas Mar Athanasius died suddenly without consecrating a successor, Kovoor Ipe Thoma Kathanar and his associates brought the Metropolitan of the Independent Church in Thozhiyoor to consecrate Titus I. www.nalloorlibrary.com (accessed January 12, 2015).

[343] This included thanksgiving after child birth, holy baptism, chrismation, holy matrimony, dedication of a House, the visitation and anointing the sick, and funeral service to Malayalam with limited copies.

[344] There are another two short liturgies for the communion, i.e. a short Thaksa for special occasion and special liturgy for the usage when the Holy Qurbana is conducted for the sick at home. The book of occasional offices were translated from Syriac in 1945 which contains the texts for baptism, marriage and funeral liturgies, thanksgiving prayer after the birth of a child, prayer for the sick and the order for the dedication of a house. The first English version was printed in 1988 and a special order of service or the burial of those who commit suicide were prepared in 1996. The seven canonical hours of daily prayer were reduced to two, especially for the use of the lay people and the text was published in 1942. The text of services conducted only by bishops (ordination rites, admission to the monastic order, and consecration of a church building) are still in manuscript form and no English translation is available. There is also a special order for the consecration of *mooron* (chrism) which is used for the consecration of a church building and for the post-baptismal anointing. Paul Bradshaw, *The New SCM Dictionary of Liturgy and Worship* (London: SCM, 2002), 295-96.

performance of other rites, in the prayers, invocations and declarations and in the resolutions of the General Assembly.

3 - Changes in the Liturgical Prayers and its Theological Significance

The MTC had to undergo a period of litigation between 1955 and 1965 on matters of its doctrines. A summary of the affidavit filed by Metropolitan Juhanon Mar Thoma[345] in this regard pointed out the doctrinal stance of the Church. The theology of the Church is embedded in the liturgy and the changes made in the liturgy witnessed the doctrinal position of the Church. The reforms, which were believed and affirmed by the MTC, as effected by the reformers of the Malankara Church, were those described in the resolutions adopted by the *Alochana Sabha* (General Assembly) at its session held in the year 1102 ME[346] (1927). It is significant to note that the District Court in Kottayam, the High Court of Kerala and the Supreme Court of India have accepted the statement of Metropolitan Juhanon Mar Thoma (1947-1976) on the doctrine of the Church.

The Church has accepted the Bible and the Nicene Creed, as the basis of its faith and doctrines. The Church believes in the doctrine of Trinity as formulated at the Synod of Nicaea. The doctrine laid down in the canons of Malankara regarding the Trinity is similar to that decided upon at Nicaea about the belief in the Trinity.[347] The Church, in tandem with the ancient faith, does not accept the western interpolation of the *"filioque clause"* which states that the Holy Spirit proceeds from the Father and the Son. The Church retains the biblical teaching of the procession of the Holy Spirit from the Father (Jn.15:26). The Church clearly holds the doctrine of the Trinity as interpreted by the creeds of Nicaea, Constantinople and Ephesus.

---

[345] XVIII Mar Thoma Metropolitan (1893-1976).
[346] Malayalam Era.
[347] Mathews Mar Athanasius Metropolitan, *Mar Thoma Sleehayude Edavakayakunna Malankra Suriyanisabhayude Canon* (Malayalam) (Thiruvalla: Church Sahitya Samithi, 2008), 18-19.

Regarding the nature of Christ, the Church believed that both the divinity and humanity of Christ were united in the same person, inseparable, but so as not to be confounded in the union. This Church is neither Nestorian nor Monophysite. Another major change was that prayers for the departed souls and Saints were removed from the liturgy and considers praying for the dead and praying to the Blessed Virgin Mary and to Saints are opposed to the canon and Scripture.[348] The Church does not validate the practice of seeking the intercession of Saints for lack of biblical reference.

In the case of the priesthood, the Church believes that the priest is only the representative of the people. The Church affirms the priesthood of the laity and believes that Christ alone is the mediator.[349] It is because of the reformation that the laity got a major role to play in the worship. This change made the worship services more people oriented and lively. Owing to the reformation, a renewed understanding of worship has emerged in the Church with a collective involvement of the people of God, not merely something done by a clergy alone for and on behalf of the people.

The Church has recorded that the Holy Eucharist is the Spiritual Sacrifice, the Sacrifice of grace, peace, and thanksgiving. It does not believe that the Holy Communion is a sacrifice in its literal sense of the term; but it is not believed to be a sacrifice attended with shedding of blood. The Church does not believe that the bread and wine in the Holy Eucharist are merely symbols of the Body and Blood of Jesus Christ. It is permissible for the members of the Church to believe, either that while they are symbols, the body and blood of Christ become present in the company of the worshippers through the medium of bread and wine, in a manner incomprehensible to human senses and beyond the reach of analytical tests, or that they do not so become present.[350] The elements bread and wine are regarded as the signs and semblance of the flesh and blood of Jesus Christ. The Church does not say the bread and wine are the "real" body and blood of Jesus Christ. The Church accepts the bread and wine set at the Holy

---

[348] Alexander Mar Thoma, The *Mar Thoma Church: Heritage and Mission,* 16.
[349] Alexander Mar Thoma, *The Mar Thoma Church: Heritage and Mission* 16-17.
[350] Thomas and Koshy, *Faith on Trial,* 15.

Qurbana as the symbols and the likeness of the body and blood of Christ. The Church denies transubstantiation and the physical presence of Christ in the body and blood. But it is believed as a divine mystery beyond human comprehension. The Lord's Supper should be conducted only when there are partakers, and it should be in the native language so that the participants could comprehend the full meaning of the service. Auricular confession was also stopped.[351]

The following are the main difference between the Mar Thoma and the Orthodox Syrian Church's Eucharistic liturgical prayers.

(a) The word sacrifice wherever it expresses the idea that the sacrifice of Christ was repeated was either dropped or explained. It was replaced by the expression "the bloodless sacrifice of grace, peace, and praise."[352] The Church does not give more importance to the concept of sacrifice, and mysterious act in Holy Qurbana, but believes in the once for all sacrifice of Christ on Calvary and the presence of Christ in the Qurbana. It is not a repetition of the same sacrifice on Calvary. Because of this, the Church removed all the words from the Jacobite liturgy, which express this meaning:

(b) With regard to the Words of Institution, the words of Christ as given in the Gospels retained (Lk.22:19, Mt.26:28). In the Words of Institution, the Church has adopted only the Gospel narratives about the last supper and avoided the rest of it. The term eternal life is not in the institutional narrative of the Gospel. That is why it is avoided.

(c) The term mystery is dropped from all places where it occurred, in order to avoid confusion among the believers or discourages them from the belief of magical change in the bread and wine during the communion service.[353] This word is dropped wherever

---

[351] K. Joseph, *A Brief Sketch of the Church of St. Thomas in Malabar* (Kottayam: CMS, 1933), 14.
[352] Alexander Mar Thoma, *The Mar Thoma Church: Heritage and Mission,* 16.
[353] Alexander Mar Thoma, *The Mar Thoma Church: Heritage and Mission* 16-17.

it followed as an unexplainable and unfathomable reality. It is a mystery revealed in Christ and through his sacrificial death on the cross. In order to avoid confusion among the faithful, the Church uses the term bread and wine instead of body and blood. This is considered a mystical and incomprehensible experience.

(d) Regarding the importance of bread and wine, the MTC believes that the elements are not mere symbols, but an "anamnesis" of the salvific act of Christ and the spiritual presence of Christ in and through the Eucharist. The Mar Thoma liturgy does not elaborate on what ways or means this presence is experienced in the Eucharist. The Church believes that, this as an inexplicable experience and a mystical one, which could be understood only through faith. There are mainly three understandings, i.e. the symbolic representation of the bread and wine as the body and blood of Christ, the remembrance of Christ's salvific act and the presence of Christ in the celebration of the Holy Qurbana. (Symbolism, anamnesis and presence of Christ). In the Mar Thoma liturgy the transformation of the body and blood (elements) in a particular way is not mentioned.[354]

(e) With regard to the *Epiclesis*, the following prayer was accepted: "May the Holy Spirit sanctify this bread and wine into the body and blood of our Lord Jesus Christ!" The word "transform" and "descended on" were specially omitted. In the Mar Thoma liturgy,

---

[354] Regarding the importance of the bread and wine, the Orthodox tradition views the bread and wine are the real body and blood of Christ. They are not treated as mere symbols. But Christ is really present in the elements, which are set on the altar before the priest. Through the invocation of the Holy Spirit, the bread and wine are transformed into the body and bold of Jesus Christ. This conversion according to Orthodox theology is a mystery. The Orthodox tradition believes in realism and it rejects the symbolic interpretation of the Eucharist. According to Orthodox faith, Christ is really presented in the bread and wine and the consecrated elements are not treated as mere symbols. The transformation into the body of Christ is possible with the help of Holy Spirit i.e., through the mediation of Holy Spirit. It is a real presence of Christ, whose being is glorified in present and future. Hence there is no difference between the incarnate presence of Christ and the Eucharistic presence. The real presence may be different from the general presence of Christ because here the presence is immediate and objective. Interview with Mathews Mar Aprem on 12th November 2013 in Dublin.

the awe-inspiring view of the descent of the Holy Spirit is omitted. This is to avoid the over dramatization of the Holy Qurbana.

(f) Regarding the priesthood, the Church believes that the celebrant is the representative of the people and affirms that Christ alone is the mediator. This Church does not recognize the "priestly mediation."[355] The Church believes that the priest is a representative of the whole community and prays for all the people. The Church gives more importance to the collective prayer rather than individual prayer.

(g) In the case of intercession, the structure is the same but in the content, the prayers that refer to the prayer for the departed and the intercession to the saints has been omitted. The Church remembers the faithful departed, but does not pray for them. The Church gratefully remembers and thanks God for the lives of the departed faithful. It considers the earthly life very important and insists everyone should lead a responsible Christian life which takes them to eternal life.

(h) The concept *Theotokos* - the Mother of God, is not acceptable to the reformed faith. The Church uses the term *Christotokos* - Mother of Christ since it is more biblical. Whenever the term *Theotokos* appears it is replaced with *Christotokos*. There are traces of Monophysite teachings[356] in some prayers and the person of Christ is not defined in such a way in the passion narrative.

---

[355] Alexander Mar Thoma, *The Mar Thoma Church: Heritage and Mission,* 16-17. The Apostle Paul wrote that there is only one mediator between God and humanity - the man Christ Jesus (1 Tim. 2:5). This is the stand of the MTC on mediation.

[356] Nestorius (386-451) was the bishop of Constantinople during 428-431 CE. He hesitated to call St. Mary as *Theotokos* instead he called her - *Christotokos* (Mother of Christ) - against the faith affirmation of the undivided Church. It was in this context that Cyril of Alexandria in the Council of Ephesus in 431 CE declared St. Mary as *Theotokos* as she bore Jesus Christ, who is fully divine and fully human. This led to the rejection of Nestorius's teachings. The MTC accepts the first three Ecumenical Councils. Both in the Council of Nicaea and Constantinople, the full humanity and full divinity of Jesus Christ was irrefutably affirmed as the official doctrine of the Church. The liturgical emphasis of the MTC is purely scriptural since the term Christotokos is generally accepted in the Church. Juhanon Mar Thoma, *Basic Christian Beliefs* (Thiruvalla: Christava Sahitya Samithi, 2008), 38-39. Daniel, *Ecumenism in Praxis,* 62-64.

Hence, this has been changed. More about reconciliation and redemption is reflected in the liturgy of the MTC.

(i) In the Orthodox service, there are mainly two processions. The first procession starts when the celebrant escorted by a host of acolytes makes a circumnavigation around the holy altar swinging the censer and finally facing to the faithful in the nave of the church. It is a ritual which is a symbolic representation of the magi who went to see baby Jesus born in Bethlehem. In the second procession, the celebrant comes towards the people carrying the holy mysteries reverentially which symbolises the second coming of Christ.[357] In the Mar Thoma Eucharistic service, the processions are not considered essential. The Church retains the liturgical vestments, candles and incense as before. The oriental form of the service and liturgy are continued.

4 - Liturgical Translation in the Mar Thoma Church

As cited above, the revision of the Eucharistic liturgy has been the starting point of the reform movement in the Malankara Church. The 21st Metropolitan Joseph Mar Thoma has remarked that:

> "the present Eucharistic liturgy brought to Malankara by the Antiochian Church and that had been used by our ancestors even after the reformation in 1836, and the later Malayalam translation of 1942 which was guided by the great endeavour of His Grace, Titus II Mar Thoma Metropolitan, who initiated this progressive effort, with the help of Very Rev. Kaniyamparambil Kurian Cor-Episcopa of the Jacobite Church, Syriac teachers like C. P. Philippose Kassesa, Olasseril Joseph Malpan, Maliyekkal M.G. Zachariah Kassesa of Karthikapally and some Hindu Malayalam pundits. They were successful in preserving the accuracy of the translation and composing the hymns to the original tunes and meter of Syriac music. That process took four years to complete and

---

[357] George Mathew Nalunnakal and Kuriakose Moolayil, *Sathyavisshwasa Padanagal* (Malayalam) (Chenganassery: Mor Adai Study Centre, 2001), 97-101.

gave new impetus for the idea of reformation and an understanding of the traditions of the Malankara Mar Thoma Syrian Church."[358]

Though there were organized attempts to revise the liturgy during the years 1900, 1913, 1924, and 1945, it was in 1954, that Titus II officially published a revised order of Holy Qurbana.[359] The revision of the liturgy took place not in an orderly manner during the early periods of the Church. Titus II Mar Thoma says about this as follows: "Since the liturgy was in Syriac, the priests who celebrated the liturgy translated it in accordance with the reformed faith. But the entire text was neither revised nor published as one book."[360] The Malayalam liturgy is the base for translations into other languages. Translating directly from the Syriac text is no longer in practice.[361] At present the liturgy of the Holy Qurbana is available in eight languages such as Malayalam, English, Hindi, Tamil, Kannada, Telugu, Marathi and Spanish.[362]

---

[358] Joseph Mar Thoma Metropolitan, Foreword in *"The MTSC Order of Worship"* published by the Mar Thoma Syrian Church in Singapore 2015, 1.

[359] Mathew, *Liturgy for Our Times,* 37.

[360] Titus II, *Qurbana Thaksa,* i-ii.

[361] Interview with Geevarghese Mar Theodosius on August 28, 2015 in Dublin.

[362] (1) The first **English translation** of the liturgy of St James was published in 1972, although prayer books had already been translated in 1940's. Juhanon Mar Thoma and Alexander Mar Thoma, authorized English versions to be used in the Church wherever it was needed. The Diocese of North America and Europe has published a version that comprises the translation of the Malayalam Thakso, Prayer Book for Divine Service and the other Sacraments and Rites. The Church authorised more than one version of translation, because of the linguistic differences in different parts of the world. (2) An official **Hindi** version of the Eucharistic liturgy was translated on behalf of the Christu Pandhi Ashram Sihora in 1967. In the preface of the official liturgy it was stated that "Rev. Gnanabharanam of Pendra Road made a complete translation of the liturgy for the ashram in 1952. (3) A **Telugu** version of the liturgy was translated mainly by the initiative of Rev. Kuruvila Philip along with Mr. K.R. Stanley in December 1987. (4) The first **Kannada** version of the liturgy is translated by Rev. M.P. Philip while he was serving as the missionary of the Hoskote region in Northern Karnataka. Later Very Rev. P. J. Thomas and Rev. P.V. Philip took the initiative and revised and reprinted it on behalf of the Ankola Ashram and for the use of the mission fields in the Karnataka State. (5) A translation of the **Tamil** version of the liturgy is undertaken by Rev. Reji Zachariah and team for the Pollachi mission filed in Tamil Nadu. (6) The **Marathi** version of the Liturgy is translated for the use of the faith community in the regions of Maharashtra, especially in the mission centers of Chackon and Jaavahar. The missionary Rev C. Thomas took the initiative of the translation and Mr. Sunny Pattolay from Pune also helped him in this endeavour. (7) A

5 - Conclusion

The liturgical revision and reforms in the MTC have been perceived as an ongoing process. The whole progression of liturgical development and revision in the Church from the time of Abraham Malpan in 1835 to Juhanon Mar Thoma in 1954 was a result of a continuing progression of theological debates, critical arguments, heated discussions and thorough study on the existing liturgical prayers and practices of the Liturgy. Even though, the influence and involvement of the Western missionaries in reforming the Syriac liturgy into Malayalam seem passive, they did make a concrete contribution to the process of revision especially from the period of 1835-1840. As pointed above, the primary aim of the "Mission of Help" was for a scriptural reformation in the Syrian Church. In order to reinvigorate the Malankara Church, the missionaries concentrated on teaching priests, opening schools in parishes, translating the Bible, and translating the Book of Common Prayer into Malayalam.

Before Abraham Malpan, the liturgical revision initiated by the CMS missionaries were very often perceived as an ignored reality. A rereading of the history of the liturgical development in the MTC proves that the CMS missionaries laid foundation for the whole process of liturgical revision and later Abraham Malpan ignited it with his passionate efforts to renew the Church rooted in the historical, apostolic and episcopal nature of the Malankara Church. As we have seen, during the period of 1836-1840 there existed two versions of reformed liturgy. The earlier one was a revised version by the CMS missionaries composed in 1836 and later the liturgy believed to be of Abraham Malpan. It is because of the close connection between Malpan and the missionaries in Seminary, Abraham Malpan might have had a role in shaping the amended liturgy of missionaries and might

---

Spanish version of the liturgy is translated and released it on 17th of January 2016 under the initiative of the North America and Europe Diocese for the mission centers in Mexico under the supervision of the Diocesan Bishop Geervarghese Mar Theodosius. A **German** version of the liturgy is translated by a Liturgical Translation Committee initiated by the Switzerland Mar Thoma Congregation under the leadership of Rev. K. Jameson and it is under the consideration of the Episcopal Synod for its authorization. Mathew, "History of the Development of the Mar Thoma Syrian Liturgy," 40-41.

have used the revised liturgy of CMS in the Seminary Chapel. Because of the absence of sufficient historical documents on the liturgy of Abraham Malpan, in considering the context of the Malankara Church, one can assume that after leaving the Seminary in 1840, Malpan might have celebrated the Holy Qurbana with the revised Thaksa in which he softened the liturgical reforms by restoring or recasting some elements which had been removed from the liturgy under the pressure of parishes who support Malpan.[363]

Even though there were many attempts to reform the texts of the Eucharistic liturgy of the Malankara Church during the years of 1873, 1900, 1913, 1924, a modern version of the service book came to be published only after 1927 with the suggestions of the General Assembly of the Church (*Sabha Pradhinidhi Mandalam*). This Thaksa was again revised and tentatively accepted, which has the unanimous support of the committee of experts, is now in use and has later received the official recognition of the Church. Hence there are significant differences between the Amended liturgy of missionaries or Abraham Malpan and the Mar Thoma liturgies of the 20th century. As a reformed and reforming Church, the MTC upholds a flexible nature in the usage of languages for the liturgical revision and translation processes. Liturgical revision is an ongoing process in the Church. Since the liturgy proclaims the faith and theology of the Church, it is being translated into different languages from Malayalam as, and when, the need arises. As has been noted, the MTC revised its Eucharistic liturgy in considering the needs of the people within the historical experiences of the community. This Church stood as a pioneer in this unique way of continuing and renewing the liturgy through reformation. The reformation in the Malankara Church was an affirmation of the Eastern doctrinal teachings based on the Bible; therefore, the MTC affirms and upholds a reformed Eastern Orthodox tradition.

---

[363] Thazhathu Chandapilla Kathanar remarks that Malpan did not deviate from the year old faith and practices of the ancient Church. Malpan was against the evil practices existed in the Church and he was not interested in incorporating new faith and practices. After the demise of Malpan, the reform school in the Church argued for changes in prayers in line with Anglican theology. Thazzhath Punnathra Chandapilla Kathanar, *Vilapangalude Cherupusthakam*, (Malayalam), 39-40

Chapter 5

The Concept of Mission in Scripture, Traditions and Liturgy

The mission of the Church is based on the mission of Jesus Christ. Jesus came with the mission to preach Good News to all nations (Mk.13:10). He proclaimed God's nearness to, and concern for, God's people. David Bosch points out that "mission has its origin in the heart of God. God is the fountain of sending love. This is the deepest source of mission. It is impossible to penetrate deeper still; there is mission because God loves people."[364] The Church, through its missionary activities works for the transformation of the world in Christ. The transformation of the world through the love of Christ is the meaning of Christian mission. Therefore, the very life of the Church is missionary in nature and its bearers witness as the agency of the Kingdom of God. This also cannot be proved in abstract theoretical concepts. Only missionary activities can prove that the Church is the agent through which the Kingdom of God continuously actualizes itself in history.[365]

1 - The Concept of Mission in Scripture
The Christian religion is a historic religion that centres on the salvific act of Jesus Christ. The main task of the Church is to communicate the good news of Christ and to make disciples of all nations (Mt.28:18-19). Even though the term mission is not appearing explicitly in Scripture, this concept permeates the entire Bible. The concept of mission in the Old Testament

---

[364] Bosch, *Transforming Missions,* 392.
[365] Paul Tillich, "The Theology of Missions," *The Journal Christianity and Crisis* (March 1955): 27.

lies in the understanding that the transcendent God is the God who is involved in the history, who acts in and through the history.[366] The record of His involvement in history indicates that His work is both revelatory and redemptive.[367] The act of God is manifested in and through the activities and mission of the Patriarchs, Judges, Prophets, Priests and Kings in the history of Israel. The Church's mission of inclusivity and universality has its roots in the Old Testament, particularly in the vision of the prophets (Gen.12:3, Isa.45:1-8, 49:1-6).[368] The New Testament reveals that the mission is the manifestation of the love of God (Jn. 3:16). The mission of the Church has its roots in the ministry and person of Jesus, who is both "evangelical" and "evangelizer,"[369] as he preached, served and witnessed to the reign of God and gathered around him a community[370] (Mk.1:14-45, 6:7-13, Lk.10:1-20). Jesus saw his purpose as being sent by God his Father to proclaim and accomplish spiritual deliverance for humankind (Lk.4:43, Jn.3:34, 8:42, 10:36). Before ascending into heaven, Jesus commissioned his disciples to go to the ends of the earth with a particular mission (Mt. 28:18-20). This great commissioning (Mt.28:16-20, Jn.20:19-23) is a mandate for mission. Hence the mission of the Church has its roots in the post-resurrection faith of the first disciples. They held the conviction of Jesus' universal Lordship as risen Christ, through whom humanity has direct access to God. The Holy Spirit is the guide and source of strength for mission (Jn.15.26, 14.26, Lk.24:49, 46-48, Acts.1:8). The Disciples of Christ created a new community of fellowship in prayer and mutual service with the power of the Holy Spirit. For them mission begins with the self-understanding in

---

[366] Robert Hall Glover, *The Bible Basis of Missions* (Chicago: MOODY, 1976), 15-22.

[367] Geevarghese Mar Theodosius, "Mission of the Church in the 21st Century," in *Challenges and Prospects of Mission in the Emerging Context,* ed. Koshy P. Varughese, (Faridabad: Dharma Jyoti Vidya Peeth, 2010), 20.

[368] Lesslie Newbigin, *The Logic of Election in the Gospel in a Pluralistic Society* (Grand Rapids, MI: Eerdmans, 1989), 80-88. George R. Hunsberger, *Bearing the Witness of the Spirit: Lesslie Newbigin' Theology of Cultural Plurality* (Grand Rapids: MI, Eerdmans, 1998), 45-112.

[369] Mortimer Arias, *Announcing the Reign of God: Evangelization and the Subversive Memory of Jesus* (Philadelphia: Fortress, 1984), 2.

[370] Hans Kung, *The Church* (New York: Sheed and Ward, 1967), 74-75.

relationship with Jesus and its manifestations.[371] For the apostles, to prove Jesus as the awaited Messiah to the Jews was the "mission." The mission outside Judaism was spontaneity, the result of a vision to Peter (Acts.10). It inaugurated new debates on the very notion of mission. It was a part of their very life and existence. They were witnessing what they experienced.[372] The religious persecution of the early Christians during the first and second centuries has pointed up another mode of mission. For them, to witness Jesus Christ was a matter of life and death, a process of persecution, dispersion and expansion that resulted in the mission (Acts.8:4). When the Romans persecuted the early Christians, they dispersed from Jerusalem. Wherever they went, they preached the good news of Jesus to everyone. apostles, and early missionaries, travelled everywhere, to the Mediterranean world, North Africa and even as far as India, with the Gospel. Paul's missionary journey in the book of the Acts of Apostles narrates a descriptive report on the growth of Christianity. When the early believers scattered because of religious persecution, they preached wherever they were dispersed[373] (Acts. 8:4). Gradually Christianity "defied territorial confinement and transcended all human constraints-political, social and cultural."[374] The mission of the Christian community is to give witness to the reality of God through the Church as a sign, foretaste, and presence of the Kingdom of

---

[371] Glover, *The Bible Basis of Missions,* 22-30.

[372] The apostles, particularly Paul and John, perceive the mystery of the plan of God for the whole creation. St. Paul envisions a new cosmic community in which God seeks to gather all things (Eph.1:10), reconcile all things (Col.1:20), reunite all things so that God will be all in all (1 Cor.15:28). The evangelist John sees the Word of God enlightening everywhere (Jn.1:9) and becoming flesh to share with us his fullness (Jn. 1:16). John also sees God making all things new, so that there will be a new heaven and a new earth, where there will be no more tears and suffering (Rev.2:1-5). The missionary journeys of St. Paul were also the result of a vision and the initiation of the Holy Spirit (Acts.13:1-3, 16.6-10). His mission to the gentile community was mainly based on his interpretation of his own conversion. He emphasized the grace element in Christian faith. It was by the grace of God that he was saved, not on merit. Therefore, mission, for St. Paul is an initiation of the Holy Spirit as well as his personal understanding of God and its manifestation. Michael Amaladoss, "Challenges of Mission in the 21st century," *Theology Digest* 47, no.1 (Spring 2000): 15-20.

[373] Sam George, "Diaspora: A Hidden Link to 'from Everywhere to Everywhere,'" *Missiology: An International Review 39, no.* 1 (January 2011): 46-55.

[374] Adrian Hastings, *'150-1550': In a World History of Christianity* (Grand Rapids, MI: Eerdmans: 1999), 58.

God. The mission of the Church must, therefore, be preoccupied with the nature of the One to whom it bears witness.

2 - Mission in Different Ecclesiastic Traditions

The term mission has no common connotation in the history of Christianity. Throughout the centuries, diverse ecclesiastical traditions defined and practiced it differently. According to Schmemann, "a theology of mission has been always the fruit of the total being of the Church and not a mere speciality for those who receive a particular missionary calling."[375] To understand the concept of mission in the MTC, it is imperative to trace the varied understandings of mission in different Christian traditions since the Church stands in between Orthodoxy and Protestantism. The acceptance of ecclesial pluralism, practice of Eastern liturgical tradition, and the affirmation of the Anglican theological emphasis shaped a theology of mission for the MTC. As noted above, this Church is indebted to the Antiochian Orthodox Church for its liturgical contributions, worship pattern and also it is obliged to the Protestant missionaries of Europe, especially the CMS, for its theological position. In order to understand the notion of mission in the MTC, it is imperative to analyse the mission concept of the Antiochian Orthodox Church and the Protestant traditions. A detailed description on the concept of mission in the Orthodox[376] and Protestant traditions are highlighted below.

---

[375] Daniel B. Clendenin, ed. *Eastern Orthodox Theology: A Contemporary Reader* (Grand Rapids, MI: Baker, 1995), 196. Alexander Schmemann, *Church, World, Mission* (New York: St. Vladimir's, 1979), 28.

[376] The title Orthodox refers to several Churches, which have been in conflict over doctrinal, administrative, and hierarchical matters. "The Orthodox Churches share the common roots, historical experiences, and cultural expressions. All these Churches are found in the eastern parts of the Christian world and therefore are sometimes called the Eastern Churches. The Orthodox Churches affirm a common Orthodox faith, life, practice and a conciliar nature of unity. While the Orthodox Church is separated by geographic and administrative jurisdictions rooted in the long history of Orthodox people across the globe, these Churches are united by shared doctrines and religious practices across jurisdictional, linguistic, and geographical locations." Frances Kostarelos, "Short Term Missions in the Orthodox Church in North America," *Missiology: An International Review* 41, no.2 (April 2013): 179-186.

2.1 - The Concept of Mission in the Orthodox Tradition

The designation "Orthodox" or the Orthodox Church provides a perspective on the ecclesiological self-understanding of the Eastern Church. The term "Orthodox" is derived from a Greek word *doxazein* (to glorify) or from *dokein* (to think, to have a perspective) and means the Church that correctly praises God or the Church of the "right faith" or "right doctrine." Both interpretations form a unity of Orthodoxy and orthopraxy that pertains to the self-understanding of the Orthodox Churches.[377] In general, the missionary understanding of the Orthodox Church derives from mainly three areas: Scripture, Church Fathers and the Liturgy. These are considered as the elements of a theology of mission.[378]

(1) **Scripture**: The Eastern Church considered Scripture to be part of the apostolic tradition, which had a living continuity and was wider than the Bible alone. The richness of tradition illuminates and interprets Scripture. For them, the liturgy and writings of the Church Fathers were the basis for understanding the Bible. The Orthodox accept the Bible as the Word of God, a record of God's will. The Orthodox view of Scripture is dynamic. God's revelation dealt with persons, patriarchs, prophets, priests, and ultimately with Jesus Christ. Authority was not usually accorded to the biblical books at the time they were composed, but came gradually over the course of centuries. Thus behind the books of the Bible lies a dynamic history of oral tradition.[379]

---

[377] For Orthodox an understanding of the unity of the Church is based on shared faith and life rather than on organizational structures. It sees membership of the Church as based on participating in the life given by God rather than through membership of an organization. John Binns, *An Introduction to the Christian Orthodox Churches* (Cambridge: Cambridge University, 2002), 42.

[378] James Stamoolis, "Mission in Orthodox Theology," *The Greek Orthodox Theological Review* 33, no.1 (Spring 1988): 63-80.

[379] T. G Stylianopoulos, *The New Testament: An Orthodox Perspective*. vol. 1 (Brookline, Massachusetts: Holy Cross Orthodox, 1997), 7-13. The mission of the Church cannot be reduced only to preaching the Gospel-it implies service, i.e. witness through deeds as well as words. He further explains that the mission of the Church in its ultimate theological meaning is an expression of the apostolic faith of the Church itself. Gerald H.

(2) **Church Fathers**: The Church Fathers bear the witness of the Orthodox to mission. In the Patristic period, the mission had not been given prominence since the Christological controversies, which consumed so much energy and time, detracted from the formulation of missionary theology. The Church Fathers had an understanding of the nature of the plan of God for the salvation of the world. According to Bosch, the monastic movement was another saving element in the Patristic and later in the Orthodox missionary tradition. Supremely, however, it has been the simple faith of thousands of ordinary believers that, to this day, gives expression to an essentially missionary dimension in Orthodoxy. [380]

(3) **The Liturgy**: In the Orthodox tradition, the liturgy is a corporate act rather than an individualistic approach. It is a means to keep their faith traditions in the midst of their challenges and persecutions. The liturgy helped them to exist in isolation from their cultural roots and it has been effective in enabling the continued identity and existence of the Church. There is an interconnection between the liturgy and the mission of the Church. The supreme liturgy, the Eucharist, is the culmination of the mission of the Church that reveals the mission imperative. The Church that gathers for worship is an act of proclamation (1 Cor.11:26). "For as often as you eat this bread and drink the

Anderson and Thomas F. Stransky, eds., *Mission Trends No. 1: Crucial Issues in Mission Today* (New York: Paulist, 1974), 59-70. The mission of the Church developed, as part of the Christian civilization, a social and personal ethos, which had itself been shaped by Orthodox Christianity. Anderson, eds. *Mission Trends No. 1*, 65-66. As Timothy Ware puts it, tradition has a broad, comprehensive meaning: "to an Orthodox tradition means the books of the Bible; it means the Creed, it means the decrees of the Ecumenical Councils and the writings of the Church Fathers; it means the Canons, the Service Books, the Holy icons- in fact, the whole system of doctrine, Church government, worship and art which Orthodoxy has articulated over the ages. The Orthodox Christians views themselves as heir and guardian to a great inheritance received from the past, and they believe that it is their duty to transmit this inheritance unimpaired to the future." Timothy Ware, *The Orthodox Church* (London: Penguin, 1969), 204.
[380] Bosch, *Transforming Missions*, 205-209.

cup, you proclaim the Lord's death until he comes." Therefore, the extent of the mission of the Church is confessed at every Eucharistic service.[381] The Orthodox theologians point out the centrality of the Eucharist in the mission understanding of the Orthodox Church.[382] Orthodoxy's liturgical-sacramental origin is the Eucharist. Currently, the Orthodox theologians widely share a Eucharistic ecclesiology.[383] The Eucharist is a single corporate action which involves the whole community.[384] In the Eucharist, "the Church becomes what it is," fulfils itself as the body of Christ, as the divine Parousia - the presence and the communication of

---

[381] Ion Bria, ed., *Go Forth in Peace: Orthodox Perspectives on Mission* (Geneva, WCC, 1986), 25-30. Stamoolis, *Eastern Orthodox Mission Theology Today*, 86-102. "The Church celebrates the Eucharist as a human response to the divine gift, its acceptance, and appropriation by humanity. This response has two aspects, i.e. the God-centered and man or world-centered. These two aspects cannot be separated for they condition each other and together constitute the dynamics of Christian life and action. The God-centered aspect is the sanctification, the growth in holiness, of both the Christian individual and the Christian community. It is the slow transformation of the old Adam in us in to the new one, the restoration of the pristine beauty, which was lost in sin. It is also the slow victory over the demonic powers of the cosmos, the joy and peace which make it partakers of the Kingdom and of life eternal. The Orthodox spiritual tradition always stressed the mystical nature of Christian life, as life hidden with Christ in God. The second aspect of the Church as response is man or world-centered. It is the understanding of the Church as being left in this world, in its time, space, and history with a specific task or mission. The Church is fullness and its home is in heaven. However, this fullness is given to the world, sent into the world as its salvation and redemption. In the Orthodox experience and faith, it is the Church and its sacrament that makes possible the Church-mission." Schmemann, *Church, World, Mission*, 199.

[382] Ware, *The Orthodox Church*, 269-314, Ion Bria, "Dynamics of Liturgy in Mission" *International Review of Mission* 82, (1993): 317-325, Ion Bria, "The Liturgy after the Liturgy," *International Review of Mission* 67, (1978): 86-90.

[383] Christoph Bottigheimer, "Unity, Yes, But which Unity?" *Theology Digest* 52, no. 2 (Summer 2005): 119-126. The Eucharistic ecclesiology places the Eucharist at the heart and essence of the very life of the Church. The nature of the Church is seen and experienced through the Eucharist and it is the meeting point of God and humanity. They consider that the nature of the Church is *koinonia* or communion. It exists through the sharing in the life of God, given in Christ and made effective through the working of the Holy Spirit. The Orthodox faith is that through the Eucharist the divine life is given to the community of the faithful.

[384] Binns, *An Introduction to the Christian Orthodox Churches,* 43. The Church is created, sustained, and visible presence in the Eucharist or liturgy or communion and at the Eucharist the Church is made complete and whole.

Christ and of his Kingdom.[385] In the Orthodox tradition, the unity, holiness, catholicity, and apostolicity of the Church are centred in the sacrament of Eucharist.[386] It is through the Eucharist that the believers celebrate their union with Christ.[387] The Eucharistic community is not part of the Church, but it is the complete Church to which nothing can be added for it to function as God intends. There is equality between communities and bishops too. The basic unity and identity of each local Church can be expressed by the slogan: One Bishop, one Eucharist, and one Church.[388]

According to Schmemann, the essence of Orthodox theology is its "sacramental, liturgical, mystical ethos. This is manifested primarily in the rite of the Eucharist, consisting of two complementary movements: one of ascension toward the throne of God, laying aside all earthly cares, to feast upon and offer Christ. Through participation in the Eucharist, the Christian experiences full participation in the divine life (*theosis*)[389] and then returns,

---

[385] "It is in the Eucharist that the Church accomplishes the passage from this into the world to come, into the Eschaton; participates in the ascension of its Lord and in his Messianic banquet; tastes of the joy of and peace of the Kingdom. Thus, the whole life of the Church is rooted in the Eucharist and it is indeed the mission of the Church." Schmemann, *Church, World, Mission,* 198.

[386] The Eucharist, in the words of John Zizioulas, is "the locus for the prophetic presence of the Eschaton in history." Aristotle Papanikoulaou, "Divine Energies or Divine Personhood: Vladimir Lossky and John Zizioulas on Conceiving the Transcendent and Immanent God," *Modern Theology* 19, no. 3 (July, 2003): 357-385.

[387] The ministry of the Eucharist is what the Church is for, and becomes the premier, even the sole, mark of the Church: "Where the Eucharist is, there is the Church or the Church makes the Eucharist, the Eucharist makes the Church." Veli Matti Kärkkäinen, *An Introduction to Ecclesiology* (Downer's Grove: Intervarsity, 2002), 21.

[388] The Orthodox life is centred on the mystery of the Eucharist. "The closed sacramental mystery of the Eucharist in the Orthodox tradition considers the Eucharist as an eschatological event, an anticipated advent of the Kingdom to come and a fullness of divine presence. This is also why any form of inter-communion - i.e., Eucharistic communion between Christians who are divided in faith and in ultimate ecclesial commitment- necessarily reduces the Eucharist to a form of human fellowship, distinct from the union in the Kingdom of God which is the Eucharist's ultimate meaning." Binns, *An Introduction to the Christian Orthodox Churches,* 41.

[389] The Orthodox theology emphasizes the notion of *theosis* that means a process of deification in the life of the believer. Through the Sacrament of Baptism, Christians share the very life of God and they are incorporated into the body of Christ. *Final*

yet mystically remains connected to the heavenly reality. The mission of the Church is bound up in the rite of the liturgy and the Eucharist, which is the presence of the Eschaton on earth, though an ontological abyss remains between the old and new worlds that will not be bridged in this aeon."[390]

In the Orthodox tradition, the history of salvation is the revelation of the glory of God. It is this glory, which is the manifestation of the will of God, communicated in Christ, in the Church and in the Parousia. Humanity responds to God by glorifying Him through worship. They considered the mission as participation in the glory of God. The Church is planted where God is glorified. Therefore, for the Orthodox, worship is the best means to witness the glory of God. Bosch defined "mission as an experience of worship."[391] Being a worshipping community, the Orthodox people proclaim their mission and witness as the glory of God in the world. He further states that, "the major manifestation of the missionary activity of the Orthodox Church lies in its celebration of the liturgy."[392] It is clear that the Orthodox worship, mission and theological framework are constructed around the theme of "glory of God." This is the focal point of the missiology of the Orthodox Church. Stamoolis explains that, in the tradition of Orthodoxy, both its history and its theology serve as guides for the construction of an Orthodox theology of mission. He asserts that, "the primary emphasis of the Orthodox understanding of missionary work is to offer glory to God."[393] For Orthodox theology, the glory of God is a continuous manifestation and worship is the culmination of the revelation of the glory of God. The love of God and the glory of God came together in the redemption of individuals. Hence for the Orthodox, mission

Report of CWME Consultation of Eastern Orthodox and Oriental Orthodox Churches (Neapolis, Greece: 1988), 18. Scherer and Bevans, eds., *New Directions in Mission and evangelization*, 235.

[390] Schmemann, *Church, World, Mission*, 209-216.

[391] Bosch, *Transforming Mission*, 206.

[392] Bosch, *Transforming Mission*, 207.

[393] Yannoulatos writes "a key to the Orthodox understanding of the process of history is, 'the glory of the most holy God' viewed in the perspective of His infinite love... the process of human history, of which the Bible speaks, begins and ends with the glory of God." Stamoolis, *Eastern Orthodox Mission Theology Today*, 49-51.

is participating in the glory of God.[394] Generally, for the Orthodox, mission equals being a worshipping community. The mission of the Church is to be *synergoi*, fellow-workers, with God (1 Cor.3:9; 2 Cor.6:1). The Orthodox Church understands that her task is to offer *Orthodoxia*, right praise, to the living God. The entire Orthodox Church affirms that they are called out to work with God in extending that worship to the ends of the earth.[395]

The Orthodox Churches also place the doctrine of the Trinity as the centre of theological thinking about the nature of the mission.[396] The Orthodox understanding of mission is Trinitarian - Trinitarian view of God, a theocentric understanding of man, and ecclesiology based on communion rather than on authority.[397] A Trinitarian theology points to the radical communal nature of God as such, and this communion overflows into an involvement with history that "aims at drawing humanity and creation in general into this communion with God's very life."[398] The mission is understood fundamentally as rooted in the continual self-giving and self-revelation of God within the history of the creation; Trinitarian processions are understood not only as movements within the mystery of God, as such, but as God moving in saving love within the world. The Church is then understood as the people that God has chosen not only to participate in the saving life of the divine community, but also to be the agent and cooperators in God's outreach to the whole of creation. The

---

[394] Stamoolis, *Eastern Orthodox Mission Theology Today,* 51.

[395] Anastasios Yannoulatos "Orthodox Spirituality and External Mission," *International Review of Mission* 52, (1963): 300-302.

[396] The documents issued by the Orthodox Church in 1986, entitled "Go forth in Peace: Orthodox Perspective on Mission" begin with the assertion that while the Church's mission is based on the mission of Christ, a proper understanding of this mission requires an application of Trinitarian theology. Orthodox Advisory group to the WCC-CWME, "Go Forth in Peace: Orthodox Perspective on Mission," in *New Directions in Mission and Evangelization 1: Basic Statements 1974- 1991,* eds. James A Scherer, and Stephen B. Bevans (Maryknoll, New York: Orbis, 1992), 203.

[397] Meyndroff, "Orthodox Theology Today," *St. Vladimir's Theological Quarterly* 13, no.1/2 (1969): 77-92. Schmemann, *Church, World, Mission,* 70.

[398] God's very nature is missionary. It is not primarily about "the propagation or transmission of intellectual convictions, doctrines, moral commands, etc.," but rather about the inclusion of all creation in God's overflowing, superabundant life of communion. It is an invitation to be bearers of divine life found in the Trinity. Scherer and Bevans, eds., *New Directions in Mission and evangelization,* 204, 289.

Orthodox theologians like Valdimir Lossky, John Meyendorf and John Zizioulas understand the Trinity as an ecstatic communion of persons, always involved in the world, always inviting all of creation to share in the triune life of communion-in-mission.[399] Such an understanding of God as Trinity is at the basis of the Orthodox theology of mission as well.

2.2 - A Historical Analysis of Mission in the Protestant Traditions[400]

Protestantism is one of the three major branches of Christianity, along with Roman Catholicism and Eastern Orthodoxy. It is formed from the split with Roman Catholicism during the Reformation in Europe in the 16th century. The main leaders of this movement were Martin Luther, John Calvin, and Huldrych Zwingli. The reformers broke from the Roman Catholic Church due to the authoritarianism of ecclesiological structures and to theological differences.[401] In the Protestant tradition, the Church is defined as a

---

[399] Vladimir Lossky, *The Mystical Theology of the Eastern Church* (Crestwood, New York: St. Vladimir's Theological Seminary, 1976). John Meyendorf, *Trinitarian Theology East and West* (Brookline, Mass. Holy Cross Orthodox, 1977), John Zizioulas, *Being as Communion* (Crestwood, New York: St. Vladimir's Seminary, 1985).

[400] The date often cited as the beginning of the Protestant movement is 1517, based on the date of Martin Luther's first act of dissent: the public posting of his 95 Theses, criticizing Roman Catholic practices and teachings. At the time, however, Luther had no intention of starting a new Christian tradition called "Protestantism" but hoped to reform the Catholic Church. Protestantism as a movement evolved in the decades following this act as Luther's ideas, theological arguments took root, and the Catholic Church resisted and rejected them. Protestants share an adherence to the centrality of Scripture (both the Hebrew Scriptures and the New Testament) as well as a doctrine of salvation through faith in Jesus Christ. Martin Luther considered certain books contained in the Catholic version of the Bible (based on the Septuagint) to be of lesser value as he used the Hebrew Masoretic Text, which also excluded these books from the canon. Therefore, the Protestant Old Testament contains 39 books whereas the Roman Catholic Old Testament contains 46 books and includes sections of common books not included by Protestants. The New Testament is the same in both traditions.

[401] The Protestant denominations formed a pattern of worship and liturgy, varying from the Roman Catholic forms of worship. The Anglican and the Lutheran Churches have maintained liturgies and rituals similar to those of the Roman Catholic Church, whereas other denominations, such as Baptists, Presbyterians, Pentecostals, and United Church of Christ, have developed less liturgical forms of worship. Most Protestants practice the Sacrament of Baptism and Communion as key rites of Christian initiation and ongoing devotion. Though originating in Europe, Protestant Christianity has spread across the globe through missionary activity and now has members from nearly every country, race, and ethnicity. Mark Juergensmeyer, ed., *The Oxford Handbook of Global Religions*

spiritual communion, a work of God, a place of gathering by the initiative of the 'Risen Christ' with the power of the Holy Spirit. Interestingly, Protestant Churches did not believe in the mission at the beginning. The early reformers like Martin Luther and John Calvin were not concerned with the mission activities. The following discourses determined their understanding of mission: (a) theologically, the concept of predestination, which they held, was not conducive to missionary outreach. (b) Their biblical exegesis considered Christ's missionary mandate as directed to the twelve only. (c) Their emphasis was on reforming, not on spreading.[402]

It was in the second half of the 17th and in the 18th century that Protestants began to develop a new idea of mission.[403] The Enlightenment and Industrialization in Europe gave a new self-understanding of humanity- man as a rational, independent and individual-capable of rational choice. Christianity made it rational, human and dependent on God. The 18th century Protestant missionary awakening was intimately associated with the birth of Evangelicalism.[404] David Bosch claims that "the entire modern missionary enterprise is, to a very real extent, a child of the Enlightenment and similarly that the entire Western missionary movement of the past three centuries emerged from the matrix of the Enlightenment."[405]

(Santa Barbara: University of California, 2006) 28-29. John Bowker, ed., The *Cambridge Illustrated History of Religions* (Cambridge: Cambridge University, 2002), 47-48.

[402] J. Herbert Kane, *Understanding Christian Missions* (Grand Rapids, MI: Baker Book, 1983), 140.

[403] Kane points out that the modern missionary enterprise was the direct outcome of the Pietist movement which began in Germany following the thirty years' war, which ended with the peace of Westphalia in 1648. As the Protestant reformation was a revolt against the corrupted doctrines and morals of the Church of Rome, so the Pietist movement was a revolt against the barren Orthodoxy and dead formalism of the State Churches of Protestant Europe. The father of Pietism was Philip Spencer (1635-1705). The Pietists in their teaching emphasized three things: a genuine conversion experience leading to newness of life, cultivating the inner life by Bible study, prayer and Christian fellowship and missionary zeal. Kane, *Understanding Christian Missions,* 142.

[404] Evangelical Christianity has been interpreted as a movement whose origins and contours owe an immense debt to the philosophical and cultural patterns of the Enlightenment. Brian Stanley, ed., *Christian Missions and the Enlightenment* (Cambridge: William B. Eerdmans, 2001), 2.

[405] Bosch, *Transforming Mission*, 274, 344. According the Bosch, emphasis derived from the enlightenment which provided the defining or paradigmatic features of the

121

Generally, Protestant tradition consists in keeping two decisive elements as criteria for mission: truth and faithfulness, i.e. "The Gospel be preached purely and that the sacraments be administered in conformity with the Gospel."[406] These two criteria, defining the Church as a place and event in which the Word is proclaimed and the sacraments are celebrated, serve as reference points for all understanding of ministry in Protestantism. The ministry of the whole Church is to proclaim the gospel through preaching and the celebration of the sacraments. They affirm that each member of the Church is assigned to that task; each baptized person has a vocation, a mission, a ministry to witness, to praise, to evangelize, to obey the commands of the Lord. Each is to take his or her part in sharing the ministry of the whole Church.[407]

The following are various features that are most frequently held to be distinctive of the conduct of Christian mission within the Protestant tradition, principally in relation to the 18th and early 19th centuries. They are (a) An almost universal belief that non-Western peoples were "heathens," lost in the degradation of sin and in need of salvation through the gospel of Christ. (b) A parallel tendency to dismiss other religious systems either as "heathen idolatry or as at best superstitions and not religions at all, and hence as devoid of any trace of the presence of God. (c) A belief in the manifest superiority and liberating potential of Western civilization in both its intellectual and its technological aspects. (d) An unshakable confidence in the regenerative capacity of rational knowledge, always provided this was linked to Christian proclamation. (e) An assumption that the Christian message was addressed principally to individuals, calling them to undergo a conscious and identifiable inner experience of personal

---

Protestant missionary movement from its origins in the 18th century until the collapse of the enlightenment rationality in the postmodernist crisis of the late 20th century.

[406] *Augsburg Confession* 7; Institute of Christian Religion iv, 2. http://www.ccel.org/ccel/schaff/creeds3.iii.ii.html (accessed August 12, 2015).

[407] Francois Clavairoly, "Protestantism and Theology of Ministries: Ecumenical Perspective," *Theology Digest* 49, no.1 (Spring 2002): 53-54.

conversion to Christ.[408] The Protestant missionaries ministered with the conviction that the non-Christian were lost in their sin and dependent on the gospel of Christ for salvation. It was grounded in the theology of the Pauline epistles and the Augustinian tradition that mediated that theology to Catholic Christendom. The Enlightenment movement stresses the values of rationality, progress, liberty and freedom. The enlightenment creed of humans' progress was constructed on the foundation of a Renaissance confident in the human creative capacity grounded in the philosophy of Aristotle.[409]

In the Protestant tradition, the slogan *Sola Scriptura* may be regarded as the common denominator. The role assigned to the written Word of God is more decisive in all matters. This principle expresses the reformers insistence on the sufficiency of the Word of God as the final authority in matters of faith.[410] The Bible is the supreme authority in all matters of faith and conduct, the highest court of appeal in questions of controversy in the reformed and Protestant traditions.[411] The Word of God is considered as the ultimate authority pertaining to the life and witness of the Church and all human opinions must submit to the voice of the Holy Spirit speaking in Scripture. An articulation of theology is very often embedded in songs, sermons, prayers and practices.[412] The Westminster Confession of Faith affirms that:

> "The supreme judge by which all controversies of religion are to be determined, and all decrees of councils, opinions of ancient writers, doctrines of men, and private spirits, are to be examined, and in whose sentence we are to rest, can be no other but the Holy Spirt speaking in Scripture." (I: X) this is because "All synods of

---

[408] Brian Stanley, ed. *Christian Missions and the Enlightenment* (Cambridge: William B. Eerdmans, 2001), 8.

[409] Anthony Pagden, *European Encounters with the New World: From Renaissance to Romanticism* (London: New Haven, 1993), 6.

[410] Eduardus Van der Borght, *Studies in Reformed Theology, vol.18: Unity of the Church: A Theological State of the Art and Beyond* (Boston: Brill, 2010), 113.

[411] Robert Letham, *Through Western Eyes Eastern Orthodoxy: A Reformed Perspective* (Ross-shire, Mentor, 2007), 175.

[412] Richards, *Foundations For Mission*, 67.

councils, since the apostles' time, whether general or particular, may err; and many have erred. Therefore, they are not to be made the rule of faith, or practice; but to be used as a help in both" (XXXI: IV). This Assembly affirms that the primary author of Scripture is the Holy Spirit, who does not and cannot err."[413]

The European Reformation stated firmly that, all members of the Church receive a vocation and that some will be especially called and formed to exercise the ministry of preaching and of celebrating the sacraments. However, this ministry is not understood as a participation in what Catholic theology calls "the priestly ministry of Christ." While the Reformation stresses the importance of ordained ministry in the service of the visible Church, it also recalls that ministry neither represents Christ not participates in his sacrificial action. For all (the minister, the Church, and each member of the Church) are completely beneficiaries of God's salvific action. Thus, their actions can be but a response through grace, proclamation of good news and the sharing of the sacraments. For them, Christ alone is the mediator and the Church and its ministers are considered as sanctified witnesses. In the Protestant tradition, a minister is not a priest because his/her ministry does not claim to participate in the priestly work of Christ. A statement of the Reformation, therefore, deliberately locates ministries in the context of the proclamation of the gospel, of the celebration of the sacraments, and in the building up of the Church. Those statements are rooted in the reading and interpretation of the biblical texts.[414]

---

[413] Westminster Assembly, *The Confession of Faith: The Larger and Shorter Catechisms with the Scripture Proofs* (Applecross, Ross-Shire: The Publication Committee of the Free- Presbyterian Church of Scotland, 1970), I: X. The Westminster Assembly was a council of divines, called by Parliament to reform the government, worship and discipline of the Church in England, Wales and Ireland, initially to defend the Thirty-Nine Articles of Religion of the Church of England against 'false aspersions and calumnies.' This assembly considered the Trinitarian and Christological pronouncements of the first six ecumenical councils to be in harmony with the Bible. Letham, *Through Western Eyes Eastern Orthodoxy*, 174.

[414] Clavairoly, "Protestantism and Theology of Ministries," 54-55.

3 - A Theological Paradigm of Mission in the Liturgy

The term "mission" refers to the action of sending. In Christian theology, sending is always a personal act prompted by the infinite love of God. Mission is a word, which tries to capture something of the inexhaustible love of the Father, the Son and the Holy Spirit permeating and energizing the Church in its own outreach of love.[415] Mission belongs to God and it is for the entire creation. God the Father initiated the process of salvation in creation through the revelation of Jesus Christ, who is the centre of God's mission to creation. The Christian mission is a participation in the mission of God. It can be understood as the work of a community (the Church), with a community (the Trinity), and for a community (God's creation). The mission of God in creation is actualized by the work of the Holy Spirit.[416]

The liturgy is a positive human response to the love of the heavenly Father revealed through Jesus Christ in history. It includes all forms of prayers and practices. The celebration of the Eucharist is the centre of Christian worship. Through the Eucharist, the Church participates in the very divine life of God. There is a dynamic interaction between the liturgy and mission.[417] The liturgy orients the worshipping community for mission. The vocation of the Church is to bear witness to the resurrection of Jesus Christ and to introduce the values of the Kingdom of God. When the faithful are gathered around the Table to break the bread, the Church proclaims and celebrates the day of resurrection.[418] Therefore, the Church by its very gathering and celebration of liturgy bears witness and proclaims the mission of Christ each time.

---

[415] James H Provost, ed., *The Church as Mission* (Washington D.C: Canon law Society of America, 1984), 88.

[416] Joe Egan, "Mission as Trinitarian Practice," in *Faithful Witness: Glimpses of the Kingdom,* eds. Joe Egan, and Brendan McConvery (Dublin: Milltown Institute of Theology and Philosophy, 2005), 342-356.

[417] Provost, *The Church as Mission,* 90.

[418] Petros Vassiliadis, "Mission and Proselytism: An Orthodox Understanding," *International Review of Mission* 85, no. 337 (April 1996): 263.

3.1 - The Doctrine of the Trinity: A Fundamental Aspect of the Liturgy

The doctrine of Trinity is a distinctive mark of the Christian faith which has very deep roots in the Christian tradition. Even though there is no explicit reference as such to the term Trinity in the Bible, this theological dogma defends the central faith of the Bible and of the Church.[419] According to McGrath, "the doctrine of Trinity is the outcome of a process of sustained and critical reflection on the pattern of divine activity revealed in Scripture, and continued in Christian experience. This is not to say that Scripture contains the doctrine of Trinity; rather, Scripture bears witness to a God who demands to be understood in a Trinitarian manner."[420] This doctrine emerged as a result of concrete theological reflection and debates throughout the centuries especially in the fourth and fifth centuries, when the early ecumenical Church councils carefully formulated creedal summaries of the Christian faith, including the Nicene Creed. There are various kinds of interpretations derived throughout the periods on this topic.[421] Generally, a Trinitarian understanding of God signifies, God in three persons, mutually

---

[419] Jurgen Moltmann, *The Trinity and the Kingdom: The Doctrine of God* (London: SCM, 1981), 16. The scriptural expression of Trinity is found in Mt.28:19 and 2 Cor.13:13. The New Testament passages link together the Father, the Son and the Holy Spirit as part of greater whole. The totality of God's saving presence and power can only be expressed by involving all three elements. See 1 Cor.12: 4-6, 2 Cor.1:21, Gal.4:6, Eph.2: 20, 2 Thess.2:13-14, Titus.3:4-6, 1 Pet.1:2. The Bible reveals that there is One God, the One who created the world and redeemed the people of Israel: "The Lord our God is one" (Deut.6:4), "the One who was with God in the beginning, and, in fact, was God (Jn.1:1), Jesus is the "exact representation of God's being" (Heb.1:1), the perfect image or 'icon' of God (Col.1:15). Acts.5:3-4 and 2 Cor.13:14 discloses that the Holy Spirit is also a divine person. There is no divided loyalties or competing interest in divine life. John D. Witvliet, "The Opening of Worship: Trinity," in *A More Profound Alleluia: Theology and Worship in Harmony,* ed. Leanne Van Dyk (Grand Rapids, MI: William B. Eerdmans, 2005), 5.

[420] It is Tertullian (155-240 CE) who is responsible for the development of the Trinitarian terminology. He argues that "the three persons of the Trinity are distinct, yet not divided, different yet not separate or independent of each other. The complexity of the human experience of the redemption is thus the result of the three persons of the Godhead acting in distinct yet coordinated manners in human history, without any loss of the total unity of the Godhead." Alister E. McGrath, *Christian Theology: An Introduction,* 2nd ed. (Oxford: Blackwell, 1997), 293-294, 297.

[421] For Irenaeus (130-202 CE), the whole process of salvation bore witness to the action of Father, Son and Holy Spirit. He used the term "the economy of salvation" to dispense the discourse of Trinity. For him, the economy of salvation means "the way in which

indwelling and indebted together.[422] Latin theology of the Christian West emphasizes the divine nature, whereas the Greek theology of the Christian East emphasizes the divine hypostases (person).[423] Western readings of the Trinity underlined the single divine substance of God and that treated the personhood within the Trinity secondarily. Consequently, the West ended up with a functionally monistic way of imagining God's engagement with the world: the Father, the Son, and the Holy Spirit act individually.[424] The Eastern tradition is seen as beginning with the relationality of the three divine persons, whose unity is found in the source or origin of the Father, as well as in their *perichoresis*,[425] or mutual indwelling.[426] Eastern theology tended to emphasize the "distinct individuality of the three persons or *hypostases*," and sought "to safeguard their unity by stressing the fact that both the Son and the Spirit derived from the Father."[427] According to this view "the relation between the persons or *hypostases* is ontological, grounded in what those persons are. Thus the relation of the Son to the

---

God has ordered the salvation of humanity in history." McGrath, *Christian Theology: An Introduction*, 296.

[422] Veli-Matti Karkkainen, *The Trinity: Global Perspective* (London: Westminster John Knox, 2007), 37. Lesslie Newbigin, *The Relevance of Trinitarian Doctrine for Todays Mission* (London: Edinburgh House, 1963), 34.

[423] Karkkainen, *The Trinity: Global Perspective*, 44-45.

[424] Leonard E. H Jalmarson, "A Trinitarian Spirituality of Mission," *Journal of Spiritual Formation and Soul Care* 6, no. 1 (2013): 95.

[425] *Perichoresis* is a Greek term, firstly used by pseudo-Cyril in the sixth century and then by John of Damascus in the eighth century. The word *"peri"* (as in perimeter) means around and *"choresis"* means dancing as in the choreography of a ballet). The term literally refers around dancing and more deeply stands for reciprocity and exchange in the mutual indwelling of the persons, to express how each person can permeate and coincide here with the others without confusion. Theologically, there is a *perichoresis* of the persons of the Trinity within the unity of their substance. *Perichoresis*, describes the mutual indwelling and the mutual inter-penetration of the Father and the Son and the Spirit. Here, the Father, the Son and the Holy Spirit are like three dancers holding hands, dancing around together in joyful freedom. It suggests that persons truly exist through their participation in each other, not as persons in relationship, but persons as a relationship. Shirley C. Guthrie Jr, *Always Being Reforming* (London: Westminster John Knox, 2008), 37. Stephen Spencer, *SCM Study Guide to Christian Mission* (London: SCM, 2007), 19. McGrath, *Christian Theology: An Introduction*, 298-299.

[426] Craig Van Gelder and Dwight J. Zscheile, *The Missional Church in Perspective: Mapping Trends and Shaping the Conversation* (Grand Rapids: Baker Academie, 2011), 103.

[427] McGrath, *Christian Theology: An Introduction*, 297.

Father is defined in terms of 'being begotten' and sonship."[428] An Eastern understanding of the Trinity deals with God's radical relatedness and the movement towards the restoration of creation. The notion of *perichoresis* invites us to think in a new way about the meaning of "one" and "personal." The oneness of God is not the oneness of a self-contained individual; it is the unity of a community of personas. In addition, "person" means by definition interpersonal: one cannot be truly personal alone, but only in relation to other persons. Such is the unity and personal character of the Father, the Son and the Holy Spirit.[429] In short, it is claimed that the East begins with the Threeness of the Trinity and the West with the oneness or unity.[430]

A Trinitarian theology stresses that God's life is one of abundant communion, a kind of fellowship that overflows to include everyone.[431] In Trinity, there is a fellowship and community of equals who share all that they are and have, each living with and for the others in self-giving love, each free not "from" but "for" the other. Here, God is God in the community, and in this divine community, there is no above or below, superior or inferior, but only the society of equals who are different from one another and live together in mutual respect and self-giving love. Unity is the basis of their existence. The term "relationality" is a key to understand the mystery of God. God, as a Trinity of persons who are mutually constitutive of and infinitely in communion with one another, is wholly constituted by relationality.[432] According to Zizioulas, relational personhood is constitutive of being: a component of essence. There is no personal identity without relationality. "The Orthodox tradition has

---

[428] McGrath, *Christian Theology: An Introduction*, 297-298.
[429] "They are not three independent persons who get together to form a club. They are what they are in relationship with one another. Each exists only in this relationship and would not exist apart from it. The Triune God, the Father, the Son and the Holy Spirit live only in and with and through one another, eternally united in mutual love and shared purpose." Guthrie. *Always Being Reforming*, 36-37.
[430] Karkkainen, The *Trinity: Global Perspective*, 44-45.
[431] John D. Witvliet, "The Opening of Worship: Trinity," in *A More Profound Alleluia: Theology and Worship in Harmony*, ed. Dyk, 8.
[432] Cunningham, *These Three are One*, 165.

stressed the generative, outward-reaching love (*ekstasis*) and communion (*koinonia*) of the three persons. The Trinity is seen as a community, whose orientation is outward and whose shared love spills over beyond itself. Moreover, the concept of *perichoresis* is a dynamic, circulating movement that has offered rich analogies for human interdependence."[433] The work of Zizioulas[434] reaches back to the Cappadocian Fathers, who understood God's being as an essentially relational achievement among the three persons (*hypostasis*) of the Trinity. Therefore, the unified being of the One God is only to be found in the relational communion of the three persons. Newbigin frames it like this: "Interpersonal relatedness belongs to the very being of God. Therefore, there can be no salvation for human beings except in relatedness. No one can be made whole except by being restored to the wholeness of that being-in-relatedness for which God made us and the world and which is the image of that being-in-relatedness which is the being of God himself."[435]

3.2 - A Trinitarian Model of Mission

The doctrine of Trinity sets the agenda for mission. A Trinitarian understanding of mission is both a Trinitarian concept and a Trinitarian practice. The mission is fundamentally *"Missio Dei,"* God's activity, which holds both the Church and the world, and in which the Church is commissioned to participate with God. The mission is primarily an attribute and activity of God the Father, whose movement through the Son and the Spirit in love towards the creation constitutes salvation and grounds the being of the Church. Bosch summarized the conclusion in this classic statement:

---

[433] Gelder and Dwight, *The Missional Church in Perspective,* 105.

[434] According to Zizioulas, "there is no true being without communion; nothing exists as an "individual" in itself. Therefore, to be a "person" in contrast to an "individual," there needs to be communion, relation and opening to the other, or as he often calls it an *ekstasis* (going out of one's self). Human existence, including the existence of the Church communion, thus reflects the communal, relational being of God." John Zizioulas, *Being as Communion* (Toronto: Novalis, 2002), 16-22

[435] Lesslie Newbigin, *The Open Secret* (Grand Rapids: Eerdmans, 1975), 70.

"Mission was understood as being derived from the very nature of God. It was thus put in the context of the doctrine of the Trinity. The classical doctrine on the *Missio Dei* as God the Father sending the Son, and God the Father and Son sending the Spirit was expanded to include yet another 'movement' Father, Son and Holy Spirit sending the Church in the world."[436]

Missio Dei indicates that there is both communion and sending within the Triune life of God. Thus, as a community of Christ, the Church is always oriented toward the other. The heart of the Trinity is the mission and the heart of the mission is the Trinity. Being sent by Jesus is the core of the mission and going where the Spirit leads is the commitment of the Church.[437]

A *perichoretic* dimension of the Trinity stands as the paradigm for Christian mission. The *perichoretic* activity of the Triune God in and through creation establishes and inspires the missionary thrust that belongs to the very nature of Christian life. Mutual indwelling and participation in love is the basis of its relation and existence. A Trinitarian perspective on mission calls for a fundamental conversion in the practice of mission and seeks to embody Trinitarian self-giving love in all its relationships. Rationality is defined by both inward and outward movement, both community and mission. Every inward movement begins an outward one, and every outward movement begins an inward one. The unifying theme is love.[438] The sending of Christ was the inevitable plan of the Holy Trinity. For Orthodox Christians, Bosch explains, "God's love, disclosed in the sending of Christ, is the 'theological - starting point' of mission."[439] The Gospel of John 3:16[440] is a representative text of this understanding of

---

[436] David J. Bosch, *Transforming Mission: Paradigm Shifts in Theology of Mission* (Maryknoll, New York: Orbis, 1988), 390.
[437] Commission on World Mission and Evangelism, *Together Towards Life: Mission and Evangelism in Changing Landscapes* (Geneva: World Council of Churches, 2013), 4-9. Egan, "Mission as Trinitarian Practice," 347-349.
[438] Jalmarson, *A Trinitarian Spirituality of Mission*, 93-108.
[439] Bosch, *Transforming Mission*, 208.
[440] "For God so loved the world that he give His one and only Son.....but have eternal life." (Jn.3:16)

mission. In this perspective, mission is grounded in the love of God and Christians, motivated by that love, seek to communicate that love with a view to bringing forth new life and the restoration of the image of God in those outside the Christian fold.[441] Jesus Christ entrusted his mission to the Church with the help of the reconciling Holy Spirit, who impels all creation to proclaim the great works of the one God. Just as Jesus sent the apostles out in the name of the Father, and of the Son, and of the Holy Spirit, so too the Church as believers, and indeed all of humanity, is sent out and commanded to live life in the name of the Trinity. Therefore, the visible Church on earth, by its very nature is missionary and that reflects the nature of Trinity. Newbigin insisted that mission should be seen in Trinitarian terms, he wrote, "the Church is not so much the agent of the mission as the locus of the mission."[442]

3.3 - The Trinitarian Emphasis in the Liturgy of the Mar Thoma Church

As is very evident throughout its celebration, the liturgy of the MTC is Trinitarian in its very nature.[443] An analysis of the liturgical prayers, rubrics, signs and symbols in the liturgy disclose the centrality of the Trinity in the worship service. The liturgy emphasizes the fact that the Trinitarian God is a God of Communion, i.e. a life of communion with the Father, the Son and the Holy Spirit. It enumerates that the incarnation of God in Jesus Christ, the sending forth of the Holy Spirit into the world, and the foundation of the Church establishes the faith of the MTC.[444] The Eucharistic celebration in the Church begins and concludes with the Trinitarian adoration. Through this adoration, the Church affirms and proclaims her faith in the Trinity.

---

[441] Stephen J. Duffy, *The Dynamics of Grace; Perspective in Theological Anthropology* (Collegeville, MN: Liturgical, 1993), 65.
[442] Lesslie Newbigin, *Gospel in a Pluralist Society* (Cambridge: Wm. B. Eerdmans, 1989), 118-119.
[443] "We praise You, the One true God, One power....One in essence, in power and truth." *Order of Worship for Divine Service, Parasyaradhana Kramam* (Thiruvalla: Mar Thoma Publication Society, 2000), 12, 22. "Christ our God, inscrutably confessed as the One True God, known in three Persons yet believed as One." Titus II, *Qurbana Thaksa,* 125.
[444] Daniel, *Ecumenism in Praxis,* 23-25.

[445] The primary response during the opening of worship is adoration of the Trinity.[446] All *sedros* in the liturgy conclude with the adoration of the Trinity. A Trinitarian adulation is pronounced while censing the altar and throughout the service. The celebrant offers blessings in the name of the Trinity.[447] Through the pronouncement of the Nicene Creed the Church affirms its faith in the Triune God.[448] According to Jacob of Edessa,[449] (640-708 CE) "the priest begins with these words to teach the unity of the nature, the essence, and the three hypostases, which are separated without separation and united without confusion."[450]

In the Mar Thoma liturgy, the celebration of the Holy Qurbana is an expression of the communion of love from the Father through the Son by the Holy Spirit. The Church prays and sings to the Trinity "through Christ," in the power of the Holy Spirit.[451] The Liturgy shows that, God

---

[445] "Give praise to the Father Almighty. To his Son, Jesus Christ the Lord, To the Spirit who dwells in our hearts. Both now and for ever." *The Order of the Holy Qurbana*, 1.

[446] "Glory be to the Father, to the Son and to the Holy Spirit. As it was in the beginning, is now and ever shall be word without end- Amen." Titus II, *Qurbana Thaksa*, 1. Juhanon Mar Thoma, *The Order of the Holy Qurbana*, (English Version) 6th ed. (Thiruvalla: The Mar Thoma Publication Society, 1996), 1. It is important to remember that every act of praise is a strong act of negation as well as affirmation. When we sing praise to the triune God, we are asserting our opposition to anything that would attempt to stand in God's place. Witvliet, "The Opening of Worship: Trinity," 12.

[447] There are four blessings in the anaphora all of which, with the exception of the second, are in the name of the Trinity. The second blessing is in the name of Jesus Christ. Contrary to the Catholic and Protestant traditions, in the Oriental Eastern worship the celebrant and faithful turn to the East side to celebrate the Liturgy. During the time of blessings the celebrant turn towards the faithful and bless the congregation by pronouncing the Trinitarian blessing with sign of the cross.

[448] The MTC accepts the teachings of the first three ecumenical councils, i.e. Nicaea, (325 CE) Constantinople (381 CE) and Ephesus. (451 CE).The creed formulated in the Council of Nicaea is pronounced in every liturgical celebrations before the beginning of the anaphora. Titus II, *Qurbana Thaksa*, 18-19.

[449] Jacob of Edessa is the most prolific and distinguished writers of Syriac literature. He has in many respects contributed to the consolidation and further expansion of the Syriac cultural heritage in the time of Islamic rule. Dirk Kruisheer and Lucas Van Rompay, "A Bibliographical Clavis to the Works of Jacob of Edessa," *Hugoye: Journal of Syriac Studies* 1, no.1 (1998): 35-56.

[450] Quoted in Baby Varghese, "Dionysius Bar Salibi: Commentary on the Eucharist," *Moran Etho*, no.10 (1980): 48.

[451] The two primary models for Christian prayer and worship are (1) prayer directed to God the Father, God the Son, and God the Holy Spirit, and (2) prayer directed to the Father, through Christ, in the Spirit. For more on these models see Josef Jungmann, *The Place of*

is active in prompting the prayers of the faithful, in receiving it and in perfecting it.[452] An active participation in the Eucharistic liturgy enables the faithful to take part in the Trinitarian mystery. The liturgy invites the faithful to engage with the fullness of the life of Christ and draws the faithful into the Trinitarian mystery of salvation. Thus, the missionary dimension of the liturgy can be perceived from the framework of the Trinity. It enunciates the importance of mission through its prayers and practices. The liturgical celebration motivates the faithful to engage with the mission of the Triune God in creation. The Trinitarian model of mission is similarly a paradigm for the mission of the MTC. As cited above, the Trinity is a community in relationship which discloses love in action. The mission of the Church is mainly to create a community of love which is united in the name of Jesus Christ and strengthened by the power of the Holy Spirit. This community is called out to live and enliven others by the values of the Kingdom of God, to reflect the divine nature for the glory of God and to move in faith towards Eternity. The liturgical emphasis of the Trinitarian community is a model of mission, which motivates the Church through its various ministries to work for the formation of communities by its diverse interactions in society. This model demands a Trinitarian way of thinking and living which means a life based on interrelationship, mutuality, respect and unity. An experience of communion is at the heart of both God's Triune life and the Christian life.[453] A Trinitarian way of worship is practiced by communities that fully embrace Trinitarian ways of

---

Christ in Liturgical Prayer, trans. A Peeler (New York: Alba House, 1965) and Graham Redding, *Prayer and the Priesthood of Christ in the Reformed Tradition* (London: T and T Clark, 2003). In liturgy the human-divine and divine-human communication workout of Trinitarian formula. The liturgical emphasis of the prayers conclude with the Trinitarian supplication but in the extempore prayer concludes with the supplication through Christ. The MTC do practice Trinitarian worship, but without much acknowledgement of highlighting of it. Very often in the extempore prayers in the Church end with the words "in Jesus name," Amen. It is not the negation of the Trinitarian doctrine rather an affirmation of divine nature of Jesus and the supplication of prayer to the Trinity through Jesus. A Trinitarian nature of worship help the faithful to grow into the fullness of biblical teaching about God.

[452] Witvliet, "The Opening of Worship: Trinity," 3.
[453] "May they be one as were one..." (Jn.17:12), "Truly our fellowship is with the Father and with his son Jesus Christ." (1 Jn.1:3)

thinking and living.[454] "Liturgical worship reflects, embodies, and enacts a rich tapestry of relationships. Christian liturgy embodies the mutuality and *koinonia* of a Trinitarian ecclesiology. At its best, it enacts and prefigures the Kingdom of God. Christian worship is an icon or window into the web of relationships that make up the Christian Church. It is an icon of our union with Christ through the work of the Holy Spirit."[455]

---

[454] Witvliet, "The Opening of Worship: Trinity," 15.
[455] Witvliet, "The Opening of Worship: Trinity," 23.

Chapter 6

An Exploration of the Prayers and Practices of the Eucharistic Liturgy: A Missiological Interpretation

1 - Introduction

The concept of Word and Table or Word and Sacrament is drawn from a theology of worship that has its roots deep in the early Church.[456] The spoken Word is built around Scripture and the embodied Word is centered on the celebration of the Eucharist. This is the basis of the MTC and its mission. This Church is a "mission-oriented Church" and its Eucharistic liturgy[457] underlines the importance of mission. The ultimate purpose of the Eucharistic liturgy is to bear witness to the redemptive act of God in

---

[456] Andrew B. McGowan, *Ancient Christian Worship: Early Church Practices in Social Historical and Theological Perspective* (Grand Rapids, MI: Baker Academic, 2014), 19-21. In the first century document *Didache* and Church orders written or compiled across the third to fifth century-prominent among them the works known as - the *Apostolic Tradition, Didascalia Apostolorum, Apostolic Constitutions, and Testamentum Domini* give detailed references to the worship pattern and theological emphasis of the early Christian community. "They devoted themselves to the apostles' teaching and fellowship, to the breaking of bread and the prayers." Acts 2:42 is the first reference to the practices of early Christians in the New Testament. Maxwell E. Johnson, "The Apostolic Tradition," in *The Oxford History of Christian Worship*, eds. Geoffrey Wainwright and Karen B. Westerfield Tucker (Oxford: Oxford University, 2006), 32-75. R.C.D. Jasper and G.J. Cuming, eds., *Prayers of the Eucharist: Early and Reformed* (London: Collins, 1975), 9-14.

[457] The Syriac word for the Eucharist is either *qurobo*, which means approach or *qurbono*, oblation or sacrifice. The Church Fathers of the West Syrian liturgical tradition especially Moses Bar Kepha (930 CE) and Dionysius Bar Salibi (1171 CE) often refers to the liturgy of the Eucharist as the *rosae qadeeshae* signifying the profound mystery of the bread and wine, which is beyond human comprehension. These two great personalities have left behind two precious commentaries on the liturgy of St. James and also gave detailed insights into the rich symbolism and profound mysticism of this liturgy. Their insights provide the basis of the liturgical interpretation of the liturgy in this study.

Christ. Therefore, the liturgical celebration needs to be comprehended in the context of mission. This chapter is a missiological analysis of the Eucharistic liturgy of the MTC with a view to understanding how the Eucharistic liturgy motivates the Church for mission. In this chapter, the general structure, content and theology of the Eucharistic liturgy is analysed within the framework of the mission. Further, the liturgical identity of the Church and its missiological motive are studied against its Antiochian background.[458]

2 - The Structure, Content, and Theology of the Eucharistic Prayers

In this study, a general structure of the anaphora of St. James is analysed. Even though there are several studies which give details of the structure, content and theology of the anaphora of St. James,[459] there are nevertheless

---

[458] The text selected for this research is mainly the Malayalam text with English translation of the Anaphora of St. James given in the Thaksa of the MTC. It explores the contents pertaining to the concept of mission. The text is allowed to speak for itself by following its structure, rather than presenting the various aspects of mission fitted in the Anaphora. Whenever necessary, the text is compared with other texts such as the Pampakuda Syriac text with the Malayalam translations of the Syrian Orthodox Church. The Pampakuda Konat Syriac collection is one of the most important and the largest collections in Kerala, numbering over 300 manuscripts, containing mostly West Syriac, but also East Syriac material. The collection contains the most ancient manuscript of the Malabar Coast, namely the oldest copy of the West Syriac Nomocanon (*Hudoye*), written by Gregory Abu'l Faraj, also called Bar Hebroyo (1226-1286 CE). This manuscript is dated 1290 CE. The following are the liturgical texts selected for the analysis of the topic: Titus II Mar Thoma, *Malankara Mar Thoma Suriyani Sabhayude Qurbana Thaksa* (Thiruvalla: Mar Thoma, 1942), Titus II Mar Thoma, *Qurbana Thaksa of the Malankara Mar Thoma Syrian Church*, (Malayalam) 6th ed. (Thiruvalla: Mar Thoma, 2001), Juhanon Mar Thoma, *The Order of the Holy Qurbana*, (English Version) 6th ed. (Thiruvalla: The Mar Thoma Publication Society, 1996), Paul Kadavil P, *The Eucharist Service of the Syrian Jacobite Church of Malabar: The Meaning and the Interpretation*, 2nd ed. (Piscataway: Gorgias, 2003), Johns Abraham Konat, *Visudha Yakobinte Kurbana Taksa: Anushtanangalum Vyakyanangalum Cherthathu* (Kottayam: MOC Publication, 2011).

[459] F.E. Brightman, "Liturgies Eastern and Western being the Texts Original or Translated of the Principal Liturgies of the Church," vol. I. *Eastern Liturgies* (Oxford: Clarendon, 1896). E.C. Ratcliff, "The Eucharistic Office and the Liturgy of St. James," in *The Eucharist in India. A Plea for a Distinctive Liturgy for the Indian Church* (London: Longmans, 1920). H.W. Codrington, "The Syrian Liturgy," *ECQ* 1, (1936):10-20, 40-49, 87-99. K.N. Daniel, *A Critical Study of Primitive Liturgies* (Kottayam: CMS, 1937). Louis Bouyer, *Eucharist. Theology and Spirituality of the Eucharistic Prayer*, Translated by Charles Underhill Quinn (London: University of Notre Dame, 1968). Kurian Valuparampil, "St. James Anaphora: An Ecumenical Locus. A Survey of the Origin and Development of

very few that deal with the missiological aspect of the liturgy. For the purpose of analysing the liturgy, the Eucharistic model of "active presence," proposed by Kevin Irvin[460] is used to substantiate the theme of mission in this study. The Eucharistic model of "active presence" refers to "the real presence of Christ in the Eucharist. It is in and through the celebration of the Eucharist that Christ is active among the believers."[461] It insists on the interrelationship of the presence of Christ and the enactment of the Eucharist, and it calls for an active witnessing life centred on the Sacrament of Eucharist.[462] It is beyond the scope of this study to provide an in-depth treatment of the origins and development of all of the Eucharistic prayers from the Christian antiquity, especially because so many other detailed resources exists already on this subject.[463] This study is an evaluation of the reformed liturgy of the Church through the framework of the mission. For the textual analysis, as mentioned earlier, the Malayalam text with English translation of the "Anaphora of St. James" is used in the Thaksa of the

---

St. James Anaphora," *Christian Orient* 8, no. 4 (1987): 30-47. John R. K. Fenwick, *The Anaphoras of St Basil and St James: An Investigation into Their Common Origin* (Orientalia Christiana Analecta, 1992). John D. Witvliet, "The Anaphora of St. James," in *Essays on Early Eastern Eucharistic Prayers,* ed. Paul F. Bradshaw (Pueblo, 1997). Phillip Tovey, *The Liturgy of St James as presently used* (London: Grove Books, 1998). George Mathew Kuttiyil, *Eucharist (Qurbana): The Celebration of the Economy of Salvation (Madabranutha) - A Theological Analysis of the Anaphora of St. James* (Kottayam: Oriental Institute of Religious Studies, 1999). Baby Varghese, *The Syriac Version of the Liturgy of St James: A Brief History for Students* (London: Grove Books, 2001). Baby Varghese, "Anaphora of St. James and Jacob of Edessa," in *Jacob of Edessa and the Syriac Culture of His Day,* Ter Haar Romeny (Leiden: Monographs of the Peshitta Institute, 2008), 41-69.

[460] Kevin W. Irwin, *Models of the Eucharist* (New York: Paulist, 2005), 238-262.

[461] Irwin, *Models of the Eucharist,* 240.

[462] The Church is commissioned to be a missionary community to propagate the Gospel. An "active presence" of the Church as a Eucharistic community in the world is indispensable in the mission of God. It is a call to incarnate the gospel through an "active presence" in the day-to-day affairs of the people. It is a vocation to be a "sacramental presence" in the world. Christ is present in the believer in and through the celebration of the Eucharist. This emphasis on the presence of Christ is a clear and continual reminder that the Eucharist is not of our own making. An active participation in the liturgy is a mandate for an active participation in the redeeming act of God. It demands commitment, openness and the willingness to be broken and shared for the world. Irwin, *Models of the Eucharist,* 324.

[463] See Enrico Mazza, *The Origin of the Eucharistic Prayer* (Collegeville, MN: Liturgical, 1995), Paul F. Bradshaw, ed., *Essays in Early Eastern Eucharistic Prayers* (Collegeville, MN: Liturgical, 1997).

MTC. Whenever necessary the text of the Thaksa is compared with other texts such as the Pampakuda Syriac text with the Malayalam translations of the Syrian Orthodox Church.

The liturgy of the Holy Qurbana of the MTC has three parts: The Preparatory service (*Thuyobo*)[464], Ante - Communion or Public Service (*Pre-Anaphora*), and Service of Eucharist (*Anaphora*). Following is a brief outline of the liturgy as a whole.

2.1 - The Service of Preparation (Thuyobo)

Schmemann remarks that, "in the beginning of the Qurbana, the Church ascent to the "table of the lord," in His Kingdom,"[465] the Church commences its ascending process to the Kingdom in the Eucharistic celebration with a service of preparation. The *thuyobo* service is a spiritual preparation of the celebrant before the public service.[466] This service is conducted behind the sanctuary veil and it represents the period of preparation for the coming of Christ.[467] By following the West Syrian liturgical tradition, the Mar Thoma Church building is usually built in the East-West direction and

---

[464] The meaning of the Syriac word *thuyobo* is preparation, which is a preparation of the celebrant. Usually preparatory service is done in private but it also can be conducted in public. J. Payne Smith, ed., *A Compendious Syriac Dictionary* (Indiana: Eisen Brauns, 1998, First Impression 1903), 169.

[465] Alexander Schmemann, *The Eucharist: Sacrament of the Kingdom*, trans., Paul Kachur (New York: Vladimir's Seminary, 2003), 37.

[466] Even though there is very little information about the origin of the preparatory service, John of Dara's, *Commentary on the Eucharist* mainly gives emphasis on the thuyobo and pre-anaphora which proves its earlier origin. (John of Dara -825 CE, a monk of the monastery of Mar Hananya (Der Zafran), near Mardin in Tur Abdin). The text that John used is an important witness to the developments that took place in St. James Liturgy between the time of Jacob of Edessa (640-708 CE) and that of Moses Bar Kepha. (813-903 CE).

[467] Panicker, "West Syrian Anaphora," 37. The practice of celebrant saying parts of the liturgy silently originated in Syria, and shows the sense of reverence and awe characteristics of Semitic cultures, which spread west to Constantinople in the sixth century. Binns, *An Introduction to the Christian Orthodox Churches*, 46.

the building layout is divided into three[468]: *Madbaho*[469] (altar, sanctuary), *Questromo*[470] and *Haikkala* (nave or congregation hall). The celebrant conducts the preparatory service in *madbaho* in front of the *thronos* [471] with the adoration of the Trinity. There are two parts in this service, i.e. the service of Melchisedc, and the service of Aaron. The first ordering bread and wine on the altar, which recalls Melchisedc's offering of bread and wine to Abraham (Gen.14:18).[472] The preparatory service is more confessional in nature[473] and the celebrant seeks the mercy and strength of God for this solemn celebration.[474] A confessional psalm, psalm 51, is recited at the beginning of this service. The emphasis of these prayers is

---

[468] This is because the tent of Israel was constructed by Moses with three parts, that is, the holy of holies, which is the sanctuary, the place of the ministers, which is the nave, and the court which surrounded the nave and the holy of holies. The people stood in the court, priest and deacons in the place of ministers, which is the nave; in the holy of holies only Aaron to minster. John of Dara, "Commentary on the Eucharist," trans., Baby Varghese, *Moran Etho* 12 (Kottayam: SEERI, 1999), 29-30.

[469] The *madbaho* reminds us of the divine presence of God (Isa. 6:1). It is constructed generally to the East side which is considered as the sanctum sanctorum (holy of the holies). *Haikala* is the main congregation hall. In the ancient Eastern tradition, the congregation stood throughout the worship. Now there are pews provided in most places. Veil or the altar curtain separates the *madbaho* from the congregational seating area. The veil is referred to as "*thirassila*" in Malayalam. The veil reminds us that the *madbaho* is a place that is to be kept and observed as holy.

[470] It is sometimes separated from the nave by a railing and one step. Originally it signified the step in front of the sanctuary. This is the space where the readings are conducted by the lay people (first and second readings) before the public celebration of the liturgy. This area and the nave are separated by railings. Those who come for the thanksgiving prayer and the communicants who come to receive the Holy elements kneel at the railings.

[471] *Thronos*: In Syrian churches, altar is raised to a higher level, with several steps leading to the sanctuary, and a curtain is drawn across to conceal the altar from view. The sense that the worshipper is approaching a defined space where holiness is located is clearly expressed by the architecture. The consecrated place in the *madbaho* is called *thronos* (throne of God) or the altar (Ps.11:4). The *thronos* is referred to as the "table of life" because the bread and wine are placed upon it representing the body and blood of the Lord Jesus Christ. This represents the self-sacrifice of Christ, Christ himself. This is the table, which is used for the consecration of the elements in the Holy Qurbana. At the center of the *thronos*, on the topmost region, the Cross is kept. On either side of it, candles are kept. The *thronos* is generally decorated with flowers. The worshipping community, including the celebrant, faces the *thronos* during the worship. There is a step at the altar and this is called the Darga. Binns, *An Introduction to the Christian Orthodox Churches*, 44-45.

[472] Spinks, *Do This in Remembrance of Me*, 157.

[473] Panicker, "West Syrian Anaphorae," 36-37.

[474] Titus II, *Qurbana Thaksa*, 4.

on the humility of the celebrant. Psalm 51 follows the prayers in order as: *Promeion*,[475] *Sedro*,[476] *Qolo*,[477] *Ethro*,[478] *Eqbo*[479] and *Huthomo*.[480]

2.1.1 - Opening Prayer[481] - In this prayer the celebrant, beseeches the merciful Lord to purify him to stand worthily before the throne of grace[482] and to serve Him with knowledge, awe and spiritual discipline. In this prayer, God is acknowledged as the Lord and Creator, who is worthy of praise and adoration. A true awareness and realization about the attribute of God makes the celebrant more genuine and serious in the liturgical celebration.

2.1.2 - *Promeion* and *Sedro*[483] - Through the *promeion* and *sedro*, the celebrant prays on behalf of the congregation, to offer themselves as a living and acceptable sacrifice to the Lord and to lead a life worthy of their calling.

---

[475] *Promeion* means preface or introduction to a prayer. Smith, *A Compendious Syriac Dictionary*, 458.

[476] *Sedro* means row or order. It is a long meditative prayer preceded by a *promeion*. These prayers are rich in theological content. It is considered as the theological exposition of the faith and doctrine of the Church. Before the reformation, there was no space for the exposition of Scripture in the liturgical celebration. After the reformation the interpretation of the word (sermon), became a major aspect in Eucharistic celebration. John of Dara is the first West Syrian writer to mentions about sedro. Other early commentators of the Eucharist, Bar Kepha and George of the Arabs, are silent about it. On the origin of the sedro and its place in the Syrian liturgy, see, Jean Le Seder, *Li Lieu de Culte et la Messe Syro-Occidentale selon le 'De Oblatione' de Jean de Dara: Etude darcheologie et de liturgie* (Rome: Pontifical Oriental Institute, 1983), 83-89. Smith, *A Compendious Syriac Dictionary*, 362.

[477] *Qolo* means sound, tune, or voice. Smith, *A Compendious Syriac Dictionary*, 505.

[478] *Ethro* means incense, smoke and sweet perfume. It is a prayer of incense. Smith, *A Compendious Syriac Dictionary*, 410.

[479] *Eqbo* means variable termination of a prayer, short form of a prayer at the conclusion of an office. Smith, *A Compendious Syriac Dictionary*, 424.

[480] *Huthomo* means the end, closing or conclusion. Smith, *A Compendious Syriac Dictionary*, 135.

[481] "O Lord, You are merciful…... both now and forever." Juhanon Mar Thoma, *The Order of the Holy Qurbana*, 1.

[482] John of Dara remarks that, when presbyters or deacons wish to enter the divine sanctuary for the Eucharist, they shall be pure form nocturnal pollution both perceptible and spiritual. Those who enter the divine sanctuary shall be carefully vigilant by beseeching God to protect them from all faults of soul and body. If they are not entering the sanctuary with dignity, they are bringing condemnation upon the children of the Holy Church. Dara, "Commentary on the Eucharist," 17-19.

[483] *Sedro* is a long meditative homiletical prayer which is one of the characteristics of the liturgical units of the West Syrian tradition. "A literary genre known as *Memre* or metrical homilies on the important fests of the liturgical year is the most remarkable contributions of the Syriac Fathers in the field of liturgical writings. *Memre* are poetical

140

"…… make us worthy to come before You with contrition and humility, purify us from all stain that we may be transformed by the renewal of our life,[484] and go forth, as did the wise virgins, to a new world, bearing the shining lamps of faith. Enable us to sing Your praises, Father, Son and Holy Spirit, now and forever"[485] (Mt.25:1-13).

They further beseech that, by their participation in the service, they be transformed by renewing their lives, holding the shining torches of faith, in the company of wise and holy people, and that they become worthy to sing praises to God. In short, sedro prayer expresses the desire of the faithful to live in the experience of salvation through the participation in the Holy Qurbana and to commit themselves for taking part in the mission of God in accordance with the worthiness of their calling.[486] This prayer expresses the desire of the faithful to live in the experience of the salvific act[487] of Jesus Christ through the participation in the Holy Qurbana.

2.1.3 - *Huthomo* - The content of the *Qolo* (hymn) before the *Huthomo* is penitence. This confessional prayer reflects the importance of the grace of God to renounce the sins of the world. The faithful beseech God to be the fortress and refuge for them from the evil one. In this prayer, Christ is addressed as the pure and spotless lamb, who offered himself to the Father, an acceptable offering for the expiation and redemption of the whole world.[488] The first part of the prayer recalls the salvific act of Christ and

---

meditations of scriptural inspiration, originally meant to be sung during the offices of the feasts. The metrical homilies together with the Syriac translation of the liturgical homilies of the Greek Fathers served as the model for the West Syrian festal homilies throughout the centuries. These festal homilies provided most of the source materials for the sedro." Varghese, "Some Aspects of West Syrian Liturgical Theology," 171-178.

[484] John of Dara remarks that, the priest or deacon when they enter the divine sanctuary should wash their heads, hands and feet, which means the purification of the intellect from all pride and worldly thoughts, the dust of the body namely the defilement and the foolish sores and their feet, that is the life of the soul which is manifest by anger, desire, rationality. Similarly, their hearts should be away from all hateful thoughts. Dara, "Commentary on the Eucharist," 19-20.

[485] Titus II, *Qurbana Thaksa*, 3-4.

[486] Kuttiyil, *Eucharist (Qurbana)*, 62.

[487] The salvific act of Christ includes his birth, life, passion, death, resurrection, ascension, sitting at the right side of the Father and the anticipation of his second coming.

[488] Titus II, *Qurbana Thaksa*, 5-6.

the second part expresses the desire of the believers to offer themselves as a living sacrifice through the participation in the Holy Qurbana.[489] Here Christ is a model for the believers to participate in the mission of God. The *huthomo* prayers express the idea that "the believers may be accounted worthy to offer sacrifice of praise and thanksgiving, and all their thoughts, words and actions are a burnt offering to Him. They pray that they may be able to stand before the Almighty, without blemish. This is a total surrender of the faithful before God."[490]

The second part of *thuyobo* service contains the prayers beginning with the washing of hands[491] and later prayers for putting on the vestments. Before wearing each part of the vestment, the celebrant offers special prayers.[492] The vestments are a symbolic representation of the preparation for the spiritual warfare for God. This points to their "renunciation of the worldly things and the perfect detachment from all mundane and corporeal things, and their stripping of the old man, who is composed of all things that are not in accordance with the Law."[493] The Holy Qurbana as a spiritual sacrifice, is an armour for the believer and a shield against the hostile powers, passions and their operations.[494] The celebrant prepares

---

[489] Kuttiyil, *Eucharist (Qurbana)*, 63.

[490] Kuttiyil, Eucharist (*Qurbana*), 63-64.

[491] Two times during the Holy Qurbana, the celebrant washes his hands, once following his vesting as part of the preparation to ready the altar for the holy Eucharist and again before the beginning of the anaphora. As the celebrant washes his hands, he thereby reminds the congregation to leave all worldly thought and become clean in heart, spirit, and mind. The second washing reminds the faithful that all should be thoroughly cleansed to offer up and share in the Lord's Supper. "Grant us, O Lord, with purified hearts ......sacrifices in true faith; in the name of the Father, and of the Son and of the Holy Spirit." Titus II, *Qurbana Thaksa*, 6. Juhanon, *The Order of the Holy Qurbana*, 4.

[492] Dara remarks that, "when the priest enters the holy of holies, his vestments should be white. That is, his senses should be pure from all adverse things which are harmful, and this will illuminate each of his senses." Dara, "Commentary on the Eucharist," 21. The traditional liturgical colour of the MTC is white. On the use of white garments in the early Christin tradition, see Cyril E. Pocknee, *Liturgical Vesture: Its Origin and Development* (Alcuin: A. R. Mowbray, 1960). Titus II, *Qurbana Thaksa*, 6-7. Clothing with the vestments symbolises the pure, holy and splendid vestments of the holy angels, whose vestment is impassibility, immortality and unlimtedness. Dara, "Commentary on the Eucharist," 20.

[493] Dara, "Commentary on the Eucharist," 20-21.

[494] Dara, "Commentary on the Eucharist," 14.

himself to enact the salvific act of Christ through the liturgical service and reminds the faithful of the life and mission of Jesus Christ. By participating in the liturgy, the Church invites and motivates the believers to be the ambassadors of the life-giving mission of Jesus Christ. After this, the celebrant sets the paten and the chalice with the bread and wine with prayers.[495]

In this meditative prayer, Jesus is pictured as a lamb lead to the slaughter house and as a sheep before the Shearer. In the Gospel of John, John the Baptist presents Jesus as one who takes away the sins of the world (Jn.1:29). The lamb-sheep imagery is taken from Isaiah's "song of the servant" or "servant of the Lord." By bringing out this imagery, the salvific death of Christ is recalled. Here the Church recalls the salvific mission of Jesus Christ to redeem the whole creation through his atoning sacrifice.[496] Mollaveetil comments that the placing of bread on the paten symbolises all that the faithful offer to God.[497] When the priest mixes the wine[498] with the water in the chalice, the Church affirms her faith in the divinity and the humanity of Jesus Christ. The incarnation of Jesus as fully divine and fully human is emphasised and recalled. The two natures of Christ are symbolically presented in the mixing of the cup. Each event in the life of Christ, including incarnation, is salvific and pointing towards the redemption wrought by Christ.[499] The death of Jesus on the cross is affirmed as salvific and redemptive. It has washed away the sins of the creation. The faithful recall the redemptive act of Christ by participating

---

[495] Titus II, *Qurbana Thaksa*, 7.

[496] While placing the holy bread, the celebrant addresses Jesus as the "first begotten of the heavenly Father." Jesus has offered himself to the Father as a first-fruit from among men (1 Cor.15:20) and he continues to offer himself to the believers through the Holy Qurbana. In turn, the faithful have to offer a pleasing offering to God by participating in the holy mysteries. In Syriac, the Eucharistic bread is known as *burko* which means first-born. This shows that human beings offer to God all that belongs to him. Christ is the image of the invisible God, the first born of all creation (Col.1: 5, Rom.8:29, Heb.1:6). Kuttiyil, *Eucharist (Qurbana)*, 60.

[497] Moolaveetil L, *A Study of the Anaphora of St. James* (Kottayam: St. Thomas Apostolic Seminary, 1976), 72.

[498] Titus II, *Qurbana Thaksa*, 7-8.

[499] Kuttiyil, *Eucharist (Qurbana)*, 60.

in the celebration of Holy Qurbana. This participation reminds them about their mission of redemption in the world with Christ.

In this second part of the preparatory service, there is another sedro prayer,[500] which enumerates the redeeming work of Jesus Christ. Here, Christ is addressed as the creator and designer of the whole creation. While using the censor, the Church recalls the incense of Aaron:[501] the priest who offered unto God in the tabernacle and withheld thereby the plague from the people of Israel (Lev. 8:16). By incensing, the Church beseeches God to receive the fragrance of the spiritual sweetness, which is offered, and supplicates God to forgive the sins and offences. In this sense, this is a propitiatory service.[502] The Service of Preparation concludes with prayers of penitence. While censing the altar the celebrant enunciates the Trinitarian adoration. This is followed by the *huthomo*, the *trisagion* and Nicene Creed. With this, the preparatory service ends.

2.1.4 - Missional Aspects in the Preparatory Service

The preparatory service enables the celebrant to understand the importance of holiness before God[503] and the worthiness of worship. True understanding of worship enables the faithful to participate in the service actively. Through the meditative prayers the Church pleads to God for the grace of holiness to offer a sacrifice worthy of Himself. The liturgy affirms that God accepts the prayers of those who are humble and pure at heart. Through the atoning sacrifice of Christ, God rescued creation and restored the holy relationship creatures once enjoyed in the Garden of Eden. Through the prayer of penitence, the Church prepares herself to enter into communion with God through Holy Qurbana. Here the Church is reminded of the responsibility

---

[500] Titus II, *Qurbana Thaksa*, 9.
[501] This service is also known as the "Service of Aaron." Moolaveetil, *A Study of the Anaphora of St. James*, 79. Barnabas, *Holy Qurbana: A Devotional Study*, 99.
[502] Kuttiyil, *Eucharist (Qurbana)*, 65.
[503] Lev.11:44-45, 19:2, 20:7, 21:8, Josh. 24:19, 1 Sam. 2:2, 6:20. *Qadosh*, the Hebrew term for holy means sacred. The Greek term *hagios* means set apart for or by God. The Church is a set apart community to reflect the holiness of God. The mission of the Church is to reflect the qualitative nature of God (light, salt..., Mt.5:13-16) through its "active presence" in the world.

for reconciliation in her life. The liturgy affirms that the world is a place for temporary life and it is the preparatory ground for eternity. Through the initial prayer in the thuyobo service, the Church prays for the grace and blessings of a life of holiness both in this world and in the world to come. An eschatological hope is affirmed throughout this prayer.

Mission is the human response to the invitation of God to participate in His mission of transformation and the establishment of the Kingdom of God. By participating in the Holy Qurbana, the Church associates itself with the redeeming act of Jesus by the power of the Holy Spirit. For instance, in the last prayer of the preparatory service, we are reminded to understand the missionary task of the worshipping community. The prayer says - "O Lamb of God, pure and spotless, who offered Himself to the Father for the redemption of the whole world, make us fit to offer ourselves to You as a pleasing living sacrifice, and thus to follow Your own sacrifice for us."[504] This prayer affirms the missionary nature of the Church. It begins with the sending of Jesus Christ, and continues with the work of the Holy Spirit, through the work of apostles, prophets, martyrs, confessors, saints and through all the children of the Church, who have been signed with the seal of baptism. Here, the Sacrament of Baptism is perceived as the entry point into this mission journey. This reiterates the missionary character of the Church and the responsibility of every baptised person is reaffirmed. The entire preparatory service symbolizes the sacrifice and salvific death of Christ and the offering of the people to the Lord as living and holy sacrifice.[505]

2.2 - Ante-Communion Service or Public Celebration

2.2.1 - *Eqbo* - The pubic celebration of the Holy Qurbana commences with a liturgical hymn.[506] This liturgical hymn expounds the holiness of

---

[504] Titus II, *Qurbana Thaksa*, 8.

[505] Kuttiyil, *Eucharist (Qurbana)*, 59.

[506] Liturgical hymns have a major role in the worship service. These liturgical hymns contain much reflection on Scripture, and usually consist of meditations on the biblical passages associated with the theme. They also contain much doctrinal statement. As a result, the liturgy has a strong biblical quality and base. This rich biblical content of the

God and it highlights the need for the purity of hearts and minds of the faithful to offer a holy sacrifice.[507] After drawing back the veil (curtain) of the *madbaho*, the celebrant pleads for the blessings of Jesus Christ. The drawing of the curtain symbolises the full revelation of God through Jesus Christ. In this prayer, the Church recalls the memory of St. Mary (mother of Jesus) and John the Baptist, and their role in the salvation history of Jesus.[508] It was Mary's response to God, which has caused the incarnation of Christ. John the Baptist was the forerunner of Jesus, who prepared the way for the ministry of Jesus and baptised him before his public ministry. Both of these figures were the nearest witnesses of the incarnation of Christ.[509] In this short prayer, the incarnation of Jesus Christ is recalled. The Church remembers the birth and baptism of Jesus and beseeches Christ to have mercy on them. Through this prayer, at the very beginning of the public celebration of Holy Qurbana, the salvific event of Christ is brought to the attention of the believers. Brown comments that, "at the beginning of the rite proper, all are recalled to the incarnation as the miracle through which alone true worship is possible."[510]

2.2.2 - The Responsary (*Manitho*) - The responsary after *Eqbo*, attributed to Mar Severus of Antioch (465-538 CE), is rich in theological content. In this response, the person of Christ and his entire dispensation are chronologically presented, i.e. the nature of Jesus, the purpose of his incarnation, and the entire salvific act of Christ. The incarnation of Jesus, his crucifixion and death, unfold before the believers. This is considered as the proclamation and the affirmation of the faith of the Church in the Christ-event.

---

liturgy has had an effect of discouraging individual interpretation and hence fragmentation of the Church. Binns, *An Introduction to the Christian Orthodox Churches*, 50.

[507] "In Your light, we see the light.....that our prayers may rise up to You." Titus II, *Qurbana Thaksa*, 10. Juhanon, *The Order of the Holy Qurbana*, 8.

[508] "O Lord Jesus Christ, Born of Mary, Baptized by John, have mercy on us." Titus II. *Qurbana Thaksa*, 11.

[509] Moolaveetil. *A Study of the Anaphora of St. James*, 94.

[510] Brown, *The Indian Christians of St. Thomas*, 218.

2.2.3 - *Trisagion* - Trisagion is the threefold praising or adoration of God.[511] This prayer emerged in early fifth century as an antiphon to a psalm and developed into a moment of great devotion, later known as the "Little Entrance."[512] In the earlier liturgical practices the trisagion was precisely a hymn of entrance, *introit,* the processional singing by the congregation while entering the Church and preparing for the proclamation of the gospel and celebration of the Eucharist.[513] In this prayer, the holiness of God is confessed and the Church remembers the crucifixion and immortality of Jesus Christ. The crucifixion is salvific in nature. That is why it is said, "O Thou that was crucified for us, have mercy on us." Here the Church recalls the redemptive mission of Christ through his death and resurrection. In the Antiochian tradition, this prayer is addressed to Christ, and not to the Trinity. After the trisagion, the celebrant and the congregation chant *Kyrie elesion.*[514]

2.2.4 - Scripture Reading - In the West Syrian tradition, reading from Scripture is very significant. It is the practice of the West Syrian tradition to follow the Jewish worship tradition of reading from the Pentateuch and the prophets.[515] Now along with the readings from the Old Testament and the New Testament, reading of epistles and the gospel possess a unique

---

[511] "Holy art Thou, O God / Holy art Thou, Almighty Lord / Holy art Thou, Immortal Lord / O Thou, that was (†) crucified for us, have mercy on us." Titus II, *Qurbana Thaksa,* 11. Juhanon, *The Order of the Holy Qurbana,* 10.

[512] The Trisagion is a song of entry, which was originally sung during the initial procession into Church. It was used in the fifth century in processions on rogation days, along with litanies. By the sixth century it was in use in Syria, Constantinople, and Jerusalem. Its common use in both the Greek and Syriac texts suggests that it had been introduced prior to Chalcedon (451 CE). However, the Syriac text has the additions of the words "who was crucified for us" which were introduced by Peter the Fuller, non-Chalcedonian Patriarch of Antioch (471-488 CE). The trisagion is repeated thrice to accord with the number of the Holy Trinity and that the word "Holy" in the trisagion is repeated nine times in reference to the nine angelic orders, whose worship in heaven is the prototype of the worship of the Church. Binns, *An Introduction to the Christian Orthodox Churches,* 46-47. Verhelst, "Commentaire liturgique," 307-309.

[513] Alexander Schmemann, *Of Water and The Spirit: A Liturgical Study Of Baptism* (London: SPCK, 1976), 111.

[514] Lord, have mercy. Complete surrender and seeking mercy by pronouncing it three times. Repeating three times affirms absolute nature of the prayer.

[515] Baby Varghese, *Abba Father* (Kottayam: Sophia, 1988), 33-43.

place in the liturgical celebration.[516] By reading Scripture in the liturgy, the Church reiterates the responsibility of the mission of proclaiming the Good News to the world. Before reading the epistle, the congregation chants a liturgical hymn, which is biblical in nature. The theme of this hymn is the sending forth of the apostles to all parts of the world to preach the Good News. By this hymn, the believers are exhorted to remain in the true faith and the teachings of the Church. They are cautioned against false teachings and heresies.[517] The Church proclaims that hearing and obeying the Word of God is salvific and is a blessing. This is considered as spiritual food for the soul. Through the prayer before Scripture reading, the celebrant beseeches God to make the hearers worthy, that with purity and holiness they may keep the commandments of God and that of the apostles and that of St. Paul.[518] The believers need grace from God to follow the commandments. This points to the importance of the proclamation of the true Gospel - Jesus Christ. Then the deacon reads a portion of the epistle of Paul or from the epistles of the other apostles, as per the Lectionary of the Church. Then the celebrant reads the Gospel passage with devotion and fear, because through reading the gospel, the celebrant evokes the memory of the life and ministry of Christ in the minds of the congregation. The Word of God, primarily, is Jesus Christ. He is the Word of God par excellence. This Word is the life force of all which came to earth for the salvation of all. The Word of God is the key biblical image referring to Jesus Christ, which expresses the truth of God's saving love towards

---

[516] "The reading of the prophets symbolizes the labours and sweats that the holy fathers and the prophets offered in order to see the incarnated Word of God, and similarly the supplications which they offer for the human race, so that God may come and save it from the hands of the enemy. The reading of the apostle symbolises the supplications which they offered for them to Christ so that He may come to their succour and to their aid in the combats and dangers that they suffered from the tyrants. Readings of the gospel symbolises what the Son had said to his Father for the sake of the holy apostles, when He wished to ascend towards Him; My Father, keep them, as I have done, I have kept them all (Jn.17:11). It is God Himself who speaks to His Church and the people are sanctified by the words they listen." Dara, "Commentary on the Eucharist," 49-50.
[517] Titus II, *Qurbana Thaksa,* 12.
[518] Titus II, *Qurbana Thaksa,* 12-13.

creation in Jesus Christ.[519] The Gospel is described in the liturgy as the channel which "proclaims life and salvation to the world."[520] The celebrant reads the gospel, standing at the centre of the sanctuary (*madbaho*) where he blesses the congregation and utters "peace be with you all." This is in remembrance of the blessings of the resurrected Christ to the disciples. This means that Christ is the real peace, the Prince of Peace. The Church believes that the Word of God proclaims life and salvation to the entire world. The gospel reading concludes with the same affirmation "peace be with you all." In the liturgical celebration, the signing of the cross is a powerful liturgical act throughout the service which reminds all that peace is possible only through the cross, and that the Church, as a community of peace, is called out to be the ambassadors of peace. The Church accepts the redemptive power of Scripture by the signing of the cross. Here the believers understand that God speaks to the people through Scriptures all the time. By reading the gospel the priest is presenting the life- giving and redemptive power of the Saviour. The Gospel gives life and salvation and redemption to the world. After the gospel reading, the congregation sings a post-gospel hymn. Here, the Church praises God for the word of life and prays for the grace to glorify God by obeying the word.[521]

2.2.5 - Meditative Prayers: (*Promeion* and *Sedro*) - This prayer is categorized into three parts. The first part is a short preface. It is an introduction to a long meditative prayer which follows. The *promeion* and *sedro* are a common feature of the West Syrian liturgy and it varies from sacrament to sacrament and according to the liturgical seasons. Several alternative prayers are provided in almost all pre-anaphoral texts. These prayers are Christological in nature. Here, the salvific role of Christ is well explained and believers are exhorted to praise and worship Him at all times, particularly at the time of divine Eucharist. A narration of the salvific act of Christ is the main theme of all *promeion* prayers.

---

[519] Dyk, "Proclamation: Revelation, Christology," 59-61.
[520] Titus II, *Qurbana Thaksa*, 23.
[521] Titus II, *Qurbana Thaksa*, 24.

The second part in this section is a prayer for pardon and grace (*husoyo*).[522] This prayer is an expression of repentance and a petition for remission of sins. The main content of *husoyo* is confession of sins and petition for absolutions. This prayer is addressed to Christ, the Lord. Here, Christ is considered as the absolution and the absolver. The celebrant beseeches God to give fullness of life which befits a Christian. The *husoyo* is the only fixed prayer in the pre-anaphora, whereas the *promeion* and the *sedro* can be varied. These prayers are all reminders of the sinful nature of humanity and beseech the Lord to make worshippers worthy of offering the Holy Qurbana. In this session, the celebrant raises up the entire congregation before God and beseeches God for cleansing and absolution. At this point the liturgy incorporates prayers of intercession for the advancement of its mission in this world. The Church prays for the well-being of all the human race and intercedes for all creation.

This is followed by the third part, sedro, with theological reflections and petitions. The importance of sedro lies in its textual quantity, doctrinal richness, and in the singularly solemn and touching way the celebrant recites this. This prayer exhorts the faithful to assume an attentive disposition so as to have a growing experience of the divine.[523] The theology of the West Syrian tradition is mainly deposited in the sedro of the Holy Qurbana. In liturgy, the sedro includes long prose prayers recited by the celebrant while putting incense in the thurible.[524] At the end of the prayer, the celebrant makes a declaration of absolution. This is a fixed formula. The prayers in the *promeion* and *sedro* vary according to the yearly cycle. The Patriarch John I of Antioch (631-648 CE) is considered as the creator of this form of prayer.[525] The majority of the *sedro* is addressed to Christ. However, it stresses the equality of the three persons in the quality of their being as the object of adoration and the receivers of prayer. In a *sedro*, one can

---

[522] *Hussoyo* means absolution that derived from the verb, to absolve or to remit. Smith, *A Compendious Syriac Dictionary*, 132.

[523] Jacob Thekkeparampil, ed., "Sedre Absolution (*Hussoyo*) and Repentence" (*Tyobuto*),'*TUVAIK*, Kottayam: (1995), 136.

[524] Thekkeparamil, *TUVAIK*, 137.

[525] Geevarghese Panicker, "West Syrian Anaphorae," *The Harp* 6, no. 1 (April 1993): 37.

distinguish two parts: the first is the theological part that contains the theology of the feast or the occasion on which it is recited. The second part, is called petitional part, and it consists of various petitions for the needs of the Church and the world. Because of the extensive theological content, sedro can be called *Loci Theologici* of the West Syrian tradition.[526]

2.2.6 - Adoration of the Trinity and Censing - While censing, the priest says, "Holy is the Holy Father, Holy is the Holy Son and the Holy is the Living and Holy Spirit."[527] The celebrant praises and declares faith in the holy Trinity. It recalls the epiphany of the holy Trinity at the baptism of Jesus Christ. After this the congregation affirms the faith of the Church in creedal form.[528]

After the Creed, the offertory takes place. The offertory is a time of rededication of the congregation. Through the offering, the Church acknowledges God as the source of all blessings. It reminds us that the mission of the faithful is to be a blessing for others. It is an essential part of the Holy Qurbana. After the offertory, there is a time for biblical exposition, as per the lectionary. The Sacrament of Confession follows the sermon. The priest invites the faithful, who have come prepared to receive the holy sacrament, to confess their sins in unison. There is a fixed confessional prayer formula in the liturgy. The confession of sins and the assurance of pardon express the heart and reality of the gospel. This sacrament is linked theologically to the fact that God has already provided for our sins, once and for all, in Jesus Christ. That is why the confession of sin is followed by

---

[526] Jacob Thekkeparampil, *Sedra and the Rite of Incense in the West Syrian Liturgy* (Paris: Unpublished Doctoral Dissertation, 1977), 104 -108.

[527] Titus II, *Qurbana Thaksa,* 18.

[528] By pronouncing the Nicene Creed, the Church affirms its apostolic faith and continuity. The first part of the creed elaborates the divine dispensation. The Church confesses the entire Christ event such as incarnation, passion, crucifixion, death, resurrection, ascension, sitting at the right hand of the Father and His second coming - Parousia. Moreover, the profession of faith in the Trinity, in the universal Church, the resurrection of the dead and the new life in the world to come are confessed. Moses Bar Kepha gives the following divisions to the creed, which are worth mentioning: "it is right to know that this faith is divided into five headings: the first, the theology, the second, the incarnation, the third, concerning baptism, the fourth, concerning the general resurrection and the fifth concerning the future judgement and recompense." Connolly and Codrington, *Two commentaries on the Jacobite Liturgy,* 38.

the pronouncement of forgiveness by the minister[529] (2 Cor.5:17, 1 Jn.1:9). It reorients the faithful to their true identity in Christ, and reorders their relationships. This part of service enact the great movements of descending and rising in the Christian faith, it is an experience of coming back to the abundance of life which Christ shares with his children.[530] In the MTC, there is no private confession, but a general confession, which admits that there is no mediator between humanity and God except Jesus Christ. The prayer of confession is an expression of repentance for the faults either in word, thought or deeds. This is a confession of one's failure and fragility. The minister, being the representative of the Church declares the remission of sins on behalf of God. The confession ends with a prayer that it may act like a bridge to eternal life.[531] Only after the confession and absolution does the celebrant enter the *darga* (steps) of the *thronos.*

In the pre-anaphora section, there are prayers that have several references to various streams of mission such as mission as adoration, mission as proclamation (reading of Scripture), mission as being an agent of purification, mission as interceding and mission as transformation, mission as social work. These missiological aspects of the liturgy inspire and motivate the Church to find new avenues and possibilities in her witnessing life.

2.3 - The Service of Eucharist (Anaphora)[532]

The West Syrian tradition has the largest number of anaphoras, larger than in any other Church, though only a few have been edited. The anaphoras

---

[529] William A. Dyrness, "Confession and Assurance," in *A More Profound Alleluia: Theology and Worship in Harmony, 47.*

[530] Dyrness, "Confession and Assurance," 51-52.

[531] George Mathew Kuttiyil, *The Faith and Sacraments of the Mar Thoma Church* (Thiruvalla: Christava Sahitya Samithi, 2005), 50-52.

[532] The term "anaphora is Greek which means the elevation or the offering presented to God. Anaphora is that part of the Eucharistic liturgy which begins with the prayer of peace and ends with the final commendation and a blessing. Panicker, "West Syrian Anaphorae," 29.

at present, according to H J. Feulner is eighty-three.[533] Not all of these anaphoras are contained in any one book, and most are no longer in use. However, this large number of anaphoras witnesses the local variations and differences co-existing and a continued tradition of compiling new Eucharistic prayers.[534]

This section deals with the structure and theological analysis of the anaphora of St. James. Even though, the MTC uses a revised form of the St. James liturgy in accordance with the Anglican Church's reformed theology, the structure and content of the liturgy is more or less the same as the liturgy of the Syrian Orthodox Church. The reformed liturgy of the MTC is simple in its content and easy to follow. The celebration of the anaphora in the Eucharist service is that most solemn part of the Holy Qurbana service which seeks the complete attention of all participants. In this service, the Church remembers and re-enacts the salvific act of Jesus Christ. The following are the structure and content of the prayers and its theological importance.

After the liturgical act of the washing of hands,[535] the celebrant solicits the prayers[536] of the faithful for the acceptance of the celebration of the Holy Qurbana. The mutual acceptance and the prayer of intercession make the service a meaningful experience. Then the celebrant ascends into the step in the *thronos* for the celebration of anaphora. There are mainly three prayers in this section such as the Prayer of the Kiss of Peace, Prayer of Inclination and Prayer of the Veil.

2.3.1 - Prayer of the Kiss of Peace - The anaphora begins with the Prayer of the Kiss of Peace that serves as an introduction to it. This prayer is

---

[533] Hans Jurgen Feulner, "Zu den Editionen Orientalischer Anaphoren," in *Crossroad of Cultures: Studies in Liturgy and Patristics in Honour of Gabriele* Winkler, eds. Hans Jurgen Feulner, Velkovska and Robert F. Taft (Rome: Pontificio Istituto Orientale, 2000), 261-274.
[534] Spinks, *Do This in Remembrance of Me,* 158.
[535] Washing hands before the celebration of anaphora indicates that, the celebrant purifies his conscience before God. This external act is a symbolic representation of the need of purity in the celebration of the Eucharist. This liturgical act reminds us of the importance of purity in the presence of God. Bar Salibi, *Commentary on the Eucharist,* 46.
[536] "Dearly beloved, pray with me that this service may be acceptable to the Lord." Titus II, *Qurbana Thaksa,* 19. Juhanon, *The Order of the Holy Qurbana,* 16.

an exhortation to the believers to be freed from all ill will, divisions and evil, so that by exchanging the peace, they may be made worthy to be gathered before God and to communicate with Him in peaceful unity which drives away from them all carnal desires.[537] The theme of this prayer is reconciliation and peace. Then comes the salutation - "peace be with you all" and the exchange of peace. It is believed that, Jesus Christ himself grants his peace through the priest in the same way Christ granted his peace to his apostles. The celebrant exchanges the Kiss of Peace by drawing a sign of the cross. This reveals that, the cross of Christ stands as the source of peace and reconciliation. There is a strong call to mission in this very liturgical act. The Church is entrusted with the responsibility of reconciliation and peace in this world. Here, the deacon receives the Kiss of Peace from the celebrant and exchanges the same to the congregation, with the words "by the love of our Lord, give peace one to another with a holy and divine kiss." The Church believes that the exchange of peace is not a worldly thing, but a divine gift, which is given out of His immeasurable grace and mercy that is not only with the body but also with the spirit. Through this liturgical act, the believers are bound together in spiritual harmony of love and tranquillity. The congregation exchange the peace with the words – "May the love and peace of our Lord Jesus Christ abide with us forever."[538] In the Syrian Church, the exchange of peace is usually by the handclasp.[539] An act of the Kiss of Peace expresses the fellowship of the believers. It is of apostolic origin and scriptural (Rom.16:16, 1 Cor.16:20, 2 Cor.13:12, 1 Pet.5:14) which exhorts the Christians "to greet one another with a holy kiss" and is used in the liturgy to signify the "fellowship of the spirit." For this reason, it was always confined to the faithful. The fellowship of the saints here on earth is expressed in this "holy kiss." The Kiss of Peace also fulfils the words of Jesus Christ, "so if you are offering your gift at the altar, and there remember that your brother has something

---

[537] Bar Salibi, *Commentary on the Eucharist*, 49.
[538] Titus II, *Qurbana Thaksa*, 22.
[539] T.S. Garrett, *Christian Worship: An Introductory Outline* (Oxford: Oxford University, 1961), 78.

against you, leave your gift there before the altar and go; first be reconciled to your brother, and then come and offer your gift" (Mt.5:23-24). This liturgical action shows the love and harmony which should exist among the Disciples of Christ. It is necessary that the faithful should be reconciled before they take part in the service of the Holy Qurbana. It affirms that the Church is a reconciled community and the exchange of the Kiss of Peace is the sign and expression of reconciliation with God and with one another.[540] Since Holy Qurbana is the spiritual meal, it begins with the Kiss of Peace. It reminds us that loving your neighbour is a necessary part of our participation in the Holy Qurbana. Communion with God brings communion with the neighbour.[541] According to Panicker, "it is a beautiful symbol of the mystical union of all in Christ." The Kiss of Peace is the sign of the newness, peace, and reconciliation that has been achieved by the redeeming work of Christ.[542] According to Cyril of Jerusalem, "it effects the co-mingling of souls and pledges, complete forgiveness, the kiss is a sign of a true union of hearts and banishing of any grudge (Mt.5:23, 24). The Kiss, then is reconciliation and therefore holy, according to Paul who said "greet one another with the holy kiss" (Rom.16:16, 1 Cor.16:20), "greet one another with a kiss of charity" (1 Pet.5:14)."[543] The prayer and the exchange of the Kiss of Peace proclaim the desire of the believers to remain in the fellowship and salvation of God and to bear witness to that salvation by the power of the Holy Spirit.

2.3.2 - Prayer of the Veil[544] - This is a commemoration of the redeeming act of God, who out of His love towards human beings sent His Son Jesus to

[540] The God who forgives iniquities through Christ and reconciled us to the Father is the source of our reconciliation (Mt.18:33). It was also the practice of the Jews to give peace before meals (Lk.7:45, Rom.16:16). The Bible points out that the believers have to approach the Table of the Lord with purity of heart.
[541] Poikail, *St. Thomas Christians and their Eucharistic Liturgy,* 114.
[542] Kuttiyil, *Eucharist (Qurbana),* 90.
[543] D.J Sheerin, ed., *Cyril of Jerusalem* (Delaware: Michael Glazier, 1986), 68.
[544] After the exchange of the Kiss of Peace, the deacon says, "Beloved brothers and sisters, let us participate in this Holy Qurbana .....in a spirit of unity and concord." Titus II, *Qurbana Thaksa,* 22. The chalice veil is lifted and waved over the bread and wine, by this act, the Church recalls the angels rolling away the stone from the tomb of Jesus and underlines the flow of grace into the holy mysteries and through them to all believers,

bring back the sheep that had gone astray. The celebrant removes the veil, which covers the holy elements while saying the prayer. Through the Prayer of the Veil, the celebrant brings forth the divine work of salvation into the mind of the faithful. The removal of the veil symbolizes the mystery of salvation that has been revealed through Christ.[545] It also represents the hard rock, which sent forth twelve rivers of water for the twelve tribes of Israel. In other words, it points towards the living water that Christ gives through his atoning sacrifice.[546]

Bar Kepha gives the following meaning for the spreading out and lifting up of the veil. "The veil is spread over the mysteries for these reasons: first, because it signifies the secrets and invisibleness of the Godhead which is hidden in the mysteries. Secondly, it is the symbol of the stone, which was placed over the tomb of our Redeemer. Thirdly, it makes known that Immanuel Himself was covered over and hidden in the sacrifice of the law and in that figurative service."[547] The prayer and

---

bestowing upon the faithful forgiveness and salvation. This action also indicates the need to remove from our hearts the blind passions surrounding our human nature in order to truly see and comprehend what is about to take place upon the altar as we relive the Sacrifice of Christ. According to Bar Salibi, "the deacon exhorts and directs people to stand in order, fear, prudence, and sanctity. Why so? Well, firstly, the mysteries are going to be revealed from behind the veil which has been covering them. Secondly, the doors of heaven are now opened and the heavenly armies and the perfected spirits of the just are descending for this event and to give honour to the mysteries. The removal of the veil symbolically reminds us of the invisible Divinity which remains hidden in the mysteries. Moreover, the veil is also figure of the stone placed on our Lord's tomb. It likewise proclaims Emmanuel who was hidden in the Old Testament sacrifice and figurative services. The Divinity hidden in the mysteries, once unknown to the uninitiated and the unfaithful, now reveals itself spiritually to the initiated and the faithful. Again the lifting of the veil calls to mind the stone rolled away by the angel which allows us to behold that Fullness which had lain hidden in the Old Testament sacrifices. Further, it states another deep truth that ultimately removable indeed is that dense cloud which stands between the human and the Divine; yes, there is for us that possibility, that in naked purity and without veil or sign, we may one day gaze upon the glorious Brightness, the veil is raised and lowered to show that the grace of the mysteries has been given for the remission of the sins of those who believe in Christ." Bar Salibi, *Commentary on the Eucharist*, 54 -55.
[545] Kuttiyil, *Eucharist (Qurbana)*, 95.
[546] Num. 20:2-11, 1 Cor.10:1-4.
[547] "But it is removed from the mysteries, first because the Godhead which is hidden in the mysteries and is not known to the uninitiated and unbelievers is revealed. Secondly, it signifies the stone which was placed over the tomb of our Redeemer, which the angel rolled away and removed; again, it declares the Immanuel who, covered over in the sacrifice

the removal of the veil over the holy mysteries reminds the faithful that this grace of God has been given for the remission of the sins of those who believe in Christ, whether they are the people of God or gentiles. It encompasses everyone irrespective of any difference. This act reminds us of the need for an inclusive mission mandate.

2.3.3 - First Blessing (*Rooshmo*)[548] - By turning to the faithful, the celebrant pronounces a Trinitarian blessing[549] with the signing of the cross three times and entrusts them to the love, grace and communion of the Holy Trinity. Since this blessing is adapted from St. Paul (2 Cor. 13:14), this is considered as an apostolic blessing.[550] In this blessing, the three persons in Trinity are remembered with praise and thanksgiving. The love of the Father is expressed by the sending of His Son Jesus who is the manifestation of the love of the Father. The grace of the only begotten Son is the complete obedience of Jesus to the will of His Father and the willingness of Jesus to summit His life for the world. The communion and the abiding presence of the Holy Spirit is the assurance of hope and privilege of the faithful in the world.[551]

2.3.4 - Introductory Dialogue and the Thanksgiving Prayer - The dialogue between the celebrant and the congregation is one of the solemn

---

of Law, revealed Himself to us by His Dispensation." Connolly and Codrington, *Two commentaries on the Jacobite Liturgy*, 44-45.

[548] In Syriac, it is known as *rooshmo* which is derived from the root, *rshm* meaning, sign or mark. Smith, *A Compendious Syriac Dictionary*, 536. There are mainly four blessings in the anaphora in which the final one is a salutation before the departure. These blessings are simple, reassuring statements that the faithful worship in the presence and through the working of the Triune God. Witvliet, "The Opening of Worship-Trinity," 12.

[549] "The love of God the Father (†); the grace of the only begotten Son (†) and the communion and abiding presence of the Holy Spirit (†) be with you all, dearly beloved forever." Titus II, *Qurbana Thaksa*, 23. Juhanon, *The Order of the Holy Qurbana*, 19.

[550] Mar Barnabas, *A Devotional Study of the Eucharist*, 127.

[551] Kuttiyil, *Eucharist (Qurbana)*, 37. Narsai interprets the meaning of the blessing in the following manner: "The grace he (priest) says 'of Jesus Christ…of the Holy Spirit be with us,' that grace which our Lord has given by His coming, may it give us confidence before His majesty, 'the love of the Father' who sent us the Son who is from Him, may it open to us the door of mercy in the days of His coming, 'the communion of the Holy Spirit,' of which we have been made worthy, may it sanctify us and purge from us the filth of our offences." Narsai, "Liturgical Homilies" in *Liturgical Homilies of Narsai*, ed. Richard Hugh Connolly, (Cambridge: Cambridge University, 1909), 11.

liturgical formulas in the anaphora of St. James.[552] When the priest says three verses, the people say three verses responsively. Here, the people are asked to lift up their hearts and minds to where Christ sits at the right hand of his Father, to which the people respond "assuredly is good and right." Through these dialogues, the celebrant and the people prepare for the thanks offering. The believers are exhorted that the holy mysteries are revealed to them, and the doors of heaven have been opened and the spiritual armies descend to honour the mysteries. Therefore, let the minds and understanding of the faithful be on the things of heaven. They are urged to abstain from the worldly thoughts and to concentrate their thoughts and minds upward where Christ sits on the right hand of the Father. The faithful are called to give thanks to the Lord for His deeds towards them. The celebrant says it is right to thank, worship, and praise the creator of the whole world who is glorified by the entire cosmos, angelic bodies, principalities, and powers.[553] In his Mystagogical Catechesis, Cyril of Jerusalem (313-386 CE) explains "Lift up your hearts" at all times we should be mindful of God, lifting up hearts high towards God and not below, occupied with the earth and the things on earth.[554]

After the introductory dialogue, prayer of the anaphora begins. This prayer starts with a simple invocation to all the powers of heaven and on earth and the angelic choirs in praise of God. This is a prayer of thanksgiving (*Eucharistia*), for the whole creation. The faithful call upon to thank God for His redeeming work of salvation. It ends with the Holy, Holy, Holy (Sanctus) acclamation by the congregation. This is based on the visions of the prophet Isaiah and St. John (Isa.6:1-9, Rev.4:8). After this

---

[552] The communication between God and human beings in the liturgy may be understood as a dialogue. The primary pattern is that of call and response, the gracious initiative residing with God. The reading of scriptures, its explanations, and application are heard as a word from God. The human response may come as a word to God in the confession of faith and in prayers of thanksgiving, petition and intercession. Geoffrey Wainwright, "Christian Worship: Scriptural Basis and Theological Frame," in *The Oxford History of Christian Worship,* eds. Geoffrey Wainwright, Karen B. Westerfield Tucker (Oxford: Oxford University, 2006), 10-11.

[553] Kuttiyil, *Eucharist (Qurbana),* 98-99.

[554] Sheerin, ed., *Cyril of Jerusalem,* 68.

hymn of adoration, the celebrant gives thanks to the Father for the mighty deeds of redemptive history and their fulfilment in Christ.

2.3.5 - Words of Institution - The pronouncement of the words of institution is the heart of any Eucharistic anaphora. It is a recital of the institution of the Eucharist at the Last Supper, which has been taken from the New Testament accounts of the Last Supper of Jesus Christ with his disciples (Mt.26:26-29, Mk.14:12-25, Lk.22:14-20, 1 Cor.11:24-25). After the praise and thanksgiving, the celebrant pronounces the words of institution.[555] The narration of the history of salvation, including the institution narrative, the anamnesis, and the *epiclesis*, forms a unit, which is the central part of the Eucharistic prayer. This has been adapted from the New Testament accounts and accompanied by the blessing and breaking of the bread and blessing of the cup.[556] There the breaking of the bread shows Christ's death on the cross, which points towards the eternal life that he has brought through his redemption. The shedding of blood on the cross was for the remission of sins and eternal life. Through this prayer, the Church recalls the redeeming act of Jesus on the cross. In this prayer, the passion and death of Jesus are recalled. Hence the Eucharist is the recalling of the redeeming act of Christ. According to Bar Kepha, for two reasons Christ said that his body is given to the faithful. First that it may pardon their sins, secondly, that it may bestow upon them life everlasting in the Kingdom of Heaven,

---

[555] "When the sinless one of his own will chose death for us sinners, he took bread in his holy hands and He gave thanks (†), blessed (†), sanctified (†) and broke it and gave it to his apostles saying 'take, eat, this is my body given for you. Do this in remembrance of me;" and in the same way he took the cup. "He gave thanks (†) blessed (†) sanctified (†) and gave it to his apostles saying drink this all of you. This is the blood of the new covenant which is shed for many for the forgiveness of sins." "Thus as often as you eat this bread and drink this cup, you proclaim the Lord's death until he comes." Titus II, *Qurbana Thaksa*, 24-25. Juhanon, *The Order of the Holy Qurbana*, 19-20.

[556] During the pronouncement of the words of institution, the celebrant takes the holy elements in his hands, blesses it with the sign of the cross and break it. This act recalls the last supper of Jesus with his disciples. Christ laid down his life for the salvation of the world and in the same way the Church is commissioned to fulfil her mission by loving others as Christ loved her. This is symbolized in the Eucharist: this is my body given for you In the Eucharist the Church participates in this self-giving love and is thus enabled to continue his mission.

as he said in another place "who so eateth my body shall live for ever"[557] (Jn.6:55-58).

2.3.6 - Anamnesis - Generally, Christian liturgy is fundamentally an act of memory or anamnesis, an act of rehearsing God's actions in history: past, and future, realized and promised.[558] This memorial aspect has always the central place in the liturgy of the Eucharist. Anamnesis comes as a conclusion to the words of institution, as one sees from the text itself. The word "anamnesis" (memorial) means the process of bringing again or back to mind the memory of a past event. It was not merely a remembrance or a record of the past, but rather a sign of an objective reality made present, the saving deeds of God.[559] The memorial involved an encounter with the historical events. It is a sense of recalling or re-presenting an act of the past. Here, the Church remembers the explicit command of Christ: "Do this in remembrance of me" (Lk.22:20, 1 Cor.11:26). This command of Christ to the apostles at the Last Supper reminds us of the memorial aspect of the Passover celebration that was the memorial of the goodness of God manifested in creation and redemption (Ex.13:9). What Christ said was not a new rite to be performed, but a new meaning of the rite. The emphasis was on doing it in the memory of Christ. Thus, the Eucharist becomes primarily a memorial celebration of the salvific event of Christ.[560] Thus, the believers proclaim his death, resurrection, and ascension until his second coming. The celebrant and the congregation together commemorate the death and resurrection, which is made present in all its saving power. It is a remembrance of the Paschal Mystery of Christ. Through the Eucharist, the Church remembers the great saving act of God in Christ. Thus the Eucharist is the memorial of the New Covenant. Thurian says that the past

---

[557] Connolly and Codrington *Two commentaries on the Jacobite Liturgy*, 52-53.

[558] Witvliet, "The Opening of Worship: Trinity," 15. The liturgical memorial is part of the salvation plan of God, which encompasses past, present and future until the eschaton. Jesus is the primary actor in the liturgy, the one who draws the community into his action of salvation.

[559] Louis Bouyer, *Eucharist: Theology and Spirituality of the Eucharistic Prayer* (Notre Dame: University of Notre Dame, 1968), 84.

[560] T. Elavanal, *The Memorial Celebration* (Kottayam: Poursthya Vidhyapetth, 1989), 118.

event became present or rather each person became a contemporary of the past event.[561] The Eucharist is thus the fulfilment of the commandment of Christ and anamnesis is the recalling or making present the salvific experience of Christ. The MTC believes that the holy elements are not merely a memorial celebration of the salvific events of Christ but that they enact communion with the Risen Lord. The elements in themselves are objectively effective, not depending upon the man who gives them or the people who receive them. Though in faith believers seek the forgiveness of their sins, it is not merely their faith that makes the elements effective, but the presence of Christ. If faith were the reason for the effectiveness, then the Eucharist would be dependent on them rather than on God who accomplished the work of redemption.[562]

The anamnesis in most of the West Syrian anaphoras is addressed to the Son. The epicleses have developed to reflect the incarnational Eucharistic theology and to reflect varied activities of the Holy Spirit.[563] Sebastian Brock has made an analysis of the *epiclesis* in some forty anaphoras and found that most were addressed to the Father and fall into three main segments: (a) An introduction either by the verb "send" or the phrase "may there come" with the Spirit as a subject. (b) The consecratory action of the Spirit, with a variety of verbs. (c) The effects of the consecrated Bread and Wine on the communicants.[564]

2.3.7 - Invocation of the Holy Spirit[565] (*Epiclesis*) - The invocation of the Holy Spirit is an important prayer as far as the Oriental churches are

---

[561] Max Thurian, *Eucharistic Memorial*, vol.1 (London: Lutterworth, 1966), 19.
[562] Poikail, *Eucharist Liturgy*, 113.
[563] Spinks, *Do this in Remembrance of Me*, 163.
[564] Sebastian Brock, "Towards a Typology of the *Epiclesis* in the West Syrian Anaphoras," in *Crossroad of Cultures: Studies in Liturgy and Patristics in Honour of Gabriele Winkler*, eds. Hans-Jurgen Feulner, E Velkovska and Robert F. Taft (Rome: Pontificio Istituto Orientale, 2000), 177.
[565] "May the Holy Spirit sanctify the bread that it may be the body of our Lord Jesus Christ / May the Holy Spirit sanctify the wine in this chalice that it may be the blood of our Lord Jesus Christ." Titus II, *Qurbana Thaksa*, 26. Juhanon, *The Order of the Holy Qurbana*, 21. As the celebrant waves his hands over the bread and wine, he signifies the descent of the Holy Spirit from above and the Holy Spirit's hovering over the Mysteries, as the Third Person did over Jesus in the Jordan at the time of his Baptism. The hands are waved in a fashion to reflect the fluttering of the wings of the Holy Spirit who descended upon the

concerned. In this prayer, the Holy Spirit is invoked to descend upon the bread and wine and to bless and sanctify the oblation.[566] The purity and holiness of the Church is effected by the coming of the Holy Spirit upon its mysteries. The Holy Spirit comes to bless and sanctify so that those who partake in the body and blood may attain sanctification through the forgiveness of sins, the great hope of resurrection from the dead and the new life in the Kingdom of Heaven. This prayer closes with a thanksgiving to God for this wonderful economy of salvation (*madabbranuta*).[567] The Holy Spirit is operative in the Church to fulfil what Christ has already accomplished and to effect in his presence. It is a prayer sanctifying the believers along with the elements.[568] The Holy Spirit is the One who sanctifies, vivifies, and makes everything perfect. According to Cyril of Jerusalem, "for whatever the Holy Spirit has touched are hallowed and changed."[569] During the prayer of the invocation of the Spirit, the celebrant waves his hands over the gifts in a fluttering motion signify the descending of the Holy Spirit. Through this symbolic act, the celebrant affirms the presence of the Holy Spirit and it invokes the attention of the people.

The *epiclesis* is introduced by a petition for mercy, followed by the plea for the Father to send the Spirit. This petition is accompanied by a review of the Holy Spirit's role in salvation history parallel to those for the Father and Son in the pre-and Post-Sanctus sections respectively.[570]The Greek

---

womb of the Virgin Mary and incarnated the Word and who now descends to make the bread and wine truly the Body and Blood of Jesus Christ. Phillip Tovey notes that the *Epiclesis* in the Mar Thoma liturgy is vague or soft and the work of the Holy Spirit is not fully acknowledged. Tovey, *Essays in West Syrian Liturgy*, 92.

[566] This Old Testament allusion; "You need make for me only an altar of earth and sacrifice on it your burnt offering......cause my name to be remembered and I will come to you and bless you." (Ex.20:24).

[567] Jose Kochuparampil, "The Missionary Dimension of the Liturgy in the Anaphora of the Apostles Addai and Mari," *Studia Liturgica* 36, no.2 (2006): 136.

[568] Poikayil, *St. Thomas Christians and their Eucharistic Liturgy*, 109.

[569] Sheerin, *Eucharist*, 69.

[570] Baby Varghese, "The Theological Significance of the Epiklesis in the Liturgy of Saint James" in *Eucharist in Theology and Philosophy: Issues of Doctrinal History in East and West from the Patristic Age to the Reformation*, eds. Istvan Perczel, Reka Forrai and Gyorgy Gereby (Leuven: Leuven University, 2005), 363-80. McGowan, *Eucharistic Epiclesis*, 61-64.

version of the *epiclesis* contains two petitions for the sending of the Spirit using different verbs. The prayer requests the Spirit's descent "upon us and upon these gifts," but the verb in St. James in any case is a form of "send" rather than "come."[571]

   The *epiclesis* is not only a prayer for the sanctification of the bread and wine as the body of Jesus Christ; it is a prayer for the sanctification of the whole congregation. The consecration of the Eucharistic elements is not simply the transformation of the body and blood of Christ, it is also the transformation of the whole universe into the body of Christ.[572] The celebrant further prays that the bodies and souls of the believers may be sanctified. Along with the holy mysteries, the faithful are sanctified and by the descent and the operation of the Holy Spirit (Gal.5:22-23). In the view of the oriental Churches, the sanctification becomes complete not by any particular event but in the total liturgical act.[573]

   The Church fulfils her mission with the constant assistance of the Holy Spirit. In the Eucharist the Church receives the Spirit of Jesus who died and rose from the dead. The apostolic energy of the Church comes from this Spirit. Schmemann remarks that, "the Church is entirely oriented toward the Holy Spirit- the treasury of blessings and giver of life. The entire life of the Church is a thirst for acquisition of the Holy Spirit and for participation in him, and in him of the fullness of grace."[574] Through the indwelling of the Holy Spirit, the believers are sanctified to bear spiritual fruits and be transformed into Christ-like stature. The Church is sanctified to bear fruits in society. It is an invitation for being transformed by the Holy Spirit and bear spiritual fruit for the glory of God. The glorification of God and the sanctification of the faithful are the purpose of worship, especially the celebration of the Holy Qurbana.

---

[571] McGowan, *Eucharistic Epiclesis,* 65. On the relationship between these two anaphoras, see Fenwick, *Anaphoras of St. Basil and St. James.*
[572] George Mathew Kuttiyil, "Liturgy for the 21st Century," in *The Mar Thoma Church: Tradition and Modernity,* 116-117.
[573] Kuttiyil, *The Faith and Sacraments of the Mar Thoma Church,* 61.
[574] Schmemann, *The Eucharist,* 37.

2.3.8 - The Great Intercession - The prayer of intercession is an integral part of the Eucharistic service. There are six sets of petitions. For each section there is a part said aloud by the deacon while the priest prays silently. Then the priest finishes loudly each section and concludes with a doxology.[575] In that sense there are altogether eighteen prayers divided into six themes. These prayers of intercession, said by the deacon: three for the living, i.e. the leaders of the Church, the faithful and political leaders/rulers of the nation. In the second part, the Church remembers the Virgin Mary, the Doctors of the Church and the faithful departed. However, when they remember the Fathers, the prayers are not offered to them, but prayers are made to God that the Church may faithfully pursue their faith.[576] It also gives the idea that the Church is not merely a group of people gathered in the present, but is also the continuation of a tradition that has gone before. The continuity of the faith and practices of the invisible Church is affirmed. Thus, the present Church is an affirmation of the past, as well as a strong pointer to the future. It is a responsibility of the Church to pray for its members to live in the experience of redemption and interceding for others. This part of the anaphora concludes with an eschatological petition and a Christological blessing.

2.3.9 - Second Blessing/ *Rooshmo*[577] - The second solemn blessing is a Christological blessing which is taken from St. Paul's Epistle to Titus 2:13. In this blessing, Jesus Christ is addressed as, the "Great God and saviour." It was a confession of the early Church that Jesus is God and saviour. It is out of His mercy towards human beings that Jesus Christ took flesh and redeemed the world from sin and death. Bar Kepha says about this blessing as "this sacrifice which was sacrificed once upon the cross is itself the mercies, and it is about to be with you now also."[578] By

---

[575] Tovey, *Essays in West Syrian Liturgy*, 45.

[576] In the MTC, they are only remembered and not prayed for. The prayer in the text has been revised in that direction, because reformed theology does not endorse the invocation of the saints and prayers for the dead and to the dead. Kuttiyil, *Eucharist (Qurbana)*, 125.

[577] "The blessing of our Great God and Saviour Jesus Christ (†) be with you all" Titus II, *Qurbana Thaksa*, 30. Juhanon, *The Order of the Holy Qurbana*, 25.

[578] Connolly and Codrington, *Two commentaries on the Jacobite Liturgy*, 66.

164

this blessing, the Church recalls the work of salvation of Jesus Christ and all his dispensations.

2.3.10 - The Litany of Intercession - This litany is mainly for peace and reconciliation in the Church among the faithful, to live out as true Christians for the effect of communion. This is in the use of almost all the liturgies of the Eucharistic celebration of the East. Generally, this litany is a supplication of the Church for its members and the world to live in the experience of the economy of salvation. In the Mystagogical Catechesis, Cyril of Jerusalem says, "When the spiritual sacrifice, the bloodless worship has been completed, over this sacrifice of propitiation, we beseech God for the common peace of the Churches, for the good estate of the world, for the emperors, for the army, for those in sickness, for those who are distressed, for all in the world who need help, we all pray and offer sacrifice."[579]

2.3.11 - Fraction (*Qasya*) - Through the breaking of the bread the Church recalls the sacrificial death of Jesus Christ on the cross for the salvation of the world. The fraction ceremony is a commemoration of the passion, death, and resurrection of Jesus Christ. It recalls the importance of the willingness of breaking fourth into the Kingdom of God in this world. Without breaking, there is no sharing at all. While breaking the bread the celebrant meditate upon the passion of Jesus Christ. The congregation sings a liturgical song during this time. The order of fraction and singing indicates that it is the action of the recalling of the entire dispensation of God through Christ. Later the Church as a whole pronounces the Lord's Prayer.

2.3.12 - Third Blessing[580]- The celebrant blesses the congregation in the name of the Trinity. In this blessing, the sevenfold attributes of the Triune God are explained. The Trinity is confessed as holy, glorious, uncreated, self-existent, eternal, adorable and one in substance. Bar Kepha comments,

---

[579] Sheerin, *Eucharist*, 69.
[580] "May the Grace and Mercy of the Holy and Glorious Trinity, Uncreated (†) Self Existent, Eternal (†) Adorable and One in Essence (†) be with you all forever." Titus II, *Qurbana Thaksa*, 35. Juhanon, *The Order of the Holy Qurbana*, 27.

"He says this to them; these mysteries which have been consecrated and completed and perfected for you, and you are about to receive have been bestowed upon you by the grace of the Holy Trinity since they are not without or apart from the Trinity but are one of the persons of the Trinity that is the Son who became Incarnate."[581]

2.3.13 - Elevation (*Zuyaho*) - After the third solemn blessing, the celebrant elevates the bread and wine (paten and chalice) by saying "holy things are given only to the holy people. The congregation responds by saying only the Triune God is holy and He is with us. With that confidence and assurance, the faithful come forward and kneel before the altar to receive the holy elements. Here the holy mysteries are elevated and thereby the ascension of Christ is recalled. Bar Kepha explains that "the priest elevates and displays the Mysteries crying and saying 'Holy things to the Holy'- That is to say: these mysteries which are holy and life giving, to the holy it is right that they be given."[582] This prayer is a proclamation to prepare the believers to make them aware of the holiness of the mysteries, before they take part in the communion. It is found in almost all the Eastern liturgies.[583] Then the people respond by saying; "One Holy Father, Only Holy Son and One Holy Spirit are Holy'. By this it means, says Bar Kepha: "But the people confess, saying: 'One Holy Father, One Holy Son, One Holy Spirit.' That is, Thou, O priest have said that it is right that these holy things be given to the holy. We confess that we are not holy; and we say that there is none holy save (except) the One Father, and His One Son and the One Spirit who is from Him."[584] In this prayer, the faith of the Church is affirmed that the Father is the creator, the Son is the redeemer, and the Holy Spirit is the One who perfects and fulfils everything.[585]

The faithful enter into a communion with the Triune God through the Holy Qurbana. The presence of the Triune God in the life of the faithful

---

[581] Connolly and Codrington, *Two Commentaries on the Jacobite Liturgy,* 86.
[582] Connolly and Codrington. *Two commentaries on the Jacobite Liturgy,* 86-87.
[583] Moolaveetil, *A Study on the Anaphora,* 245, Kuttiyil, *Eucharist (Qurbana),* 139.
[584] Connolly and Codrington, *Two commentaries on the Jacobite Liturgy,* 87.
[585] Baby Varghese, "West Syrian Anaphor as an expression of the Trinitarian Doctrine," *Harp* 4, no.1-3 (1991): 215-223.

is affirmed here. This section of prayer is addressed to the adorable name of the Trinity who holds universal authority and power - who is worthy of praise from every mouth, and thanksgiving from every tongue because the Trinity created the world. The Church offers thanks to God for all the favours received through salvific act of Christ. This part expresses the great love of God underpinning everything: God created the world by His grace and its inhabitants by His compassion. The creative forces of God consist of grace and compassion, which are to be reciprocated by creation i.e. all inhabitants of the earth. The anaphora highlights that all are bound to praise and thank God for this creative and providential grace and love. The universal dimension of the power of God as well as of the praise and glory are highlighted here. The text affirms the existential relation of all creation to God. It prepares a solid ground for the missionary thrust.[586] God's extension of mercy and great grace towards human beings is expressed in the act of redemption. A Trinitarian mission is unfolded step by step in this part of anaphora: creation, redemption and the sending of the Son. The mission begins in Heaven, in the context of the heavenly liturgy, and towards which the mission is directed.[587] Another aspect of this affirmation is the "presence of Trinity" in the life of the believer. It is by the assurance of the presence of God, that the faithful are strengthened to cooperate with God in His mission of salvation. The Church proclaims this reality in and through the celebration of the liturgy.[588] The universal character of the mission of the Trinity is unfolded through the three Trinitarian blessings where the actions of creation by the Father, redemption by the Son, and sanctification by the Holy Spirit are recounted.

As the holy mysteries are brought down from the altar to the congregation for the communion, the second coming of Christ is foreshadowed and the faithful are reminded of the glorious second coming of Christ. As he turns from the altar, the celebrant holds the Mysteries with his hands crossed to

---

[586] Jose Kochuparampil, "The Missionary Dimension of the Liturgy in the Anaphora of the Apostles Addai and Mari," *Studia Liturgica* 36, no.2 (2006), 130-131.
[587] Kochuparampil, "The Missionary Dimension of the Liturgy," 133.
[588] Kuttiyil, *Eucharist (Qurbana),* 140-142.

signify that these are the united body and blood of the crucified Christ for the remission of sins.

2.3.14 - Reception of the Holy Elements - This is the final stage of the sacramental pilgrimage. At this time, the celebrant partakes of communion and then distributes it to the believers by saying "the body and blood of our Lord Jesus Christ, broken and shed on the cross for the forgiveness of sins, is given to the health of body and soul."[589] The act of participation in the Holy Qurbana is not merely partaking in the death and resurrection experience of Christ. It is also an expression of Christian life in the world as to how it should continue to be in the world. The goal of the mission of the Church is to have full communion between God and human beings, and between human beings, expressed through a life of love and sharing. The celebration of the Eucharist initiates this communion. In the Eucharist, the faithful are united with God and among themselves by receiving the holy mysteries. By participating in this communion the faithful commit themselves to restore the Divine goodness to the whole of creation.

2.3.15 - The Prayer of Thanksgiving - Through this prayer, the celebrant offers thanks to God on behalf of the congregation for enabling them to participate in the heavenly banquet. The priest beseeches abundant blessings for the assembled believers. The liturgy affirms that the Trinitarian God is the source of all blessings and grace. This means, God will bless those who are faithful. Here blessings are not used in a material term, but as the presence and guidance of God in the life of the faithful. The participation and reception of the Eucharist is a means of divine grace and blessing. In this prayer, the Church remembers the life and witness of the people who remain in Christ (saints) and considers them as blessed people. Likewise in this prayer, the celebrant prays for the spiritual effects of the Eucharist.

2.3.16 - Final Blessing and Dismissal[590] - With the fourth blessing the service of anaphora ends. Here by touching the *thronos*, the holy seat of

---

[589] Titus II, *Qurbana Thaksa*, 40.

[590] "My beloved brethren, I commend you to the grace and blessings of the Holy and Glorious Trinity. Depart now in peace (and serve the Lord (†) with the gifts......depart in peace, (†) filled with gladness and rejoicing." Titus II, *Qurbana Thaksa*, 44. Juhanon, *The Order of the Holy Qurbana*, 34. In this blessing, the faithful are dismissed with the

divine sacrifice of grace and mercy, the celebrant turns to the congregation and pronounces a Trinitarian blessing by the signing of the cross. The faithful are reminded that they are saved by the victorious cross of the Lord and sealed with the seal of holy baptism and assures them that the Trinitarian God will forgive their sins and comfort their souls. Later, the celebrant beseeches prayers of the congregation to receive the divine mercy and help. This is known as the commendation.[591] Through this commendation, the believers are reminded of the Economy of Salvation through Christ. This blessing commends them to go to the world with peace and lead a life worthy of their calling. This blessing entrusts the people with the responsibility of continued Christian life and mission in the world. The celebrant dismisses the congregation with the blessing of God and assures them of the guidance of the Trinity. This liturgical action points towards its mission of living out what it has celebrated.

This blessing asks that the Eucharist may be fruitful in producing moral, spiritual and eschatological effects. The participants, who are entrusted with the task of bringing about these effects is evident and of revealing to the world the new face of humanity, that of the Lord's disciples. The blessing in the name of the Trinity is summarized in a significant way by which the richness of God's gifts have been savoured during the Eucharistic celebration. It offers these gifts as a *viaticum*[592] in which the congregation partakes and communicates to the world.

Finally, the formula of dismissal "Go in peace" expresses both an invitation to cherish the gift received and also a challenge to live the

---

reassurance of salvation in Christ and commitment to Him through Baptism, a reassurance extended not only to those present, but encompassing all who have been baptized into Christ, both near and far, living and those who are resting in Christ.

[591] Kuttiyil, *Eucharist (Qurbana)*, 153.

[592] The term *viaticum* is taken from the Latin, which means food for the journey. Here this term is used not in the traditional meaning of a food which strengthens the Christian for the passage though death to life in the assurance of hope of the resurrection, rather, it is a spiritual food which gives strength and nourishment to the believer to cooperate with God in His redemptive mission.

Church's mission.[593] When we observe the liturgical celebration, there are two complimentary movements, the movement of ascension, and the movement of return. The Eucharist begins as ascension toward the throne of God, toward the Kingdom, where the visible and invisible Church join together and offer worship to God. The second movement begins with a return to the world, when the celebrant says "let us depart in peace" as he leaves the altar and leads the congregation outside the church building.[594] Schmemann comments that when our liturgy ends, we are again in the beginning, where our ascent to the table of Christ, in his Kingdom, began. We depart into life in order to witness and to fulfil our common ministry, common liturgy- in communion of the Holy Spirit.[595]

3 - Signs and Symbols in the Liturgy and its Theological Significance

In the Oriental Orthodox tradition, the signs and symbols play a major role in communicating the Divine Liturgy. It gives a visible form of the invisible reality and thereby injects life into the worship. The immanent presence of God has been portrayed through the symbolic representation in the worship. The most important feature of symbols lie in their richness of expression.[596] According to Heising, symbolism is "the very life breath of religion. It is through symbols that religions survive in our midst and through symbols that we gain access to the religious life of past or alien cultures."[597] Now signs and symbols have integrated considerably into the worship life of the congregation. This is because people are so attached to their representations. The liturgy is both a dramatic and symbolic re-living of the events of salvation. It is an invitation to the worshipper to share in the life of heaven which the saving events made possible. The

---

[593] Joachim Meisner, "Eucharist and Evangelization," *Christ Light of Nations* (Sherbrooke: Paulines, 1994), 73.
[594] Ion Bria, *The Liturgy After the Liturgy: Mission and Witness from an Orthodox Perspective* (Geneva: World Council of Churches, 1996), 34.
[595] Schmemann, *The Eucharist,* 245.
[596] Thomas Fawcett, The Symbolic Language of Religion (London: SCM, 1970), 28.
[597] Mircea Eliade, ed., *The Encyclopedia of Religion,* vol.14 (London: Mac Millan, 1997), 198.

words and actions employed in the liturgy signify the spiritual realities which lie behind them, and can be appropriated by the believer as they are purified and initiated in order to become participants in the heavenly liturgy.[598] Through sight, smell, sound, words, taste, gestures and idea one can experience symbols in the religious traditions. Through the symbols and symbolic actions, the faithful experience the richness of worship and the presence of God.

The liturgy of St. James is enriched with different signs, symbols and various verbal and non-verbal liturgical actions. These signs and symbols stand for something true and they communicate to the people. One cannot express all the feelings through words, which is why the Church use material symbols or symbolic actions in order to communicate spiritual truths. The symbols, which are non-verbal in nature, are called non-verbal symbols. The non-verbal signs and symbols are helpful to communicate any sort of meaning which is not accomplished through words. This is mostly accomplishing through material symbols, body movements, gestures, facial expressions, postures, touch and smell. A detailed note on the signs, symbols, gestures and postures employed in the liturgy is mentioned below.

3.1 - Symbols in the Holy Qurbana

During the worship, the people are able to have communion with God and, moreover, experience the presence of God through symbols and symbolic

---

[598] The symbolic meaning of the Eucharist was explored in a succession of commentaries written by some of the great figures of patristic theology: Theodore of Mopsuestia, Dionysius the Areopagite, Maximus the Confessor, Germanus Patriarch of Constantinople, Nicholas of Andida, Symeon of Thessaloniki, and Nicholas Cabasilas are few of them. There were two methods of interpretation. The first is that, at the Eucharist, we are led to union with God. This may be called the mystagogical approach and was set out by Dionysius. The whole action of the Eucharist points towards the results of Christ's work of salvation in uniting us to God. Another understanding is a literal approach to the Bible mainly by the Antiochian theologians. This is a symbolic re-enactment of the salvific act of Christ. The point of a symbolic approach to liturgy is that it does not set out to explain the simple plain significance of the service. Instead it explores and meditates on the words and the actions, and discovers different layers of meaning. This enables the worshipper to find different ways in which he/she can appropriate and make sense of the rich action of the liturgy. Hence according to John Binns the two different styles of symbolic interpretation belong together. Binns, *An Introduction to the Christian Orthodox Churches*, 51-54.

actions. In the Eucharistic celebration of the Mar Thoma Church a person gets involved with his/her five senses and that helps him/her to experience the message, i.e., hearing (language, music), seeing (pictures, sign), touching (kissing, stroking), tasting (bread and wine) and smelling (incense). All these give a life to worship. The liturgy of St. James maintains an ongoing dialogue between the celebrant and the worshippers through its symbolic richness and so it can be called the liturgy of the people. The following are some of the important symbolic expressions in the Holy Qurbana.

3.1.1 - Cross - Cross has been given a central place in the Mar Thoma worship. It becomes a symbol for the saving act of God and the sign of the cross is a seal for Christians. There are different interpretations about the meaning of the cross. It is a means of salvation, freedom from slavery of sin, reconciliation, victory over cosmic powers, evil and death, hope and life to the dead are the meanings given in the liturgy of St. James.[599] All these interpretations give a kind of eschatological hope to the worshipper. This hope is not only for the individual, but also for the whole universe. The liturgical prayers in the anaphora of St. James depict the idea of cosmic salvation and the symbol and signing of the cross stands for the liberation of humankind from sin and death. The barren cross on the altar symbolizes the divine presence of the resurrected Christ and it gives hope to the faithful. It affirms the resurrection of Christ and the Church lives with the eschatological hope of His second coming to save the world.[600] The cross placed on the altar is not an object of worship, but a symbolic representation of the salvific act of Christ. The Church proclaims that Christ is the centre and ultimate hope for the people. The MTC uses the cross, not the crucifix. The cross without the corpus signifies the risen Lord Jesus. Hence it is also referred to as the "Easter-Cross" (Col.1:19-20).

Jesus redeemed the world through his death on the cross. The message about the cross for those who are being saved is the power of God (1

---

[599] Kadavil P. Paul, *The Eucharist Service of the Syrian Jacobite Church of Malabar: The Meaning and the Interpretation.* 2nd ed. (Piscataway: Gorgias, 2003), 89.
[600] Kuriakose Moolayil, *Suriyani Sabha Charithravum Sathayangalum* (Malayalam) (Thiruvalla: Christava Sahitya Samithi, 1982), 38.

172

Cor.1:18). Cross points to the ultimate victory of Jesus over death, sin and all sorts of fear. Cross is a symbol of salvation. It reminds us of the intimate love of God for the world and God's redeeming plan of salvation through Christ. In the signing of the cross the faithful are assured of the gift of salvation. This liturgical act motivates them to be channels of peace and reconciliation. The symbol of the cross is an invitation to participate in the redemptive action of God by reflecting the nature of Christ which is love, compassion and forgiveness.

3.1.2 - Candles - The lighted candles symbolize the presence of God during the worship. God is the source of light and reminds the believers that they are called out to be the light of the world. It had been introduced in the Church with a specific purpose and it stands for communicating the truth. "This has been a practice of the early Church because when they conducted the Holy Qurbana in caves and houses during the time of persecution, candles were used for giving light. Moreover, it was given a theological significance as well and later on, it became a tradition for them to continue."[601] In continuation of this ancient practice, the MTC uses candles during the worship. The candles lighted at the beginning of the Holy Qurbana symbolize the presence of God, who is the source of light.[602] The wax of the candle is made out of honey, which is collected from different kinds of flowers. It signifies the unity of believers irrespective of their differences. The Church is commissioned to enlighten others by renouncing its own identity. It is a willingness to die for others because the mission and life of Jesus was service for others. As candles provide light, it represents the Lord Jesus Christ (Jn.8:12, 1:9). In the same way the faithful are reminded of their vocation to renounce themselves to enlighten others through a sacrificial life. The number of candles is not fixed in the MTC. Generally twelve candles are placed, six each, on both sides of the altar with a cross at the centre, which symbolizes the twelve apostles of Christ

---

[601] Mathew David, *Vishudha Qurbana- Maanavodharathinulla Daivapadathat* (Malayalam) (Bombay: Mar Ignatius Orthodox Fellowship, 1995), 54.
[602] M J Joseph, ed., *Gleanings* (Madras: Printon, 1994), 29.

and also the twelve tribes of Israel. However, owing to space and other constraints, some churches have less than twelve candles.

3.1.3 - Incense - The use of incense is one of the key factors in the Holy Qurbana. It was used in ancient days to pay honour and respect. It has been used for the solemn blessing during the Holy Qurbana, which symbolizes the elevation of prayers to God as incense. Dara comments that, "it symbolises the divine actions which are granted to the children of the Holy Church, and thus all the filthiness of sin and its passions shall be removed from them."[603] The fragrance of the incense is meant to do more than merely appeal to the sense of smell. It denotes the offering of a sweet smelling sacrifice of God (Lk.1:11) and the Gospel. Here the incense is closely related to forgiveness of sins. The incense is a means to invoke the presence of God. It is believed that, when the Church uses incense, the prayer will be taken to heaven as a fragrance.[604] The use of incense reminds the faithful of their responsibility for propagating the Gospel like a sweet smelling sacrifice.[605]

3.1.4 - *Chittola* - In Syriac "*Chittola*" means is richly coloured cloth. The *thronos* is covered with a richly coloured cloth which represents the glory of God. It usually has three divisions, signifying the Trinity and a cross in its centre represents the Lord Jesus Christ. There could be embroidery work generally signifying wine, bread, dove, and the cross. The dove, if portrayed, signifies the Holy Spirit.[606]

3.1.5 - *Tablito* - It is considered as a "portable altar," that is a consecrated wooden plank. It symbolizes the cross on which Christ was crucified. It is a reminder that the Holy Qurbana is a sacrifice without blood. From the fourth century onwards, the Church used a wooden cross for the celebration

---

[603] "The fire in the censor and the smoke symbolize the holy apostles; the fire indicates the gift of the Holy Spirit which is in them; the smoke, the preaching of the Gospel which they announced and by it they have rooted out the filthiness of the idolatry from humanity." Dara, "Commentary on the Eucharist," 47-48.

[604] Varghese, *West Syrian Liturgical Theology*, 161.

[605] Johns Abraham Konat, *Visudha Yakobinte Kurbana Taksa: Anushtannangalum Vyakyanangalum Cherthathu* (Malayalam) (Kottayam: Malankara Orthodox Church Publications, 2011), 8-9.

[606] Konat, *Visudha Yakobinte Kurbana Taksa*, 5-6.

174

of the Holy Qurbana.[607] At the consecration of a new church building, the Metropolitan of the Church consecrates the *tablito* for the particular parish. Each *tablito* has an inscription by the consecrating bishop that reads "For the Glory of God in the name of the Father, the Son and the Holy Spirit." It is consecrated with Holy Mooron by the bishop. This represents the unity of the Church and the relation between the parish and the head of the Church. The Church is a community united in the love of God. By using the wooden portable altar in the celebration of the Qurbana, the Church affirms apostolic faith and the unity of all believers in Christ. The paten and chalice are placed upon the Tablita. A *viri-kootu* is a richly embroidered cloth that is spread over the *thronos*. The *tablito* is placed at the centre on the *viri-kootu* in the pouch. The *viri-kootu* is spread only at the time of the liturgical celebration by the celebrant.[608]

3.1.6 - Vessels and Vestments - The sacred vessel and vestments used in the liturgy have symbolic meanings. The vestments signify the dignity and righteousness with which the priest is dressed up, in order that he may stand worthily in the presence of God, representing the people.[609]

3.2 - Postures and Gestures

3.2.1 - Standing Facing the East - Standing and facing towards East while praying was a normal practice of prayer among the Jews and the early Church. Like other Oriental Churches the MTC followed this custom and it is still practiced. It means facing the cross and expresses the joy of the Church in the resurrection of Christ. The cross embodies in itself the whole theology of the East. Orientation in the Eucharistic liturgy is not just a waiting turned to the East; rather it is the movement towards the East.[610] As an oriental mark of respect and adoration, the faithful stand and worship the Lord who is present with the congregation. It also indicates

---

[607] Konat, *Visudha Yakobinte Kurbana Taksa,* 6.
[608] Dara, "Commentary on the Eucharist," 34-35. In this commentary, John of Dara gives a detailed description of the symbolic meaning of the articles used in the liturgical space.
[609] Joseph, *Gleanings,* 29.
[610] Louis Bouyer, *Liturgy and Architecture* (Notre Dame; University Press, 1967), 34-35.

an active participation of the laity in the liturgy along with the clergy who also stand.[611] There is an eschatological significance in the facing towards the east. "For as the lightning comes from the East and flashes as far as the West, so will be the coming of the Son of Man" (Mt.24:27). According to Bouyer, in the liturgical celebration, the most dynamic activity of the early assembly is its eastward movement expressed all throughout the liturgy. In the human-divine encounter, orientation becomes the most dynamic human attitude.[612] The position of Eden being in the East, the idea of facing Paradise during worship is the longing for paradise. "And the Lord God planted a garden in Eden, in the East; and there he put the man whom he had formed" (Gen.2:8). So, longing for Christ and longing for communion with God in paradise, are a symbolic meaning of facing East during worship. The bowing down of the heads during worship symbolises the bowing down of the angels and the spirits who worship the divine. The bowing down of people during the worship indicates submission and thereby beseeches the blessings of God.[613]

3.2.2 - Signing of the Cross - The faithful make the sign of the cross with three fingers of the right hand, the thumb and the second finger joined below the first finger. This shows that there are three distinct persons in the Trinity of One God. It communicates the idea that the Son of God came down from heaven, saved the people from the darkness of the left, and brought to the light on the right. The signing of the cross reminds one of the salvific act of Christ.

3.2.3 - Celebrant - The Church offers the Eucharist to God the Father, and Christ is the celebrant of this great event. The Church represents the whole of creation and Christ is the redeemer of all creation. It is believed that Christ is the one who first offered communion. Because of the leadership of Christ, prayers are addressed to God the Father. It is believed

---

[611] George Mathew Kuttuyil. *Sabhayude Kudashakalum Aaradanayaum: Oru Padanam* (Malayalam) (Thiruvalla: Mar Thoma Yuvajana Sakhyam, 1995), 56.
[612] Pauly Maniyattu, *Heaven On Earth: The Theology of Liturgical Space-Time in the East Syrian Qurbana* (Rome: Mar Thoma Yogam, 1995), 184.
[613] Bar Salibi, *Commentary of Eucharist*, 52.

that the priest is the representative of the people as well as Jesus Christ. The deacon is a representative of the serving Church of God. The choir represents the heavenly choir who praise God always. The believers are the representatives of the whole of humanity and the Church. The worship is complete only when these groups join together. According to Timothy Ware, the liturgical celebration embraces two worlds: the celestial and the temporal worlds. For both in heaven and on earth, the Liturgy is one and the same - one altar, one sacrifice, and one presence. In every celebration, the faithful are taken up into the heavenly realm and the invisible Church joins with the visible Church for the celebration of the mysteries.[614]

4 - Theology of the Eucharist in the Mar Thoma Church

The Eucharist is fundamental to the life and ministry of all Christian Churches, which is an act of worship, an object of worship and an experience of worship. In one sense, it is the vehicle of grace. In and through the Holy Qurbana, the Church celebrates the paschal mystery of Christ and proclaims the Divine Dispensation - the *Madabranutha*.[615] In every Eucharist, the faithful encounter the risen Christ mystically. This encountering experience reveals them new truth about life and its mission. The Eucharist is a continuation and participation in Christ's sacrifice on Calvary. This is not a repetitive sacrifice of Christ, but a continuation and the participation of the same sacrifice. Through the Eucharist, Christ's sacrifice becomes a present day reality, so that people can experience this through partaking in the elements.[616] An analysis of the Mar Thoma liturgy reveals that, the reformed theology of the Western Europe made a great influence in the revision of the Eucharistic liturgy and the formation of the

---

[614] Ware, *Orthodox Liturgy of the Pre-Sanctified*, 270.

[615] George Mathew Kuttiyil, *Eucharist (Qurbana): The Celebration of the Economy of Salvation (Madabranutha)* (Kottayam: Paurastya Vidhyapitham, 1999), 162.

[616] Here the priest represents Jesus Christ and offers symbolically the bread and wine to God. Thus, the priest sacramentally re-enacts the oblation of His passion, which the saviour originally presented to the Father. Therefore, the Eucharist is the bloodless sacrifice. Hence, the Eucharist is not a sacrifice but it is an enactment of the same sacrifice, through which Christ offered Himself to God.

doctrines of the MTC. The following are the general understanding of the Eucharistic theology of the MTC:

The Eucharist is a memorial or anamnesis of the Christ-event. Jesus commands his followers, "Do this in remembrance of me" (Lk.22:19). It is much more than a ritualistic repetition of the past. It is rather a literal re-membering of Christ's body, a knitting together of the body of Christ by the participation of many in His sacrifice. The Church gratefully remembers the salvific-work of Jesus Christ that means the believers commemorate the whole life of Jesus Christ - from incarnation to his second coming.[617] In the Eucharist, through eating and drinking of the bread and wine, Christ grants communion with Himself.[618] The Eucharist meal is accepted not simply as remembrance but as participation, participation in the sufferings of Jesus, participation in the Kingdom of God, participation in the relationship with Jesus shared with the Father, and belief in the resurrection of Jesus.[619]

The Eucharist is a comprehensive act of thanksgiving.[620] By celebrating it, the Church offers thanks to the Father for everything accomplished through the birth and the mission of Jesus Christ on earth. The Eucharist is the benediction by which the Church expresses its thankfulness for all God's benevolence. Through the Eucharist, the Church speaks on behalf of the whole creation.[621] The Eucharist is a celebration of the gratitude to the Father Almighty for sending Jesus to the world and his self-offering for the salvation of the whole creation. It is a celebration of commitment on the part of all who participate to sacrifice themselves for Christ and His people.

---

[617] Titus II Mar Thoma Metropolitan, *Qurbana Thaksa of the Malankara Mar Thoma Syrian Church*, 6th ed. (Thiruvalla: Mar Thoma, 2001), 11.

[618] God Himself acts, giving life to the body of Christ and renewing each member, in accordance with Christ's promise. Each baptized member of the Church receives the assurance of forgiveness of sins through the Eucharist. Titus II, *Qurbana Thaksa*, 40.

[619] Brant Pitre, *Jesus and the Jewish Roots of the Eucharist* (New York: Image, 2011), 32.

[620] Titus II, *Qurbana Thaksa*, 23. Max Thurian, ed. *Churches Response to BEM: Official Response to the Baptism, Eucharist, and Ministry Text*, vol. IV (Geneva: Faith and Order Paper, 137, WCC, 1987), 8.

[621] *Baptism, Eucharist and Ministry, Faith and Order*. Paper No. III (Geneva: WCC, 1982), 10-11.

The Eucharist is the foretaste of His Parousia and of the final Kingdom.[622] It proclaims the hope that in the future all faithful gather at the eternal banquet table of the Lord. The Eucharist is a heavenly meal. It opens up the vision of the divine rule, which has been promised as the final renewal of creation, and is a foretaste of it.[623] It is a proclamation of the promise of never ending unity with God. [624]

The Eucharist has an eschatological dimension, which includes communion with all saints and martyrs. The Eucharistic celebration demands reconciliation and sharing among all those who are regarded as brothers and sisters in one family of God. It is a constant challenge in search for appropriate relationships in social, economic and political life.[625] It also proclaims the mission and vision for a harmonious world. Whenever the Church celebrates the Eucharist, she upholds the eschatological hope of a final union with God. It always contains an eternal dimension, the promise of never ending unity with God.[626] During the Eucharistic meal, in the eating and drinking of the bread and wine, Christ grants communion with himself. God Himself acts, giving life to the body of Christ and renewing each member, in accordance with Christ's promise, each baptized member of the body, the Church receives in the Eucharist the assurance of the forgiveness of sins (Mt.26:28) and the pledge of eternal life (Jn.6:51-58).

The Eucharist is a celebration of the victory of life over death, forgiveness of sin, and unity in place of division. In Christ, the Church celebrates his unique role as the redeemer, which is the central theme of the Eucharistic liturgy. It is also the celebration of the relation between God

---

[622] The Church gratefully recalling God's might acts of redemption beseeches God to give the benefits of these acts to every human being. In the memorial of the Eucharist, the Church offers its intercession in communion with Christ.

[623] "In the Eucharist, the Christians are called to be in solidarity with the outcaste and to become signs of the love of Christ who lived, sacrificed himself for all, and now gives himself in the Eucharist. The very celebration of the Eucharist is an instance of the Church's participation in God's mission to the world." *BEM.*15.

[624] Kuttiyil, *Eucharist (Qurbana)*, 20.

[625] All kinds of justice, racism, separation, and lack of freedom are radically challenged when people share in the body and blood of Christ. The Eucharist involves the believer in the central event of the world's history. BEM.14.

[626] Kuttiyil, *Eucharist (Qurbana)*, 20.

and human beings, and at the same time the relations among the faithful people through the person of Christ.[627]

The Eucharist is mainly an epiclesis. The Holy Spirit makes the crucified and risen Christ present to the believers in the Eucharistic meal, fulfilling the promise contained in the words of institution. The presence of Christ is clearly the centre of the Eucharist, and the promise contained in the Words of Institution is therefore fundamental to the festivity.[628] The above meaning of the Eucharist deserves much commendation because it links the Eucharist with each person of the Trinity and it links the believer with the past, the present and the future.

5 - Conclusion

The Eucharist is the central act of the Church. It is always the End, the sacrament of the Parousia, and yet it is always the beginning, the starting point of the mission (Lk.24:8). The Church is called out to witness the resurrection of Christ. By the celebration of the Eucharist, the Church proclaims the salvific act of Jesus Christ. An analysis of the liturgy of St. James reveals that, there is an inseparable connection between the Eucharist and mission. The prayers in the liturgy affirm the missionary nature of the Church. It begins with the sending of Jesus Christ, and continues with the work of the Holy Spirit, the work of apostles, prophets, martyrs, the confessors, saints and through all the faithful members of the Church, who have been signed with the seal of baptism. This reiterates the missionary character of the Church, and the responsibility of all baptised persons are reaffirmed. This liturgy provides a Trinitarian model of mission. It affirms that, the mission of the Church is an extension of the mission of the Triune God, which is revealed in the life of Christ by the power of the Holy Spirit. In the Holy Qurbana, the transmission of the life of communion that

---

[627] Kuttiyil, *Eucharist (Qurbana,* 25.
[628] Titus II, *Qurbana Thaksa,* 26. It is the virtue of the living word of Christ and by the power of the Holy Spirit that the bread and wine become the sacramental signs of Christ's body and blood. The Holy Spirit through the Eucharist gives a foretaste of the Kingdom of God; the Church receives the life of the new creation and the assurance of the Lord's return. *BEM.*13

exists in the Trinity is experienced. This enables the Church to continue the mission of the God in this world.[629] The Trinitarian dimension of the liturgy shows how the faithful community can be in relation with God and with their fellow beings. It is a twofold relationship: vertical relation of the faithful to God and the horizontal relation of the faithful to fellow beings.

---

[629] Karl Muller, Theo Sundermeier, Stephen B. Bevans, Richard H. Bliese, eds., *Dictionary of Mission: Theology, History, Perspectives* (New York: Orbis, 1999), 435.

Chapter 7

Missional Aspects in the Eucharistic Liturgy

The liturgy of St. James is enriched with many missiological themes. An analysis of the prayers, signs and symbols reiterates the missional aspect deposited in the liturgy. Following are the major missiological themes reflected in the liturgy which are categorized under six titles such as mission as reconciliation, mission as incarnation, mission as intercession, mission as eschatological, mission as liberation, and mission as transformation. As mentioned earlier, the Church is commissioned to propagate the gospel and to make disciples of all nations. The Holy Spirit strengthens the believers to participate with God in His mission of salvation through Christ. The celebration of the Eucharist reminds the faithful about their Christian vocation and responsibility. It is a fuel in their mission journey. The following are the major missional aspects in the anaphora of St. James.

1 - Reconciliation Aspect of Mission
Reconciliation is an important theological concept in the New Testament in connection with the mission of Jesus Christ. It is primarily the communication of the message that the death of Christ on Cross established peace between God and humanity (creation). The ultimate purpose of the mission of Jesus was to restore the broken relationship between the creation and the Creator, which happened because of the disobedience of Adam and Eve in the Garden of Eden (Gen.3:1-10). Jesus, through his atoning sacrifice on Calvary, made peace with God. The Triune God, in Christ, has reconciled the world to Himself. This divine reconciliation is further expressed in a ministry of reconciliation, whereby God has entrusted the message of reconciliation to the Church as ambassadors of

Christ. Their service as ministers of reconciliation is intrinsically bound to God's act of reconciliation and righteousness, a gracious gift freely given, with no distinctions attached - since God is one (Rom.3:21-30). For Paul, the ministry of reconciliation is connected with the Greek word *parakalein* - which implies consolation, exhortation, and encouragement. These are the central ideas of the Pauline mission and praxis (1 Cor.14:3, 31).[630] Peace and reconciliation are mandatory to worship of God in spirit and truth. Jesus says: So if you are offering your gift at the altar and there remember that your brother has something against you, leave your gift there before the altar and go. First be reconciled to your brother, and then come and offer your gift (Mt.5:23, 24). This paradigm of reconciliation entails also a kenotic dimension. Pauls exhorts that "Christians should be Christ-like, doing nothing from selfish ambition or conceit, but in humility regarding others as better than themselves" (Phil.2:3, Mk.8:35, Lk.9:23). Paradoxically, weakness may in fact be the utmost strength, and at the Last Supper, Jesus instructs his disciples that greatness is to be "as one who serves" (Lk. 22:27, 22:24-27).

1.1 - Reconciliation in the Liturgy

Reconciliation aspect of the mission is strongly rooted in the liturgy. The Eucharistic liturgy points to the need of reconciling with God and human beings. This is similar to two sides of the same coin. Reconciliation with God is possible through repentance. Participation in the liturgy exhorts the faithful to have reconciliation with God and human beings.[631] The core of the preparatory service is confessional in nature which helps the celebrant to be reconciled with God for celebrating the Eucharist. The recital of Psalms 51, promeion, sedro and following prayers[632] enumerate this aspect strongly. The prayers in the *ethro* emphasise the significance

---

[630] Jacques Matthey, "Reconciliation as God's Mission: Church as reconciling community," *Theology Digest* 52, no.2 (Summer 2005): 111-118.
[631] Titus II, *Qurbana Thaksa*, 22.
[632] "At your door I knock and from Your treasure-store, O Lord, I ask for mercy......Protect us under the wings of Your mercy" Titus II, *Qurbana Thaksa*, 4. Juhanon, *The Order of the Holy Qurbana*, 3.

of reconciliation of the whole of creation.[633] Reconciliation can be effected only by God. Since God's mission includes all of humanity and creation, different people and movements in the service of justice and peace and care for the creation can be considered 'called' and in this sense are active in God's mission. The societal process of reconciliation is fundamental because they are involved in the necessary healing of wounds, memories and identities, healing which is demanded for building peace in the sense of the biblical "Shalom." Whenever Christians are involved in these processes, they answer their call to the ministry of peace[634] (Rom.12, 1 Thess. 5).

The confessional prayer before the celebration of anaphora invites the congregation to repentance and reconciliation with God and thereby human beings. The prayer before the Kiss of Peace and the exchange of peace signify reconciliation with brothers. There are two aspects in the reconciliation, that is, vertical and horizontal. The vertical reconciliation stands for reconciliation with God and the horizontal reconciliation stands for reconciliation with others, which means reconciliation with whole creation. The cross is the culmination of these two relationships, that is, the source of reconciliation. The greeting 'peace be with you all' denotes the reconciled nature of the Church. The first blessing, an invitation to share the divine responsibility, is addressed to a reconciled community. It is indicated in the first prayer of anaphora - prayer for peace. This prayer is for peace and reconciliation in the Church. Through the prayer of confession, the community is reconciled to God and through the act of the Kiss of Peace, peace and reconciliation are passed on to the community.[635]

In the Eucharistic liturgy, *rooshmo* (blessing) and the signing of the cross are an expression of reconciliation. There are mainly three blessings in the liturgy. Each *rooshmo* is preceded by blessing of peace - "peace be with you." Throughout the gospel, it portrays that the resurrected Christ

---

[633] "Have mercy, O Lord. Reconcile the whole creation to Yourself.....an acceptable sacrifice of praise and thanksgiving." Titus II, *Qurbana Thaksa,* 5. Juhanon, *The Order of the Holy Qurbana,* 3.
[634] Matthey, "Reconciliation as God's Mission," 112.
[635] Eapen Varghese, "Missional Vision in the Liturgy of St. James," in *St. James Liturgy: A Liturgical Study,* ed. Shaiju P. John (Thiruvalla: Christava Sahitya Samithi, 2013), 18-19.

greeted the disciples with this greeting (Jn.20:19,21,26). It indicates the significance of the cross and resurrection in the redeeming mission of Jesus Christ. St. Paul writes, "for he himself is our peace, who has made us both one and has broken down in his flesh the dividing wall of hostility by abolishing the law of commandments expressed in the ordinances, that he might create in himself one new man in place of the two, so making peace, and might reconcile us both to God in one body through the cross, thereby killing the hostility."[636] The greeting "peace be with you" also indicates Jesus' victory over death and enmity. This victory is passed on to the faith community through the greeting. It enjoins that the community continuously to work out salvation through victory over forces of death and reconciliation (Phil.2:12). In the West Syrian liturgical tradition, peace is always connected with "peace and reconciliation." The term *Slomo* means peace and *Shyno* means reconciliation. Therefore, peace and reconciliation go together and there is no peace without reconciliation. The faith community is always reminded to cherish the peace of God attained through the cross and the resurrection of Christ. Worship is a celebration of peace and reconciliation. Through peace and reconciliation the Church is one with God and one with each other; not in an ideal way but always by renewing and rejuvenating the relationship. The Church is commissioned to the mission of reconciliation through the blessing - "peace be with you." At the same time, the celebrant blesses peace existent in a reconciled community. The mission of the Church is to be a channel of peace and reconciliation in a world as is. Family, Church, society, nations, and the environment are the victims of violence and hatred today. These are some of the areas where peace and reconciliation are needed. The Church is a reconciled community which must work for peace and reconciliation within the self, family, Church, society and for the entire creation. Peace

---

[636] Eph.2:14-16. Paul called his work' the ministry of reconciliation, the cross being the means by which the reconciliation is accomplished (Rom.5:8) the mainspring of this conviction lies in the love of God, reached out to the concrete human situation in which humankind is alienated from the image and spirit of God. Dean S. Gilliland, *Pauline Theology and Mission Practice (*Michigan: Baker, 1983), 13, 25.

and reconciliation are not given as a finished product; but the faithful need to work for it continuously. Hence the greeting is repeated on several occasions in the anaphora.[637]

1.2 - Mission of Reconciliation

We the Church are summoned to be the ambassadors of reconciliation. Today the Church is a fragmented Church. There are divisions in the name of doctrines, rituals, practices, and cultures. The fact that the good news of reconciliation preached by Christians is divided among themselves weakens their witnessing. In a world torn by enmity and hatred, discrimination and inequality, injustice and poverty, war and terrorism the reconciliation paradigm of mission is of high importance on both local and global levels. The mission of reconciliation is to be affirmed. Christians should therefore persevere to find new ways and means of closer cooperation in carrying out their common mission of evangelisation, as circumstances of time, place and culture permits. As an agent of God's mission of reconciliation, the Church should be a living witness to the unity which she confesses. The Holy Qurbana demands reconciliation and sharing among all those who are regarded as brothers and sisters in the one family of God. The Lord's Supper is the sacrament which builds up community. All kinds of injustice, racism, estrangement, and lack of freedom are radically challenged when we share in the body and blood of Christ. By participating in the Eucharist, the partakers are renewed, transformed, and they are spiritually nourished. Through the participation in the mystery of salvation, the faithful are incorporated into Christ and empowered for mission. The gift of unity in the Eucharist - partakers in the same table without any discrimination - is a prophetic sign for the ministry of reconciliation. The Church is an agent of reconciliation. In short, we can conclude that the Triune God wants a reconciling community; the work of God in creation and salvation calls

---

[637] Varghese, "Missional Vision in the Liturgy of St. James," 19.

for reconciliation, the redemptive work of Jesus as reconciliatory, and the Church's mission as reconciliation.[638]

2 - Incarnation Aspect of Mission

The doctrine of incarnation is central to Christian faith. This precise theological term refers to a divine being taking on humanity. In the incarnation, God acts in and through the flesh and blood of Jesus Christ. The incarnation of Christ encapsulates the Father sending the Son Jesus to live among us. It is a radical, self-expression of divine love towards humanity. The incarnation is part of God's unique redemptive plan of salvation at work in Christ.[639] The triune God came into the world in the person of Jesus Christ and comes into the very lives of the Church through His Spirit.

The incarnation of Christ is the embodiment of God in person. In the New Testament, the Gospel of John is the first place that exposes the incarnation and its role within the *Missio Dei*. John 1:1-18 unfolds the mysterious nature of the pre-existence of Christ in creation. As John 1:14a says, "the Word became flesh and lived among us." The Father had sent Jesus into the world. God's act of becoming incarnate in Christ is unique. It calls the Church to follow Jesus Christ. St. Paul reveals the kenotic nature of Jesus Christ, for the purpose of highlighting the notion of imitating the action of becoming incarnate. [640] Christopher Wright mentions the "uniqueness of Jesus," who came to complete the redemptive plan for humanity that began with the people of Israel.[641] The mission of the Church

---

[638] Robert J. Kennedy, *Reconciliation:The Continuing Agenda* (Collegeville, MN: Liturgical, 1987), 31.
[639] Christopher Wright, *The Mission of God* (Nottingham: Inter-Varsity, 2006), 385.
[640] Phil.2:5-7, "In your relationships with one another, have the same mind set as Christ Jesus: Who, being in very nature God, did not consider equality with God something to be used to his own advantage; rather, he made himself nothing by taking the very nature of a servant, being made in human likeness." This passage is the base of the theology of kenosis, which is a model of mission. Kenosis means emptied himself. It is a call for self-renunciation.
[641] Wright, *The Mission of God*, 386-388.

is to reflect the uniqueness of Jesus' redemptive life through its self-emptying witness and life.

2.1 - Incarnation and Mission

Incarnation is the very heart and nature of the mission. As Frost and Hirsch says, the incarnation of Christ "is an absolutely fundamental doctrine, not just as an irreducible part of the Christian confession, but also as a theological prism through which we view our entire missional task in the world."[642] Through the incarnation, Jesus entered into the world for salvific mission. This is to say that without the incarnation, the fundamental truth of the gospel - crucifixion, resurrection, ascension or second coming, of which the New Testament's understanding of the mission is developed, would not have come into being. The incarnation of Christ to humanity is therefore significant.[643]

The incarnation is not an effort of the self, but it is possible only by the power of the Holy Spirit. It is not our own incarnation, but the Holy Spirit who makes Christ present in us and beyond us. In the concluding thanksgiving prayer, the celebrant reminds all that the faithful enter into a communion with the Holy Spirit. It is with the communion of the Holy Spirit that the Church becomes a missionary community. Living in the presence of Christ means embracing the Holy Spirit that Jesus promised the Father would send (Jn.14:16). It is to understand that God is with every disciple until the end of the age (Mt.28:20). It is also about recognizing that those who have faith in Christ have him living in them. The incarnated Christ now dwells in the lives of believers, and thus incarnational mission is to live in the presence of Christ. The Holy Spirit makes the witness of the Church effective. The Church is equipped with the Holy Spirit to represent Christ to the world. The Church is united to Christ as branches are united

---

[642] Michael Frost and Alan Hirsch, *The Shaping of Things to Come* (Massachusetts: Hendrickson 2003), 35.
[643] Darrell Guder, *Missional Church* (Michigan: William B. Eerdmans, 1998), 4. Bosch, *Transforming Mission*, 9.

to the vine (Jn.15). "In Christ" means united to the death, resurrection, and ascension of Jesus (Rom.6:3-11, Eph.2:6). Hence the followers of Jesus join with God in incarnational mission; they live as "sent out people" (Jn.17:18), with an outward movement of one community or individual to another.[644] They embody the gospel which means that they have Christ living in them, and therefore their lives express incarnational mission.

2.2 - Liturgy and Incarnation

The incarnation of Christ is a prominent theme in the liturgy of the MTC. It was necessary for the second person of the Trinity - Jesus Christ - to assume human flesh to communicate the message of salvation through his salvific act. Through the incarnation, the truth of God entered into the lives and thoughts of the people. Throughout the liturgy, especially in the *promeion*, the Church commemorates the incarnational nature of Jesus Christ and appeals for his grace and mercy.[645] For instance, in the preparatory service, the *promeion* deals with the theme of the incarnation of Jesus Christ. This *promeion* reflects the very nature of God such as "a saving, redeeming, and life-giving God."[646] He is the One who budded forth from the virgin womb (his incarnation), who quickens the dead by his voice, is worthy of praise, honour, and adoration at all times. The Church affirms her faith in the incarnation of Christ through the celebration of the Eucharist.[647]

In the *anaphora*, after the prayer of the Kiss of Peace and before the first blessing, there is a liturgical act called "*Sosappa Aghosham*"- elevation of the veil - from the mysteries in which the celebrant removes the veil placed over the paten and chalice. This act is an explicit example of the symbolic representation of the incarnation of Christ.[648] *Sosappa* is used to cover the bread and wine - the holy body and blood of Jesus Christ.

---

[644] Guder, *Missional Church,* 129.
[645] Titus II, *Qurbana Thaksa,* 120-134.
[646] Titus II, *Qurbana Thaksa,* 9.
[647] Kuttiyil, *Eucharist (Qurbana),* 65.
[648] Titus II, *Qurbana Thaksa,* 23.

It is the divine mystery. This divine mystery is hidden, and unveiling the sacred mysteries symbolize that the hidden things are now being revealed. Incarnation is the revelation of divine mystery. Hence St. John says "no one has ever seen God; the only God, who is at the Father's side, he has made him known" (Jn.1:18). The covering of the mysteries symbolizes the time before the incarnation of the Word, who was concealed and hidden from humanity and uncovering the mysteries indicates the time after his incarnation, in which he was revealed and known to humankind.[649] The first *rooshmo*[650] in the Holy Qurbana indicates another aspect of the incarnation. The attributes of God such as love, grace and communion are remembered and the gifts and abiding presence of the Triune God is being wished to the faithful. These virtues are personal feelings. By attributing these qualities to the Trinity, the *rooshmo* demonstrates the incarnation in a telling way to the congregation.[651] The wording of this *rooshmo* is taken from St. Paul's second letter to the Corinthians. Paul concludes his letter with the following greetings: "The grace of the Lord Jesus Christ and the love of God and the fellowship of the Holy Spirit be with you all" (2 Cor.13:14).

Incarnation means being one with humanity which is the core of the Christian mission. The Words of Institution in the liturgy are a classic example of Jesus being one with humanity. After this, the consecration of the bread is followed. The words of institution with the prayer "when the sinless One of His own will, choose to suffer death for us sinners, He took bread in His holy hands..." This denotes the ultimate identification of Christ with humanity through His death. By its very nature death denotes an inherent weakness in creation. Human beings are helpless when they face this reality. Through dying on the cross, Jesus Christ identified with the weak nature of the world and humanity and revealed his complete

---

[649] Varghese, *Bar Salibi*, 98.
[650] "The love of God the Father, the grace of the only begotten Son and the communion and abiding presence of the Holy Spirit be with you all dearly beloved, forever." Titus II, *Qurbana Thaksa*, 23. Juhanon, *The Order of the Holy Qurbana*, 19.
[651] Varghese, "Missional Vision in the Liturgy of St. James," 21.

human nature. He incarnated into the most trivial experience of humanity - death. The prayer of "anamnesis" is a culmination point of the incarnation of Jesus. "O Lord, we remember your death, burial, resurrection and your ascension into heaven."[652]

The incarnation aspect of the mission is incomplete with just identification. The incarnation is not to end in identification with human triviality. It is to transcend and transform humanity. Otherwise, there will not be any salvation. In the incarnation there is transcendence in humanity's life situation. In *epiclesis*, humanity is united with the very nature of Jesus Christ. The invocation of the Holy Spirit to sanctify the bread and wine indicates this transcendence.[653] Through the sanctification of bread and wine, which is an offering of the faithful, the community of the faithful is sanctified and is identified with Jesus Christ. Here the humanity is lifted up to the divinity of Christ. This process of *theosis* is the divinization of humanity. Humanity does not become God. Instead, the humanity is no more the sinful humanity, but the one that is identified with the divine humanity of Christ. This divine humanity is part of the Trinity. St. Paul explains it in the kenotic Christology in Philippians: "and being found in human form, he humbled himself by becoming obedient to the point of death, even death on a cross. Therefore God has highly exalted him and bestowed on him the name that is above every name, so that at the name of Jesus every knee should bow, in heaven and on earth and under the earth, and every tongue confess that Jesus Christ is Lord to the Glory of God the Father" (Phil.2:8-11).

There is a downward movement and an upward movement in incarnation. The God who stooped down and became human did not end up there. The prayers before distributing the holy elements[654] accompanying the act of ascending and descending from the steps of the *thronos* signify

---

[652] Titus II, *Qurbana Thaksa*, 25.

[653] May the Holy Spirit, sanctify the bread...." Titus II, *Qurbana Thaksa*, 26. Juhanon, *The Order of the Holy Qurbana*, 27.

[654] Standing with the paten and chalice in his hands the celebrant says, "O Son of God who came for......your own atoning sacrifice." Secondly, turning west, he continues, "O Lord God, graciously bless ....presence forever." Finally, descending from the steps,

the *theosis* experience of the Church. The downward moment signifies the Christ's incarnation and ascending the step denotes the divinization of humanity through Christ. The mission of this is a two-way process: It incarnating downward into every human situation and rising up again from it. This transcending and transforming affects deeply the weakness of human nature, just as Jesus transformed the death of disobedience into the death in obedience. The mission of the Church is to incarnate in every human situation. God identifies himself with humanity in its fullness, thus making humanity a part of divine Godhead. Therefore, the incarnation invites the congregation into a mission, that is, to present Jesus into every trivial human situation and to transform it. This is a challenge of the mission in the liturgy.

3 - Eschatological Aspect of Mission

Eschatology occupies a pivotal place in Christian theology. It is the culmination of Christ's saving work. Christology according to the New Testament is deeply eschatological in character, centred on the resurrection of Christ and on His return in glory, the Parousia (1 Thess.4:14-17). The term eschatology derives from the Greek word *"Eschaton,"* meaning the end time or the end of time. It refers to the end of time on earth, but also since that includes the "new heavens and a new earth" (2 Pet.3:13), it denotes the heavenly dimension as well. The Church believes that, the earthly liturgy is a mirror image of the heavenly liturgy.[655] The sacraments of the Church are not the only signs that commemorate the salvific act of Christ, nor simply operative symbols of God's grace in the present moment. Indeed, it constitutes a promise of future glory, a prefiguration of the hoped-for parousia.[656] "The eschatological character of Christian faith means that we have hope in the power of God over all that would hurt

---

the celebrant proclaims that "the blessings of Jesus.....both now and forever." Titus II, *Qurbana Thaksa,* 39-40. Juhanon, *The Order of the Holy Qurbana,* 31.
[655] Giles Dimock, *The Eucharist (*New York: Paulist, 2006), 135-137.
[656] Paul O'Callaghan, *Christ Our Hope-An Introduction to Eschatology* (Washington D.C: The Catholic University of America, 2011), 230.

and destroy. Eschatology is not about idle speculation about who will be left behind, at the second coming; it is about our hope in God. Christian eschatology affirms not only that we have hope that God will triumph over evil in some future time, but also that we participate already in that future. One way in which we participate in God's future now is by coming to the table to "proclaim the death of the Lord until he comes again."[657]

3.1 - Eschatological Emphasis in the Liturgy

The Holy Qurbana is the foretaste of the Kingdom of God and an anticipation of the future coming of Jesus Christ.[658] It is an act of thanksgiving to the Father for the inauguration of the Kingdom of God through Jesus Christ. The Church believes that Jesus Christ inaugurated the Kingdom of God in history and it will be completed in its final, authentic and glorious form in the Eschaton. It is in the Holy Qurbana, that the Church foreshadows the coming of the Kingdom of God. There is an interaction wherein the past, the present and the future are manifested. An anticipation of the world to come is clearly presented. This is the point where the mission of the Church originates. The mission of the Church is seen as the dynamic journey of the people of God as a whole towards the Eschaton, with the Eucharist as the point of departure. Here we have a perfect synthesis and a dialectical presence of "history" and "eschatology." Indeed, the Church has always believed that the "New Jerusalem," the Kingdom to come, was not only a gift of God, but also a seal and a fulfilment of all the positive, creative efforts of humankind to cooperate *(synergy)* with the Creator throughout the entire process of history. The author of the letter to the Hebrews mentions that the present Church is only an image (icon) of the truth, which is to be revealed only in the Eschaton. "... the law has but a *shadow* of the good things *to come* instead of the *true* form of these realities" (Heb.10:1). In other words, truth is no longer connected with the past but with the future, with the Eschaton. The Holy Qurbana is always giving importance to this

---

[657] Martha L. Moore-Keish, "Eucharist: Eschatology", in *A More Profound Alleluia*, 111.
[658] O'Callaghan, *Christ our Hope,* 67.

great anticipation. St. Paul the Apostle exhorts the Church to celebrate the Eucharist as the "culmination of its very existence, proclaiming the Lords death until he comes"[659] (1 Cor. 11:26) when, in the fullness of time, the Lord will hand over the Kingdom of his priestly people to the Father and God will be all in all (1 Cor.15:28). The Eucharistic celebration not only applies all the power and efficacy of the sacrifice of Christ on the cross, but in a very real way provides the faithful with an anticipation of the Parousia, as it invites us to look forward to the second coming of Christ.[660] "The Antiochian anaphora stresses the economy of salvation, the looking forward to the end of time, and the splendour of the glory of God. This eschatological thrust is perhaps one of the clearest characteristics of the anaphora of St. James."[661]

This liturgy points to the reality that the Holy Qurbana unites the heaven and the earth. It is a cosmic reality. Heaven comes to earth each time when the Eucharist is celebrated and yet it has not come in its fullness since the end of time has not yet come - the future is here, but not yet in its fullness.[662] The veiling and unveiling in the *madbaho* during the celebration of the Eucharistic liturgy symbolises this reality. The liturgy affirms that the Church participates with the heavenly host, with angels, archangels, thrones and dominations, virtues and powers and principalities, Cherubim and Seraphim - all nine choirs of angels join the assembly on earth in singing the praise of God through Christ and in the Spirit.[663] In the celebration of the Holy Qurbana, the visible Church on earth is in union with the invisible Church in heaven. It is an awesome moment of heaven appearing on earth. Heavenly choirs of the great cloud of witness who have

---

[659] O'Callaghan, *Christ our Hope*, 329-332.
[660] O'Callaghan, *Christ our Hope*, 231.
[661] Irenee Henri Dalmais, *The Eastern Liturgies* (London: Burns and Oats, 1960), 40. Alexander Schmemann, *Church, World, Mission* (Crestwood. New York: St. Vladimir's, 1979), 199.
[662] Dimock, The *Eucharist*, 135-137.
[663] Titus II, *Qurbana Thaksa*, 24-25,

gone before us (Heb.12:1) join with the earthly assembly in their song of praise.[664]

In the *sedro* prayer during the preparatory service, the celebrant prays "make us worthy to come before You with contrition and humility, purify us from all stain that we may be transformed by the renewal of our lives, and go forth, as did the wise virgins, to a new world, bearing the shining lamps of faith."[665] By the celebration of the Eucharist, the Church anticipates entering into a new world with Christ. The Eucharist is considered as a spiritual food for the journey towards eternity; *Vazhiyahaaram* - viaticum - it is believed that Christ is actively present with the believers on their way to eternity. After this prayer, the celebrant prays "protect us under the tender mercies of Your wings when you separate the good from the wicked people."[666] The Church faithfully hopes for the final judgement and the separation of the righteous from the wicked. In the Eucharistic liturgy, all prayers concluded with the petition of *hosho vabkulsban lolmin* which means "now and forever." This is a supplication with eschatological hope. It means prayers offered at this moment and until eternity.[667]

In the pre-anaphora, during the confessional prayer in between *promeion* and *sedro,* the celebrant prays for the good ending of the children of peace.[668] Here the good ending means a life in fullness with Christ in this world and in the world to come. Before distributing the holy mysteries, descending from the steps of the altar, the celebrant pleads for the blessings of Jesus Christ to the faithful not only in this world but also in the world to come.[669] The Church celebrates and participates in the liturgy with an eschatological hope. Hence the common practice of the celebrant, who significantly faces the East during the celebration of the Eucharist, for it is

---

[664] Dimock, *The Eucharist,* 135-137.

[665] Titus II, *Qurbana Thaksa,* 4.

[666] Titus II, *Qurbana Thaksa,* 5.

[667] Varghese, "Missional Vision in the Liturgy of St. James," 21.

[668] Titus II, *Qurbana Thaksa,* 16.

[669] "The blessings of Jesus Christ our great God ....grace of God be on us all, both now and forever." Titus II, *Qurbana Thaksa,* 40. Juhanon, *The Order of the Holy Qurbana,* 31.

from there that Christ, the Sun of Justice will come.[670] The liturgy speaks of the second coming of Jesus, which is the glorious and wonderful return of Christ in the fullness of time.

The third blessing in the Holy Qurbana is pronounced in the name of Trinity. It is different from the first Trinitarian blessing in its content. It affirms the transcendence of the Trinity, i.e., uncreated, self-existent, eternal, adorable and one in essence. It is very different from the temporal world that is created, dependent, finite, and fragile. The Trinity is not only personal and attached to humanity but has a transcendental and eschatological aspect. It is beyond human comprehension, a mystery, an eschatological reality. The eschatological dimension of the Trinity is glorified here. The Trinity is transcendental and at the same time, it becomes immanent. The prayers that follow establish the immanent nature of the Trinity. "The Holy Father, who created the world in his mercy, is with us. The one Holy Son, who saved it by his precious passion, is with us. The one living Holy Spirit who perfects and fulfils all that is and that has been, is with us."[671] The transcendental mystery, the Triune God, is with the believers. This transcendental mystery is beyond the world, but is the foundational reality of the world (Heb. 11:2).Thus, mystery touches history. Through this relationship, history becomes a continuum of the mystery. This is eschatology. When history is touched by mystery and mystery becomes the foundational reality of history, eternity breaks into history. The situation is eschatological. Therefore, the third *rooshmo* and the following prayers indicate the eschatological dimension of the mission. Hence the celebrant steps down from the *thronos* for the distribution of the holy elements, which signifies the presence of the transcendental Trinity within our world of humanity. The descent of the celebrant from the steps symbolizes the descent of the transcendental Trinity into the world and into the life of all humanity.[672]

---

[670] J. Ratzinger, *The Spirit of the Liturgy* (San Francisco: Ignatius, 2004), 74-84.
[671] Titus II, *Qurbana Thaksa*, 35.
[672] Varghese, "Missional Vision in the Liturgy of St. James," 22.

In the Eucharist, the faithful receive the holy elements of the same bread. This signifies the unity of the Church and reminds that the faithful are members of the one mystical body of Christ. The unity of the faithful is affirmed by the breaking of the bread. Unity is not only essential to the mission of the Church; it is an essential reflection of its eschatological nature. Unity in the Church is a foretaste of the unity of all humanity with God in the Eschaton. The Church is to be the nucleus of the new humanity, a humanity in which all nations, tribes, and all tongues are reconciled with God. The Church is to be united as "a sign and a sacrament of the unity of humankind."[673] A divided Church contradicts its destiny as the nucleus of the new redeemed humanity. The Eucharist, on the other hand, is the measure of the unity of the local congregation. The fellowship around the same cup and the same loaf is the supreme evidence of unity. As the Eucharist is the supreme testimony to the unity of the Church, baptism is the supreme witness to the mission of the Church.

Eschatology does not mean otherworldly, but trans-worldly, beyond the world. Eternal and adorable is identified with finite, created beings and thus transcends them. This is the sanctification. In the anamnesis, the sanctification of the body and blood symbolizes the sanctification of the whole Church and the faithful. This sanctification is for sanctifying the world. Thus the community is symbolically identified with the eschatological community. In eschatology, where history becomes a continuum of mystery, humanity gets a dimension beyond the world. This eschatological dimension of humanity also makes mission eschatological. The mission is eschatological. It cannot have an end in the achievement of certain goals on earth. The mission is in the world, and for the world, but its dimension is far beyond the world. The Christian mission is not something that begins and ends with a person. It is eschatological. It is lifting up humanity and the entire creation of the Lord that is an ongoing process. At the same time it could experience the fulfilment. It is this continuity and

---

[673] Lesslie. Newbigin, "What Kind of Unity?" *National Christian Council Review* 95, (1975): 487- 491, www.newbigin.net (accessed November 18, 2015).

fulfilment in the mission that is referred to as an eschatological dimension of the mission.[674]

4 - Intercession Aspect of Mission

Intercession is a prayer offered to God on behalf of someone or on behalf of a group for God's goodness and mercy. In the Old Testament, the role of the mediator in prayer is prevalent, especially in the cases of Abraham, Moses, David, Samuel, Hezekiah, Elijah, Jeremiah, Ezekiel, and Daniel. The New Testament portrays Jesus Christ as the ultimate intercessor (Jn.17). The apostles Paul and Peter urged the Church to pray. Because of this, all Christian prayers become intercession since it is offered to God through Jesus Christ. Jesus closed the gap between Creation and God when He died on the cross. Because of the mediation of Jesus, the Church can intercede in prayer on behalf of others. The Church is a community interceding for others. The very identity and mission of the Church reveals this nature.

4.1 - Emphasis of Intercession in the Liturgy

The liturgy of the Church reflects the importance of intercession. The Church celebrates the Holy Qurbana as a thanksgiving to the Father on behalf of the entire creation. The Church intercedes for the world since the world is the arena of its mission. The mission of the Church is mainly redemptive ever urging for the salvation of all creation. The world is the agenda for mission. The Church celebrates the liturgy on behalf of the world and for the world. The liturgy portrays the mediation of Christ through its prayers and practices. For instance, the second blessing of the Holy Qurbana is a Christo-centric blessings in which the mediation of Christ is affirmed. The faithful receive the blessings of Jesus Christ with fear and concord. Through this blessing, the Church affirms that "Jesus the great God and saviour" is the mediator between God and the entire creation. "For there is one God and one mediator between God and men, the man Christ Jesus" (1 Tim.2:5). "Who is he that condemns? Christ Jesus, who died - more than that, who

---

[674] Varghese, "Missional Vision in the Liturgy of St. James," 23.

198

was raised to life - is at the right hand of God and is also interceding for us" (Rom.8:34). The Church has become one in Christ, who is the only Mediator and Intercessor, and offers intercession through its liturgical celebration. This is one of the reasons for not interceding to Mother Mary or to the Saints. The Church, both far and near, living and the departed, has become one in Christ the mediator. Through *epiclesis*, the bread and wine, along with the congregation, are sanctified and identified with Christ. The whole body has become one in Christ. Incarnation has absorbed the community and the elements in Christ. This identity of the congregation and the elements is represented through the Christo-centric blessing.

The principle of identification and the principle of mediation is important in intercession. When the Church intercedes, she identifies with the parties for whom she intercedes. The *thubden* prayers (great intercession) are an integral part of the Eucharistic service. There are six sets of petitions. These prayers of intercession are said by the Deacon: three for the living, i.e. the leaders of the Church, the faithful and political leaders, rulers of the nation. In the second part, the Church remembers Virgin Mary, the Doctors of the Church and the faithful departed. It is the responsibility of the Church to pray for its members to live in the experience of redemption and intercession for others. This part of the anaphora concludes with an eschatological petition and a Christological blessing. After the second blessing, in the litany of intercession, the Church continues to pray for reconciliation and peace in the world, for unity in the Church and harmony between all people and communities, for the sick, for the distressed, for the prisoners, for the travellers, and for unity and love for those who are estranged. By this litany, the Church identifies with the wounded people and the wounded world. After the litany, there is a time for silent prayer to intercede and which concludes with the pronouncement of the Lord's Prayer by the whole congregation. By giving space for silent prayer, the entire congregation participates in the mission of intercession both personally and corporately.[675]

---

[675] Varghese, "Missional Vision in the Liturgy of St. James," 24.

In the first part of the service, the celebrant intercedes for the community through Christ. At this time, the celebrant offers prayer in submission - Godward position - i.e. hands clasped. This means, the Church cries out to God, pleads for His mercy, longs for His grace, remembers the promise of God, and in faith clings to His goodness. In the second part of the service, from the celebration of anaphora, there is an up-ward position of the hands - stretched hands - of the celebrant, which signifies heaven came down through Jesus Christ. The liturgy affirms that through the identification of Jesus with humanity and his mediation on behalf of the entire creation on the right side of the Father atonement has been made for all.

In the third section of the final blessing, the celebrant says "pray for me, my brethren, weak and sinful as I am that I may obtain mercy and help. Depart in peace, filled with gladness and rejoicing."[676] This part affirms the intrinsic relationship between the celebrant and the congregation. It is a classic example of intercession. It affirms that the mission is an ongoing responsibility and a mutual commitment of both the laity and the clergy. The celebrant admits his feeble human nature and requests the congregation to pray for him to discharge his responsibilities. It is to them that the priest turn requesting their prayers. Those not implementing mission are not *Laos* (people of God); they are still *Oklos* (crowd). Here the term "mission" refers to the action of sending. This sending is always a personal action prompted by the limitless love of God. The word mission tries to capture something of the inexhaustible love of the Father, of the Son and of the Holy Spirit permeating and energizing the Church in its own outreach of mission.[677]

Intercession is an important mission of the Church. It is an inclusive mission in which all faithful - the children, aged, differently abled, mentally challenged, physically challenged, widows, the bedridden are all capable of participating in intercessory prayers. In other words there are no barriers on the basis of socio-economic or other status for participating

---

[676] Titus II, *Qurbana Thaksa*, 44.
[677] Provost, *The Church as Mission*, 90.

in intercessory prayers. Intercessory prayer is not a means of coaxing something out of God. Rather, such prayers could change our self-centred and narrow mindedness so that there is more room in our hearts to take care of the needs of others. When the Church intercedes, she identifies with the people for whom she prays. It is an expression of solidarity with others. Intercessory prayers help the Church to embody and promote the values of the Kingdom of God (peace, justice, equality, service...) by conforming our will to the will of God. The Spirit of God prays in our spirit as we offer prayers of intercession for ourselves and for others in need.[678]

5 - Liberation Aspect of Mission

Liberation is a major theme in Scripture and in the liturgy. In the Old Testament, the Exodus of Israelites from Egyptian bondage is the foundational narrative of the Jewish nation. The God of Israel hears the cries of the poor and the marginalised. God is on the side of Israel and against Egypt not simply because Israel is His people, but because God sides with the downtrodden. The Exodus reveals Yahweh as the God of the slaves, and the rest of the scripture shows that the mission of God is universal, not merely local. God selected Israel with a mission, that is, that, through them, God is made known among the nations. The God of Israel is the God of all the earth who has compassion on all He has made (Ps.33:13-15, 145:9, 146:6-9). The Bible reveals a God who hears the cries of the oppressed and loves to bring deliverance. The prophets exhorted the people of God for the need of liberation in relation with God. In the New Testament, Jesus inaugurated his ministry by announcing that he had come to release the oppressed (Lk.4:18-19). The ultimate purpose of the Incarnation of Christ is to liberate the creation from the clutches of sin and death.

In the liturgy, the proclamation of the Good News is understood as a form of liberation. Proclaiming the Word to the community is integral to the mission aspect of the Church. There is a close connection between

---

[678] Varghese, "Missional Vision in the Liturgy of St. James," 24.

the liturgy and Scripture. The liturgy communicates the life-giving Word to the faithful. The community of the faithful, in turn, receives the word in order to continue its proclamation in a broader sense. The preaching of Jesus must be seen in this light. Evangelizing the poor liberates them with the spoken word.[679] The reign of God cannot remain merely on a conceptual level, rather it should be experienced. The Christian preaching takes place in the context of ecclesia, the people of God. It is the "Word and the Table" that forms a community of believers, and conversion follows upon proclamation. A ministry of preaching occurs in a community. By participating in the paschal mystery, the participants are helped to see their suffering inserted into that same paschal mystery of transformation. Resurrection takes on both a comprehensive and radical significance. It does not bespeak reference to Eternity alone; it also refer to time and space in which manifold injustice arising from selfishness and greed causes the desperate struggle of those millions of man and women yearning and searching for justice and peace. From this realization, mission depends largely on worship. In the MTC, reading of the Bible and an exposition of Scripture has a major role. The Church communicates the Word through its liturgy, preaching, and its exemplary life. Listening and preaching the Word of God is not an isolated moment, but it is a way of life. The liturgy affirms that the faithful community is called out to share God's concern for justice and reconciliation throughout human society, and for the liberation of humanity from all kinds of oppression.[680]

6 - "Go in Peace" - Implementation Aspect of Mission

The final blessing in the liturgy is a threefold blessing[681] which marks the conclusion of the Eucharistic service. It is meant to disperse the faithful. Just as the absolution in confession assures the remission of sin and thereby the new status of the believing community as a reconciled body, this

---

[679] Kennedy, *Reconciliation*, 255.
[680] Varghese, "Missional Vision in the Liturgy of St. James," 25.
[681] "My beloved brothers and sisters, I commend you to …" Titus II, *Qurbana Thaksa*, 44. Juhanon, *The Order of the Holy Qurbana*, 34.

absolution addresses a new community, as one entrusted with the mission. It reminds every one of the responsibility of the new community to bear witness of the salvific act of Christ. The faithful are exhorted to depart in peace with the assurance of the presence of Christ in their lives. They are assured by the grace and blessings of the holy and glorious Trinity in their missionary life. The faithful are a redeemed community in Christ and called out for the mission of redemption and salvation. The celebrant blesses the redeemed community. Thus they become the custodians of the grace and the blessings of the holy and glorious Trinity, through the atoning sacrifice of Christ. They are supposed to dispense the grace and blessings to the world.

The commendation, "Go in peace" is the action of sending out the congregation with a purpose. It is a biblical exhortation. Jethro had sent out Moses with the same greeting, when Moses had the vision of the burning bush (Ex.4:28). It was a mission of liberation and formation of the slaves in Egypt into a people of God. "You shall be to me a kingdom of priests and a holy nation" (Ex.19:6). In the New Testament, the woman who was a sinner also received the same commissioning dispensation by Jesus Christ (Lk.7:50). The dispensation is a commissioning too. The faith community embodies the salvific act of Jesus Christ. The celebrant assures the renewing presence of Christ in the last part of this benediction.[682] This is biblically supportive. Moses asked God to reveal God's way while he was leading the Israelites through the desert to the Promised Land. God did not answer to this request. Instead, God assured His presence with him. "My presence will go with you and I will give you rest" was God's answer (Ex.33:13, 14).

The community dispensed with the Lord's commissioning is a fragile community. But they are "saved by the victorious cross" and they were "sealed with the seal of Holy Baptism." Still, they may fail in their mission and err in the life in this world. However, the exhortation reminds us that

---

[682] "You both near and far, who are saved by the victorious cross......will forgive your sins and comfort your souls." Titus II, *Qurbana Thaksa*, 44. Juhanon, *The Order of the Holy Qurbana*, 34.

203

the Holy Trinity will re-instate them and comfort them. This is what the second section of the *rooshmo* assures. In the third section, the celebrant says "pray for me, my brethren, weak and sinful as I am that I may obtain mercy and help. Depart in peace, filled with gladness and rejoicing."[683] This part affirms the intrinsic relationship between the celebrant and the congregation. It affirms that the mission is an ongoing responsibility and a mutual commitment of both the laity and the clergy. The celebrant admits his feeble human nature and requests the congregation to pray for him to discharge his responsibilities as a follower of Jesus Christ.[684] It is the commissioned new community which has inherited the grace and blessings of the Trinity, and which imparts it through faith, life and practices. The priest beseeches the people for their prayers. Those who are not implementing the mission of God are not *Laos* (people of God), they are still *Oklos* (crowd). Here the term, mission, refers to the action of sending. This sending is always a personal one, prompted by the unlimited love of God.[685]

7 - Conclusion

As we have seen, the liturgy of the Holy Qurbana has three main parts. During the first part, the priest prepares himself for the celebration of the Holy Qurbana. The second part, the pre-anaphora contains the scripture reading, long meditative prayers, sermon, and general confession. It is followed by the third part which consists of the Kiss of Peace and it ends with the Dismissal and Blessings. The phrase "Go in Peace" in the final blessing of the liturgy calls for the mission of believer to be ambassadors of Christ in the world. The breaking of bread and distribution of communion takes place during this section. The liturgy of the Holy Qurbana in fact serves as the central thread and brings the believers close to the Lord Jesus as well as to the Church, which is His body. The symbols used in the Holy Qurbana communicate the theological richness and the traditions of

---

[683] Titus II, *Qurbana Thaksa*, 44.
[684] Varghese, "Missional Vision in the Liturgy of St. James," 25.
[685] Provost, *The Church as Mission*, 90.

204

the Church. As we have seen, this liturgy is a deeply moving and richly symbolic spiritual drama in which the salvific act of Jesus Christ is relived and shared. The liturgy is, both in its character and in its mystery, appealing to both the physical and mystical senses. The symbolism of word and act, of vestment and voice, of jingling of the censer, burning of the incense, lighted lamps in the sanctuary, and the veil, transports the faithful before the very throne of God. It is in the "table of life," where the glorification of God and the sanctification of people are taking place. It is the solemn occasion where the heaven and the earth are reconciled. It is on this Table that the Church proclaims the resurrection of Christ, and this process will continue until He comes back in his glory.

The celebration of the liturgy of the anaphora of St. James contains and transmits powerful imagery and exhortations of Christian mission, and the key aspects of the mission are reconciliation, incarnation, eschatology, intercession, and liberation. The prayers, signs, and symbols are rich in missional vision and establishes the missional aspect more emphatically. This liturgy, undoubtedly, provides many opportunities for the participation of the congregation. Still, it is often criticised as lengthy, monotonous and for its lack of variety. The prayers are replete with idioms, images, and it echoes the Bible. An active participation in the Eucharistic liturgy strengthens the participants to discharge their God-given mission. The Eucharist involves a thankful remembrance of the mighty deeds of God in history, a sending forth into the contemporary world to be with the God as He continues his saving deeds, and we are looking forward for the end which He is bringing about.

The message of life-long purity and holiness deriving from Gospel and the mysteries permeating all ranks and rules within the Church is confessed by the congregation and guides faithful towards the ecclesiological and sacramental dimension of mission. In presenting the role of the Holy Spirit in effecting sanctification, the anaphora leads to the hope of eschatological fullness which will be attained in the Kingdom of Heaven. Hence, the participants find a movement from heaven to earth by the creative, redemptive and sanctifying actions of the Father, Son and the Holy Spirit in this anaphora. In this liturgy, there, one can highlight, so to speak, the letter "M": naming "Mission" is effected through "Messenger," the Son. The "Message" of holiness and knowledge of truth comes down to all in time and space through the traditions and the mysteries of the Church. Finally, the "Mission-goal" is the attainment of new life in the world to come through communion with and by means of the body and blood of Christ. Therefore, we could conclude that the anaphora of St. James presents a well-substantiated theology of mission. Overall, the liturgy of St. James gives us the impression that the mission of the Church flows from the Eucharistic liturgy.

Chapter 8

Paradigms of Mission in the Malankara Mar Thoma Syrian Church: An Assessment

1 - Introduction

The MTC is a mission-oriented Church. The reformation (1836 CE) in the Malankara Church motivated them to carry out the mission of Christ seriously and it ignited them to move out from its caste scenario[686] of Kerala. As we have seen, the ecclesial identity and the mission theology of this Church were reshaped by its encounter with the CMS missionaries and also by the social and political changes that took place in Kerala during the first half of 18th century. An encounter with European Protestant Christianity encouraged them to accept evangelism, social service, and struggles for justice and peace as goals for the mission. [687] The mission of the MTC is significant because it is the pioneering Church among the Malankara Christians who initiated the first cross-cultural mission in the Indian sub-continent.[688] The translation and renewal of the Eucharistic

---

[686] The Malankara Christians in Kerala enjoyed a privileged position in the social terrain of Kerala with the privileges of the upper class. They were confined and found themselves comfortable in their own social set up. The Reformation process gave impetus to move out from its own area to the non-Christian communities like Dalits, Adivasi's and oppressed communities in the country.

[687] The term mission is expressed by the use of verbs meaning "to send," normally with God as the expressed subject. The Hebrew verb *salah* and the Greek term *apostello* emphasize an authoritative, commissioning relationship involved. The Scriptures also employ the cognates *apostolos* ('apostle,' the one sent) and *apostole* ('apostleship,' the function of being sent), referring to the one sent and his function. Horst Balz and Gerhard Schneider, ed., *Exegetical Dictionary of the New Testament*, trans. Virgil P. Howard, James W. Thompson, John W. Medendorp and Douglas W. Stott. vol. 1 (Grand Rapids: Eerdmans, 1993), 141-42.

[688] Thomas, *A History of the First Cross-Cultural Mission,* 100-101.

liturgy on the basis of Scripture gave a strong impetus for the Church in its mission.

A missiological analysis of the Eucharistic liturgy in the previous chapter highlighted various missional themes treasured in the liturgy. Since the Eucharistic liturgy is a liturgical foundation for mission, it is imperative to understand how the Church used the themes of mission enshrined in its liturgy in its mission journey. Hence, this chapter focuses on how the Church employed these missional aspects for the continuance of its mission. After the formation of this Church (1889), the leaders of the community recognized the necessity of keeping revival as an ongoing process. To meet this end they initiated Bible conventions especially Maramon Convection, instituted Ancillary Organizations and established Ashrams. Hence the leaders of the Church gave special attention to integrate the Liturgy and Mission in the background of its historic apostolic spiritual heritage. This chapter is a descriptive analysis of the historical development and continuity of mission in the MTC and the role of liturgy in carrying out its mission. It is an investigation to discover how the Eucharistic liturgy became a source of strength in the Church in its mission initiatives. Further, it explores various models of mission employed by the Church to carry out through its various ministries.[689]

2 - Mission Patterns of the Mar Thoma Church and its Liturgical Influence

The Christian Church is commissioned with the privilege and responsibility of participating in the mission of Jesus Christ by the power of the Holy

---

[689] Mission and Ministry are not synonymous. The mission is the agenda of God and ministry is the option of the ambassadors of Christ guided by the Holy Spirit. There is an intrinsic relationship between mission and ministry. The Church has a mission but has many ministries. The mission is an inclusive term which includes every aspect of human life, but ministry is a term which refers to a particular aspect of the mission of the Church. For instance, the ministry of teaching, preaching, healing, serving. All these ministries are coming under the mission of the Church. The Church does not exist for itself, but for its mission. A ministry is the means by which mission is achieved. Mathew Mar Makkarios, "Mission of the Church: Contextual and Universal," *Mar Thoma Seminary Journal of Theology* 1, no.1 (June 2012): 59.

Spirit.[690] The starting point of Christian mission is the divine commission to proclaim the Lordship of Christ over all creation. That calls for our active involvement in all aspects of human life. The proclamation of the Gospel is about using both word and deed to express the love of God to all. There are numerous missionary approaches to deal with the task of mission.[691] Hendric Kraemer has identified the ideal missionary approach of mission as the combination of "a prophetic, apostolic, heraldship of truth for Christ's sake, with a priestly, apostolic ambassadorship of love for His sake."[692] While the Church is assigned to proclaim the good news of Jesus Christ, the context is the deciding factor in shaping the paradigm for its mission. The mission of the MTC is a continuation of the mission of Jesus Christ. The Constitution of the Church clearly states that:

> "the ministry of the Church is the gift of the Risen Christ. The responsibility to fulfill this ministry, in history, is entrusted with the Church. The Church affirms that the people of God are sent all over the world and that they partake in the salvation work of God, to unite everything in Jesus Christ through the ministry of reconciliation begun in Jesus Christ. The Church receives the power of the Holy Spirit, which enables the Church to fulfill the redemptive work of God, who directs and controls the events in history. The Holy Spirit guides the offices of the ministry, originated (through) divine plan and ordains the people of God to build the Church which is the body of Christ, in order that they

---

[690] Nugent, "Theological Foundation for Mission Animation: A Study of the Church's Essence," 7-18.

[691] The Churches Together in Britain and Ireland (CTBI) identified the marks of mission as "to proclaim the Good News of the Kingdom; to teach, baptize and nurture new believers; to respond to human need by loving service; to seek to transform unjust structures of society; to strive to safeguard the integrity of creation and sustain and renew the life of earth and peace and reconciliation.. Further they identified mission as "proclamation of Jesus as Universal Saviour or 'Proclamation,' mission as participation in the Triune God or *Missio Dei;* mission as liberating service of the Reign of God or Kingdom mission. Anne Richards, John Clark, Martin Lee, Philip knights, Janice Price, Paul Rolph and Nigel Rooms, *Foundations For Mission: A Study of Language, Theology and Praxis from the UK and Ireland* Perspective (London: Churches Together in Britain and Ireland, 2010), 15-16, 56.

[692] George K. Zachariah, "Mission of the Church," in *Mar Thoma Messenger* (October 2004): 17-18.

may attain maturity, akin to the fullness of Christ, through faith and knowledge in the Son of God and the Unity of the Holy Spirit. The Church believes and proclaims the above basic principles of the ministry of the Church."[693]

The Metropolitan Joseph Mar Thoma, during his presidential address of the *Sabha Prathinidhi Mandalam* (the supreme administrative body of the Church) in 2009 reiterated the mission of the Church in the following words:

> "We should never forget that we are appointed by God to share the core values of the Gospel to each and every corner of the world. The hallmark of the MTC once was lay missionary work. The emphasis of the Church was for sharing the Gospel values, rooted in the reformation principles, with others. However, we should search our conscience to find out whether we are distancing ourselves from the gospel values by conforming to the world."[694]

This is a clear indication of the priority of the Church in its mission. The Church designs its mission strategy in considering the context and the need of the time.

The identity of the Church as an "Apostolic Christian Community" gives an impetus for its mission. As mentioned in the first chapter, it is believed that the Apostle St. Thomas is the architect of the Christian community in the Malankara region. This apostolic identity and spiritual heritage provide an originality and authority to the Church in its mission. The Apostle was a missionary by himself with a vision. The post-resurrection experience of St. Thomas was unique and his missionary thrust was based on this experience (Jn.20:26-29). His experience was a result of his deep encounter with Christ. He knew Christ very personally and came to India with this Christ experience with which he communicated

---

[693] *The Constitution of the Mar Thoma Syrian Church of Malabar, Division 1, Chapter 1, Declaration Part. 2, Clause 5* (Thiruvalla: Mar Thoma Press, 2000), 4-5.
[694] *Minutes of the Sabha Prathinidhi Mandalam*, 2009 at Thiruvalla, *Mar Thoma Messenger*, (October 2009): 14.

and shared the Gospel. The missionary thrust of St. Thomas is the mission motivation of the MTC. The Church believes that, this mystical experience of St. Thomas is entrusted with the Malankara Church.[695] In the same way that the Apostle Thomas experienced Christ, the Church now experiences and encounters resurrected Christ in the Eucharist. It is in and through the Eucharist that the Church now experiences the divine. By participating in the liturgy, the faithful partake in the salvific act of Christ. The Eucharist is the culmination of human and divine fellowship which provides that solemn space where the Church encounters the resurrected Christ. It is from this mystical encounter that they are empowered and strengthen for communicating the Gospel. In short, the Christ-experience of the faithful through the Eucharist strengthens and motivates them to participate in the mission of God. The liturgy enables the people of God to internalize and enliven this Christ experience. In the final blessing in the Eucharistic liturgy, the celebrant assures the peace of Christ and exhorts them to be channels of peace and divine presence in the world. ".....depart in peace filled with gladness and rejoicing."[696] The Eucharist calls for a "liturgy after the liturgy." This Christ experience in the liturgy is the missionary thrust of the Church. In this sense, the Eucharist is the liturgical foundation for mission in the MTC.

The MTC follows the scriptural pattern of mission. This means, the Church included the various patterns of mission expressed in the Bible, such as: the Matthean model of mission as "making disciples" (Mt.28:18-20), Lukan model of mission as "social transformation" (Lk.4:16-21), Pauline Model of mission as "ambassadors of Christ" and Johannine model of mission as "life and love" (Jn.3:16). The mission understanding of the Gospel of Mathew is disciple-centred and Luke's is boundary-centred. A general view of the mission understanding of Paul is time-centred. The Apostle Paul is supremely conscious of the fact that through Christ, God the Father has inaugurated a cosmic grace period, a suspension of his

---

[695] Iinterview with Joseph Mar Barnabas Episcopa on September 08, 2015.
[696] Titus II, *Qurbana Thaksa,* 44.

judgement for a set time[697] (Rom.1:5, 15:5, Gal.1:1-5). In the Gospel of John, the emphasis of mission is "the incarnational love." The focus of the overall scriptural mission is God's new action in the Messiah, who calls for a new response from everyone. The key text is: God sent Jesus and he sends his messengers.[698]

The MTC keeps tradition and Scripture in its mission journey. The mission understanding of this Church is dual in nature, which is based on the Liturgy and the Bible. It is not contradictory, but complementing each other for relevant mission. As mentioned in the previous chapter, the spirit of reformation ignited the Church to take up the command of Christ seriously and that motivated them to find out new ways of engaging in mission contextually. In other words, the reformation motivated the Church to locate mission activity at the centre of the Church. The Church was open enough to receive the CMS mission's ideas and strategies for mission along with its own Oriental liturgical base. The Church combines the emphasis on Scripture and evangelism with the traditional Eastern Church forms of worship and ways of life. The Church believes that the Christian community enters into the life and love of God by celebrating the Eucharist.

2.1 - A Historical Survey of Mission in the Mar Thoma Church

As pointed out in the earlier chapters, the Christian community in Kerala during the 19th century accommodated itself to the caste structure of the society, and there was no possibility for the so-called outcastes to become members of the Church. The MTC remained as an exclusively "high caste Church" with members consisting of the Syrian Christian tradition. This caste identity resulted in the exclusion of the so-called low caste people. Later, from the final decade of the 19th century, interaction with the modern protestant missionaries had a drastic influence on the mission thinking and identity of the Church. In the beginning, the Church shared the purpose and

---

[697] Stan Nussbaum, *A Reader's Guide to Transforming Mission* (New York: Orbis, 2005), 33.
[698] Nussbaum, *A Reader's Guide to Transforming Mission,* 42.

goal of most of the Protestant mission of that time, which is, a soteriological focus on saving souls from eternal condemnation.[699] The first half of the 19th century to the first decades of the 20th century was known as the "great century of missions."[700] In line with the Keswick[701] spirituality, which emphasized the individual conversion, holy living, and the immediate salvation through accepting Jesus Christ, inspired the members of the MTC and its evangelists to venture forth on missionary work along those goals of direct evangelism. Later, a paradigm shift[702] occurred in the

---

[699] Alex Thomas, "The Mar Thoma Church: Then and Now," in *In Search of Christian Identity in Global Community,* 45.

[700] The main outcome of the evangelical awakening of the 18th and 19th centuries was the rise of modern missionary movements in Europe. They were mainly: The London Missionary Society (LMS) in 1795, the Scottish Missionary society-1796, the Netherlands Missionary Society-1797, the Church Missionary Society (CMS) -1799, the British and Foreign Missionary Society -1804, the American Board of Commissioners for Foreign Missions (ABCFM)-1810, the American Baptist Foreign Mission Society -1814, the Basel Mission -1816, the Wesleyan Methodist Missionary Society-1817-18, the Danish Missionary Society-1821, the Berlin Missionary Society -1824, the Rhenish Missionary Society -1828, the Swedish Missionary Society -1835 and the North German Missionary Society -1836. Most of these organizations were voluntary societies independent of the Church. These institutions considered themselves as separate institutions concerned with Christian missions in overseas. William Anderson, *Towards a Theology of Mission* (London: SCM, 1955), 15. Stephen B. Bevans and Roger P. Schroeder, *Constants in Context: A Theology of Mission for Today* (New York, Maryknoll: Orbis, 2004), 212. Herbert J. Kane, *Understanding Christian Missions* (Grand Rapids, MI: Baker Book, 1983), 142.

[701] The Keswick movement is an evangelical movement emerged in England in the late 19th century. The term Keswick derives its name from a small community in the Lake District of England who urged for personal holiness and high moral values. They stressed the possibility of victorious Christian life and the need for a definitive crisis experience. They conduct a spiritual convention with a view to promote personal holiness and spiritual victory. The aim of the Keswick movement is the "Promotion of Practical Holiness. From Keswick the teaching quickly spread over England, Canada and the United States, with Moody himself being key to the propagation of Keswick teaching in the U.S. Keswick is not a doctrinal system, much less an organization or a denomination. Though leading churchmen and noted scholars led the movement, like Hudson Tayor, Andrew Murray, Amy Carmichael, Handley Moule, F.B. Meyer,.L. Moody, Robert McQuilley, no Keswick leader has written a treatise on its teaching. There is no official doctrinal statement and a broad variety of doctrinal positions have been held and taught by those associated with the name Keswick. Mark Steven Rathe, *The Keswick Movement its Origins and Teachings,* M.A. Thesis (San Francisco: Simpson College, 1987).

[702] A paradigm shift takes place when there is a leap from one world-view to another which allows the world to be explained and interpreted in a new way. A paradigm is defined as "an entire constellation of beliefs, values, techniques, and so on, shared by the members

understanding of mission and the Church searched for new ways to make the mission relevant to the community along with direct evangelism. Later, the Church had developed a theological vision for mission, considering the pluralistic context of India. By adopting an incarnational model of mission, the Church attempted to challenge the evils of the caste structure, serving the poor through hospitals, destitute homes and other like social institutions. The Church started day care centres for poor children, orphans and the socially deprived communities and initiated many programmes for the development of villages. The Church also attempted to provide education for all people irrespective of their caste or religious status.[703] According to Thomas, several factors contributed to the shift in the mission understanding of the MTC. A shift in the mission theory has taken place from the Willington Conference of the International Missionary Council in 1952.[704] The mission of the Church came to be understood as the work of God in the world (*Missio Dei*[705]) rather than an agenda of the Church. The concept of the Kingdom became the frame of reference of the mission of the Triune God. Jesus embodied the Kingdom of God through acts of healing, redemption and reconciliation. The Church is no longer seen as the goal of mission, but as an instrument of God's mission.[706] The mission is

---

of a given community. It is an entire worldview." Spencer, *SCM Study Guide to Christian Mission,* 40-41.

[703] Thomas, "The Mar Thoma Church: Then and Now," 45.

[704] The Willington Statement was clear that "the Missionary calling of the Church is derived from the mission of God; the Church has a missionary calling rather than a mission, and that calling is to engage in God's mission. Our mission therefore has no life of its own, only in the hands of the sending God alone. The Church is both part of what God is doing, as a particular expression or embodiment of the work of God flowing from the very nature of God, and the Church has a particular vocation to engage with God in this work, in and for the world." Richards, et al., *Foundations For Mission,* 53. Bevans and Roger, *Constants in Context,* 284-285.

[705] Karl Barth was the key figure behind the coining of the phrase '*Missio Dei*' as a summary of mission's dependence on the initiative of God himself. Mission was not to be seen as one of humanity's building projects, carried forward by its own strength and reason, but as a divine movement in which the Church was privileged to participate. It is his student Dietrich Bonhoeffer (1906-1945) who has been described as 'the architect' of new way of understanding the mission of the Church. Bosch, *Transforming Mission,* 375. With Barth, he saw that the foundation of faith, mission, the Church and theology is not human enquiry, reason or science but God's revelation in Jesus Christ.

[706] Thomas, "Mar Thoma Church: Then and Now," 46.

witness to the fullness of the promise of God's Kingdom, and participation with Christ in the ongoing struggles between the Kingdom of God and the power of darkness and evil in the world. Bosch observed that all Churches, including the Roman Catholic Church, embraced the paradigm shift of the Church-centred mission to a Kingdom-centred mission. Since Vatican II, the missionary nature of the Church had been defined on the Trinitarian foundation where the focus of mission is the Kingdom of God.

The MTC has undertaken mainly two models of mission. By following the methods of Western missionary movements like London Missionary Society (LMS), CMS, Basel mission, this Church firstly adopted a Church-centric paradigm of mission, and later shifted to a Kingdom-centric paradigm corresponding to the growth of its missiological and theological understanding. For instance, the cross-cultural mission in the North Kanara, South India, reflects these shifts in its missiology with a gradual movement towards an incarnational pattern of mission. In this pattern, the gospel becomes a way of life and its message transforms life.[707] By the middle of the 20th century, the Church had formed five mission fields altogether in Kerala and in Karnataka viz: South Travancore Mission, Central Travancore Mission, North Travancore Mission, Palakkad Mission, and Kanara Mission.[708] The paradigm shift of the Kingdom-centred mission came into the MTC considerably through the preaching of E. Stanley Jones, (1884-1973) who was a regular speaker at the Marmon convention for half a century. His theology of mission was grounded in the biblical theology of the Kingdom of God. He understood the Kingdom of God as expressed in the Nazareth manifesto of Jesus Christ (Lk.4:18) as a model for Christians to follow. He introduced the sermon of Jesus at Nazareth[709] as a missionary paradigm to the MTC. Thus, the Church focused on witness to the reign

---

[707] Thomas, *A History of the First Cross Cultural Mission,* 129.
[708] Y.T. Vinaya Raj, "When the 'Mission Field' writes the History," in *In Search of Christian Identity in the Community, of the Church,* ed. Joseph, 149-153.
[709] The reign of God has its transforming influence on the economic, the social, the political, and the moral and spiritual life of the people.

of God as its goal of mission. The Metropolitan Alexander Mar Thoma rightly pointed out that,

> "Jesus Christ came to preach good news to the poor, to proclaim liberty to the captives, to give sight to the blind and to set free the oppressed. Evil is found both in individuals and in the structures of the society. The gospel has to be presented as the power of God which saves individuals and changes social structures; it is the duty of the Church to work on both levels."[710]

The MTC believes that the Church is present in the world to work for the Kingdom of God established through the person and work of Christ. The Church considers that the Christian mission is both proclamation and engaging in activities that liberate people. Evangelism, social service, struggles for social justice and truth, and uplifting of the depressed class is the inevitable responsibility of the Church. Thus, the goal of the mission of this Church is the total redemption of individuals and the society. The missionary outreach programmes of the Church are both personal and social. It involves both evangelism and social development. In the beginning, the mission understanding of the Church was of the affirmation of the Church and activity of establishing churches. Unlike western mission societies,[711] it was a mission of the Church and through the Church. It planted churches in different part of India. Later, the concern of the Church extends to the welfare of all individuals and their salvation, which is to be realized in their social life, employment, physical growth, and social, cultural and economic development. The role played by the Metropolitans of the Church, especially Abraham Mar Thoma and Juhanon Mar Thoma, to identify the social dimension of mission is noteworthy. The Church

---

[710] Alexander Mar Thoma, *The Mar Thoma Church: Heritage and Mission*, 26.
[711] "Very often the missionary movements during the 18th and 19th centuries considered mission as sending missionaries from the west to east and making them similar to the west in religion and culture. It was associated with western imperialism. Therefore, most of the missionaries who came to India were not able to find the rich religious and cultural heritage of India. It was on the basis of their missionary consciousness; the modern missionaries have not found the same western missionary consciousness in the Mar Thoma Church." Daniel, *Ecumenism in Praxis*, 56.

believes that the love of God spills over from the Christian community in all directions. It is not an accident, but a deliberate intention of corporate worship and a necessary result of it. They extend to society, culture, the state, and even the world of nature.

2.2 - Mission Models[712] in the Mar Thoma Church

The model of mission that emerges in the Church today is a result of a theological reflection on missionary practice in current multicultural, multi-religious, globalized and religiously polarized world.[713] As the Church moves forward as a witnessing community in the 21st century, there are various approaches communicating the Gospel, witness such as proclamation, liturgical action and contemplation, inculturation, interreligious dialogue, working for justice and peace, commitment to reconciliation. Later, models of mission emerged in considering the need of the time such as a dialogue model, an institutional, an ecumenical model etc. All contribute to a missionary practice that is both dialogical and prophetic, faithful to contemporary context as well as to the constants of Christian faith.[714] A new understanding of mission as expressed in the statement "mission belongs to God and not ours," motivated the Church to find new avenues for mission engagements.[715] It is about God's gracious

---

[712] Mission models are the result of systematic reflection on mission strategies. Models have provided answers for understanding a reality which is not immediately accessible to the senses. Through the models theologians present the different aspects of the same reality. Mission models are employed for the purpose of explanation, and this in a more comprehensive way. These models help us to articulate and present the ideas in a systematic way. James Empereur, *Models of Liturgical Theology* (Nottingham: Grove Books, 1987), 9-12. Sallie McFague, *Metaphorical Theology: Models of God in Religious Language* (Philadelphia: Foretess, 1982), 104-105.

[713] Philip Jenkins, "The Next Christianity," *Atlantic Monthly* 290/3 (October 2002): 53-72.

[714] Bevans and Roger, *Constants in Context*, 284-285.

[715] In his edited book, *Classic Texts in Mission and World Christianity*, Norman E. Thomas enumerated the contemporary paradigms of mission in a detailed way i.e. mission as the Church-with others, as *Missio Dei*, as mediating salvation, as quest for justice, as evangelization, as contextualization, as liberation, as inculturation, as common witness, as ministry by the whole people of God, as interfaith witness, as theology, as hope in action. Studying each of these paradigms are beyond the scope of this work. Norman E. Thomas, ed., *Classic Texts in Mission and World Christianity* (New York: Orbis, 2002), 81-304. Against the earlier models of evangelization of the whole world, modern understanding

invitation to humanity to share in the dynamic communion that is at the same time God's self-giving missionary life. It is more urgent because in a world of globalized poverty, militant religious fundamentalism and new appreciation of local culture and subaltern traditions, the vision and praxis of Jesus of Nazareth can bring new healing and new light.[716] The MTC has been employing many models to communicate the Gospel. The following are some of the more prominent mission paradigms endured by the Church.

2.2.1 - The Church Model of Mission

This model of mission states that the Church engages in mission and mission is for the sake of planting and building the Church.[717] This mission model put forward the three self-understanding principles of the Church, i.e. The Church as self-governing, self-propagating, self-sustaining. The Church and mission paradigm of the ecumenical movement during 1910-1938 goes along with this line. The first meetings of the World Missionary Conference in Edinburgh, 1910, and the Tambaram meeting of International Missionary Conference (IMC) gave primary emphasis to this mission model. Missionary methods and praxis are to a great extent determined and theologically sustained by the theological foundations of mission and evangelization. The Church believes that communicating the gospel is the primary task of her mission. In this model proclamation of the gospel or Evangelism[718] is considered as the heart of all missionary

---

of mission is most represented by the phrases of presence, humanization, dialogue, and liberation, etc. In Asia, Kim Yong-bock (1982) defines God's mission as the suffering people of Asia; Marlene Perera (1992) asserts that mission is to inaugurate the reign of God among human beings; and Prakai Nontawasee (1989), a former president of Christian Conference of Asia (CCA), sees mission in terms of mutual solidarity, meaning the work of enabling a meeting of different souls and persons, and allowing for the lives of people to be touched by one another.

[716] Bevans and Roger, *Constants in Context*, 284-285.

[717] A focusing biblical text for this model is Mt.28:19-20 "Go therefore and make disciples........ to the end of the age." It affirms that every person converted to Christ becomes a member of the universal Church and individual churches are local expressions of that One Catholic Church. The members are added to the Church only as they are joined to Christ by faith. Kane, *Understanding Christian Missions*, 300.

[718] There are two words in the New Testament, which are pertinent to evangelism. The noun *Evangelion* means good news which occurs seventy five times in the New Testament and

endeavours. The very heart of the gospel lies in its mission and it is the mark of the Church.[719] In Evangelism, the term "missionary methods" refer to the procedure through which the reign of God is established on earth, the Church is planted in the people and the gospel is proclaimed among those who have not yet heard it.[720] In a critical view, a Church centric model of mission aimed at proselytism and church planting later proved to be inadequate for the multi-religious community of Indian society. In a cross-cultural context, this model was very often criticized as an exclusive approach towards Church planting.[721]

2.2.2 - The Kingdom Model of Mission

The Kingdom model of mission is a highly appreciated paradigm in mission theology. The Christian Church is a community commissioned to represent the Kingdom of God in history. The Church itself is not the Kingdom of God, but it is its agent, its anticipation, and its fragmentary realization. Jesus Christ, according to Christian conviction, is the centre of history.[722] Therefore, the mission of the Church is to invite others to experience the new life in Jesus Christ (2 Cor.5:17). The model of Kingdom in the Bible describes it as the one that encompasses all of life that welcomes the most unlikely subject, exposes every pocket of evil and liberates from every injustice and oppression (Lk.9:2, 14:13,21, Jn.18: 36). The life, ministry, passion, death and resurrection of Jesus enables the Church to identify with him today. This criterion leads the Church not only to discover who Christ is, but where he is to be found today; i.e. among the poor, the powerless, and the oppressed- and what he is doing; healing their wounds, breaking the chains of oppression, demanding justice and peace, giving life and

---

the verb *evangelizomai* means "to publish good news" which appears twenty four times. The word evangelism derived from the term *evangelion*. The gospel is the evangel, the good news. Evangelism is the act of proclaiming the good news. Kane, *Understanding Christian Missions*, 298, 303.

[719] Kane, *Understanding Christian Missions*, 298.
[720] Muller et al., *Dictionary of Missions*, 316-320.
[721] Thomas, *A History of the First Cross-Cultural Mission*, 130.
[722] Tillich, "The Theology of Missions," 25.

imparting hope to the hurting. This model of mission affirms that the Church is commissioned to comfort the grieving, encourage the lonely, feed the hungry, minister to the handicapped, help the aged, the abused and the confused. Jesus entered into human history to redeem the whole creation and to establish the Kingdom of God. This model suggests a holistic transformation towards Christ. The involvement of the Church with the conciliar ecumenical movement provided the idea that Jesus embodied the Kingdom of God through acts of preaching, healing, reconciliation and redemption. The Church was no longer the goal of mission but an instrument of God's mission. Thus the MTC began to focus on witnessing to the Kingdom of God in its mission thought. The Church incorporated evangelism and church planting within a wider vision of a Kingdom-centered model of mission. [723]

2.2.3 - An Incarnational Model of Mission

Incarnation is the very heart and nature of the mission. Incarnational model of mission means that just as God became fully human in the person of Jesus Christ, the followers of Christ become fully at home in their own particular space and time. It calls for an intimate, incarnational identification with people in a particular culture where the Church communicates the Gospel. The Church is often defined as the extension of Christ's incarnation. The Church is equipped with the Holy Spirit to represent Christ to the world. The faithful embody the Gospel which means that they have Christ living in them, and therefore their lives express incarnational mission. The MTC adopted an incarnation pattern in mission, in which the goal of mission is neither proselytism nor widening the boundaries of the Church; rather, the mission is witnessing to the reign of God by identifying with the marginalized and providing opportunities for them to grow as human beings. The incarnation of God through Jesus Christ invites the Church "to become living members of Christ's earthly community and to begin a

---

[723] Thomas, *A History of First Cross Cultural Mission*, 130.

life of service to others."[724] This would bring a new social order in which the values of the Kingdom of God dominate.[725] This new social order is not limited by any earthly institution, and even by the Church. The MTC's mission, therefore, is to witness the message of "incarnation-identification" of God with the people and world realities. As a witnessing community in a multi- cultural and religious pluralistic context, the Church adopted an incarnational pattern of mission as its suitable model of mission in the religious pluralistic context of India.[726] The concept of incarnation is used as a criterion for evaluating the contextual nature of the mission.

2.2.4 - An Institutional Model of Mission

The Church envisioned changes occurring in society. Society was becoming modern with the realization of self / individual, secular space, democracy, equal right of citizens, and institutionalization. In line with this modern trend, the Church itself was organized as an institution. The adoption of the constitution of the Church is a classic example of this. The MTC established many institutions to propagate the gospel. These institutions are considered as instruments of mission. The Mar Thoma Evangelistic Association itself is an institution. When we reflect on the institutional nature of the Church there are mainly three areas to which the Church gave special focus, i.e. education, health and social work.

The value of education has always been an integral part of the missionary movement. Besides preaching the gospel to the outcast, the Church gave attention to their educational and economic progress. The programme of education has been considered as an important aspect of the mission of the Church.[727] The MTC took a major role in it. Rev. K. E. Oommen (1881-

---

[724] Bosch, *Transforming Missions,* 10-11.
[725] Orlando E. Costas, "Christian Missions in the America," in *New Directions in Mission and Evangelization-Theological Foundations,* eds. James A. Scherer and Stephen B. Bevans (Marknoll, New York: Orbis, 1994), 9.
[726] Thomas, A *History of the First Cross Cultural Mission,* xiii.
[727] The Western missionaries, Churches and religious organizations were in the forefront of education in India. The Anglican missionaries marked the beginning of a new deal in education. During the colonial time, education had been the traditional prerogative of the higher castes in the social context of Kerala. It was a monopoly of the high caste

1984) states that the reason for starting the schools under the auspices of the MTC was "the desire of its members to read the Bible."[728] He says, "people had Bibles and they wanted to read, but there were only very few people who could read and write. Therefore, they wanted their children to learn to read the Bible at home. Hence, primary schools were started wherever possible with the grant-in-aid system. It resulted in the Church beginning several schools in various places. The Church has shown great enthusiasm to start English-medium schools also with a view to equip children to read the commentaries of the Bible."[729] A Christian sense of mission impels the Church to give a preferential option for the poor and the marginalized and for the education of their children.[730] The early Mar Thoma community established more than 120 primary schools in Kerala. The Church runs many village schools to cater to the needs of the less privileged, especially in the North Indian villages.[731]

---

people. The vision that low castes also have the right to education gave an impetus for their emancipation and liberation from the social and political context. It created a space for social transformation and change. With the aim of uplifting people through education, the primary school education was given a forward thrust.

[728] K. K. George, George Zacharia, Ajith Kumar, *Grants-in-Aid' Policies and Practices Towards Secondary Education in Kerala* (New Delhi: National Institute of Educational Planning and Administration, 2002), 1-3.

[729] The MTC started schools to provide learning to read and mediate the Bible with the assistance of commentaries through the medium of English and in the vernacular, and to provide elementary education to the converts from the "lower castes." The educational institutions are not limited to formal learning, but to the training of the students in a variety of fields and thus enabling them to be active participants in the building up of a new society. It strives to achieve the integral development of the human personality. George, Zacharia and Kumar, *Grants-in-Aid*, 1-3. A. Sreedhara Menon, *A Cultural Heritage of Kerala*, (Madras: V. Subramanayam, 1996), 163. K.E. Oommen, M.T and E.A Schools, in *Mar Thoma Schoolukal* (Malayalam) 1-3, 89. *Mar Thoma Schoolukal Charithra Samkshepam*, 1-159. This book contains the concise history of the Mar Thoma schools.

[730] Pauly Kannookadan, ed., *The Mission Theology of the Syro-Malabar Church,* (Kochi: Liturgical Research Centre, 2008), 250.

[731] The Mar Thoma Gram Jyoti Education and Development Society which was started in 1997 meant to establish village schools (Gram Jyoti Schools) in North India is a typical example of continuing the spirit of mission. It is a matter of witnessing the Christian presence and message. The schools become landmarks, symbols, and milestones of faith and witnessing. Along with the secular education, the Church gives priority to the theological education. The main purpose of the theological institutions is to impart biblical, theological, liturgical and pastoral training to candidates for the ministry of the Church. The principal theological institution of the Church is the Mar Thoma Theological

Under the institutional model of mission, a medical mission[732] is a part of the missionary outreach programme of the Church. It is an integral part of the witness of the Church. The medical mission started in 1947. Through the medical mission, the evangelistic concern for the sick and suffering is being fulfilled. The medical mission is closely connected with the Evangelistic Association of the Church. To convert people to Christianity is not the purpose of the medical mission but to render them Christian love and stewardship through their service and medical care. The medical service in itself is a part of the mission of the Church. It is an expression of the healing ministry of Christ. The Church has 49 social welfare institutions, 14 destitute homes and 9 hospitals.[733]

2.2.5 - A Charity and Developmental Model

An act of service is an integral part of the proclamation of the Gospel. The Church has to work for the growth of society and contribute her share in nation building. The charity model of mission is significant in the Church. It is distinguished by at least three characteristics. (a) It is always self-giving. (b) It is done in the name of Jesus. (c) Its final consequence one cannot fully comprehend or calculate in the here and now. Love of God and love of neighbour is closely connected.

The MTC gives special attention to the holistic development of the people and their life conditions. The salvific act of Christ is directly related to the world, and this is fundamental to both development and mission. In

---

Seminary, established in 1926, at Kottayam. Currently, The Church owns 14 colleges, 6 Higher Secondary Schools, 8 High Schools, 1 Vocational Higher Secondary School, 4 technical institutes, 1 Teachers Training Institute, 15 U.P. Schools and 114 primary schools. Besides, there are several schools and other educational institutions owned and managed by individual parishes. Joseph, *Malankara Mar Thoma Syrian Church: Sabha Directory 2015*, 23. Zac Varghese, ed., *Christian Witness: Revisiting the Mission Mandate of the Church*, Prathinidhimandalam 2009 Study (Thiruvalla: Mar Thoma Syrian Church, 2009), 35.

[732] The modern missionaries, taking its cue from Jesus, has actively promoted medical missions, including clinics, dispensaries, rest homes, hospitals, and in a few cases medical schools. In fact, the modern scientific medicine and surgery were introduced to the third world by Christian missionaries.. Kane, *Understanding Christian Missions*, 308.

[733] Joseph, *Malankara Mar Thoma Syrian Church: Sabha Directory*, 24.

the person and works of Jesus, God proclaims sovereignty over the whole of life and not just over a religious sector of it. Likewise the Church is concerned with all spheres of life; and so it is not the Church development services which brings transformation, but, on the contrary, it is the Holy Spirit which injects transformation in the service.[734] The Development Department of the Church is the most recent organization formed with a missionary concern.[735] The "Bhoo-bhavana Dana "movement (gift of land and house) initiated by Metropolitan Juhanon Mar Thoma in 1968 has now completed forty seven years. The Church, through this project, envisages building and providing houses to the people who suffer due to lack of proper housing. Around 8400 houses have been constructed and given to the needy ones irrespective of caste and religion in Kerala and other states outside Kerala.[736] The Church runs several orphanages and destitute homes to give asylum to the needy; all these provide many opportunities for the

---

[734] At the World Conference for Church and Society in 1966 and at the Fourth Assembly of the WCC in Uppsala in 1968, the phase "responsible society" coined in Amsterdam in 1948, was taken up, and focus was on justice as such as society's constitutive element. The Uppsala assembly called on the Churches to allocate five percent of their budgets for development. The creation of a just society is possible only through a sustainable development that must be based on peace and justice. Muller, et al., *Dictionary of Missions*, 102-108.

[735] The work of this department is done through a registered society named Christian Agency for Rural Development (CARD). Its main objective is to act as a facilitator, an agent for change, or catalyst, to motivate and equip rural people to organize themselves for economic, educational and cultural development for social justices. There are over 40 social institutions in the Church, which are located in different geographical areas. They include counselling centres, hospital guidance centres, hospice for the terminally ill, schools for the mentally and physically challenged children. Through these institutions, the Church shows its distinctive character as a visible sign of its concern for the less privileged and the needy. It is an attempt in the area of social witness. Zacharias Mar Theolophilus, "The Pastoral Ministry of the Mar Thoma Church," in *In Search of Christian Identity in the Community*, 35-38.

[736] Joseph Mar Thoma Metropolitan, *Circular No.245*, dated 01st February 2016. Later, as part of the "home for the homeless" project in commemorating the silver jubilee of episcopal ministry of the Metropolitan Emeritus Philipose Mar Chrysostom Mar Thoma, with the cooperation of the Kerala government, the Church constructed around 5,000 houses for the homeless irrespective of caste and religion. There is also the Marriage Aid Fund started in 1972, to render financial aid to the poor for the marriage of their daughters. The relief fund designed to give immediate relief to individuals and groups who are affected by calamities such as floods, cyclone, tsunami etc. has responded well in times of need.

members in far-flung corners of the world to participate in the mission model of charity in the Church.

2.2.6 - A Dialogue Model of Mission

Dialogue is a part of the evangelizing mission of the Church. In dialogue, there is a space for listening and speaking, learning and teaching, understanding and respecting, mutually helping and collaborating. Dialogue fosters mutual enrichment, fecundation and harmony among the followers of different religions. Besides, it challenges participants to grow deeper in their religious convictions and faith.[737] Dialogue is part of the living relationship between people of different faiths and ideologies as they share in the life of the community.[738] In the midst of the plurality of faith and multiplicity of cultural and ethnic communities, the Christian community can fulfill its prophetic role only in collaboration with others. This is a practical reason for dialogue of the Church with another religion.[739]

---

[737] Even though the term dialogue is not in the Bible, the warm relationships and the intense personal encounters suggested by the active verb are very prominent throughout the Bible. The basis on which Christians enter into and continue their dialogue with others is their faith in Jesus Christ. Christian participation in dialogue is a part of the concrete living out of the view of life and the way of life that stem from faith in Jesus Christ Kannookadan, *The Mission Theology of the Syro-Malabar Church*, 274. S. J. Samartha, "Dialogue as a Continuing Christian Concern," in *Mission Trends No. 1: Critical issues in Mission Today,* eds. Gerals H.Anderson, Thomas F. Stansky (New York: Paulist, 1974), 259.

[738] Anderson, *Mission Trends,* 247.

[739] Dialogue is a positive attitude and profound reason to recognize the presence and action of God in other religions. A dialogue can promote mutual respect, acceptance, transformation and enrichment as well as collaboration in the fight against injustice and evil structures. Through dialogue one understands his own religion and faith in a better way. Mission as dialogue requires that vulnerability, humility, and openness to other faiths encountered. In a multi- religious and plural cultural context of the world, the mission of the Church calls for it to be a truly dialogical community. It demands an attitude of openness and respect to other faiths and the role of being an agent of reconciliation and peace among the various groups. The Church has to create a common forum of dialogue and liberalize action through which mutual misunderstanding, hatred, discord and discrimination could be opposed, a forum which could together build up a nation with justice, peace and harmony. The primary task of the Church in this context is to build up a human community, which is based on freedom, fellowship, equality, justice, and peace. The mission of the Church, then, is universal reconciliation. Amaladoss,"Challenges of Mission in the 21st century," 16-20.Anderson, *Mission Trends,* 247-262. Stephen B. Bevans and Roger P. Schroeder, *Prophetic Dialogue: Reflections on Christian Mission Today* (Maryknoll: Orbis, 2011), 37-38.

The New Delhi assembly of the World Council of Churches (WCC) in 1961 referred to "dialogue as a form of evangelism which is often effective today."[740] Uppsala 1968 pointed out that "the meeting with men of other faiths or of no faith must lead to dialogue. A Christian dialogue with another implies neither a denial of the uniqueness of Christ, nor any loss of his own commitment to Christ, but rather that a genuinely Christian approach to others must be human, personal, relevant and humble."[741] Listening and participating in dialogue can be a form of proclamation in the quest for truth. The MTC follows a dialogue model of mission. The Church is engaged in dialogue with other religions and groups to foster unity and peace in society. The Church believes that dialogue affirms the other and at the same time helps to grow in relation, not in isolation. The Church established many dialogue centers for creative engagements with other faith communities. The Alexander Mar Thoma Centre for dialogue in Kottarakkara, Kerala is a classic example of this mission.

2.2.7 - The Sacramental Model of Mission

The Church is a sign, foretaste and instrument of God's reign in Christ entrusted with the responsibility to shape and direct the world with the power of the sacraments. Since sacraments are a visible expression of the invisible grace, (reality), the Church reveals the power of the sacraments through its very identity and mission. Sacraments point to the eternal blessings, which are meant to understand the divine grace. Sacraments are effective in two ways: culturally effective in organizing human life and theologically effective in integrating human persons into the life of God. Cultural efficacy is not divine power, but human beings encounter the Trinity in human culture, through the incarnation and sacrament. Jesus Christ is the center of every liturgical celebration. The ecclesiological understanding of the Church as the sacrament, sign and instrument was very much dominant in the debate dealing with the missiological

---

[740] World Council of Churches, *New Delhi Report: Section III* (London: SCM, 1961), 84.
[741] *The Uppsala Report 1968* (Geneva: WCC, 1968), 29.

226

nature of the Church. The Church continually proclaims Christ and his Paschal Mystery through its liturgical celebrations. The worship is not just something the Church does alongside witnessing the Good news; worship itself is a witness to the world. It is a sign that all of life is holy, that hope and meaning can be found in offering ourselves to God (Rom.12:1). The celebration of Eucharist proclaims Christ's death until he comes (1 Cor.11:26). The liturgical life of the Church is a vital dimension of the mission calling.[742] The worship and liturgy proclaim the mission of the Church both internally and externally. Internally, it gives the assurance of the presence of God personally to the faithful and externally it proclaims their identity and vocation.

Stamoolis speaks of the liturgy as a method for mission. It is the source of Christian witness because at liturgy the faithful open themselves to the Spirit, through communion with the Lord's body and blood.[743] The liturgy is always the entrance into the presence of the Triune God and always ends with the community being sent forth in God's name to transform the world in God's image. Hence the mission is conceived, in other words, as "the liturgy after liturgy," the natural consequences of entering into the divine presence in worship.[744] As the document, "Go Forth in Peace put it, "the liturgy is not an escape from life, but a continuous transformation of life according to the prototype of Jesus Christ, through the power of the Spirit. The liturgy does not end when the Eucharist assembly disperses. "Let us go forth in peace;" the dismissal is a sending off of every believer to mission in the world where he or she lives and works, and of the whole community in the world, to witness to what they are and to the truth that the Kingdom is coming."[745]

---

[742] Richards, *Foundations of Mission*, 56.

[743] Bevans and Roger, *Constants in Context*, 295.

[744] Bria, *Liturgy after the Liturgy*, 27-32.

[745] Ion Bria, ed., *Go Forth in Peace: Orthodox Perspectives on Mission* (Geneva: WCC, 1986), 226.

2.3 - Models of Mission: A Critical Assessment

Since, the MTC has extended considerably as a multi-cultural and multi-ethnic community around the world, it is imperative that, they have to design appropriate models of mission in considering its context. Otherwise the mission of the Church becomes irrelevant and the identity of the Church seems to become just a multi-ethnic minority institution. Very often the traditional pattern of mission such as Church planting, direct evangelism, emphasis on proselyticism etc., seems to be rejected by the community at large because of the arising religious intolerance, fundamentalism, inequality and injustice. At present, there is no common strategy or pattern for mission in the Church. For instance, it is important to analyse critically how far the Church could do justice to her calling of liberation of the Dalit Christians within the Church.[746] A liberational approach of mission is the need of the hour which urges the Church to consider socio-economic injustice as unacceptable to the justice of God. Our faith in a liberator God compels us to involve ourselves to affirm solidarity with the poor and liberating them from the unjust structures. The mission strategy of the Church is not that of extending its boundaries; rather it has to share the true spirit of unity, cordiality, solidarity of the people in their struggle for justice and peace and equality and to focus on God's Kingdom revealed in Christ. In this juncture, the mission of the Church must be holistic and it should address all aspects, threats and challenges of the whole of humanity. [747]

---

[746] It is unfortunate to note that there are segregation and the practice of casteism within the MTC. Very often Dalit Marthomites left the Church in large numbers because of the casteism within it. The formation of the "Prathyaksha Raksha Daiva Sabha" by Poikayil Yohannan is a protest against this. It was only in 1981 that Dalit Marthomites were given the status of parishes in the Church. For a long time they were called Sabha, almost with a segregationist connotation, but in 1971, they came to be called chapels which later was upgraded to parishes. Currently, the constitution of the MTC ensures representation of Dalits in decision-making bodies of the Church, such as Sabha Council, (Executive body of the Church) and Diocesan Councils. There are several development programmes being carried out for the holistic development of Dalit and Adivasi communities through the agencies like STARD, Christian Agency for Rural Development (CARD), and BPDP (Backward People's Development Programme) in the Church. Interview with Rev. K.Y Jacob, the director of the CARD on December 15, 2015. Joseph, "Abraham Malpante Naveekaranam," in Sabha Directory-2015, 353-355.

[747] Amaladoss, "Challenges of Mission in the 21st Century," 18-20.

The Church has to discover new patterns of mission in considering the needs of the context. There is a fundamental distinction between the Church and the Kingdom of God in the present context. This distinction radically changes the traditional absolutists and the exclusivist understanding of the Church and its mission. The values of the Kingdom of God is radically a new reality and order, and the Church is commissioned to be a sign and servant of the Kingdom of God. Hence, the Kingdom and the historical Church are not identical. The Church has to give way to the Kingdom of God.[748] The goal of the Mar Thoma mission activity is to witness the redeeming power of God in Jesus Christ through its very life. As we have seen, the focus of the Eucharist liturgy is the incarnational nature of Christ and his salvific act for the redemption of whole creation. Since the Church employs the incarnational model in its mission activities, their renders Church considerably more relevant in the transformation of society. Hence an emphasis on the incarnational pattern of mission has to be reiterated in the Church.

It is worth noting the positive role played by the institutions and ancillary organizations of the Church in its mission. The institutions employed a charity and developmental model of mission in the Church. A caution here: even though the Church could make a great impact in society through its institutions, it has nevertheless to be cautious of the danger of secular ideologies in its witnessing life. At present, institutions very often tend to become so timid and seem to keep a deliberate silence against evil practices in society such as corruption, discrimination, and injustice. There is a growing tendency that appears to move in line with the secular institutions; that is to say maintain the priority of making profit, over the communication of Christian values. Although the Church had taken education as part of ministry and mission, it worked in a hierarchical frame of paternalism (enlightened to the less enlightened - Missionaries to

---

[748] Kuncheria Pathil, "A Response to Religious Pluralism," in *In Search of Christian Identity in Global Community*, 89-90.

Syrian Christians and Syrian Christians to the new believers) challenging the spirit of mission itself.

In a multi-religious and pluralistic context like India, there is a need to affirm the Kingdom values of justice, peace, love, respect, and tolerance for creating a peaceful co-existence. In other words, to witness is to search for the eternal truths of the Kingdom of God and become partners in fighting for common Christian causes, celebrating festivals together and working to re-establishing and sustaining the integrity of creation. Thus acknowledging the presence of God in other religious traditions is included in the area of witnessing.[749] In the present context, the Church should make all efforts to remove every trace of triumphalism, exclusivism and any attitude of superiority in its teachings, structures, evangelizing activities and the style of the functioning of its institutions. Particularly, it has to ensure that its educational enterprises, charitable activities, health care services and social involvements are geared to the genuine promotion of people's well-being and progress and not in any way to convert from their religions. However, it should be pointed out that the Church always defends the right of individuals to profess the religion of their choice. All the same, it denounces proselytisation through the use of questionable means, such as fraud, force and allurement.

The religious pluralist[750] context demands new policies for Church mission. The attitude of the Church vis-à-vis another religion had been apologetic and missionary. She defended her uniqueness and invited others

---

[749] Zac Varghese, ed., "Christian Witness: Revisiting the Mission Mandate of the Church," *Prathinidhimandalam 2009 Study* (Thiruvalla: Mar Thoma Syrian Church, 2009), 28-29.
[750] Plurality has existed in India for centuries but pluralism is a modern reality. Traditional India had been a land in which peoples and communal groups who followed different religions, lived according to different cultural values and social patterns, and spoke different languages, coexisted. There was a religious tolerance and mutual acceptance, and respect prevailed in the social and personal scenarios. Nevertheless, throughout the periods of history, a general dominant tendency came to birth due to colonial situations, unequal social structure, and the politicization of religion. It influenced the social fabric of Indian society. The movement from co-existence to dialogue existence is the movement from plurality to pluralism. This movement of plurality to pluralism is not only national but also local as well as worldwide. M. M Thomas, *The Church's Mission and Post Modern Humanism: Collection of Essays and Talks 1992-1996* (New Delhi: ISPCK, 1996), 129.

to join her; co-existence, collaboration and solidarity in the common struggle against atheism and evil materialism in an effort to build a better world were not within her scope.[751] In a multi-religious context, the Church must consciously build up a multi-religious society, in which every religious community is recognized, accepted and respected and in which this new order allows each group to contribute its riches to the good of all.[752]

Pattern of dialogue is a crucial aspect in the mission in the present context, since the Church faces various challenges in the face of nascent fundamentalism and religious intolerance. In a pluralistic context, the Church has to consider the dialogue model of mission more seriously when it encounters other faith communities. Dialogue between world-views becomes possible and indeed necessary for life. Dialogue then becomes the only possible mode of co-existence.[753] The Malankara Church reacts to the reality of Indian religious plurality by way of two major paradigms of the modern world, viz., inclusivism and pluralism.[754] In the present context, instead of ecclesio-centrism which is exclusive in nature, Inclusivism or Karl Rahner' classic term of "Anonymous Christian"[755] is a meaningful and effective attitude for the communication of the Gospel.

In a diverse cultural context of India, the Church has to create a common platform to have healthy dialogue and liberalized action through which mutual misunderstanding, hatred, discord and discrimination could be identified and opposed. The primary task of the Church in this context is to build up a human community, which is based on freedom, fellowship, equality, justice, and peace. The mission of the Church then

---

[751] Gregory Karotemprel and Jacob Marangattu, eds., *Evangelizing In The Third Millennium, Series No-1* (Rajkot: Deepti Publication, 2006), 55.

[752] Thomas Malipurathu and L. Stanislaus, eds., *A Vision of Mission in the New Millennium* (Mumbai: St Paul's, 2001), 77.

[753] Karl Rahner, *Theological Investigations*, vol. 6, trans. David Bourke (London: Darton, Longman and Todd, 1976), 35.

[754] Daniel, *Ecumenism in Praxis,* 57.

[755] Christ's salvation and grace is given to all, even outside the boundaries of the visible Church; it is present also in other religions, though they do not know it. This expression denotes people, who live in the state of Christ's grace through faith, hope and love, yet who have no explicit knowledge of the fact that his life is orientated in grace-given salvation to Jesus Christ. Rahner, *Theological Investigations*, vol. 14, 283.

is universal reconciliation.[756] Building a genuine human community that brings together people of all religions and cultures with the dialogical framework of pluralism is the common historical responsibility of the time. The uniqueness of each human person and diversity in the community invite us to the possibility of accepting the "other" as "other."[757] In a multi-religious context, the Church must consciously build up a multi-religious society, in which every religious community is recognized, accepted and respected and in this new order allowing each group to contribute its riches to the good of all. The witness of the Church is to follow the lifestyle of the cross in the context of respecting differences and accepting pluralities. For effective Christian witness, it is necessary to have increased trust and unity between faith communities. There is a need to re-engage and continue conversations with other religions and churches. There is an urgent need to affirm the Kingdom values of justice, peace, love, respect, and tolerance for creating a peaceful co-existence. In other words, to witness is to search for the eternal truths of the Kingdom of God and become partners in fighting for common Christian causes, celebrating festivals together and working to re-establishing and sustaining the integrity of creation.[758] Thus acknowledging the presence of God in other religious traditions is included in the area of witnessing.

In the present context, the Church should make all efforts to remove every trace of triumphalism, exclusivism and any attitude of superiority in its teachings, structures, evangelizing activities and the style of

---

[756] An approach of interreligious dialogue demands oneness and a vision of inclusive approach towards other religions and culture. It is based on the realization that Christ is present and active among all peoples and all religions and that the saving grace of Christ is present and operative in them; hence we need to enter into dialogue with them. The Church, while accepting Christ as God's final and full revelation, is at the same time aware of the fact that our realization of the fullness of the mystery of Christ will be possible only at the end of time, and that it is her task to grow in the realization of this mystery through sharing with others. D.S. Amalorpavadass, "Approaches, Meaning and Horizon of Evangelization," in *Light and Life We Seek to Share* (Patna: All India Consultation on Evangelization, 1973), 54-55. Thomas Malipurathu and L. Stanislaus, eds., *A Vision of Mission in the New Millennium* (Mumbai: St Paul's, 2001), 77.

[757] Joseph, *In Search of Christian Identity in the Community,* 89-92.

[758] Zac Varghese, ed., "Christian Witness: Revisiting the Mission Mandate of the Church," *Prathinidhimandalam 2009 Study* (Thiruvalla: Mar Thoma Syrian Church, 2009), 28-29.

the functioning of its institutions. Particularly, it has to ensure that its educational enterprises, charitable activities, health care services and social involvements are geared to the genuine promotion of people's well-being and progress and not in any way to convert from their religions.[759] The Christian task to witness and not to convert is important in the pluralistic context of India. However, there is nothing wrong in inviting those who respond positively to the person of Christ to experience fellowships around the Table of the Lord and the Table of the word as 'part of the Church' within their religious and cultural community-settings.

3 - Conclusion

As stated earlier, the Church is missionary by her very nature and purpose, and all the members of the Church are missionaries. The mission of the Church is mainly the proclamation of the universal salvific act of God unveiled in and by Jesus Christ, fructified by the Holy Spirit. The Evangelisation, thus, is a Trinitarian and ecclesial act of announcing the Good News of integral salvation for all humans. The Church exists in order to proclaim the Good News revealed through Christ. To witness the salvific life of Christ is the ultimate mission of the Church. Thus, the Eucharistic participation invites the faithful to render a Eucharistic presence in the world by the power of the Holy Spirit. As demonstrated above the Eucharist liturgy of the Church is treasured with missional models. The Church used these models extensively and thereby participating in the redemptive mission of God actively. The theological and liturgical paradigms of mission treasured in the Eucharistic liturgy is the guiding principles for mission in the Church. Particularly two mission strategies applied by the MTC in India are visible at this point: the incarnational model of mission and the Kingdom of God model of mission. An incarnational pattern of mission is the most effective model of mission in the Church where the

---

[759] Rienze Perera, "Religion, Cultures and Peace: The Challenge of Religious Pluralism and the Common Life of Asia," in *Faith and Life in Contemporary Asian Realities,* eds. Feliciano V Carino and Marina True (Hong Kong: Christian Conference of Asia, 2000), 112-113.

Gospel can be communicated in its best way by identifying with the people and to their cultural and social set up. The ashrams in the Church and their incarnation model of mission bear witness to this fact. The extension of mission work among the so-called outcastes of the community is also a classic example of this model of mission. It is obvious that the Church attempted to incarnate the Gospel through challenging the evils of the caste structure, serving the poor through hospitals and destitute homes, thereby focusing on the development of villages though several humanitarian programs. It aims at adopting the life and engagements of Jesus Christ as the mission of the Church. A major mission mandate in the village of India is to work for social and economic justice, peace and development with a strong emphasis on liberating the poor, from oppressive structures. It is an invitation to share the joy of Christ in His Kingdom. Participation in issues such as human rights, minority problems, social and economic injustice which we commonly face, gives a basis for dialogue.

Chapter 9

An Integration of Liturgy and Evangelism: A Historical and Liturgical Overview

After the formation of the MTC in 1889, the leaders of the community felt
the need for a spiritual renewal in the Church in the changing social context
of Kerala. They desired to have a spiritual renewal through revival of the
Church in the light of the Bible within the Oriental liturgical premises. The
Church leaders suggested three means to achieve this goal: conducting
revival meetings, founding mission fields among the so-called "outcast"
and starting secular schools and social institutions.[760] There are mainly
three agencies - Maramon Convention, Ancillary Organizations and
Ashrams - which gave an impetus for Church in its mission. An analysis
of the mission strategy of these institutions show that there is a clear
integration of Liturgy and Mission in its course of growth. The MTC along
with its Oriental Eastern liturgical tradition, moves forward with the Bible
to communicate the Gospel through its Eucharistic presence.

1 - The Maramon Convention and Mission (1895)

The Maramon Convention is an annual spiritual gathering which
contributed immensely to shape and design the identity and mission of
the MTC.[761] It is the most visible expression of the *koinonia* of the MTC

---

[760] Daniel, *Ecumenism in Praxis*, 107.

[761] The Maramon Convention, the largest Christian convention in Asia, is held at Maramon,
Kerala, India annually on the vast sand-bed of the Pampa River next to the Kozhencherry
Bridge. The missionary wing of the MTC, the Mar Thoma Evangelistic Association is the
organizer of this convention. This Bible convention is considered as a "Festival of Word"
with forty five bible studies and devotional sessions, intercessory prayers, dedication
services, worship services and Holy Qurbana services in three of the Churches nearby. It
extends from Sunday to Sunday usually on the second week of February every year. More

in general.[762] As mentioned earlier, the Christian community is built up through the proclamation of the Word of God and the celebration of the Liturgy. It is the Table and Word that unite the people of God. An engagement with Scripture is always central to the identity of a Christian community. The Christian communities are not just hearers of the Word, but also the proclaimers of the Word. Hence the pioneering endeavour of the MTC in spreading the Word of God is the formation of the Maramon Convention.

The Maramon Convention is the venue where the ministry of the Church is being planned and flourished in the premise of Scripture and Liturgy.[763] It is noteworthy that the various ancillary organizations of the Church like Sevika Sangham (Women's wing), Sunday School, Yuvajana Sakhyam (Youth Fellowship), Young Family fellowship, Voluntary Evangelistic Association, Baskiomos Fellowship[764] and Senior Citizen's fellowship arose in the Church for spiritual nurturing and Christian action after the

---

than 150,000 believers come together to listen to the Word of God. Theodosius, "Maramon Convention: Mission and Ministry," 28-31.

[762] *Koinonia* comes from the initiative of God in establishing communion with human beings by the power of the Spirit. The early Church continued to practice the *koinonia* of Christ by gathering together for worship and by the breaking of bread. They shared everything and fellowship in Christ was their strength (Acts.2:44-45). There are different dimensions of *koinonia*, such as *martyria* (witness), *diakonia* (service) and *leiturgia* (worship), fulfilment in the communication of the gospel, and in the celebration of the sacramentality of life. The theological concept of *communio* refers fundamentally to communion with God through Jesus Christ in the Holy Spirit. This communion occurs in the Word of God and in the sacraments. Figura, "The Works of Communion: Christian Community in Act," 231. Craig L. Nessan, *Beyond Maintenance to Mission: A Theology of the Congregation*, 2nd ed. (Minneapolis: Fortress, 2010), 4-5. Bradley, *From Memory to Imagination*, 113-115. Nessan, *Beyond Maintenance to Mission*, 4..

[763] .J. H. Bishop, "Past and Present of the Travancore and Cochin Mission," *The Church Missionary Intelligencer* XXI (October, 1896): 762. C.M. Agur, *Church History of Travancore* (New Delhi: Asian Educational Services, 1990, 186. T.C. Chacko, *Ayroor Achen Athava C.P.Philipose Kassisa* (Malayalam) (Kozhencherry: Mar Thoma Samajam, 1949), 36-39. Thomas, *A History of the First Cross Cultural Mission*, 49-50. Agur, *Church History of Travancore*, 186 -187, A.T. Philip, "Origin and Significance of the Maramon Convention," *Indian Church History Review* XXIX, no.2 (December 1995): 147-148. Karinjappally, *Roots and Wings*, 64-65.

[764] The Syriac term *Baskiyamo* means the daughter of the covenant. In the MTC, wife of a priest (popularly called Kochamma) has a special consideration as a daughter of the covenant who is expected to assist the priest in his pastoral ministries.

236

commencement of the convention. The hearing of the Gospel through the proclamation of the Word and experiencing the Word in the liturgy at Maramon helped the members to respond with loving Christian care and service to the needs for evangelization within the Church and outside it.[765] Thus Maramon Convention initiated a missionary movement within Kerala society, crossing caste boundaries.[766] The Maramon Convention is now a forum where the faithful and missionaries from various parts of the world gather together for homecoming, greater fellowship, and to renew their mission enthusiasm. In addition to the Metropolitan and bishops of the Church, eminent biblical scholars and popular preachers of various Christian denominations share the Word of God.[767] There has been significant contributions emerged from this convention, the first being the idea of voluntary contributions and the other voluntary evangelists. The idea of voluntary contribution enabled the members to contribute from their own resources to support the Church and her missionary activities.[768]

---

[765] Theodosius, "Maramon Convention, Mission and Ministry," 30-31.

[766] This Convention has inspired the members of the Church to take the Gospel to different parts of India which have different languages, cultures, manners and religious background; thus the gospel was preached in Karwar, Ankola, Hoskote, Sihora, Satna, Tibetan Border, Nepal and such other places of North India and South India. Initially the Evangelistic Association came up to support these mission centres. Now there are sixty two mission fields, reaching out to two thousand six hundred Indian villages that are supported by the various organizations of the Church, and different dioceses. They established many schools, medical clinics, and caring centres for Mother and child, etc.

[767] The prominent preachers in the Marmon Convention includes Thomas Walker, England (1900–1912), Sadhu Sunder Singh, Punjab (1918), Dr. G. Sherwood Eddy (1919), Dr. E. Stanley Jones, USA (1920–1968), Dr. Toyohiko Kagawa, Japan (1938), John R. Mott, Nobel Peace Prize winner (1946) and President of World Alliance of YMCAs, Dr. Bob Pierce, founder and president of World Vision (1964 and 1966), Astronaut Colonel James Irwin (1985), Dr. John Haggai, founder president of Haggai Institute (1973), Bishop Donald Jacobs, Mennonite church (1974), the Most Revd Dr. Robert Runcie, Archbishop of Canterbury (1986), the Most Revd Dr. George Carey, Archbishop of Canterbury (1995), Dr. Samuel Kobia, WCC General Secretary (2007), the Revd Dr. A. B. Masilamani, the Rev. Dr. Samuel Kamaleson

[768] The MTC is a self-supporting missionary Church with the contribution of its own members. The idea of voluntary evangelism later found concrete expressions in an organization known as the Mar Thoma Voluntary Evangelist Association founded in 1924. All other organizations in the Church like Sunday School Samajam and the Sevika Sangam emerged from this convention. They all grew out of the missionary zeal of the members, mostly the laity, in the early part of the last century. The Maramon Convention thus has a particular role in designing the ministry of the MTC. It helps the people to

The Maramon Convention stands as a space for enhancing the ecumenical relations of the Church. Every year the morning session on Wednesday is set apart as an ecumenical gathering and the church dignitaries of all Christian denominations including the Catholics, Orthodox and Protestant communities gather to share their view on ecumenism and strengthening one another by the Word of God.[769] The Maramon Convention is a space which calls for social reform and community development. In the early years, there were many people, coming to the Pampa riverbed asking for alms. This enabled the Church to respond to it by starting hospitals, old age homes, hospices, rehabilitation centres, institutions for physically and mentally challenged people, and initiated various awareness programmes, rehabilitation programmes, empowering programmes for the members. This convention for the last one hundred and twenty years challenges the Church to grow with a vision of the New Church without walls and penetrate into the wider society, welcoming all sorts of people to the house of worship. In the words of Mar Theodosius, "the Maramon Convention is a symbol and it acts as a guideline and a model for every parish to open its walls and doors to accommodate all people wanting to listen to the Word of God."[770] There exists also in the Church a practice whereby revival meetings and Bible conventions are held annually in each parish of the MTC and at diocesan and regional levels, before the Maramon Convention.

---

know and experience Jesus Christ and go out into the world with the power of the Holy Spirit to translate the "Word" into "Deed" for the ministry of the total transformation of the whole world.

[769] All these years, the leaders of various political parties, social groups and organizations, irrespective of their religious background, attend it. It provided an opportunity for the people of various castes to gather in a common platform to hear the Word of God. It initiated a great movement that transcended the high caste mentality and called for the dignity of the so-called low caste people. This convention is an opportunity to affirm the oneness in Christ, irrespective of any caste or class differences. Through this convention, the Church stands as an umbrella in which all human beings irrespective of their caste, class, sex, gender, and faith come together and share their common views on social justice and Kingdom values. Thomas, *A History of the First Cross-Cultural Mission,* 49-53.

[770] Theodosius, "Maramon Convention, Mission and Ministry," 28.

1.1 - The Maramon Convention: Liturgy in the Premises of Revivalism

Even though the Marmon Convention is a "Festival of the Proclamation of the Word," the celebration of the Eucharist is the culmination of this Spiritual gathering.[771] This 'Sunday to Sunday' celebration symbolically expresses the idea that the faithful gather and disperse by the power of the Table and Word. The faithful are strengthened by the Word of God and disperse with the conviction that their ultimate vocation is to proclaim the Kingdom of God by rendering a Eucharistic presence in the world. An integration of the Liturgy and Scripture is very evident in the Maramon Convention. The Liturgy and Scripture keep the members together as a community. Through participation in the Eucharist, the members of the Church experience a mystical union with Christ. It connects the individual with the wider fellowship of the community of believers. The Bible is the Word of God, in the sense that it helps the faithful to realize the presence of God in their life experiences. As a sacramental word, Scripture presents Christ to the believing community.[772] As a sacramental word, Scripture is not only a witness to the revelation that has taken place in Christ; rather, it draws the faithful into the presence of Christ and invites them to be transformed into his image. It opens the possibility of relationship between the divine and the human. In this view, the Bible forms the community into the body of Christ through this liturgical gathering. Scripture becomes a means by which Christians are gathered into the body of the living Lord. Lathrop remarks that, "a community gathers in prayer around the scriptures read and proclaimed. This community of the word then tastes the meaning of that word by celebrating the meal of Christ, giving thanks over bread and cup and eating and drinking. It is this word-table community, the body of Christ, which gathers other people to its number, continually teaching both itself and these new comers the mercy and mystery of God

---

[771] This Convention begins on Sunday after the Holy Qurbana in the parishes and concludes with special liturgical worship in the *pandal* itself and Holy Qurbana in nearby parishes. Each sessions of the Convention follow a liturgical order and format i.e., *Kauma*, Prayer, Intercession, Bible reading, proclamation of the Word, Exhortation of the Bishops and Benediction.

[772] Dyk, "Proclamation: Revelation, Christology," 65-66.

and washing them in the name of that God."[773] The spirituality of the Maramon Convention integrate the Eucharist and Scripture.

The missional themes enshrined in the Eucharistic liturgy determine the content and style of this gathering. Through this spiritual gathering, the faithful are nourished and strengthened by the table of the Word and table of the Body of Christ.[774] One of the characteristics of the Oriental methodology for the proclamation is the catechetical and liturgical approach. It is through the liturgy that the Church communicates its faith and theology. The biblical emphasis ensures a clear direction for rendering a Eucharistic presence. Here mission is an incarnational living of the liturgical, ascetical and mystical spirituality to make visible the Trinitarian-Eucharistic experience of God's saving action.[775] Therefore, the liturgical worship and proclamation of the Word is a creative expression of witnessing. As mentioned in the previous chapter, the ultimate calling of the Church is to render a sacramental presence in the world. Therefore, the liturgy and the proclamation of the Word through the Maramon Convention is specifically designed to bring God's life to His people, restoring His image in them. God's plan for the future of the cosmos is present in the Church through the liturgy in the background of Scripture. To translate the love and life of God into the world is not an accident, but a deliberate intention of corporate worship and a necessary result of it. The Eucharist and Scripture proclaim the mission of the Church both internally and externally. Internally, it gives the assurance of the presence

---

[773] Scripture is a means of grace used by the Holy Spirit to nourish and build up the community of faith. The Holy Spirit uses Scripture as a sacramental element, as it were, to unite the believers to Christ. Scripture unites believers to Jesus Christ, himself the Word of God. The Bible is the Word of God in a sacramental sense, uniting us to Christ, the one true Word of God. It brings Christ to believers. Gordon Lathrop, *What are the Essentials of Christian Worship?* (Minneapolis, MN: Augsburg Fortress, 1994), 22. Dyk, "Proclamation: Revelation, Christology," 66-67.

[774] The community of faithful is entrusted with the responsibility to share the good news of Christ through its very life. They proclaim their faith in society through lifestyle. It is an expression of self. The search for this identity is manifested in the relationship between God and the human within the setting of liturgy. The faithful realize it through participating in the Liturgy. A celebrated faith is proclaimed and proclamation aims at gathering people for celebration.

[775] Kannookadan, *The Mission Theology of the Syro-Malabar Church,* 21.

of God personally to the faithful and externally it proclaims their identity and vocation._Hence one can say the Maramon Convention is a source of spiritual strength in the Church for its mission, spiritual and liturgical life. A former general secretary of the MTEA Rev. K.T. Jacob, in his article, *the Maramon Convention- Origin and Growth* claims that the message from the MTC's conventions was a major reason for the Church's focus on spiritual revival of its members in its early missionary efforts.[776]

2 - Ancillary Organizations of the Mar Thoma Church

The Church is a community of believers united and it exists with a diversity of ministries.[777] At present, there are seven official organizations in the Church with a mission outreach agenda. They are: The Mar Thoma Evangelistic Association (1888) that carries out the evangelistic work among the exterior regions and communities such as Dalits, Adivasis and other non-Christian regions of India and abroad. 2) The Mar Thoma Voluntary Evangelistic Association (1924) that animates the missionary and evangelistic task of the parishes within the Church. 3) The Mar Thoma Suvisheshaka Sevika Sangham (1919) take care of the ministry among the women's wing. 4) The Mar Thoma Sunday School Samajam (1905) that is responsible for the Christian education of the children. 5) The Mar Thoma Yuvajana Sakhyam (Youth wing) (1933) which orients towards the spiritual growth of the youth in the Church and society. 6) The Department of Sacred Music and Communications (1969) focuses on the music ministry of the Church. 7) The Mar Thoma Student Conference focus on the spiritual growth of the college students. Apart from the ancillary organizations, each diocese has its own mission initiatives in its own territorial regions. Along with the dioceses, there are mission initiates in the centre and parish level.

---

[776] K.T. Jacob, a priest of the MTC, who served as a missionary, a managing committee member of MTEA and the Clergy Trusty of the Church. K T. Jacob, "Maramon Convention Uthbhavavum Valarchayum" George Alexander, ed., *Maramon Convention Sathabdhi Valyam* (Thiruvalla: Mar Thoma Evangelistic Association, 1995), 58-74.

[777] Ministry is a term which refers to a particular aspect of the mission of the Church. For instance, the ministry of teaching, preaching, healing, serving. All these ministers are coming under the mission of the Church. A ministry is the means by which mission is achieved.

2.1 - The Liturgy and Organizations of the Church

The primary role of the Church is to give glory to God through its liturgical gatherings. From a liturgical perspective, the above mentioned organizations function as strong units of worship. The liturgy organizes the people of God and unifies the ministries of the Church. More profoundly, it is in the context of liturgy that all the organizations of the Church are initiated. They are designed to render sacramental presence in the world. The liturgy is the umbrella through which each organization is initiated and fostered for mission. Each organization is connected with the overall mission of the Church through the liturgical celebrations. The ministries of each organization arranges its programme for this purpose. The liturgy is the centre of all its ministers. For instance, the Church sets apart a special Sunday for each organization to celebrate and communicate its ministries to the entire Church. The lectionary and programmes of the Church are designed accordingly. In this special Sunday, each organization prepares an order of worship with the consent of the Metropolitan. The members of the particular organization lead the worship in each parish, and organize various programmes related to the motive of the organization. This means that the worship is the source of each organization's ministry in the Church. There is a dedication service conducted for the newly elected office bearers and committee of each organizations every year during the Holy Qurbana service. It affirms that the ministry of all ancillary organizations in the Church stems from the power of the Table. Apart from it, all the programmes of the organizations are commenced and concluded with liturgical worship. Even though each organizations concentrate on specific ministries the liturgical worship is the centre of its ministries which play a great role in the overall mission of the Church.

3 - Ashrams in the Mar Thoma Church and its Mission Strategy

In the ancient Indian tradition, ashrams were the abode of ascetics who lived a solitary life in devotion and meditation. These abodes were either in the forests or on the banks of rivers. The ancient ashrams in India never became institutions.[778] The ashrams adopted a form of education known as *Gurukula* (Guru's family) in which the students lived with their teachers. The teachers looked after the temporal and spiritual welfare of their students. No caste distinction was allowed within an ashram.[779]

During the second half of the 19th century, a number of socio-religious and political developments in modern India revived the ashram movement. The new spirit of Indian nationalism and a search for Indian identity revitalized the old ashram concept.[780] The emergence of several Hindu revival movements[781] was a result of the interaction with Western ideas

---

[778] Paul Pattathu, *Ashram Spirituality: A Search into the Christian Ashram Movement against its Hindu Background* (Indore: Satprakashan Sanchar Kendra, 1997), 4. K.V. Varghese, *A Vision for Wholeness: Ashrams and Healing in India* (Delhi: ISPCK, 1999), 1-2.

[779] The term ashram is derived from two Sanskrit words such as *Aa* and *Shram* mean well-labour. It denotes a place where the labour is well done, a place worthy of staying or establishing a tent. It is associated with a place where a teacher-guru lives and imparts religious or secular knowledge. It is an institution where a preceptor passes on spiritual knowledge as well as professional training to the seekers and assists pupils to live a purposeful life, physical as well as economical. Indian Ashram is a place for silent prayer and meditation. Irrespective of religions, the ashram model has a role in shaping the spirituality of the Indian religious traditions especially among Christians. An ashram in its present understanding is a place where spiritual growth, devotion, training and religious culture take place. Prayer and devotion are the centre of ashram life. Savarirayan Jesudason, *Ashrams, Ancient and Modern; Their Aims and Ideals* (Vellore: Sri Ramachandran Press, 1937), 9-15.

[780] Helen Ralston, *Christian Ashrams: A New Religious Movement in Contemporary India* (Lewiston, Queenston: The Edwin Mellen, 1987), 15-22.

[781] (a) The Brahmo Samaj was the earliest reform movement of the modern type which was greatly influenced by Western ideas. Raja Ram Mohan Roy was the founder of Brahmo Samaj. He has been rightly hailed as the father of modem Indian nationalism. The Brahmo Samaj is a social and religious movement founded in Kolkata in 1828 by Raja Ram Mohan Roy. The Brahmo Samaj movement thereafter resulted in the Brahmo religion in 1850 founded by Debendranath Tagore. (b) The Arya Samaj movement, basically revivalist in nature, was an outcome of the reaction to Western influences. The Samaj was organised by Swami Dayanand Saraswati in 1875 who strove to rouse the patriotic feelings of the people by the revivalist slogan "Back to the Vedas." (c) Prarthana Samaj aimed at reforming Hindu society. The Samaj suggested the worship of one Almighty. In order to end social evils it started many institutions like orphanages etc. It also condemned ban on widow remarriage. With this end in view it opened widow ashrams and supported the cause of widow remarriage. It also started a plan for adult literacy. (d) Ramakrishna Movement by Sri Ramakrishna and Swami Vivekananda. The Ramakrishna Movement has great dynamism and absorbing power. This movement urges the transformation of human consciousness. (e) Neo-Vedanta by Swami Vivekananda was a central personality in the development of neo-Hinduism (also called Neo-Vedanta) in late 19th century and

and revived interest in Oriental studies, which brought about a renaissance among Hindus. These movements made a great impact and injected new life to ancient India's culture and religious values. These movements sustained India's spiritual and cultural identity as it moved away from British imperialism.[782] All modern Hindu ashrams had a central personality, the founder of inspirer of the institution, such as Rabindran Natha Tagore of Shantiniketan, Mahatma Gandhi of Sathyagraha ashram and Ramana Maharshi of Ramana ashram.[783]

3.1 - The Christian Ashram Movement

Several factors motivated Christians in India to start Christian ashrams.[784] According to Alex Thomas, "the modern Hindu ashrams founded by Mahatma Gandhi, Tagore and others influenced the emergence of Christian ashrams. The growing spirit of nationalism accelerated the process of indigenization in India. Most importantly, Indian Christian leaders demanded equality with foreign missionaries and searched for indigenous methods of evangelization."[785] In the context of rising nationalism, people discarded Christianity as Western and imperialistic. According to Stanley Jones,[786] the awakening of the national spirit in India demanded a new

---

the early 20th century. His ideals and sayings have inspired numerous Indians as well as non-Indians, Hindus as well as non-Hindus.

[782] The spread of English education sowed seeds of democratic socialism among young educated Indians. In the religious sphere, the growth of the spirit of nationalism brought about an impulse to rebuild India within Hinduism. Seeds of change sprouted within many socio-religious movements. Groups began to provide social services to Indian people. According to Paul Pattathu, the Hindu renaissance influenced Rabindranath Tagore, Mahatma Gandhi, Aurobindo and others in their attempt to reform India on the basis of the ancient ashram tradition. Thomas, *Christian Indians and Indian Nationalism 1885-1950*, 14, 28-35. Paul Pattathu, *Ashram Spirituality*, 9.

[783] The inmates observed celibacy and renounced their personal possessions. They practiced non-violence to keep a harmonious relationship with the universe. The ashrams employed social service in their agenda, such as medical work and self-employment programmes like Khadi manufactures in the Sabarmathi ashram of Gandhi. Jesudason, *Ashrams, Ancient and Modern*, 9-15.

[784] Philipose Thomas, "Christian Ashrams and Evangelisation of India," *Indian Church History Review* XI, no, 3 (December 1977): 206-207.

[785] Thomas, *A History of First Cross Cultural Mission*, 98.

[786] One of the pioneers of the ashram movement in the world was E. Stanley Jones, a friend of Martin Luther King and Mahatma Gandhi. He was a Methodist in the mould of Wesley

244

approach in the mission method: to relate the Christian movement to Indian culture and to Indian national consciousness.[787] In order to remove the prejudice against Christianity, Indian Christians attempted several ways to present Christ and Christianity in the culture and forms of Indian society. The Christian ashrams were one of those attempts.[788] Through Christian Ashrams, the Indian Christians envisaged national reconstruction and the establishment of a community in line with the Kingdom of God on earth. Stanley Johns and others promoted the ashram ideal for the evangelization of India, and they put emphasis on radical social changes.[789] He started an ashram at Sat Tal, in the foothills of the Himalaya in 1930. He was with the Mahatma Gandhi in the Sabarmati ashram in the early 1920's, and he spent several months at Shanthinikethan, the ashram founded by Rabindranath Tagore in 1923.[790]

When we analyse the ashram movement in the context of the Indian Church, there are three models to take note of (a) Fr. Bede Griffith and his Christ Kula Ashram,[791] (b) Evangelist Stanley Jones and his Sat Tal Ashram, (c) The Christ Panthi Ashram.[792] Both the ashram Christkula and the Christ-Panthi reveal their particular *Sadhana* (religious aim/goal of religious practices) through the names they have given to their ashram;

---

brothers, Charles and John, with a burden to preach the Gospel of Christ and he adopted the ashram system more as a resort where people can come and stay and attend his Bible classes and meditation/sermon session. He also toured different parts of India and had meetings with students in Christian colleges. His interaction with Mahatma Gandhi made him popular with the college students. He was a good friend of the MTC and a regular preacher in the Marmon Convention.

[787] E. Stanley Jones, "The Ashram Ideal," in *Indian Churches Problems of Today,* ed. Brenton Thoburn Badley (Madras: Methodist Publishing House, 1930), 44.

[788] Firth, *An Introduction to Indian Church History,* 255. Thomas, *A History of the First Cross Cultural Mission,* 99.

[789] Johns believed that the ashrams constituted an ideal way to produce a Christianity that was truly Christian and truly Indian. Jones, "The Ashram Ideal," 48-50. Thomas, *A History of the First Cross Cultural Mission,* 100.

[790] Richard W. Taylor, *The Contribution of E. Stanley* Johns (Madras: The Christian Literature Society, 1973), 13. Thomas, *A History of the First Cross Cultural Mission,* 100.

[791] Kristu Kula means family of Christ and Christ Panthi means followers of the way of Christ.

[792] Ravi Tiwari, "Christi Panthi Ashram, Sihora Revisiting Ashram Movement," *Mar Thoma Messenger* XXXIV, no.2 (April 2015): 25-29.

both aspire to be following the way of devotion- *Bhakthi Marga* - to realize the continues presence of Christ in their midst. The Sat Tal ashram, however, denotes its location only. Bade Griffith, on the other hand, followed ascetic practices of a yogi and combined it with scriptural studies along the *Upanishadic*[793] line. Much influenced by Raman Maharshi, he tried to move along with the Christian mystics, and his ashram became a centre for Christian-Hindu meeting point which was later carried on by Swami Abihshiktanand.[794]

The inspiration to start Christian ashrams within the MTC came from early Protestant ashrams, and their search for indigenous methods of evangelization.[795] Most of the Mar Thoma Ashrams were established during the time of Abraham Mar Thoma (1917-1947), who was known as a missionary bishop. In the MTC, ashrams have been set up very much along Gandhian principles like nonviolence, truth, simplicity and social service. The ashrams in the Church are the missionary outreach demonstration centres that work hand in hand in the mission fields. It is a centre of the evangelization of the Church. However, ashrams are not considered as gospel propaganda centres, but rather as gospel demonstration centres. They are places of new family relationships, centres of social and economic unity, study, training, worship, meditation, social service and village evangelism. These Christian ashrams came to be known as "cells of the Kingdom of God."[796] The ashrams have been closely connected with the local people who undertake medical, social and educational work and outreach programmes.[797]

---

[793] One of the Scriptures of Hindu religion.

[794] Tiwari, "Christi Panthi Ashram, Sihora Revisiting Ashram Movement," 26.

[795] Joseph, *Mar Thoma Sabha Directory* - 2015, 341.

[796] Karinjappally, *Roots and Wings,* 68-69.

[797] In 1924, the MTC started a mission in Palghat and established an ashram there in 1928 with the name, Christu Dasa Ashram. Another Ashram began in 1931 at a place in Kerala known as Perumbavoor, to manage a high school in that area. The first Mar Thoma ashram that was founded outside of Kerala was the Christa Mitra ashram at Ankola in 1940. In subsequent years, several ashrams were established in different parts of India: The Christa Panthi Ashram at Sihora, in Madhya Pradesh (1943), The Christu Sishya Sangham at Hoskote near Bangalore (1947), The Christiya Bandhakulam at Satna in Madhy Pradesh (1952), The Christu Shanthi Sangham in Nepal (1952), The Shanthi Mandiram in Anshra

3.2 - Ashrams: A Paradigm of Incarnational Pattern of Mission

The ashrams mainly employed the incarnational model of mission through its very life and activities. The emphasis of the ashrams was to create a Kingdom-centred mission strategy in the Indian context. The ashrams are a place of meditation, evangelization, celebration of liturgy and social service. Everyday life in the ashrams begin with meditation and thereupon liturgical celebration. An incarnational aspect enshrined in the Eucharistic liturgy is the model of mission in the ashrams. The members of the ashrams integrate with the community as a catalyst for evangelism and social service. In other words, ashrams witnesses a foretaste of the Kingdom of God through its various activities. Ashrams were also a place of liturgical experimentation in the process of which they took initiative in translating the liturgy from Malayalam into other vernaculars. For instance, the translation into Hindi was the initiative of the Sihora Ashram.

The MTC adopted an Ashram model of mission to exemplify its Kingdom-centered mission thought. The Mar Thoma ashrams are evangelistic in nature and founded for the evangelistic, medical, educational, social and economic development of Indian villages.[798] The members of the ashram consisted of priest, evangelists, doctors, nurses, and other medical staff. The Church adopted an ashram model as a distinctive Indian mission model. It became a powerful catalyst for social change and development. These ashrams give equal importance to worship and social service.[799] The Ashram model of mission is very inclusive in nature where both women and men actively participate in the ashram activities.[800] For example in the Sihora and Ankola ashrams the women inmates are actively involved in the medical mission and other social development programs.

Pradesh (1955), and The Christa Prema Kulam at Bhopal (1955). Joseph, *Mar Thoma Sabha Directory-2015*, 341-345.Varghese, *A Vision for Wholeness*, 52-53.

[798] Helen Ralston, *Christian Ashrams: A New Religious movements in Contemporary India* (New Delhi: ISPCK, 1998), 80-84.

[799] Thomas, *A History of the First Cross Cultural Mission*, 102-103.

[800] Very often, the members who participate in the mission of the Church are male. The women are not able to take an active role in the mission of the Church in various mission centers because of the patriarchal nature of the Church and the conditions of male-dominated Indian society. Thomas, *A History of the First Cross Cultural Mission*, 127.

4 - An Integration of the Liturgy and Evangelism in the Church

Since the Eucharistic liturgy is a liturgical foundation for mission in the Church as highlighted above, the MTC triggered its missionary thrust through the channels of the Maramon Convention, Ancillary Organizations and Ashrams in the Church. Even though the mission strategies of these agencies are varied such as: revivalism,[801] personal evangelism, proclamation of the Word, social service, teaching, worship, witness and holistic development, they uphold the distinctiveness of Liturgy along with its scriptural footings.

In the initial development of the Church, the leaders found it difficult to connect effectively its traditional oriental liturgical piety with the major changes in its evangelical revival context.[802] This resulted in some less-informed preachers criticising the Church's unique nature of blending evangelical faith with its oriental liturgical mooring. Instead, they wanted to emphasize spirituality based on individualistic pietism, over and above the oriental liturgical positioning. This provided a space for some of the Church members to try to lessen its liturgical corporate worship base. This eventually developed into tension within the Church between its liturgical heritage and the newfound revivalism, which emphasised adult baptism, speaking in tongues and the second-coming of Christ. This tension prepared the ground for churches such as Baptist and Brethren to work among the members of the MTC since the last decade of the 19th

---

[801] Revival meetings and conventions instilled a special importance of keeping personal piety among the Church members. These meetings were open to all communities including the so-called "outcastes". The revivalism in the Church helped the members to maintain a serious personal piety with a new emphasis on spontaneity and to interpret the Bible in the light of the contemporary context. A former Vicar General of the Church, Rev. K. E. Oommen described the influence of the revival meetings at the Church as: "they had come to set a very high value of the daily readings and study of the Bible and also to accept the Bible as the primary authority in the doctrinal matters. In public worship, on Sundays and other holidays, a sermon came to be an inevitable part of the service." Jacob, "Maramon Convention Uthbhavavum Valarchayum" (Malayalam), 61-62.

[802] Daniel, *Ecumenism in Praxis*, 109-110.

century. Added to this were other reasons which resulted in a fresh schism within the Church in 1961.[803]

Hence, the primary task before the MTC was to integrate its Eastern liturgical base to the new evangelical fervour. In the initial stage of evangelization, the missionary approach of mission organizations particularly MTVA was mainly through conducting prayer meetings, visiting houses, and conducting community development programmes.[804] Along with these, later the Church took initiative to translate the Malayalam Eucharistic liturgy and introduced liturgical worship in their own vernacular.[805] According to Daniel, the MTC's integration task was dual in nature. Primarily it was an assimilation of the Eastern liturgical and evangelical faith of the CMS as well as the integration of the Church and mission to create a Church with a missionary zeal.[806] The vision of the Church combined the "evangelical faith and experience within the framework of corporate life" with the "liturgical devotion of the Oriental Eastern Church."[807] Therefore, the MTEA had to assert its independence from Western missionary societies and Churches in thought and action. According to Daniel, the Eastern liturgical basis of the MTC led the Church to devote time for integrating the Church's sacramental life and missionary consciousness in its teachings followed by the integration of the Church and the MTEA.[808] As to the leaders of the MTC, the integration of the

---

[803] A critical analysis of the influence of revivalism in the MTC shows that there was a certain lack of ecclesiological and liturgical emphasis in the annual conventions at the parishes as well as in the conventions in the regional and diocesan levels, and the Marmon Convention. Having influenced by evangelicalism, some member of the Church showed reluctance to integrate evangelical and liturgical base in the Church. They gave more emphasis on evangelicalism. This lead to an internal struggle within the Church and later the friction resulted in a schism in the Church and subsequent formation of the St. Thomas Evangelical Church in 1961. Its headquarters is at Manjadi, Thiruvalla, Kerala.
[804] Malabar Mar Thoma Syrian Christian Evangelistic Association, *Annual Report 2012-13*, 14.
[805] A detailed description on translation of liturgy is highlighted in the second chapter.
[806] Daniel, *Ecumenism in Praxis*, 101.
[807] The Malabar Mar Thoma Syrian Evangelistic Association was a registered organization under the Indian companies act VI, under the Travancore Regulation I, of 1882, in 1904. Mathew and Thomas, *Indian Christians of St. Thomas*, 89.
[808] Daniel, *Ecumenism in Praxis*, 102.

Church with the MTEA was a main concern as it faced the autonomous existence of Western missions and organizations.[809] The leaders of the Church were very much open and particular in this integration process. For instance Thomas Mar Athanasius, the then Metropolitan wholeheartedly supported the integration process.[810] Besides, MTEA leaders like Thomas Kottarathil,[811] Mathai Edavanmelil, and Yohannan Kottoorethu were loyal churchmen and had been known for their efforts to amalgamate the missionary spirit and Eastern liturgical ideals in their thoughts and actions.[812]

According to Daniel, the Church employed two methods for integrating the missionary spirit and Eastern liturgical ideas. It started an "educational phase to edify the Church whereby it prepared teachings on "mission" and "Eastern liturgical practices" for Sunday worship, Bible convention meetings, and conferences. Convention meetings and conferences used to conclude with the Holy Qurbana, explaining the Church's paramount importance of the Eastern liturgy. Along with it, constitutional efforts were made to safeguard the Church's integration with the MTEA by providing checks and balances. For instance the third annual meeting of the MTEA made a decision that the reports of all meetings of the MTEA shall be submitted to the Metropolitan.[813] The purpose of this decision was to bring all proceedings of the MTEA before the Metropolitan for his perusal and approval. This was later included as a clause in the MTEA constitution. Similarly, the Church's sacramental life made its oriental liturgical faith lively and the Church's constitution made its liturgical

---

[809] Most of the missionary organizations including the CMS were voluntary societies independent of the Church. These institutions considered themselves as separate institutions concerned with Christian missions in overseas.

[810] George Alexander, "Malankara Mar Thoma Suvishesha Prasanga sangham," in *Maramon Convention Sathabdhi Valyam*, 160-302. Rev. George Alexander is a clergy of the MTC. He was the General Secretary of the MTEA during 1981-1987 and he wrote a concise history of the MTEA since its inception in 1995.

[811] Thomas Abraham Kottarathil was a clergy of the MTC, who was one among the twelve instrumental in the formation of the MTEA.

[812] Daniel, *Ecumenism in Praxis*, 102.

[813] *Report of the Third Meeting of the MTEA*, M.E. Dhanu 27, 1064. (February 7, 1889). Daniel, *Ecumenism in Praxis*, 102-103.

observance mandatory.[814] C. P. Philipose (1868-1948), the first General Secretary of the MTEA, helped the Church to keep the balance of these two elements by integrating missionary spirit and oriental liturgical piety in the MTEA's mission praxis.[815] Instead of keeping the independent nature of the organizations who initiated the evangelisation process, the MTC bases all mission work at the centre of her very life from its inception, which is in contrast to the administrative pattern of the Church Missionary Society.[816] The leaders of the Church were very cautious to avoid the possible division of the Church-mission dichotomy as it appeared in Western missionary societies.[817] The MTC continues to struggle with all those sectarian tendencies in the name of a Church-centred evangelicalism. [818]

5 - The Eucharistic Liturgy: A Foundation for Mission in the Mar Thoma Church.

An analysis of the historical development of mission strategy and mission models employed in the Church demonstrates that the Eucharistic liturgy is the foundation of the Church in its mission. The missional themes enshrined in the Eucharistic liturgy motivates the Church to design new strategies and models of mission contextually. Even though the Church still struggles to maintain a balance between the evangelical pietism and Oriental liturgical

---

[814] "the ministry of deacon, priest and episcope, rites of the Church viz., Church dedication, Church consecration, holy baptism, holy communion(Qurbana), holy matrimony, unction of the sick, funeral services and observance of Lents, Sundays and dominical feasts shall not be abolished at any time" *Constitution, Mar Thoma Syrian Church,* Declaration, Part. I, (Thiruvalla: Mar Thoma Church, 2002), 1.

[815] Daniel, *Ecumenism in Praxis,* 103.

[816] The Travancore mission of the CMS was an independent mission agency and therefore it was not under the Anglican Dioceses of Cochin. Stephen Neill, *Creative Tension* (Duff Lectures) (Edinburgh: Edinburgh Press, 1959), 86.

[817] The "evangelical-oriental liturgical" and "church-mission" integration stood in contrast to the organizational pattern of the ministry enterprises in the West. This was an expression of the Indian Church's assertion of autonomy and independence in the new missionary context. *Report of the Third Meeting of the MTEA,* M.E. Dhanu 27, 1064 (February 7, 1889); the Malabar Mar Thoma Syrian Christians Evangelistic Association: Memorandum and Articles of Association, as amended in 1106 M.E. (1931), reprinted, 1-12; cited in *Mar Thoma Sabha Directory,* ed. Thomas, 150. Daniel, *Ecumenism in Praxis,* 104-106.

[818] Mathew and Thomas, *Indian Christians of St. Thomas,* 102-103, Mathew, *Malankara Mar Thoma Sabha Charithram* vol. II, (Malayalam), 174-175.

moorings, it is clear that the missional nature and identity of the Church derive from its Liturgy.

The Holy Qurbana is fundamental to the life and ministry of the MTC, which is an act of worship, an object of worship and an experience of worship. In one sense, it is the vehicle of grace. In and through the Eucharist, the Church celebrates the paschal mystery of Christ and proclaims the Divine Dispensation - the *Madabranutha*.[819] In every Eucharist, the faithful encounter the risen Christ mystically. This encountering experience reveals them new truth about life and its mission. The Eucharist is a continuation and participation in Christ's sacrifice on Calvary. This is not a repetitive sacrifice of Christ, but a continuation and the participation of the same sacrifice. Through the Eucharist, Christ's sacrifice becomes a present day reality, so that people can experience this through partaking in the elements.[820]

The Church is entrusted with mission of salvation through Christ by the power of the Holy Spirit. Whenever it celebrates the Eucharist it partakes and reflect the mission of Jesus Christ. The Eucharistic liturgy affirms that the community gathered for worship must be dispersed for mission. It orients the believing community towards new responsibilities such as witness to Jesus Christ, preservation of creation, and service to society. These new responsibilities are carried out in various spheres of life, such as family, Church, society, environment and the entire creation. The praxis of the Church in the community symbolizes the Christian identity. The liturgy, traditions, institutions, and other outreach programmes such as development and charity proclaim the nature and identity of a community. A ministry in the Church is a response and a commitment to the call and commission of the Lord of the Church. It is within the community and by the community that the ministry of the Church is nurtured and proclaimed.

---

[819] Kuttiyil, *Eucharist (Qurbana):The Celebration of the Economy of Salvation,* 162.
[820] Here the priest represents Jesus Christ and offers symbolically the bread and wine to God. Thus, the priest sacramentally re-enacts the oblation of His passion, which the saviour originally presented to the Father. Therefore, the Eucharist is the bloodless sacrifice. Hence, the Eucharist is not a sacrifice but it is an enactment of the same sacrifice, through which Christ offered Himself to God.

The Eucharistic liturgy through its prayers, signs and symbols reveal the missional nature of the Church. Hence, one can say that the Church is a Eucharistic community and its identity and mission derive from the Eucharist. The Eucharist is a symbolic act of the abundance of divine love. It expresses Christians' identity as a Eucharistic community based on their relationship to God and to their fellow human beings. Basically, the Eucharist brings together two basic aspects of the entire mystery, i.e. the Eucharist strengthens and deepens the bonds of community and also Eucharistic sharing means that one must divide, separate and give to another what is shared and this denotes the self-giving of Christian life.[821] In this sense, the Church is a Eucharistic community and its mission and identity derives from the Eucharist. An example of this basic formula would be the theological rationale for the shape of the Eucharistic action. For instance, in the preparation service of the Eucharist (pre-anaphora), the faithful gather to be formed into a community, ready to attend to God. This recognition of who and where we are prepare us to incorporate our story into the story of what God has done for us. The key moment of this incorporation and engagement in the celebration is the proclamation of the gospel at the climax of the Liturgy of the Word. Then in the anaphora, in the Eucharistic action, God who has come to share our life in the Word made flesh, catches us up into his transforming action of grace as we, the broken fragments of his body, are made one as we receive his body broken for us. Renewed by this mystery, the faithful are motivated to share this life of engagement and transformation. The final blessing in the Eucharistic liturgy is the key to the mission of the Church.[822] Through the Eucharist, the Church reminds us that sharing is possible only through breaking and

---

[821] Koch, "Principles for a Christian theology of Baptism," 235-236.
[822] David Stancliffe, "The Making of the Church of England's Common Worship," *Studia Liturgica* 31, no.1 (2001): 16. "A tradition common to both the East and the West is that all ordinations must be related to a concrete community and must take place within the context of a Eucharistic assembly. Both of these point to the close relation between ministry and community. The Eucharistic assembly is the natural milieu for the birth of ministry understood in this broader soteriological perspective." Zizioulas, *Being as Communion*, 211-212.

the Church prepares herself for the mission of sharing by breaking. It is the mission of self-emptying. "Caring by sharing" is an integral part of the mission.[823] The paschal mystery as celebrated in the Eucharist and the enduring presence of Christ as the Redeemer in the world helps the Church to connect the Eucharist and mission. The Christian community being missionary in its proclamation, liturgy and service to the neighbour, it testifies its missionary calling by entering into the various needs of people. This community is called together for worship and send forth to minister to the community within their context. The MTC in line with the Oriental Orthodox tradition goes along with the concept of worship as offering glory to God. The gathered community experiences the life and love of Christ mystically through the liturgy and moves out into the world to share this abundant life through their interactions with fellow human beings. The Church shares the glory of God through its transformative actions by its various ministries.

Mission is an ecclesial act. The mission commitment of the Church derives from the words of the Lord "as the Father sent me, so I send you" (Jn.20:21). The final dismissal of peace and exhortation in the Eucharistic liturgy of the Church - "Go in peace"- mainly focuses on this aspect. The ultimate calling of the Church is to bear witness to the salvific act of Christ. To render a sacramental presence in the world. The concept of "liturgy after the liturgy"[824] is important at this juncture. This means, after worship the faithful move out to proclaim the good news and become a channel for transformation. This is reflected through the everyday life and the actions of the believers. It radiates their entrusted divine mission through their active involvement in the society. Through the exemplary actions and behaviour of the Christian community, the love and the life of God spill over in all directions. They extend to society, culture, the state, and to the whole world. "Not only humanity, but also the whole universe participates

---

[823] Geevarghese Mar Theodosius, "Mission of the Church in the 21st Century," in *Challenges and Prospects of Mission in the Emerging Context,* ed. Koshy P Varughese (Faridabad: Dharma Jyoti Vidya Peeth, 2010), 26.

[824] Bria, *Liturgy after the Liturgy,* 27-32.

in the restoration and finds its orientation again in glorifying God."[825] The mission theology of the Church is firmly grounded on the concept of mission as ecclesial proclamation of the economy of salvation in the present context. The teaching, life and worship of the Church is characterized by its missionary nature. The most valuable heritage of the MTC, known as the way of Thomas, is the intimate and personal Christ experience of St. Thomas the Apostle. The legacy of St. Thomas is to believe with conviction, confess with enthusiasm and witness with courage. This has to be a permeating presence in the life and activities of the missionaries. The West-Syrian liturgy and spirituality, Anglican theological and missional influence and Indian culture and lifestyle etc., have been enhancing the faith experience, identity and mission of the Church.

In responding to the mission call of the Bible, the MTC affirms that it is fundamentally entrusted with a mission of salvation that Christ offered in history. The Church believes that Jesus Christ is at work in and through the Church and striving towards the goal of establishing his Kingdom. The mission theology of the Church is firmly grounded in Scripture and the Liturgy. As a bridging Church in between the Orthodox and Protestant traditions, the mission emphasis or the understanding of the mission of the Church, is dual in nature, i.e. mission as proclamation through Word and deed and mission as witnessing through the very act of the celebration of the Liturgy. Privileged with the West Syrian liturgy and Anglican theological emphasis the MTC has developed a unique way of witnessing the Gospel. The teaching, life and witness of the Church is characterized by its missionary nature. A celebrated faith is proclaimed and proclamations aim at gathering people in celebration of the Holy Qurbana. This missionary thrust of the Church is expressed in its liturgy, especially in the final benediction and the blessings of the liturgy "Go in peace" - liturgy after the liturgy. This thesis reiterate the fact that the revised Eucharistic liturgy of the MTC is the foundation for its renewed way of doing mission in different contexts.

---

[825] Nussbaum. *A Reader's Guide to Transforming Mission*, 206.

6 - Conclusion

An integration of Liturgy and Revivalism was a major task of the Church in its initial stage. Even though there were challenges to address revivalism in the background of Liturgy, the Church could successfully integrate the Word and Sacrament together in its identity and mission. The Maramon Convention is an instance of the integration of Liturgy and Word. A major missiological imperative employed by CMS missionaries in India was solely centred on Scripture. Against this popular understanding, the MTC, through its own reformation process showed that Liturgy can likewise be an imperative for mission. The mission theology of the Church is firmly grounded on the concept of mission as ecclesial proclamation of the economy of salvation here and now. The Church strongly held an approach of mission as "brotherly communion and service." The MTC accepted the supreme Liturgy- Eucharist- as the culmination of mission. The Church has employed many mission models enshrined in its Eucharistic liturgy to make its mission relevant and fruitful. The mission activities of the Church were not simply copying the mission strategy of the CMS mission or any other foreign missions operating in India. It was developed as an approach in considering the need of the Indian context with a view to render a Eucharistic presence. Initially there are mainly two strategies of mission applied in India that are the Church-centric model and the Kingdom-centric model. A paradigm shift in the understanding of mission later gained prime importance over the Church-centric model. In the Kingdom-centric approach, the Church promoted an incarnation model of mission in India by founding its own ashrams in different parts of India, so as to bring all communities, including the lower caste, higher caste, and out-caste communities under the guidelines of its mission work. The Kingdom-centered mission praxis was actualized through its development department and charity model of mission. In the course of time, the Church was open enough to accept the dialogue model and institution model in its mission journey. The history of mission endeavours in Malankara proves that Christian mission in India is not very Western, foreign and imperialistic; it is indigenous, culturally authentic, and struggles to create a meaningful witness to the reign of God.[826] In this juncture, the translation and revision of the Eucharistic liturgy on the basis of Scripture gave a strong impetus to the Church in its mission.

---

[826] Thomas, *A History of the First Cross Cultural Mission*, xi.

General Conclusion

The centre of every liturgical celebration is Jesus Christ and his pervading Paschal Mystery. The Church continually proclaims Christ and his salvific-act through its liturgical celebrations. The mission of the Church is to participate in the mission of God. More precisely, the Church is commissioned with a mission that comes from God and that belongs to God. A Christian community which actively participates in liturgical worship cannot remain thoughtlessly closed in on itself, but must progress in the practice of His mission. The mission is first and foremost, God's turning towards the world in creative love, redemptive healing and transforming power. God's mission, as experienced in the Eucharist, embraces the entire human race and indeed all creation.[827] Through an active participation in the liturgy, the faithful experience communion and fellowship with the Triune God and with their fellow believers. Further, an active participation in the liturgy reminds the faithful of their responsibility to witness the salvific act of Christ both individually and collectively. It motivates the Church to impart a Eucharistic presence in the world and thereby accommodates others into a communion with the Triune God. The Eucharist is a *viaticum* and a source of strength in the lives of the witnesses.

The purpose of this research was to find out how the Eucharistic liturgy of the MTC is observed as the foundation for mission in its course of growth. In order to accomplish this objective, I have examined the historical evolution and the developmental process of the Eucharistic liturgy of the Church which is a revised version of the Liturgy of St. James. This study is an appraisal of various missiological themes reflected in this Eucharistic liturgy. The liturgy of the Church is studied in the perspective of mission and Kevin Irvin's theory of Eucharist - "An active presence model'" is employed for the analysis of the liturgy in general. In

---

[827] Swan, *The Eucharist, communion and Formation*, 575-576.

its course, various mission models engaged in the Church are considered and came to a conclusion that, the incarnational model of mission is the most effective model of mission in the Church in the context of rising religious fundamentalism and aggressive secularism. The formation of the MTC as a missionary community and the influence of the liturgy in its missional identity is a matter of study, in which the role of the CMS missionaries are also evaluated. By considering the role of liturgy in the mission of God, it is imperative to understand how the Eucharistic liturgy functions as a liturgical foundation for mission.

The first two chapters of this book dealt with the question of how the Malankara Christians in Kerala existed as a faith community in the midst of its caste based social set up and the nature and identity of the Mar Thoma Church in general. The MTC is believed to be a historic apostolic faith community, strongly rooted in the spiritual heritage of St. Thomas Christians in continuity with the apostolic faith handed over to them from generation to generation. Throughout the centuries, the Malankara Church was connected to the various ecclesial traditions such as the East Syrian (4th C), the Roman Catholic (16th C), the West Syrian (17th C) and the Anglican (19th C). An interaction with these faith communities influenced and shaped the theology, faith and practices of the Malankara Church from time to time. The reformation in the Malankara Church was a landmark in the history of the St. Thomas Christians. During the 19th century, because of the influence of the British rule, English education and the activities of the CMS missionaries made a remarkable change in the social, cultural, political and ecclesial landscape of Kerala, especially in the Central Travancore region. The missionary activities and inspiration of the CMS missionaries were instrumental to commence a revival process in the Malankara Church. The translation of the Bible to the vernacular, its availability to the common people, and the reformed doctrines of the Anglican Church made a great impact in the spiritual life of this Non-Roman wing of the Malankara community. A deeper understanding of Scripture, liturgy, faith and practices of the Church gave impetus for a process of revival in the Malankara Church. The reformation in the Church caused the formation of a new faith community with a renewed enthusiasm for the mission of God. The translation and revision of the Eucharistic liturgy is the basic visible expression of reformation in the Malankara Church. The Bible is the foundation of the liturgical revision in the Church.

The reformation in the Malankara Church was a process of redefining the definition of worship from ritual to experience. It helped the faithful to experience the abiding presence of Christ in their lives which motivated them to cooperate with God in His mission. A renewed understanding of worship derived in this context; i.e. worship is not a mere ritualistic act rather it is an expression of one's dynamic relationship with the Risen Lord. It is an experience of being empowered by the Holy Spirit to ascribe praise and glory to the Triune God in every moment of one's life. The concept of "liturgy after liturgy" is most important in this juncture. Every encounter that Jesus had with the people helped them to have new understanding about life, existence, and one's calling. It is this new understanding of life that helps a person to have the concept of mission in life. But this concept of mission comes only when we redefine worship and participate in the Paschal Mystery actively. In the MTC, the reformation process ignited the people with new understanding of worship and thereby new awareness of its mission in the society. The reformation of the 19th century motivated the Church to locate mission activity at the centre of the Church. The Church was open enough to receive the ideas and mission strategies of the CMS along with its own Oriental liturgical base. The reformation process in general and the Eucharistic liturgy in particular gave a new impetus for the Church in constructing an ecclesial identity and pattern of mission. The anaphora of St. James is the model of the liturgical ordo of this Church. Since the MTC follows the West Syrian liturgical tradition and uses the liturgy of St. James for its liturgical celebrations, a close examination on the distinctiveness of the West Syrian liturgical tradition and historical and theological emphasis of the reformed liturgy of St. James is evaluated in the third chapter. The development of the revised Eucharistic liturgy of the Church is not a sudden outbreak of a historical movement but it is an outcome of a concrete and systematic study and research in its faith journey. In the fourth chapter, a close examination of the origin, historical development, liturgical revisions, major theological and doctrinal emphasis and various translations of the Eucharistic liturgy of the Church is examined.

The fifth chapter dealt with the concept of mission in Scripture, in various ecclesial traditions and in the liturgy. A Trinitarian model of mission is the focus of the revised liturgy. The Eucharistic celebration creates a communion of believers with the Trinity. The Eucharist not only conforms the believer to Christ individually, but transforms them collectively into His body by the power of the Holy Spirit. The mutual indwelling of Christ in the believer and the believer in Christ is expressed in the liturgy and that leads to a deeper assimilation of the believer to Christ and a complete immersion into Trinitarian life. This liturgy provides a Trinitarian model of mission. It affirms that the mission of the Church is an extension of the mission of the Triune God, which is revealed in the life of Christ by the power of the Holy Spirit. In the Mar Thoma liturgy, the celebration of the Holy Qurbana is an expression of the communion of love from the Father through the Son by the Holy Spirit. The Church prays and sings to the Trinity "through Christ," in the power of the Holy Spirit. An active participation in the Eucharistic liturgy enables the faithful to take part in the Trinitarian mystery. The model - Trinity as a community - stands as a paradigm for the formation and sustenance of witnessing communities in the Church. The sixth and seventh chapters highlight how the Trinitarian model of mission and various missional themes in the liturgy gave direction to the Church in its mission. For which, the structure, content and theology of the prayers, signs and symbols are studied. Along with this, the influence of major missional aspects enshrined in the liturgy is dealt in detail and came to a conclusion that the reformed Eucharistic liturgy is the liturgical foundation for mission in the MTC.

An analysis of the historical developments, structure, content and theology of prayers, signs and symbols in the revised Eucharistic liturgy of St. James proves that there is a strong sense of mission flowing from it. This anaphora is enriched with missional elements which centre primarily on the four-fold pattern of the central Eucharistic act of Christian worship: gathering, word, table and sending. The reformed liturgy contains and transmits powerful imagery and exhortations of Christian mission. This liturgy reveals that there is an inseparable connection between Eucharist and mission. The prayers in the liturgy affirm the missionary nature of the Church. It begins with the sending of Jesus Christ, and continues with the work of the Holy Spirit, the work of apostles, prophets, martyrs, the confessors, saints and through all the faithful members of the Church, who have been signed with the seal of baptism. This reiterates the missionary character of the Church and reaffirms the responsibility of all baptised persons. In short, the Christ-experience of the faithful through the Eucharist strengthens and motivates them to participate in the mission of God. The liturgy enables the people of God to internalize and to enliven this Christ experience. For instance, in the final blessing in the liturgy, the celebrant assures the peace of Christ and exhorts them to be channels of peace and divine presence in the world. "…..depart in peace filled with gladness and rejoicing." This is an explicit call for mission in the revised liturgy. The Eucharist calls for a "liturgy after the liturgy"; this Christ experience in the liturgy is the very missionary thrust of the Church. In this sense, the Eucharist is the liturgical foundation for mission in the MTC.

The Eucharist is not only the source and nourishment of the mission of the Church, but also it determines its content and method. Hence the ministry of the Church must be appropriate and designed as per the need of a particular region and context. The missiological elements in the Eucharistic liturgy play a catalytic role for the mission in the Church. The major missiological themes reflected in the liturgy are categorized under six titles; i.e. mission as reconciliation, mission as incarnation, mission as intercession, mission as eschatological, mission as liberation, and mission as transformation. The Church made an effort to bring these missional themes employed in the liturgy into the practical realm by its ancillary organizations, convention gatherings, and socio-charitable works. While the MTC moved out as a mission oriented faith community, it is imperative to understand how the concept of mission is historically developed and being practiced in the Church. The last two chapters dealt with how this Church practices the missional aspects that is highlighted in its liturgy. Further, various mission models employed in the Church were analysed in detail and various ministries through the ancillary organizations of the Church and ashrams were investigated. The Church continues the mission of Christ through its organizations. All her activities are means of sharing the good news, sharing God's love. All individual and organizational engagements in mission flow from the tradition of the Church. The ministries of the organizations are aimed at communicating the Gospel in various ways. Through the activities of its institutions and organizations the Church aims for this holistic transformation. The organizational activities help to foster the relationship between Christ and its members and to guide them as they reach out to others in the love of Christ. The Eucharistic liturgy has a unifying role in the functioning of the organizations. The ashrams in the Church and their activities bear witness to the incarnational model of mission. The extension of mission work among the so-called outcastes of the community is a classic example. The MTC's new policy to launch missionary work among the "outcast" community might be seen by some as a departure from its centuries-old mission policy in a caste-conscious Indian society. The Church attempts to incarnate the Gospel through challenging the evils of the caste structure, serving the poor through hospitals, destitute homes and day care centers for poor children; in short, it thus focuses on the development of villages though humanitarian programs. In other words the Church attempts to incarnate.

The auxiliary organizations of the Church through its various ministries could effect a great impact in the socio-religious sphere of the community at large. These institutions employ a charity and developmental model of mission in the Church. Through the socio-charitable institutions like schools, hospitals, orphanages etc... the Church tried to address pertinent issues of the society and also greatly involved in the liberative aspect of mission. The Bible conventions and revival meetings in the Church, especially, the Maramon Convention, provides a platform for sharing the ecumenical and missional vision of the Church. These meetings are a solemn space which initiates dialogue with other faith communities and thereby fosters unity, harmony and mutual learning in the pluralistic context of Kerala. The liberal and pluralistic mission outlook, which is independent of the Western theology in relation to other religions helped the Church to develop a mission pattern of inclusive paradigm in mission. The Church always showed solidarity with the people who struggle for equality, liberty, justice and freedom. The Church seriously address the socio-political issues emerges in its due course. The Church was always been an agent of reconciliation in the time of conflict between Churches and social institutions.

The reformation is not just a historical and one time venture in the history, rather it should be an ongoing process in the Church. Being a missionary community, the Eucharistic centred life of the Church is a liturgical foundation of its mission. Through a systematic liturgical orientation, liturgical affirmation and a Eucharistic centred life style, the Church can exist as a true missionary community. In order to keep the concept of mission relevant, the Church has to develop a liturgical Eucharistic spirituality and to practice it through its very life. Eucharistic centred spirituality always seeks the "other" and invites others to the heavenly banquet of God and the communion of saints. An active participation in the Eucharistic celebration motivates the faithful to lead a Eucharistic living, which means a life grounded on the Eucharistic values. It is an enactment of the Eucharistic life style which is more self-transcending and self-giving. The celebration of the Eucharist should help the faithful to see the world from the perspective of the gospel and enable them to lead a sacramental life in the midst of the challenges of living in the world.[828] Currently the Church must come to grips with various realities like fundamentalism, secularism and communalism. In addition, on the deeply internal level, there lurk destabilizing dangers like theological ambivalence and an attitude of relativism, all of which pose a potential crisis of Christian identity and an erosion of faith itself and Christian value.

---

[828] Irwin, *Models of the Eucharist*, 295.

Reformation today is to address all issues arising from the geographical spread of the Church to almost all continents, including the issues of migration and the consequent plurality.

The Church is commissioned to be a "Community of Witness" through its very liturgical celebrations in its varied cultural and geographical contexts. The MTC in line with the Oriental Orthodox tradition goes along with the concept of worship as offering glory to God. The celebration of the Eucharist is not just the proclamation, but it is the Gospel itself. It is through the Eucharist that the Church witnesses the mission of God. The gathered community experiences the life and love of Christ mystically through the liturgy and moves out into the world to share this abundant life through their interactions with fellow human beings. The Church shares the glory of God through its transformative actions by its various ministries. Mission means sharing the faith through Christ, sharing his life. An emphasis on Eucharist-centred ecclesiology guides and motivates the faithful to enliven a mission-oriented life. The Eucharist is the central expression of the Church's identity as the sacrament of God's unconditional love, manifested in Christ. Mission is not only the conclusion of the Eucharist, but a concrete living out of that mystery of divine love. In order to guide the people for a sacramental living, the Eucharist centred approach of mission is the need of the time and it is crucial for accomplishing a relevant mission.

Bibliography

BOOKS AND JOURNALS

Abbot, Walter M. ed. *The Document of Vatican II, Sacrosanctum Concelium.10.* New York: The America Free, 1966.

Abraham, K.C. "Mission and Ministry of the Church: A Liberative Perspective." *Bangalore Theological Forum* 29, no.3 (September 1989): 41-46.

Abraham, T.P. *Malankara Mar Thoma Syrian Church: Journey Through Centuries.* Thiruvalla: Christava Sahitya Samithi, 2012.

Adam Adolf. *The Eucharistic Celebration: The Source and Summit of Faith.* Collegeville, MN: Liturgical, 1994.

Adam, Adolf. *The Liturgical Year: It's History and it's Meaning After the Reform of the Liturgy.* New York: Pueblo, 1981.

Aerthayil, James. *The Spiritual Heritage of the St. Thomas Christians.* Bangalore: Dharmaram, 2001.

Aerthayil, James. "The Liturgical Spirituality of the Syro-Malabar Church." In *The Spirituality of the Syro-Malabar Church,* edited by Sebastian Naduthadam. Kochi: Liturgical Research Center, 2009.

Agur, C.M. *Church History of Travancore.* New Delhi: Asian Educational Services, 1990.

Aiya, Nagam V. *The Travancore State Manuel,* Vol.2. Trivandrum: The Travancore Government, 1906.

Alexander, George. ed. *Maramon Convention Sathabhdhi Valyam.* Thiruvalla: Mar Thoma Evangelistic Association, 1995.

Alexander, P.J. ed. *The Mar Thoma Church: Tradition and Modernity.* Thiruvalla: Mar Thoma Syrian Church, 2000.

Allmen, Jean-Jacques Von. *The Lord's Supper.* Cambridge: James Clarke and Co, 2002.

Amalados, Michael. "Challenges of Mission in the 21st Century." *Theology Digest* 47, no.1 (Spring 2000):15-20.

Amalados, Michael. "Our Mission in India Today." *Vaigarai* 6, no. 2 (September 2001):18-23.

Amalorpavadass, D.S. "Approaches, Meaning and Horizon of Evangelization." In *Light and Life We Seek to Share*. Patna: All India Consultation on Evangelization, 1973. 54-57.

Amalorpavadass, D.S. "Indigenization and the Liturgy of the Church." *International Review of Mission* 65 (1976):164-167.

Anastasios, Archbishop. *Mission in Christ's Way*. Geneva, World Council of Churches, 2010.

Anderson, Gerald H., and Thomas F. Stransky, eds. *Mission Trends No.1: Crucial Issues in Mission Today*. New York: Paulist, 1974.

Anderson, William. *Towards a Theology of Mission*. London: SCM, 1955.

Athyal, Jesudas M., and John J. Thattamannil, eds. *Metropolitan Chrysostom on Mission in the Market Place*. Thiruvalla: Christava Sahitya Samithi, 2002.

Baago, Kaj. "Indigenization and Church History." *Bulletin of the Church History Association of India* (February 1976): 24-28.

Baldovin, J.F. *Liturgy in Ancient Jerusalem*. Nottingham: Grove Liturgical Study, 1989.

Balz, Horst., and Gerhard Schneider, eds. *Exegetical Dictionary of the New Testament*. Vol. 3. Virgil P. Howard, James W. Thompson, John W. Medendorp and Douglas W. Stott, trans. Grand Rapids: Eerdmans, 1993.

Baptism, Eucharist, and Ministry. Faith and Order Paper No. III, Geneva: WCC, 1982.

Bar Salibi, Dionysius. *Commentary on Eucharist*. Baby Varghese, trans. Kottayam: St. Ephrem Ecumenical Research Institute, 1998.

Barnabas, Mathews Mar. *Vishuda Qurbanayude Oru Padanam*. 5th ed. Kottayam: OSSAE, 1992.

Barsoum, Ignatius Aprem I. *History of Syriac Literature and Sciences.* Pueblo: Passeggiata, 2000.

Bates, Barrington J. "Expressing What Christians Believe: Anglican Principles for Liturgical Revision." Anglican Theological Review ATR/92:3, 455. www.anglicantheologicalreview.org/static/pdf/articles/bates.pdf (accessed December 08, 2015).

Bauckham, Richard. *Bible and Mission: Christian Witness in a Postmodern World.* Grand Rapids: Baker, 2003.

Baum, Wilhelm and Dietmar Winkler. *The Church of the East: A Concise History.* London: Routledge, 2010. http://www.peshitta.org/pdf/CoEHistory.pdf (accessed November 14, 2014)

Baumstark, A and West F. *On the Historical Development of the Liturgy.* Collegeville, MN: Liturgical, 2011.

Bevans, Stephen B, and Roger P. Schroeder. *Constants in Context: A Theology of Mission for Today.* New York, Maryknoll: Orbis, 2004.

Bevans, Stephen B, and Roger P. Schroeder. *Prophetic Dialogue: Reflections on Christian Mission Today.* New York, Maryknoll: Orbis, 2011.

Binns, John. *An Introduction to the Christian Orthodox Churches.* Cambridge: Cambridge University, 2002.

Bishop, J H. "Past and Present of the Travancore and Cochin Mission." *The Church Missionary Intelligencer* 21 (October, 1896): 12-15.

Blauw, Johannes. *The Missionary Nature of the Church: A Survey of the Biblical Theology of Mission.* New York: McGraw-Hill Book Company, 1961.

Bordeyne, Philippe, and Bruce T. Morrill. "Baptism and Identity Formation: Convergence in Ritual and Ethical Perspectives: A Dialogue." *Studia Liturgica* 42 (2012): 154-175.

Bosch, David J. *Transforming Missions: Paradigm Shifts in Theology of Missions.* New York: Orbis, 1992.

Bottigheimer, Christoph. "Unity, Yes, But which Unity?." *Theology Digest* 52, no.2 (Summer 2005): 119-126.

Bouyer, Louis. *Eucharist: Theology and Spirituality of the Eucharistic Prayer.* trans. *Charles Underhill Quinn.* Notre Dame, Indiana: University of Notre Dame, 1968.

Bradley, C. Randall. *From Memory to Imagination: Reforming the Church's Music* Cambridge: Grand Rapids, 2012.

Bradshaw, Paul F, and Maxwell E. Johnson. *The Eucharistic Liturgies: Their Evolution and Interpretation.* Collegeville, MN: Liturgical, 2012.

Bradshaw, Paul F. "Patterns of Ministry." *Studia Liturgica* 15, no.1 (1982): 55-58.

Bradshaw, Paul F. ed. *Essays in Early Eastern Eucharistic Prayers.* Collegeville, MN: Liturgical, 1997.

Bradshaw, Paul. *The New SCM Dictionary of Liturgy and Worship.* London: SCM, 2002.

Bria, Ion. "Unity and Mission from the Perspective of the Local Church: An Orthodox View." *The Ecumenical Review* 39 (1987): 265-270.

Bria, Ion. ed. *Go Forth in Peace: Orthodox Perspectives on Mission.* Geneva: WCC, 1986.

Bria, Ion. *The Liturgy after the Liturgy: Mission and Witness from an Orthodox Perspective.* Geneva: WCC, 1996.

Brightman, F. E. *Eastern Liturgies,* Oxford: Clarendon, 1896.

Brightman, Frank Edward. "Liturgies Eastern and Western being the Texts Original or Translated of the Principal Liturgies of the Church." Vol. I. *Eastern Liturgies.* Oxford: Clarendon, 1896. https://archive.org/details/liturgieseastern01unknuoft (accessed November 17, 2014).

Brink, Ten E L. *"The CMS Mission of Help to the Syrian Church in Malabar, 1816-1840: A Study in Protestant Eastern orthodox Encounter"* PhD Thesis, Hartford Seminary, 1960.

Brink, Laurie. "In Search of the Biblical Foundations of Prophetic Dialogue: Engaging a Hermeneutics of Otherness." *Missiology: An International Review* 41, no.1 (January 2013): 9-21.

Broadley, George and Howard. *The Christians of St. Thomas and their Liturgies*. London, John Henry and James Parker, 1864.

Brock, Sebastian P. "An Introduction to Syriac Studies." In *Horizons in Semitic Studies,* edited by John Herbert. Birmingham: University of Birmingham, 1980. 8-40.

Brock, Sebastian P. "The Earliest Syriac Literature." In *Early Christian Literature,* edited by Young, F, L Ayres, and A. Louth. Cambridge: Cambridge University, 2004. 161-171.

Brock, Sebastian P. *Fire from Heaven: Studies in Syriac Theology and Liturgy*. Aldershot: Ashgate, 2006.

Brock, Sebastian P. *The Bible in the Syriac Tradition*. Kottayam: SEERI, 1988.

Brock, Sebastian P. *The Luminous Eye, the Spiritual World Vision of St. Ephrem*. Kalamazoo: Cistercian, 1985.

Brock, Sebastian. P. "An Early Syriac Commentary on the Liturgy." *Journal of Theological Studies* 37 (1986), 387-403.

Brock, Sebastian. P. *A Brief Outline of Syriac Literature*. Kottayam: St. Ephrem Ecumenical Research Institute, 1997.

Brown, Leslie W. *The Indian Christians of St. Thomas: An Account of the Ancient Syrian Church of Malabar*. Cambridge: Cambridge University, 1956.

Brunk, Timothy M. *Liturgy and Life: The Unity of Sacrament and Ethics in the Theology of Louis-Marie Chauvet*. New York: Peter Lang, 2007.

Buchanan, Claudius. *Christian Researches in Asia with Notices of the Translation of the Scriptures into the Oriental Language*. London: T. Caddell and W. Davide, 1814.

Buchanan, Claudius. *The Works of the Rev. Comprising His Christian Researches in Asia*. New York: Whiting and Watson, 1812. http://search.library.utoronto.ca/details?1445955 (accessed March 20, 2014).

Buchanon, Collin. ed. *Anglican Eucharistic Liturgies 1985-2010*. London: Canterbury, 2011.

Burns, Stephen. *The SCM Study Guide to Liturgy.* London: SCM, 1996.

Callaghan, Paul O. *Christ Our Hope: An Introduction to Eschatology.* Washington D.C: The Catholic University of America, 2011.

Casey, Damien. "Liturgy Matters: Liturgy and Scripture as the Mirrors of Catholicity." *Australian eJournal of Theology* 4 (2005): 1-7.

Chacko, M.C. *Thaksa Committee Report.* Thiruvalla: R.V. 1925.

Chacko, T. C. *The Concise History of the Mar Thoma Church.* Malayalam. 5th ed. Thiruvalla: Episcopal Jubilee Institute, 2001.

Chacko, T.C. *Ayroor Achen Athava C.P.Philipose Kassisa.* Kozhencherry: Mar Thoma Samajam, 1949.

Chaillot, C. *The Syrian Orthodox Church of Antioch and the All the East: A Brief Introduction to its Life and Spirituality.* Geneva: Inter-Orthodox Dialogue. 1988.

Chaillot, Christine. "The Ancient Oriental Churches." In *The Oxford History of Christian Worship,* edited by Geoffrey Wainwright, Karen B Westerfield Tucker. Oxford: Oxford University, 2006. 131-169.

Cherian P, *The Malabar Syrians and the Church Mission Society: 1816-1840.* Kottayam: Church Missionary Press, 1935.

Chupungco, Anscar J. *Handbook for Liturgical Studies,* Collegeville, MN: Liturgical, 2000.

Clarke, Sathianathan. *Dalits and Christianity: Subaltern Religions and Liberation Theology in India.* Calcutta: Oxford University Press, 1998.

Clavairoly, Francois. "Protestantism and Theology of Ministries: Ecumenical Perspective." *Theology Digest* 49, no. 1 (Spring 2002): 51-56.

Clement of Alexandria, *Paedagogus,* Part 2, 4 and 8, 441; trans. Roberts, A. and Donaldson. J. http://www.ellopos.net/elpenor/greek-texts/fathers/clement-alexandria/default.asp (accessed November 25, 2015).

Clendenin, Daniel B. ed. *Eastern Orthodox Theology: A Contemporary Reader.* Grand Rapids, MI: Baker Book, 1995.

Clergy conference. *Self-formation through Worship and Sacraments.* Thiruvalla: Christava Sahitya Samithi, 2008.

Code of Canons of the Eastern Churches. Washington DC, Canon Law Society of America. 1992

Commission of Faith and Order, World Council of Churches. "Towards Koinonia in Worship: Consultation on the Role of Worship within the Search of Unity." *Studia Liturgica* 25, no.1 (1995): 1-31.

Commission on World Mission and Evangelism. *Together Towards Life: Mission and Evangelism in Changing Landscapes.* Geneva: World Council of Churches, 2013.

Common Witness: A Study Document of the Joint Working Group of the Roman Catholic Church and the World Council of Churches. Geneva: World Council of Churches, 1984.

Congar, Yves. *Tradition and Traditions: An Historical and Theological Essay.* New York: Macmillan, 1967.

Connolly, Richard Hugh. ed. *Didascalia Apostolorum: The Syriac Version. trans. Verona Latin.* Oxford: Clarendon, 1929.

Connolly, Richard Hugh., and Humphrey William Codrington, eds. *Two Commentaries on the Jacobite Liturgy by George Bishop of the Arab Tribes and Moses Bar Kepha: Together with the Syriac Anaphora of St. James and a Document Entitled the Book of Life.* Oxford: Williams and Norgate. 1913.

Conway, Stephen. ed. *Living the Eucharist: Affirming Catholicism and the Liturgy.* London: Longman and Todd, 2001.

Crawford, David S. "Christian Community and the States of Life." *Communio-International Catholic Review* XXIX (2002): 337-365.

Crockett, William R. "Christianity and Culture in Modern Secular Society." *Studia Liturgica* 20 (1990): 28-35.

Cyril of Jerusalem. *Mystagogical Catechesis. In a Select Library of the Nicene and Post- Nicene Fathers of the Christian Church. Second Series.* Vol. VII. eds., Schaff Philip and Henry Wase, Edenborough: T and T Clark, 1955. 1-157.

Daniel, I. "The Syrian Church of Malabar." In *The Nazranis*, edited by George Menacherry. Thrissur: SARAS, 1998. 334-362.

Daniel, Joseph. *Ecumenism in Praxis: A Historical Critique of the Malankara Mar Thoma Syrian Church.* Frankfurt: Peter Lang, 2014.

Daniel, K. N. *Malankara Sabhayum Naveekaranavum.* Vol. I. Thiruvalla: K. N. Daniel, 1949.

Daniel, K.N. *A Critical Study of Primitive Liturgies*, Kottayam, RPT, 1937.

Danielou, Jean. *The Bible and the Liturgy.* Notre Dame: University of Notre Dame, 1973.

Darragh, Neil. "Hazardous Missions and Shifting Frameworks." *Missiology: An International Review* XXXVIII, no.3 (July 2010): 271-280.

Davies, John Gordon. "The Missionary Dimension of Worship." *Studia Liturgica* 6, 2 (1969): 79-84.

Davies, John Gordon. *Worship and Mission.* London: SCM, 1966.

Davis, Charles. *Sacraments of Initiation, Baptism, and Confirmation.* New York: Sheed and Ward, 1964.

Davis, Stephen T., Daniel Kendall, and Gerald O'Collins, eds. *The Trinity.* Oxford: Oxford University, 1999.

Day, A.H. *Dawn in Travancore: A Brief Account of the Manners and Customs of the People and the Efforts that are being made for their Improvement.* Kottayam: Church Missionary Society, 1860.

Day, Peter D. *The Liturgical Dictionary of Eastern Christianity.* Kent: Burns and Oates, 1993.

Deiss, L. *Springtime of the Liturgy: Liturgical Texts of the First Four Centuries.* Collegeville, MN: Liturgical, 1979.

Dharma Jyothi, Vidya Peeth. *At The Master's Feet: A Study of the Faith and Practice of the Mar Thoma Church.* Faridabad: Sabina, 2007.

Dimock, Giles. *The Eucharist.* New York: Paulist, 2006.

Doe, Michael. *Saving Power: The Mission of God and Anglican Communion.* London: SPCK, 2011.

Dorn, Christopher. "Lord's Supper in the Reformed Church in America: Tradition in Transformation." *American University Studies VII: Theology and Religion.* Vol. 264. New York: Peter Lang, 2007.

Draper, Jonathan A. "The Apostolic Fathers: The Didache." *Expository Times* 117:5 (Feb. 2006): 177-181.

Egan, Joe., and Brendan McConvery, eds. *Faithful Witness: Glimpses of the Kingdom.* Dublin: Milltown Institute of Theology and Philosophy, 2005.

Elavanal, T. *The Memorial Celebration.* Kottayam: Pourathya Vidhyapetth, 1989.

Elavathingal, Sebastian. *Inculturation and Christian Art: An Indian Perspective.* Rome: Urbiana University, 1990.

Eliade, Mircea. ed. T*he Encyclopaedia of Religion.* Vol.14. London: Mac Millan, 1997.

Engineer, Asghar Ali. *On Developing Theory of Communal Riots.* Bombay: Institute of Islamic Studies, 1984.

Ernest Falardeau. *A Holy and Living Sacrifice: The Eucharist in Christian Perspective.* Collegeville, MN: Liturgical, 1996.

Ervvine, Roberta R. *Some Distinctive Features in Syriac Liturgical Texts.* New York: St. Nersess Armenian Seminary, 2006.

Faith and Order Paper No.210. *One Baptism: Towards Mutual Recognition-A Study Text.* Geneva: World Council of Churches, 2011.

Farquhar, J N. "The Apostle Thomas in North India," in *The Nazranis, edited by* Menacherry in the *Bulletin of the John Rylands Library* 11, 1926. 313-322.

Fawcett, Thomas. *The Symbolic Language of Religion.* London: SCM, 1970.

Federov, Vladimir. "Orthodox Mission Today." *Together in Mission: Orthodox Churches Consult with the Church Mission Society.* Mosco (April 2001): 13-14.

Fenwick, John R K. "The Missing Oblation." *The Contents of the Early Antichene Anaphora* Grove Liturgical Study 59. Nottingham: Grove Books, 1989.

Fenwick, John R. K, and Bryan D. Spinks. *Worship in Transition: The Liturgical Movement in the Twentieth Century.* New York: Continuum, 1995.

Fenwick, John R. K. *The Forgotten Bishops: The Malabar Independent Syrian Church and its Place in the Story of the St. Thomas Christians of South India.* Piscataway, New Jersey: Gorgias, 2009.

Fenwick, John R.K. *Liturgy for Identity and Spirituality.* Kottayam: Thomas Mar Athanasius Memorial Research and Orientation Centre, 2008.

Fenwick, John R.K. *The Anaphoras of St. Basil and St. James: An Investigation into their Common Origin.* Roma: Pontificium Institutum Orientale, 1992.

Ferguson, Everett. *Backgrounds of Early Christianity.* 2nd ed. Grand Rapids, MI: Eerdmans, 1993.

Ferguson, Everett. ed. *Encyclopedia of Early Christianity.* London: St. James, 1990.

Figura, Michael. "The Works of communion: Christian Community in Act." *Communio-International Catholic Review* XXIX (2002): 220-238.

Fink, Peter. ed. *The New Dictionary of Sacramental Worship.* Collegeville, MN: Liturgical, 1990.

Firth, Bruce Cyril. *An Introduction to Indian Church History.* Delhi: ISPCK, 1961.

Flannery, Austin. ed. *Sacrosanctum Concilium* 14, Vatican Council II: Conciliar and Post –Conciliar Documents. New York: Costello, 1975.

Francis, Mark R. *Liturgy in a Multicultural Community.* Collegeville, MN: Liturgical, 1991.

Frost, Michael and Alan Hirsch. *The Shaping of Things to Come.* Massachusetts: Hendrickson, 2003.

Fuller. C.J. *The Nayars Today*. Cambridge, Cambridge University, 1976.

Garrett, T.S. *Christian Worship: An Introductory Outline*. Oxford: Oxford University, 1961.

Garrigan, Siobhan. "A New Model for Ecumenical Worship." *Studia Liturgica* 43, no.1 (2013): 32-53.

Geevarghese, K.E., and Mathew T. Thomas, eds. *Beyond the Diaspora*. Thiruvalla: Mar Thoma Church Diocese of North America and Europe, 2014.

Geisler, Norman L, and Ralph MacKenzie. *Roman Catholics and Evangelicals: Agreements and Differences*. Grand Rapids, MI: Baker Books, 1995.

Gelder, Craig Van, and Dwight J. Zscheile. *The Missional Church in Perspective: Mapping Trends and Shaping the Conversation*. Grand Rapids: Baker Academie, 2011.

Gelineau, *Joseph*. "New Models for the Eucharistic Prayer as Praise of All the Assembly." *Studia Liturgica 27 (1997): 79-87.*

Gelston, A. "The East Syrian Eucharistic Prayers." In *The Serious Business of Worship: Essays in Honour of Bryan D. Spinks*, edited by Ross M. and Jones, S. London: T and T. Clark, 2010. 55-64.

George, Alexander. ed. *Maramon Convention Sathabdhi Valyam*. Malayalam. Thiruvalla: Mar Thoma Evangelistic Association, 1995.

George, M.C. *Palakunnathu Abraham Malpan*. Thiruvalla: Church Literature Society, 1985.

George, M.V. *Communion in the Body of Christ and the St. James' Liturgy*. Vellore: The St. Luke's Orthodox Parish, 1969.

Gilliland, Dean S. *Pauline Theology and Mission Practice*. Grand Rapids, MI: Baker Book, 1983.

Glasser, Arthur F, and Donal A. McGavran. *Contemporary Theologies of Mission*. Grand Rapids, MI: Baker Book, 1983.

Glover, Robert Hall. *The Bible Basis of Missions*. Chicago: MOODY. 1976.

Gopalakrishnan. P. K. *A Cultural History of Kerala.* 4th ed. Thiruvananthapuram: State Institute of language, 1991.

Guder, Darrell L. "Missional Church." *International Catholic Review* XXIX (2002): 220-238.

Guder, Darrell L. ed. *Missional Church: A Vision for the Sending of the Church in North America.* Grand Rapids: Eerdmans, 1998.

Guthrie, Shirley C. *Always Being Reforming.* London: Westminster John Knox, 2008.

Guy, L. *Introducing Early Christianity: A Topical Survey of its Life, Beliefs, and Practices.* Illinois: Inter Varsity, 2004.

Hastings, Adrian. *'150-1550': In a World History of Christianity.* Grand Rapids: Eerdmans, 1999.

Hellwig, Monika K. *Encyclopedia of Religion.* Vol. V. Collegeville, MN: The Liturgical. 2004.

Hesselgrave, David J, and Edward Rommen. *Contextualization: Meanings, Methods and Models.* California: William Carey Library, 2000.

Hofinger, Johannes. ed. *Liturgy and the Missions: The Nijmegen Papers.* New York: P J. Kennedy and Sons, 1960.

Hopko, Thomas. *The Orthodox Faith.* Vol 4. Crestwood, New York: Vladimir Seminary, 1984.

Hough, James. *The History of Christianity in India: From the Commencement of the Christian Era.* London: R.B. Seeley and W. Burnside, 1839.

Howard, George Broadley. *The Christians of St Thomas and their Liturgies: Comprising the Anaphora of St. James, St. Peter, The Twelve Apostles, Mar Dionysius, Mar Xystus and Mar Evannis, together with the Ordo Communis.* Oxford: John Henry and James Pakker. 1864. http://cerziozan.ru/the-christians-of-st-thomas.pdf (accessed November 14, 2014).

Hunt, E. J. *Christianity in the Second Century.* London: Routledge. 2003

Irwin, Kevin W. *Models of the Eucharist.* New York: Paulist, 2005.

Jalmarson, Leonard E. "Trinitarian Spirituality of Mission." *Journal of Spiritual Formation and Soul Care* 6, 1 (2013), 93-109.

Jeffery, Peter. "The Meanings and Functions of Kyrie eleison." In *The Place of Christ in Liturgical Prayer: Trinity, Christology, and Liturgical Theology,* edited by Bryan D. Spinks and Martin Jean. Collegeville, MN: Liturgical, 2008. 127-194.

Jeffrey, Robin. *The Decline of Nayar Dominance.* New York: Holmes and Meier, 1976.

Jenkins, Philip. "The Next Christianity." *Atlantic Monthly* 290/3, (October 2002): 53-72.

John, Mathai. "The Reformation of Abraham Malpan and Assessment." *Indian Church History Review* 24/1, (1990): 31-65.

John, Zacharia. *"The Liturgy of the Mar Thoma Church of Malabar in the Light of its History."* Master's thesis, University of Durham, 1994.

Johnson, Dale A. "Lectionary", Syriac Orthodox Resources, http://sor.cua.edu/Lectionary/ (accessed February 12, 2016).

Johnson, Maxwell E. "The Apostolic Tradition." In *The Oxford History of Christian Worship,* edited by Geoffrey Wainwright and Karen B. Westerfield Tucker. Oxford: Oxford University, 2006. 32-75.

Johnson, Maxwell E. *The Rites of the Christian Initiation: Their Evolution and Interpretation.* Collegeville, MN: Liturgical, 1999.

Jones, J. P. *The Year Book of Missions in India, Burma and Ceylon.* The Christian Literature Society for Asia, 1912.

Joseph, K. *A Brief Sketch of the Church of St. Thomas in Malabar.* Kottayam: Church Missionary Society, 1933.

Joseph, M. J. ed. *In Search for Christian Identity in Global Community.* New York: Dioceses of North America and Europe, 2009.

Joseph, M. J. ed. *Malankara Mar Thoma Syrian Church: Sabha Directory 2015.* 4th ed. Thiruvalla: Mar Thoma Syrian Church, 1915.

Joseph, M. J. ed., *Gleanings.* Madras: Printon, 1994.

Joy. K T. *The Mar Thoma Church: A Study of Its Growth and Contributions.* Kottayam: Good Shepherd, 1986.

Jungmann, Josef. *The Place of Christ in Liturgical Prayer.* trans. A Peeler. New York: Alba House, 1965.

Jurgen Feulner, Hans. "Zu den Editionen Orientalischer Anaphoren." In *Crossroad of Cultural Studies in Liturgy and Patristics in Honour of Gabriele Winkler,* edited by Hans Jurgen Feulner, E Velkovska, and Robert F. Taft. Rome: Pontificio Istituto Orientale, 2000.

Kane, Herbert J. *Understanding Christian Missions.* Grand Rapids, MI: Baker Book, 1983.

Kanjappally, Koshy Mathew. *Roots and Wings.* Bangalore: Word Makers, 2004.

Kannookadan, Pauly. ed. *The Mission Theology of the Syro-Malabar Church.* Kochi: Liturgical Research Centre, 2008.

Kärkkäinen, Veli Matti. *An Introduction to Ecclesiology.* Downer's Grove: Intervarsity, 2002.

Karkkainen, Veli-Matti. *The Trinity: Global Perspective.* London: Westminster John Knox, 2007.

Kawashima, Koli. *Missionaries and a Hindu State:* Travancore: *1858-1936.* Delhi: Oxford University, 1998.

Keay, F.E. *A History of the Syrian Church in India.* Delhi: ISPCK, 1960.

Kennedy, David J. *Eucharistic Sacramentality in an Ecumenical Context: The Anglican Epiclesis.* Aldershot: Ashgate, 2008.

Kennedy. Robert J. ed. *Reconciliation: The Continuing Agenda.* Collegeville, MN: Liturgical, 1987.

King, Archdale. *The Rites of the Eastern Christendom.* Rome: Catholic Book Agency, 1948.

Kirk, Andrew J. *The Mission of Theology and Theology as Mission-Christian Mission and Modern Culture.* Series, 6. Pennsylvania: Trinity Press International, 1997.

Kirk, Andrew J. *What Is Mission? Theological Explorations.* Minneapolis: Fortress, 2000.

Klauser, Theodor. *A Short History of the Western Liturgy.* London: Oxford University, 1969.

Knight, Douglas H. ed. *The Theology of John Zizioulas.* Aldershot: Ashgate, 2007.

Kochuparampil, Jose. "The Missionary Dimension of the Liturgy in the Ananphora of the Apostles Addai and Mari." *Studia Liturgica* 36, 2 (2006): 129-137.

Kochuparampil, Xavier. "The Liturgical Dimension of Evangelisation." *Questions liturgique* 72 (1991): 218-230.

Kollaparambil, Jacob. *The Babylonian Origin of the Southists Among the St. Thomas Christians.* Roma: Pont.Institutum Studiorun Orientalium, 1992.

Konat, Johns Abraham. *Visudha Yakobinte Kurbana Taksa: Anushtannangalum Vyakyanangalum Cherthathu.* Kottayam: Malankara Orthodox Church Publications, 2011.

Koodapuzha, Xavier. ed. *Eastern Theological Reflection in India.* Kottayam: Oriental Institute of Religious Studies, 1999.

Kruisheer, Dirk, and Lucas Van Rompay. "A Bibliographical Clavis to the Works of Jacob of Edessa," *Hugoye: Journal of Syriac Studies* 1, no.1 (1998): 35-56

Kung, Hans. *The Church.* New York: Sheed and Ward, 1967.

Kunjukunju, Jameson. *"Theological Difference Reflected in the Eucharistic Prayers and Practices of the Malankara Mar Thoma Church and Malankara Jacobite Syrian Church."* B.D thesis., The United Theological College, Bangalore, 2003.

Kurian, Prema. "Denominationalism to Post-Denominationalism: Changes in American Christianity." *Mar Thoma Messenger 30*, no.2 (April 2011): 23-27.

Kuruvila, Abraham. *An Indian Fruit from Palestinian Roots: Towards an Indian Eucharistic Liturgy.* Thiruvalla: Christava Sahitya Samithi, 2013.

Kuruvilla, K. K. *A History of the Mar Thoma Church and its Doctrines.* Madras: Christian Literature Society, 1951.

Kusuman, K. K. *Slavery in Travancore.* Trivandrum: Kerala Historical Society, 1973.

Kuttiyil, George Mathew. *Eucharist (Qurbana): The Celebration of the Economy of Salvation (Madabranutha) - A Theological Analysis of the Anaphora of St. James.* Kottayam: Oriental Institute of Religious Studies, 1999.

Kuttiyil, George Mathew. *Liturgy for Our Times.* Kerala: Christava Sahitya Samithi, 2006.

Kuttiyil, George Mathew. *The Faith and Sacraments of the Mar Thoma Church.* Thiruvalla: Christava Sahitya Samithi, 2005.

Labourt, H. *Dionysius Bar Salibi, Expositio Liturgicae,* CSCO 13-14. Paris: Harrassowitz. 1903.

Lathrop, Gordon. *What are the Essentials of Christian Worship?* Minneapolis, MN: Augsburg Fortress, 1994.

Lefebvre, Solange, Denise Couture, and K. Gandhar Chakravarty. eds. *Concilium.* London: SCM, 2014.

Letham, Robert. *Through Western Eyes- Eastern Orthodoxy: A Reformed Perspective.* Wales: Mentor, 2007.

Liturgical Commission of the Church of England. *New Patterns for Worship.* London; Church House, 2002.

Lossky, Vladimir. *In the Image and Likeness of God.* Crestwood, New York: St. Vladimir's Theological Seminary, 1974.

Lossky, Vladimir. *The Mystical Theology of the Eastern Church.* Crestwood, New York: St. Vladimir's Theological Seminary, 1976.

Lott, Eric J. ed. *Worship in an Indian Context.* Bangalore: United Theological College, 1986.

Lutheran World Federation. "Nairobi Statement on Worship and Culture: Contemporary Challenges and Opportunities." *Studia Liturgica* 27 (1997): 88-93.

Malipurathu, Thomas., and L. Stanislaus, eds. *A Vision of Mission in the New Millennium.* Mumbai: St Paul's, 2001.

Maniyattu, Pauly. *Heaven On Earth: The Theology of Liturgical Space-Time in the East Syrian Qurbana.* Rome: Mar Thoma Yogam, 1995.

Mannion, Francic M. *Masterworks of God: Essays in Liturgical Theory and Practice.* Illinois, Chicago: Hillenbrand Books, 2004.

Mannooparambil, Thomas. "Liturgical Spiritualty." In *Eastern Theological Reflection in India,* edited by Xaviour Koodapuzha. Kottayam: Oriental Institute of Religious Studies, 1999. 220-225.

Mar Athanasius, Thomas Suffragan, and T. P. Abraham. *Navvekaranavum Sabhayude Dwuthyavum.* Malayalam. Thiruvalla: T. A. M, 1984.

Mar Makkarios, Mathews. "Mission of the Church: Contextual and Universal." *Mar Thoma Seminary Journal of Theology* 1, no.1 (June 2012): 58-61.

Mar Theodosius, Geevarghese. "Mar Thoma Church." In *Mar Thoma Church: Tradition and Modernity,* edited by P.J. Alexander. Thiruvalla: Mar Thoma Syrian Church, 2000. 98-102.

Mar Theodosius, Geevarghese. "Maramon Convention: Mission and Ministry." *Mar Thoma Messenger* (2009): 28-31

Mar Theodosius, Geevarghese. "Shifting meaning in Public, Religion and Domestic Spaces: Theological, Ministerial and Missional Challenges." *Mar Thoma Messenger* 34, no. 3 (July 2015): 14-17.

Mar Thoma, Juhanon. *Christianity in India and a Brief History of the Mar Thoma Syrian Church.* Madras: K.M. Cherian, 1973.

Mar Thoma, Juhanon. *The History of the Mar Thoma Church and the Christian Church in India.* Thiruvalla: Christava Sahitya Samithi, 1973.

Mar Thoma, Titus II. *Malankara Mar Thoma Suriyani Sabhayude Qurbana Thaksa.* Thiruvalla: Mar Thoma, 1942.

Massey, James. *Roots - A Concise History of Dalits*. New Delhi: CISRS, 1991.

Mateer, Samuel. *The Land of Charity: A Descriptive Account of Travancore and its People*. New Delhi: Asian Educational Services, 1991.

Mathew, C.P, and M. M. Thomas. *The Indian Churches of St. Thomas*. Delhi: ISPCK, 1967.

Mathew, Geevarghese. "Mar Thoma Theological Seminary: A Retrospective Reading." Mar Thoma Seminary Journal of Theology 1, no. 1 (June 2012):9-12.

Mathew, K. V. *Viswaasaacharangal Marthoma Sabhayil*. Kottayam: Mar Thoma Seminary, 1993.

Mathew, N. M. *Malankara Mar Thoma Sabha Charithram*. Vol. I.II.III. Thiruvalla: Mar Thoma Episcopal Jubilee Institute of Evangelism, 2003.

Mathew. C.P. *Thaksa Nirupanam*. Malayalam. New Delhi: Dharma Jyothi Viddya Peeth, 2008.

Mathew, Sunni E. "History of the Development of the Mar Thoma Syrian Liturgy," in *Roots and Wings of Our Liturgy, Mar Thoma Clergy Conference 2008*, edited by A. T. Zachariah. Kottayam: WiGi, 2008. 18-41.

Mazza, Enrico. *The Origin of the Eucharistic Prayer*. Collegeville, MN: Liturgical, 1995.

Mc Guckin, John Anthony. T*he Orthodox Church: An Introduction to its History, Doctrine, and Spiritual Culture*. Sussex: Wiley-Blackwell, 2011.

Mcanus, Frederick R. *Liturgical Participation: An Ongoing Assessment*. Washington: The Pastoral, 1988.

McGowan, Anne. *Eucharistic Epiclesis, Ancient and Modern*. London: SPCK, 2014.

McGrath, Alister E. *Christian Theology: An Introduction*. 2nd ed. Oxford: Blackwell, 1997.

McKenna, J. H. *The Eucharistic Epiclesis: A Detailed History from the Patristic to the Modern Era.* Chicago, Illinois: Hillenbrand, 2009.

Meisner, Joachim. "Eucharist and Evangelization." *Christ Light of Nations.* Sherbrooke: Paulines, 1994.

Menacherry, George. ed. *Indian Church History Classics. The Nazranis.* Thrissur: SARAS, 1998.

Menachery, George. ed. *The St. Thomas Christian Encyclopaedia of India.* Vol.1, Thrissur: St. Thomas Christian Encyclopedia, 1982.

Meno. "Syrian Orthodox Church." In *The Encyclopedia of Christianity,* Vol. 5, edited by E. Fahlbusch. Grand Rapids, MI: Eerdmans, 2008. 281-284.

Menon, A. Sreedhara. *A Survey of Kerala History.* Kottayam: Sahitya Pravartthaka Cooperative Society, 1967.

Menze, Volker L. *Justinian and the Making of the Syrian Orthodox Church.* Oxford: Oxford University, 2008.

Metropolitan, Mathews Mar Athanasius. *Mar Thoma Sleehayude Edavakayakunna Malankra Suriyanisabhayude Canon - 1857.* Malayalam. Thiruvalla: Church Sahitya Samithi, 2008.

Metropolitan, Titus II. Mar Thoma. *Qurbana Thaksa of the Malankara Mar Thoma Syrian Church.* Malayalam. 6th ed. Thiruvalla: Mar Thoma Sabha, 2001.

Meyendorf, John. *Trinitarian Theology East and West.* Brookline: Holy Cross Orthodox, 1977.

Michael, John Britto. *"The Church's Marian Profile and Evangelization in India: In the Light of the Federation of Asian Bishop's Conferences' Documentation on Evangelization."* PhD diss., St. Patrick's College, 2014.

Milne, Rae George. *The Syrian Church in India.* Edinburgh: William Blackwood and Sons, 1896.

Mingana, Alfonso. *The Early Spread of Christianity in India. Bulletin of the John Rylands Library.* Manchester: Manchester University, *1926.*

Mohan, P. Chandra. "Growth of Social Reform Movements in Kerala." In *Perspectives on Kerala History. Kerala State Gazetteer.* Vol. II, edited by P. J. Cheriyan. Trivandrum: Government, 1999.

Moltmann, Jürgen, "The Mission of the Spirit: the Gospel of Life." In *Mission: An Invitation to God's Future,* edited by Timothy Yates. Sheffield: Cliff College Publishing, 2000. 19-34.

Moolan, John. "Death Rite Customs of St. Thomas Christians in Malabar." *Studia Liturgica* 38, no.2 (2008):197-205.

Moolaveetil, L. *A Study of the Anaphora of St. James.* Kottayam: St. Thomas Apostolic Seminary, 1976.

Moosa, Matti. *The Maronites in History.* Piscataway: Gorgias, 2006. http://www.syrianorthodoxchurch.org/library (accessed October 15, 2015).

Moreau, Scott. ed. *Evangelical Dictionary of World Missions.* Grand Rapids: Baker, 2000.

Muller, Karl, Theo Sundermeier, Stephen B. Bevans, and Richard H. Bliese. eds. *Dictionary of Mission: Theology, History, Perspectives.* New York: Orbis, 1999.

Mundadan, Mathias A. *History of Christianity in India, From the Beginning up to the Middle of the Sixteenth Century.* Vol. I. Bangalore: Church History Association of India, 1989.

Mundadan, Mathias A. *Indian Christians: Search for Identity and Struggle for Autonomy.* Bangalore: Dharamaram Publications, 1982.

Mundadan, Mathias A. *Traditions of St. Thomas Christians.* Bangalore: Dharmaram College, 1970.

Naaman, Paul. *The Maronite: The Origins of an Antiochene Church.* Collegeville, MN: Liturgical, 2011.

Naduthadam, Sebastian. ed. *The Spirituality of the Syro-Malabar Church.* Kochi: Liturgical Research Centre, 2009.

Neill, Stephen. *A History of Christian Missions.* 2nd ed. New York: Penguin, 1986.

Neill, Stephen. *A History of Christianity in India: The Beginning to AD 1707.* Vol.1 Cambridge: Cambridge University, 1984.

Neill, Stephen. *Creative Tension: Duff Lectures.* Edinburgh: Edinburgh Press, 1959.

Nessan, Craig L. *Beyond Maintenance to Mission: A Theology of the Congregation.* Minneapolis: Fortress, 2010.

Newbigin, Lesslie. *The Household of God.* New York: Friendship, 1954.

Newbigin, Lesslie. *The Open Secret: An Introduction to the Theology of Mission.* Grand Rapids, MI: Eerdmans, 1975.

Newbigin, Lesslie. *The Relevance of Trinitarian Doctrine for Todays Mission.* London: Edinburgh House, 1963.

Ninan, K. I. *Sabhacharithra Vichinthanagal: Anglican Kalaghattam.* Malayalam. Thiruvalla: Christava Sahitya Samithi, 1997.

Nugent, Vincent J. "Theological Foundation for Mission Animation: A Study of the Church's Essence." *World Mission* 24, no.1 (Spring 1943): 7-18.

Nussbaum, Stan. *A Reader's Guide to Transforming Mission.* Maryknoll, New York: Orbis, 2005.

Oborji, Francis Anekwe. *Concepts of Mission: The Evolution of Contemporary Missiology* Maryknoll, New York: Orbis, 2006.

Old, H.O. *Worship: Reformed According to Scripture.* Louisville, Kentucky: John Knox, 2002.

Panicker, Geevarghese and John Vellian. *A Historical Introduction to the Syriac Liturgy.* Kottayam: SEERI, 2010.

Panicker, Geevarghese. *The Holy Qurbanao in the Syro-Malankara Church.* Kottayam: St. Ephraem Ecumenical Research Institute, 1991.

Panicker, Geevarghese. "West Syrian Anaphora." In *The Harp: A Review of Syriac and Oriental Studies*, Vol. VI, no.1, edited by V.C. Samuel, Geevarghese Panicker and Jacob Thekkepparampil. Kottayam: SEERI, 1993: 37-45.

Panicker, Geevarghese. "West Syrian Anaphorae." *The Harp* 4, no.1 (April 1993): 35-39.

Service of the Syrian Jacobite Church of Malabar: The Meaning and the Interpretation. 2nd ed. Piscataway: Gorgias, 2003.

Payton, James R. JR, *Light from the Christian East: An Introduction to the Orthodox Tradition.* Illinois: Inter-Varsity, 2007.

Pecklers, Keith F. *Worship, New Century Theology.* London; Continuum, 2003.

Pfatteieher, H. Philip. *Liturgical Spirituality,* Pennsylvania, Trinity International, 1997.

Philip, A. T. "Liturgical Imperatives of the Mar Thoma Church." In *A Study on the Malankara Mar Thoma Church Liturgy,* edited by M.V. Abraham and Abraham Philip. Manganam: Thomas Mar Athanasius Memorial Orientation Centre, 1993. 22-42.

Philip, A. T. *The Mar Thoma Church and Kerala Society.* Thiruvananthapuram: Juhanon Mar Thoma Study Centre, 1991.

Philip, A.T. "Origin and Significance of the Maramon Convention." *Indian Church History Review 29,* no.2 (December, 1995): 147-149.

Philip, T. V. *The Mar Thoma Church in the St. Thomas Christian.* Thrissur: National, 1973.

Philip, T.V. *East of the Euphrates: Early Christianity in Asia.* New Delhi: ISPCK, 1998.

Pieris, Aloysius. "The Church, the Kingdom of God and the other Religions." *Dialogue* 22 (1970): 3-7.

Pitre, Brant. *Jesus and the Jewish Roots of the Eucharist.* New York: Image, 2011.

Pocknee, Cyril E. *Liturgical Vesture: Its Origin and Development.* Alcuin: A. R. Mowbray, 1960.

Podipara, Placid J. *Reflections on Liturgy.* Kottayam: Oriental Institute of Religious Studies, 1983.

Poikail, George. *ST. Thomas Christians and their Eucharistic Liturgy.* Thiruvalla: Christava Sahitya Samithi, 2010.

Pothen, S.G. *The Syrian Christians in Kerala.* London: Asia Publishing House, 1963.

Power, David Noel. "Liturgy and Culture Revisited." *Worship* 69 (1995): 225-243.

Power, David Noel. *Love Without Calculation: A Reflection on Divine Kenosis.* New York: The Crossroad, 2005.

Price, Charles, and Ian Randall. *Transforming Keswick.* London: OM, 2000.

Provost, James H. ed. *The Church as Mission.* Washington D.C: Canon law Society of America, 1984.

Rae, George Milne. *The Syrian Church in India.* Edinburgh: William Blackwell and Sons, 1892.

Rampan, Paul K.P. *The Eucharist Service of the Syrian Jacobite Church of Malabar: The Meaning and the Interpretation.* Malayalam. Trivandrum: YMCA, 1961.

Ratcliff, E.C. "The Eucharistic Office and the Liturgy of St. James." In *The Eucharist in India. A Plea for a Distinctive Liturgy for the Indian Church.* London: Longmans, 1920.

Rausch, Thomas P. *Eschatology, Liturgy, and Christology: Towards Recovering an Eschatological Imagination.* Collegeville, MN: Liturgical, 2012.

Redding, Graham. *Prayer and the Priesthood of Christ in the Reformed Tradition.* London: T and T Clark, 2003.

Renaudot, Eusebe. *Liturgiarum Orientalium Collectio.* Paris: Coignard, 1716.

Roberson, Ronald G. *The Eastern Christian Churches. A Brief Survey.* 5th ed. Rome: Edizioni Orientalia Christiana, 1995.

Romanides, J. "The ecclesiology of the St. Ignatius of Antioch." *Greek Orthodox Theological Review* 7 (1961): 63-65.

Rompay, L. V. "Past and Present Perceptions of Syriac Literary Tradition." *Hugoye* 3, no.1 (2000): 71-103.

Saka, Ishaq. *Commentary on the Liturgy of the Syrian Orthodox Church of Antioch,* trans. *Matti* Moosa. Piscataway, New Jersey: Gorgias, 2009.

Saldanha Ulian. *Attempts of Evangelization in Mission History.* Mumbai: St. Paul's, 2009.

Samarth, Stanley J. "Abraham Mar Thoma." In *Biographical Dictionary of Christian Missions,* edited by Gerald H. Anderson. Cambridge: William B. Eerdmans, 1999. 3-4.

Samarth, Stanley J. *One Christ Many Religions.* Bangalore: SATHRI, 1992.

Samuel, A. Y. *The Anaphora According to the Rite of the Syrian Orthodox Church of Antioch.* Hackensack, New Jersey: Syrian Orthodox Archdiocese, 1967.

Scherer, James A, and Stephen B. Bevans. eds. *New Directions in Mission and Evangelization: Theological Foundations.* Maryknoll, New York: Orbis, 1994.

Schmemann, Alexander. *Church, World, Mission.* New York: St. Vladimir's Seminary, 1979.

Schmemann, Alexander. *For the Life of the World.* New York: St. Vladimir's Seminary, 1973.

Schmemann, Alexander. *Of Water and the Spirit: A Liturgical Study on Baptism.* Crestwood, New York: St. Vladimir's Seminary, 1974.

Searle, Mark. *Called to Participate: Theological, Ritual and Social Perspectives.* Collegeville, MN: Liturgical, 2006.

Senn, Frank C. *Christian Liturgy: Catholic and Evangelic.* Minneapolis: Fortress, 1997.

Shattauer, Thomas, ed. *Inside Out: Worship in an Age of Mission.* Minneapolis: Fortress, 1999.

Sheerin, D.J. ed. *The Eucharist, The Message of the Fathers.* Vol. 7. Delware: Michael Glazier, 1986.

Shirasthaar, Varghese J. *Mathews Mar Athanasius- Biography.* 2nd ed. Thiruvalla: Mar Thoma Press, 2011, First Impression, 1920,

Shorter, Aylward. ed. *Evangelisation and Culture.* London: Geoffrey Chapman, 1994.

Smith, David. *Mission After Christendom.* London: Longman and Todd, 2003.

Smith, Payne J. ed. *A Compendious Syriac Dictionary.* Indiana: Eisen Brauns, 1998.

Southgate, Horatio. *Narrative of a Visit to the Syrian (Jacobite) Church of Mesopotamia.* New Jersey: Gorgias, 2003.

Spencer, Stephen. *SCM Study Guide to Christian Mission.* London: SCM, 2007.

Spindler, M. R, F. J. Verstraelen, A. Camps, and L.A. Hoedemaker. eds. *Missiology: An Ecumenical Introduction.* Grand Rapids, MI: Eerdmans, 1995.

Spinks, Bryan D. "Eastern Christian Liturgical Traditions: Oriental Orthodox." In *The Blackwell Companion to Eastern Christianity,* edited by Parry, K. Oxford: Blackwell, 2007. 339-367.

Spinks, Bryan D. *Do This in Remembrance of Me: The Eucharist From the Early Church to the Present D*ay. London: SCM, 2013.

Stamoolis, James. J. *Eastern Orthodox Mission Theology Today.* Eugene: Wipf and Stock, 2001.

Stancliffe, David. "The Making of the Church of England's Common Worship." *Studia Liturgica* 31 (2001):14-25.

Staniforth, M. "The Didache." In *Early Christian Writings: The Apostolic Fathers,* edited by A. Louth. London: Penguin, 1987. 191-199.

Stanislaus, L, and Thomas Malipurathu. eds. *A Vision of Mission in the New Millennium.* Mumbai: St Paul's, 2001.

Stanley, Brian. ed. *Christian Missions and the Enlightenment.* Cambridge: William B. Eerdmans, 2001.

Stansky, Thomas F, and Gerals H. Anderson. eds. *Mission Trends No.1: Critical Issues in Mission Today.* New York: Paulist, 1974.

Stephen Conway. *Living the Eucharist: Affirming Catholism and the Liturgy.* London: Darton, Longmand and Todd, 2001.

Stock, Eugene. *The History of the Church Missionary Society: Its Environment, Its Men and Its Work.* Vol.1. London: MS, 1899.

Stringer, Martin. *Rethinking the Origins of the Eucharist.* London: SCM, 2011.

Stylianopoulos, T.G. *The New Testament: An Orthodox Perspective. Vol. One: Scripture, Tradition, Hermeneutics.* Brookline: Massachusetts: Holy Cross Orthodox, 1997.

Swan, Billy. *The Eucharist, Communion and Formation: Proceedings of the International Symposium of Theology: The Ecclesiology of Communion Fifty Years after the Opening of Vatican II.* Dublin: Veritas, 2013.

Taft, Robert F, H-J Feulner, and E Velkovska. eds. *Crossroad of Cultural Studies in Liturgy and Patristics in Honour of Gabriele Winkler.* Rome: Pontificio Istituto Orientale, 2000.

Taft, Robert F. "Some Notes on the Bema in the East and West Syrian Traditions." *Orientalia Christain Periodica,* 34 (1968): 326-359.

Taft, Robert. F. *The Liturgy of the Hours in East and West: The Origins of the Divine Office and Its Meaning for Today.* Collegeville, MN: Liturgical, 1986.

Taylor, William D. ed. *Global Missiology for the 21ˢᵗ Century.* Grand Rapids, MI: Baker Academic, 2000.

Thazhayil, Thomas. "The Church at Crossroads." *Mar Thoma Messenger 32, no 3 (*July 2013): 31-33.

The Constitution on the Sacred Liturgy, *Sacrosanctum Concilium* No.24, Promulgated in December 4, 1963. http://www.stolivers.com/ReligiousEd/constitution.pdf (accessed September 10, 2015).

Thekkedathu, Joseph. *History of Christianity in India.* Vol. II, Thiruvalla: Christian Literature Society, 1983.

Thekkeparamil, Jacob. ed. "Sedre Absolution (Hussoyo) and Repentence (Tyobuto)." *TUVAIK,* Kottayam: 1995. 136-139.

Thekkeparampil, Jacob. *"Sedra and the Rite of Incense in the West Syrian Liturgy."* Phd diss., University of Paris, 1977.

Thomas K.G. *Vishudha Qurbana: Charithrathiloode Oru Padanam.* Haripadu: St. Thomas Orthodox Mission Centre, 1989.

Thomas, Alex. *A History of the First Cross Cultural Mission of the Mar Thoma Church 1910 - 2000.* Delhi; ISPCK, 2007.

Thomas, George. *Christian Indians and Indian Nationalism 1885-1950.* Frankfurt: Peter D. Lang, 1979.

Thomas, K.T, and Koshy, T.N. eds. *Faith on Trial. Kottayam:* Mar Theomotheos Memorial Publishing House, 1965.

Thomas, K.T. "Mar Thoma Evangelistic Association: Outside of Kerala." *Malankara Sabha Tharaka* 70, no. (September, 1963):18-21.

Thomas, M.M. *The Church's Mission and Post Modern Humanism: Collection of Essays and Talks 1992-1996.* New Delhi: ISPCK, 1996.

Thomas, M.M. *Abraham Malpante Naveekaranam: Oru Vyakyanam.* Malayalam. Thiruvalla: TLC, 1979.

Thomas, M.M. *Towards an Evangelical Social Gospel: A New Look at the Reformation of Abraham Malpan.* Madras: Christian Literature Society, 1977

Thomas, Norman E. ed. Classic Texts in Mission and World Christianity. *American Society of Missiology.* Vol.20. Maryknoll, New York: Orbis, 1995.

Thumpamon, Mathew Varghese. ed. *Diary of Puthanpurackal Mathai Kathanar.* (Malayalam) Thiruvalla: Christava Sahitya Samithi, 2014.

Thurian, Max. *Eucharistic Memorial.* Vol.1. London: Lutterworth, 1966.

Thurian, Max. ed. *Churches Respond to BEM: Official Response to the "Baptism, Eucharist and Ministry." Text,* Vol. IV, Faith and Order Paper No. 137.Geneva: World Council of Churches, 1987. 7-13.

Tillich, Paul. "The Theology of Missions." *The Journal Christianity and Crisis* (March 1955): 27-34.

Torre, L. Della. *Understanding the Liturgy.* Athlon: St. Paul's, 1967.

Tovey, Phillip. "The Reformed Qurbana." *The Harp* XIV (2009): 253-258.

Tovey, Phillip. *Essays in West- Syrian Liturgy.* Kottayam: Oriental Institute of Religious Studies, 1997.

Tovey, Phillip. *Inculturation: The Eucharist in Africa.* Nottingham: Grove Books, 1988.

Tovey, Phillip. *The Liturgy of St. James as Presently Use.* Cambridge: Grove Books, 1998.

Tovey, Philip. "Abraham Malpan and the Amended Syrian Liturgy of CMS." *Indian Church History Review* 29/1 (June 1995): 38-55.

Ussbaum, Stan. *A Reader's Guide to Transforming Mission.* New York: Orbis, 2007.

Vadakkan, Joseph. *A Priest's Encounter with Revolution.* Bangalore: ATC, 1974.

Valuparampil, Kurian. "St. James Anaphora: An Ecumenical Locus. A Survey of the Origin and Development of St. James Anaphora." *Christian Orient*, 8, no. 4 (1987): 30-47.

Varghese, Baby. "Some Aspects of West Syrian Liturgical Theology." *Studia Liturgica* 31, no.2 (2001): 171-178.

Varghese, Baby. "St. James' Liturgy: A Brief History of the Text." *The Harp* II, (December 1989): 129-134.

Varghese, Baby. "West Syrian Anaphora: As an Expression of the Trinitarian Doctrine." *The Harp* IV (1991): 1-3.

Varghese, Baby. *The Syriac Version of the Liturgy of St. James.* Cambridge: Grove Books, 2001.

Varghese, Baby "The CMS Missionaries and the Malankara Church (1815-1840)" The *Harp,* XX (2006): 399-446.

Varghese, Baby. "Anaphora of St. James and Jacob of Edessa." In *Jacob of Edessa and the Syriac Culture of His Day,* edited by Bas ter Haar Romeny. Leiden: Brill, 2008, 239-264.

Varghese, Baby. "The Theological Significance of the Epiklesis in the Liturgy of Saint James." In *Eucharist in Theology and Philosophy: Issues of Doctrinal History in East and West from the Patristic Age to the Reformation,* edited by Istvan Perczel, Reka Forrai and Gyorgy Gereby. Leuven: Leuven University, 2005.

Varghese, Baby. "West Syriac Liturgy: One Hundred Years of Research." *The Harp* 27, (2011): 53-72.

Varghese, Baby. "West Syrian Anaphora as an Expression of Trinitarian Doctrine." *The Harp* 4, (1999): 2-3.

Varghese, Baby. *In Spirit and Truth: A Study of Eastern Worship.* Kottayam: OTC, 1987.

Varghese, Baby. *The Syriac Version of the Liturgy of St James: A Brief History for Students.* London: Grove Books, 2001.

Varghese, Baby. *West Syrian Liturgical Theology.* Aldershot: Ashgate, 2004.

Varghese, Eapen. "Missional Vision in the Liturgy of St. James." In *St. James Liturgy: A Liturgical Study,* edited by Shaiju P. John. Thiruvalla: Christava Sahitya Samithi, 2013. 18-25.

Varghese, J. *Biography of Mathews Mar Athanasios.* Thiruvalla: Mar Thoma Publication Society, 2011.

Varghese, Ninan. "Mar Thoma Medical Mission." *Malankara Sabha Tharaka* (February 2003): 21-22.

Varghese, V. Titus and P. P. Philip. *Glimpses of the History of the Christian Churches in* Churches in India. Thiruvalla: Christian Literature Society, 1983.

Varghese, Zac, and Mathew A. Kallumpuram. *Glimpses of the Mar Thoma Church History.* New Delhi: Kalpana Printing, 2003.

Varughese, Koshy P. ed. *Challenges and Prospects of Mission in the Emerging Context.* Faridabad: Dharma Jyoti Vidya Peeth, 2010.

Vellian, Jacob. ed. *The Malabar Church: Symposium in Honour of Rev. Placid J. Podipara.* Roma: Pont. Institutum Orientalium Studiorum, 1970.

Vellian, Jacob. *History of the Syro-Malabar Liturgy.* Kottayam: Powrasthya Vidhya Peeth, 1967.

Viswanadhan, Susan. *The Christians of Kerala: History, Belief and A Ritual Among the Yakoba.* Oxford: Oxford University, 1993.

Wainwright, Geoffrey. "Christian Worship: Scriptural Basis and Theological Frame." In *The Oxford History of Christian Worship,* edited by Wainwright, Geoffrey and Karen B. Westerfield Tucker. Oxford: Oxford University, 2006. 1-31.

Walls, Andrew F. *The Missionary Movement in Christian History: Studies in the Transmission of Faith.* Maryknoll, New York: Orbis, 1996.

Wanner, Kim Aldi. *Preparing the Assembly to Celebrate.* Collegeville, MN: Liturgical, 1997.

Ware, Timothy. *The Orthodox Church.* London: Penguin, 1969.

Webster, John C.B. "History of Christianity in India: Aims and Methods." *Indian Church History Review* 13, no.2 (December 1979): 87-122.

White, James F. *Introduction to Christian Worship.* 3rd ed. Nashville: Abingdon, 2000.

Whitehouse, Thomas. *Lingering of Light in a Dark Land.* London: William Brown, 1873.

Witvliet, John D. "The Anaphora of St. James." In *Essays on Early Eastern Eucharistic Prayers,* edited by Paul F. Bradshaw. Pueblo, 1997.

Witvliet, John D. "The Opening of Worship-Trinity." In *A More Profound Alleluia: Theology and Worship in Harmony,* edited by Leanne Van Dyk. Grand Rapids, MI: William B. Eerdmans, 2005. 5-23.

Wright, Christopher J. H. *The Mission of God: Unlocking the Bible's Grand Narrative.* Downers Grove: InterVarsity, 2006.

Yannoulatos, Anastasios. "Orthodox Spirituality and External Mission." *International Review of Mission* 52 (1963): 300-302.

Zachariah, George K. "Mission of the Church." *Mar Thoma Messenger.* (October 2004): 17-19.

Zakka I, Patriarch. "A Short Overview of the Common History of the Syrian Church with Islam through the Centuries." *Patriarchal Journal* 33, no.146 (June 1995): 324-326,

Zetterholm, Magnus. *The Formation of Christianity in Antioch.* London: Routledge, 2003.

Zizioulas, John. *Being as Communion.* Crestwood, New York: St. Vladimir's Seminary, 1985.

REPORTS/ MINUTES/ LETTERS/ MANUSCRIPTS
Alappuzha Civil Court, Kerala. *Mar Thoma Church- O.S. No. 439 of M.E. 1054(1879),* Thiruvalla: The Mar Thoma Syrian Church Archives, 1879.

Mar Thoma Syrian Church. *Judgement of the Royal Court of Malabar, Seminary Case.* Kottayam: Mar Thoma Theological Seminary Archives, 1889.

Report of the Third Meeting of the MTEA- (M.E. Dhanu 27, 1064) February 7, 1889. Thiruvalla: Mar Thoma Evangelistic Association, 1889.

Letter of Thomas Walker to Mrs. Walker, dated 15th February 1900. Thiruvalla: Mar Thoma Evangelistic Association, 1900.

Annual Report of the Mar Thoma Evangelistic Association. (23rd) 1911. Thiruvalla: Mar Thoma Evangelistic Association, 1911.

The Malabar Mar Thoma Syrian Christian Evangelistic Association: Memorandum and Articles of Association, as Amended in 1106 M.E. Thiruvalla: Mar Thoma Evangelistic Association, 1931.

Mar Thoma Syrian Church Samudayalochana Sabha. Resolution of the Mar Thoma Syrian Samudayalochana Sabha, May 5-6, 1936. Thiruvalla: Mar Thoma, 1936.

The Malabar Mar Thoma Syrian Christian Evangelistic Association Memorandum and Articles of Association: as Amended in 1106. Thiruvalla: TAM, 1960.

Annual Report of the Mar Thoma Evangelistic Association. Thiruvalla: Mar Thoma Press, 2011.

Annual Report 2012-13, Malabar Mar Thoma Syrian Christian Evangelistic Association, Thiruvalla: MMTSCEA, 2013.

Annual Report of the Church Council of the Mar Thoma Church for the Years: 1945-2010. Mar Thoma Church Office. Thiruvalla, India.

Mar Thoma, Abraham. "Metropolitan's Letter". In: *Malankara Sabha Tharaka,* all issues from 1945-1975.

Mar Thoma, Alexander. Metropolitan's Letter". In: *Malankara Sabha Tharaka,* all issues from 1976- 2000.

World Council of Churches. *Minutes of the Commission on Faith and Order,* New Haven, 1957, Faith and Order Paper No. 25. Geneva: WCC, 1957.

New Delhi Report of the WCC. London: SCM, 1961.

St. Thomas Centenary Souvenir, Ernakulum, Kerala 1972.

Lambeth Conference and the Lutheran World Federation, *Pullach Report.* London: SPCK, 1973.

Mar Thoma Syrian Church, *Minutes of the Second Meeting of the Joint Theological Commission of the CSI-CNI-MTC,* held at Ranson Hall of the United Theological College, Bangalore on 3rd and 4th June 1975. Bangalore: 1975.

Seminar Report of the Liturgical Committee on 16th November 1977. Kottayam: CPMM Ecumenical Study Centre, 1977.

Final Report of CWME Consultation of Eastern Orthodox and Oriental Orthodox Churches. Neapolis, Greece: 1988.

Constitution of the Mar Thoma Syrian Church of Malabar. Thiruvalla: Mar Thoma, 2002.

Joint Working Group between the Roma Catholic Church and the World Council of Churches. Ecclesiological and Ecumenical Implications of Common Baptism: A JWG Study Eighth Report. Geneva: WCC, 2005.

Annual Reports of the CARD: 1980-2012. Thiruvalla: Christian Agency for Rural Development.

The Malankara Mar Thoma Syrian Church, Constitution. Thiruvalla: V.G.C, 1998.

The Service Book of the Holy Sacraments. Udayagiri: Seminary Publications, 1999.

Unpublished liturgy of the Mar Thoma Episcopal Consecration, *Amalogia.* Thiruvalla: Kerala.

Mar Chrysostom, Philipose. Metropolitan's Letter". In: *Malankara Sabha Tharaka,* all issues from 2000-2008.

Mar Thoma Sleehayude Edavakayakunna Malankara Suriyani Sabhayude Canon, 2nd edition. New Delhi: Dharma Jyothi Vidhya Peedh, 2008.

Minutes of the Sabha Prathinidhi Mandalam, Thiruvalla, *Mar Thoma Sabha,* 2009.

The Service Book of Holy Eucharist (Anaphora). Puthencruz: JSC, 2010

CBCI Inter-Ritual Committee. Baptism and Confirmation. Bangalore: Theological Publications in India, 2010.

Mission Report of the Mar Thoma Church, Diocese of North-America and Europe -2011. New York: North America Europe Dioceses of the Mar Thoma Church, 2011.

Letter to the Metropolitan Joseph Mar Thoma on 10th December 2013 by the Liturgical Commission of the Mar Thoma Church, Thiruvalla, Kerala.

Mar Thoma, Joseph. "Metropolitan's Letter." In: *Malankara Sabha Tharaka,* All issues from 2005-2015.

Annual Report of the Malankara Mar Thoma Syrian Church 2014-2015. Thiruvalla: Mar Thoma Sabha Council, 2015.

Annual Report of the Council of Mar Thoma Parishes in Europe. London: COMPE, 2015.

Report of the Liturgical Commission of the Mar Thoma Church: 2014-2015. Thiruvalla: Mar Thoma, 2015.

Circular No. DC/568/15, by Dr. Geevarghese Mar Theodosius Episcopa, Dioceses of North America and Europe on 20th September, 2015.

Mar Thoma Sabha Diary 2016, Thiruvalla: Mar Thoma Press, 2016.

SPECIAL COLLECTIONS FROM CMS ARCHIVES, CADBURY RESEARCH CENTRE, BIRMINGHAM.

Letter of Mathew Maramon, dated 18.03.1840 (J Tucker MSS C 2/5).

Letter of J. Tucker, dated.15.04.1843.

Letter of Athanasius to J. Tucker from Puthencavu, dated.5.10.1843.

Letter to Col. Frazer by the reformists of Malankara Church 1836, CMS/ C I, 2/0 253/59/19.

Report on the Travancore Mission by Rev. S. Lambrick on 08/10/1832, CMS/ C I 2/0 149/1.

Translation of Syrian Services (Liturgy of St. James - 1837) by Rev. J. Peet, CMS/ 2/0185/2.

A Brief History of the Syrian Church in Malabar by CMS, CMS/C I 2/0148/3.

Kottayam Report 01/10/1825 by Benjamin Bailey, CMS/C I 2/0110/4.

Proceeding of the Church Missionary Society for 1818-1819. London: CMS College, 1819.